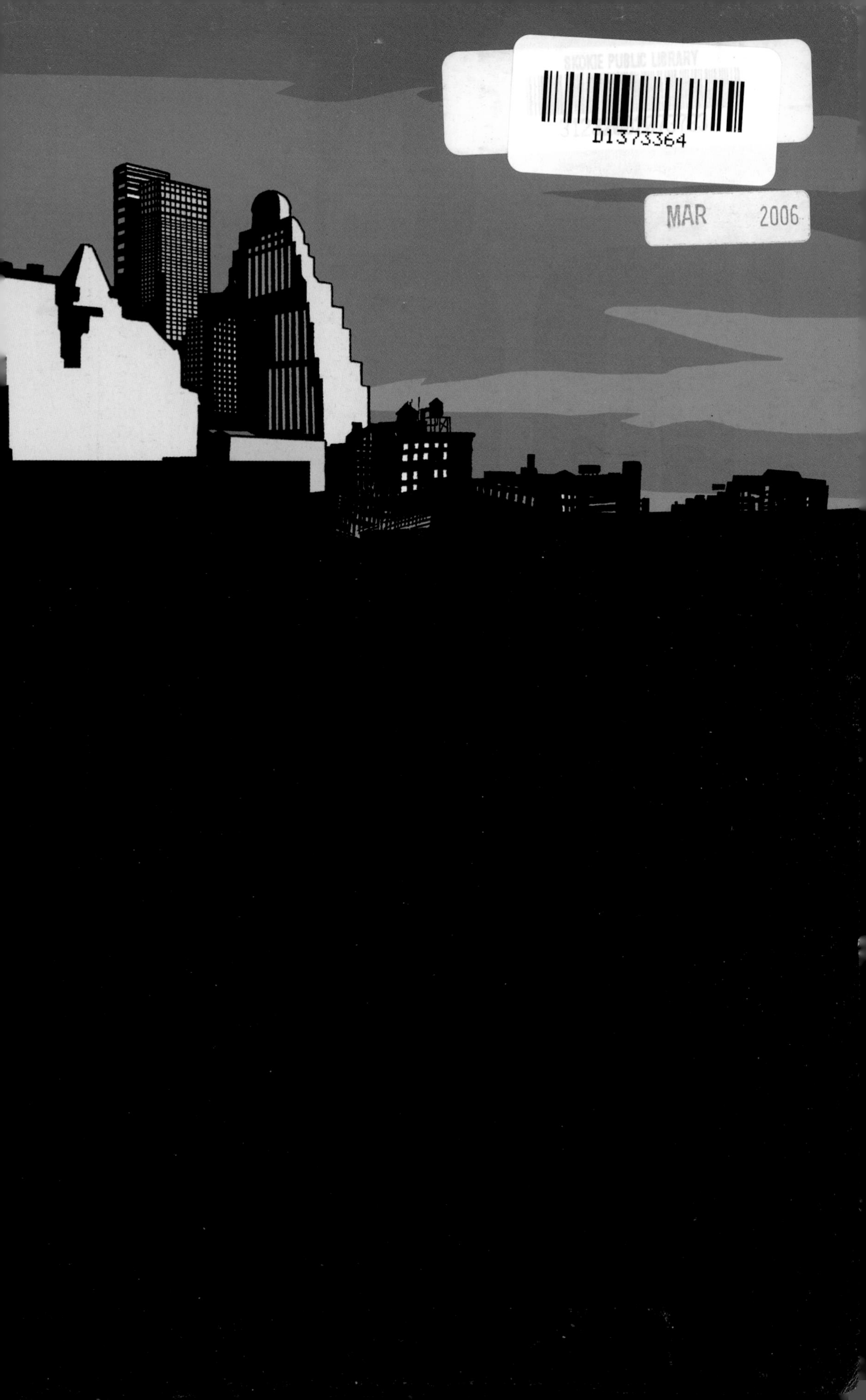

POW

CREATED AND PRODUCED BY
BRIAN MICHAEL BENDIS
AND
MIKE AVON OEMING

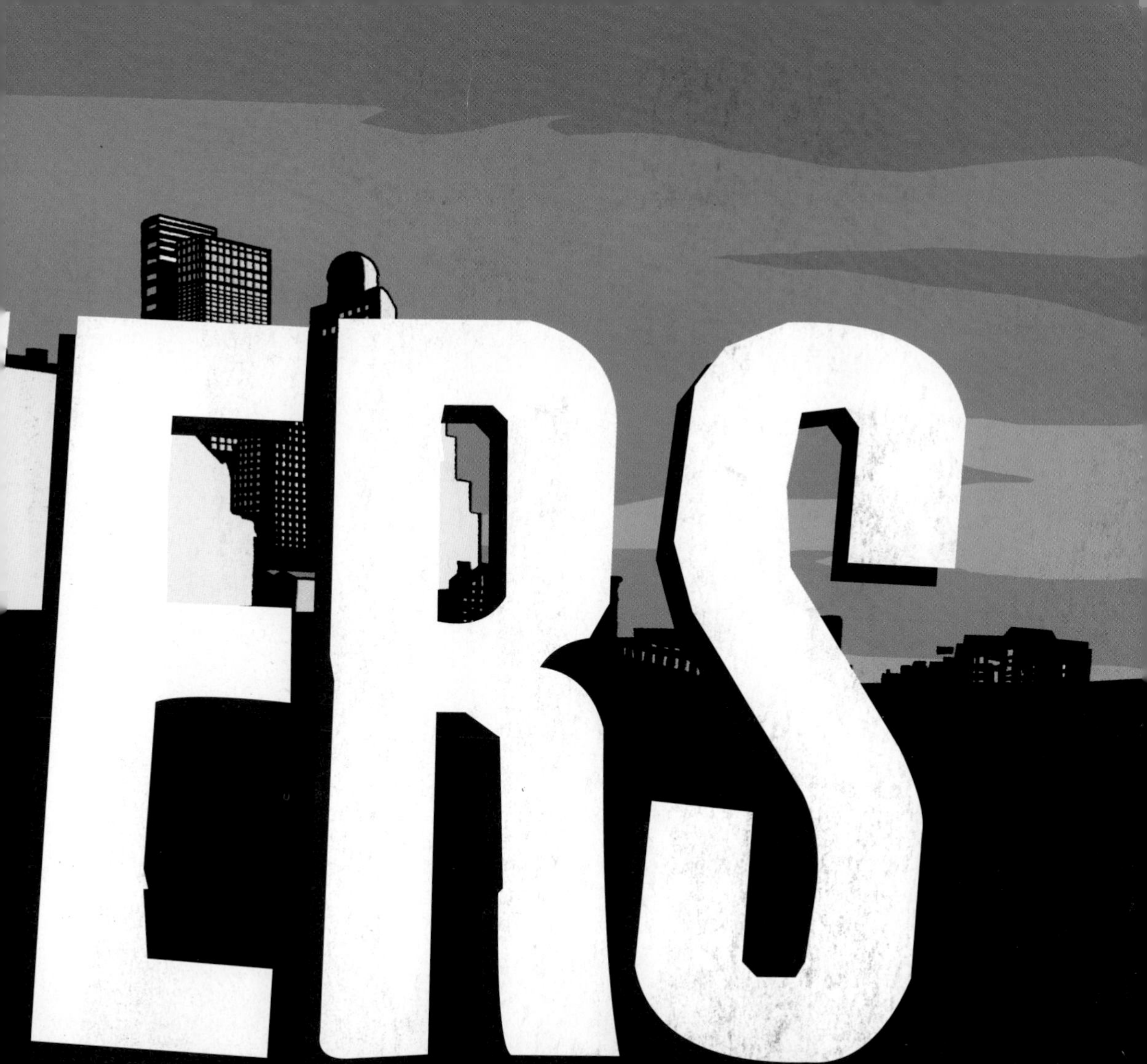
ERS

COLOR ART
PETER PANTAZIS

TYPOGRAPHY
KEN BRUZENAK

EDITORS
KC MCCRORY AND JAMIE S. RICH
WITH JAMES LUCAS JONES

BUSINESS AFFAIRS
ALISA BENDIS

DESIGN ASSISTANCE
KEITH WOOD

Previously in Powers

Homicide Detectives Christian Walker and Deena Pilgrim investigate murders specific to superhero cases--powers.

Walker, once the superhero named "Diamond," has a long and mysterious past that even he doesn't fully recall. In Deena's very first case with Walker, they solved the case of the murder of Retro Girl, an iconic figure like none other before her. It's a case that has haunted both detectives.

After a once beloved power, Supershock, decided to commit genocide in the name of "justice" the United States government quickly put together a law banning all powers. Deena Pilgrim, caught in the center of Supershock's nightmare, was killed and brought back to life and has been off the

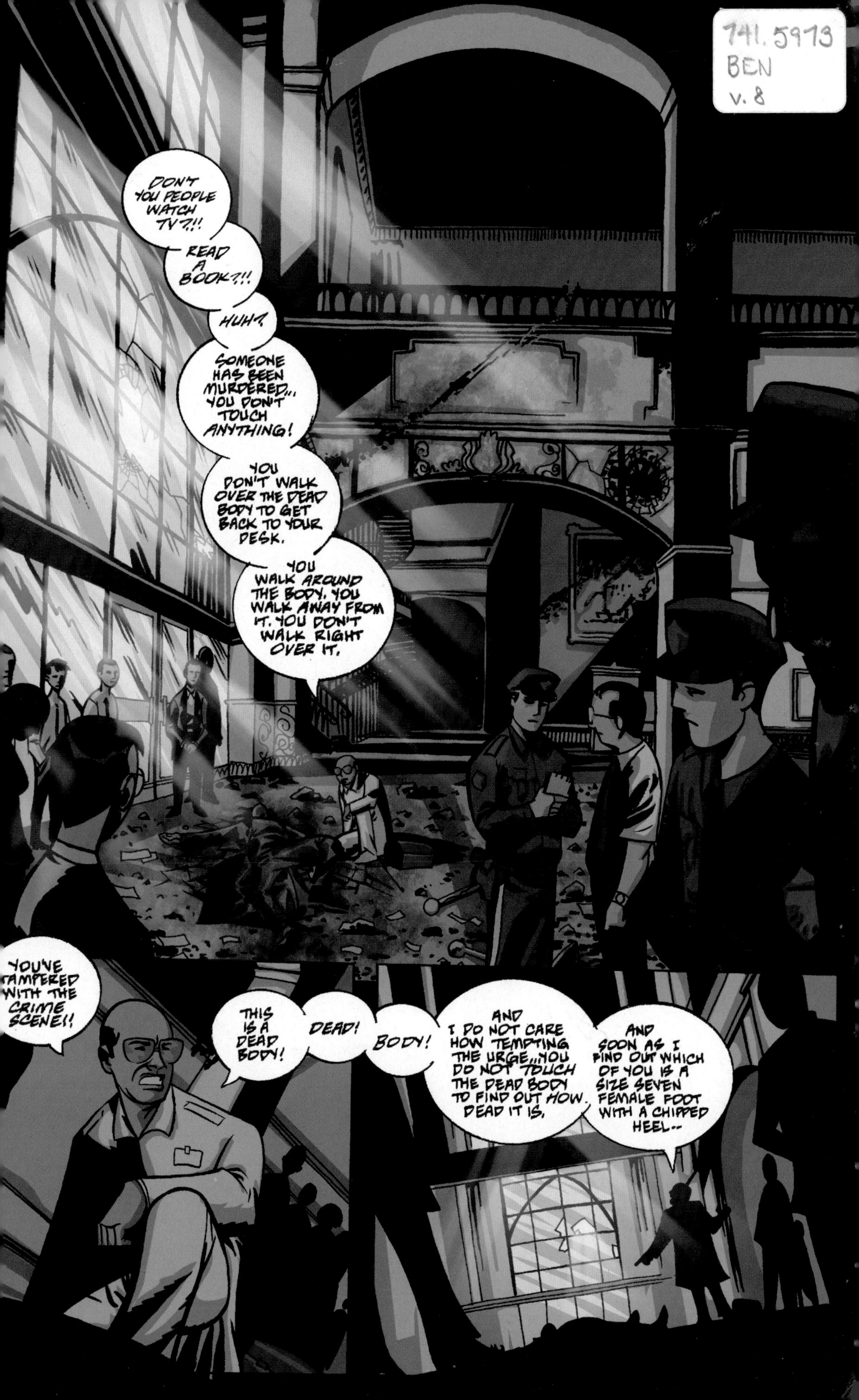
DON'T YOU PEOPLE WATCH TV?!!
READ A BOOK?!!
HUH?
SOMEONE HAS BEEN MURDERED... YOU DON'T TOUCH ANYTHING!
YOU DON'T WALK OVER THE DEAD BODY TO GET BACK TO YOUR DESK.
YOU WALK AROUND THE BODY. YOU WALK AWAY FROM IT. YOU DON'T WALK RIGHT OVER IT.
YOU'VE TAMPERED WITH THE CRIME SCENE!!
THIS IS A DEAD BODY!
DEAD!
BODY!
AND I DO NOT CARE HOW TEMPTING THE URGE... YOU DO NOT TOUCH THE DEAD BODY TO FIND OUT HOW DEAD IT IS.
AND SOON AS I FIND OUT WHICH OF YOU IS A SIZE SEVEN FEMALE FOOT WITH A CHIPPED HEEL--

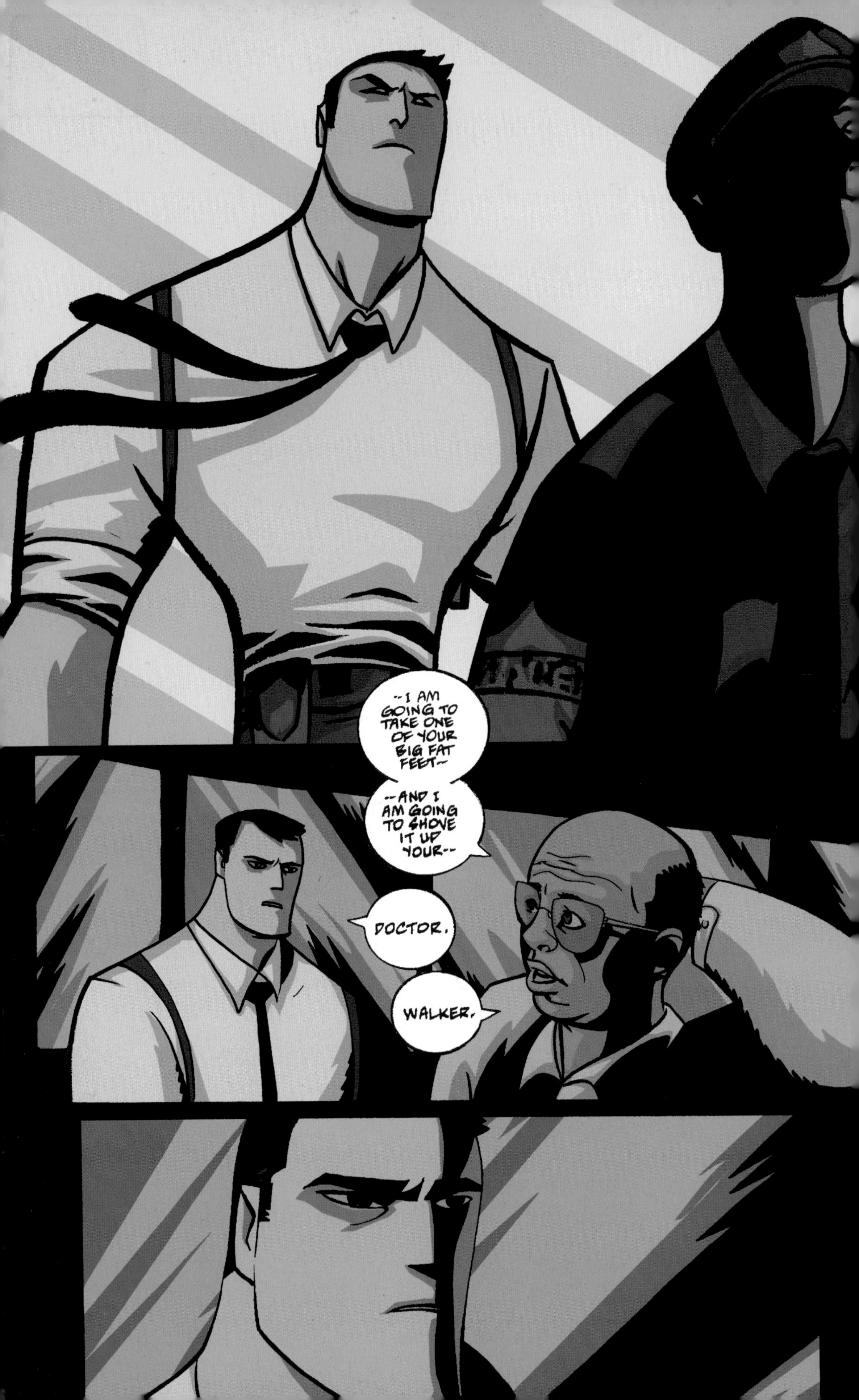
--I AM GOING TO TAKE ONE OF YOUR BIG FAT FEET--
--AND I AM GOING TO SHOVE IT UP YOUR--
DOCTOR.
WALKER.

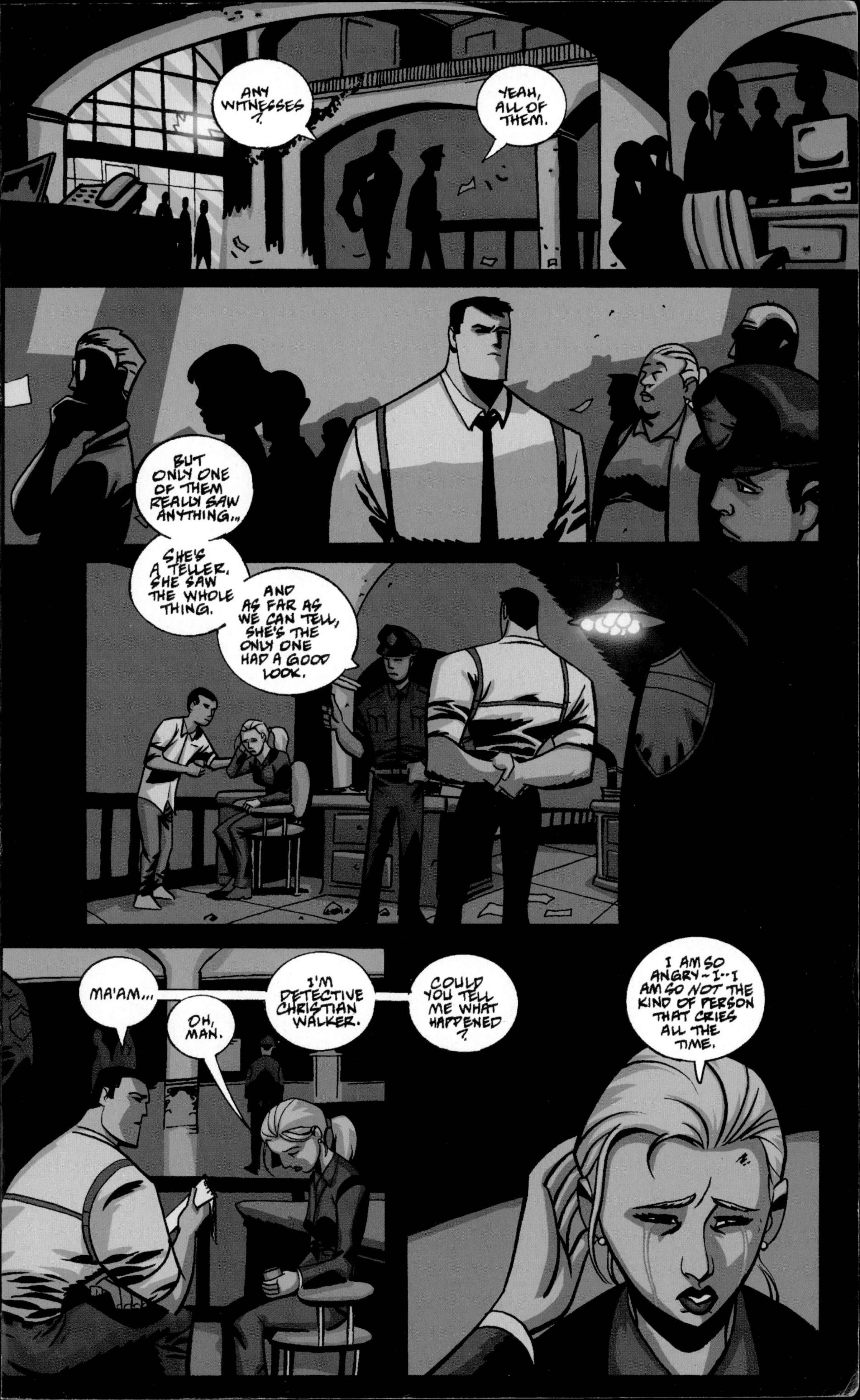
ANY WITNESSES?
YEAH, ALL OF THEM.
BUT ONLY ONE OF THEM REALLY SAW ANYTHING...
SHE'S A TELLER. SHE SAW THE WHOLE THING.
AND AS FAR AS WE CAN TELL, SHE'S THE ONLY ONE HAD A GOOD LOOK.
MA'AM...
OH, MAN.
I'M DETECTIVE CHRISTIAN WALKER.
COULD YOU TELL ME WHAT HAPPENED?
I AM SO ANGRY-- I-- I AM SO NOT THE KIND OF PERSON THAT CRIES ALL THE TIME.

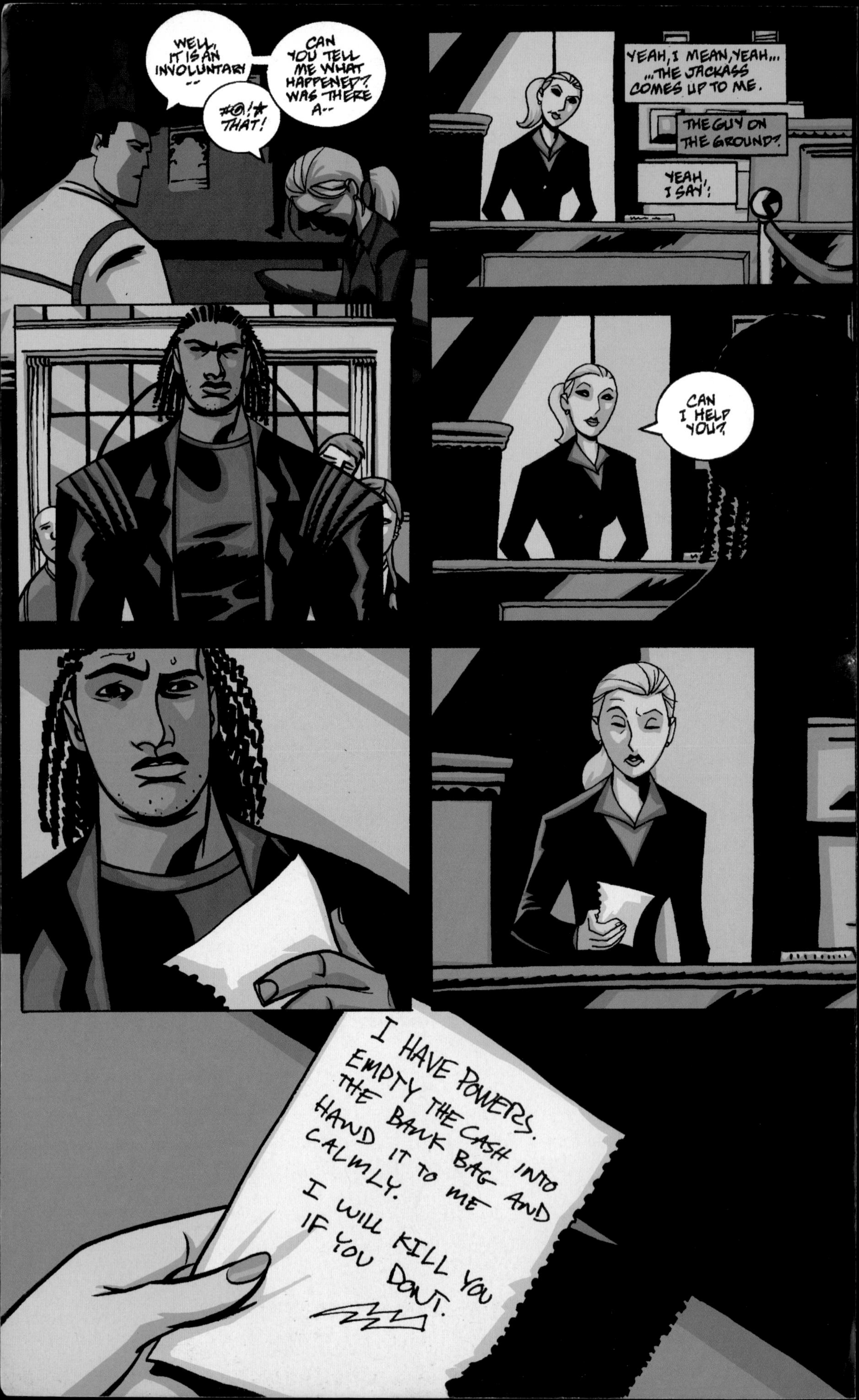
WELL, IT IS AN INVOLUNTARY --
CAN YOU TELL ME WHAT HAPPENED? WAS THERE A--
#@!* THAT!
YEAH, I MEAN, YEAH... ...THE JACKASS COMES UP TO ME.
THE GUY ON THE GROUND?
YEAH, I SAY:
CAN I HELP YOU?
I HAVE POWERS.
EMPTY THE CASH INTO THE BANK BAG AND HAND IT TO ME CALMLY.
I WILL KILL YOU IF YOU DON'T.

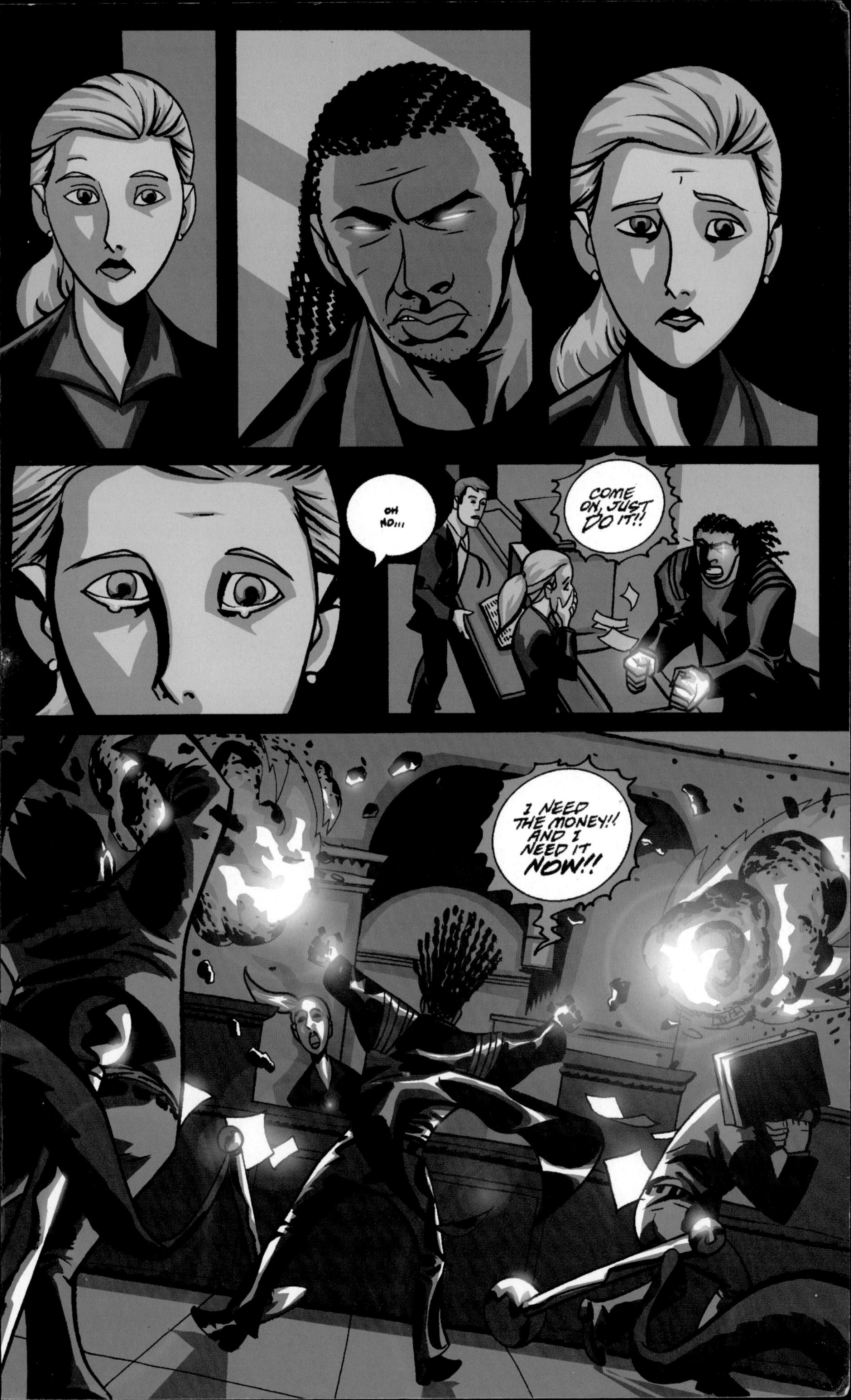
OH NO...
COME ON, JUST DO IT!!
I NEED THE MONEY!! AND I NEED IT NOW!!

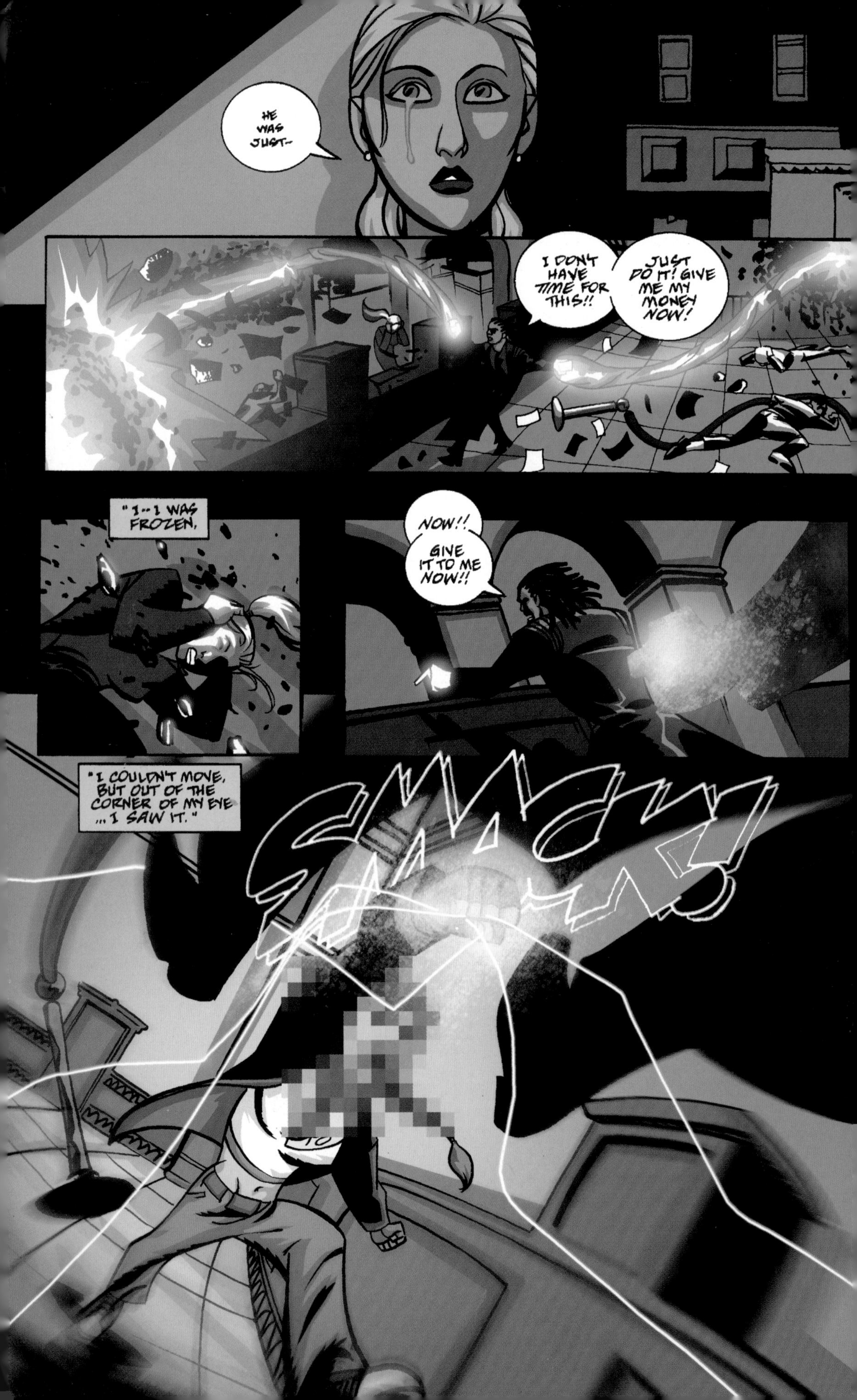
HE WAS JUST--
I DON'T HAVE TIME FOR THIS!!
JUST DO IT! GIVE ME MY MONEY NOW!
"I-- I WAS FROZEN.
NOW!!
GIVE IT TO ME NOW!!
"I COULDN'T MOVE, BUT OUT OF THE CORNER OF MY EYE ...I SAW IT."

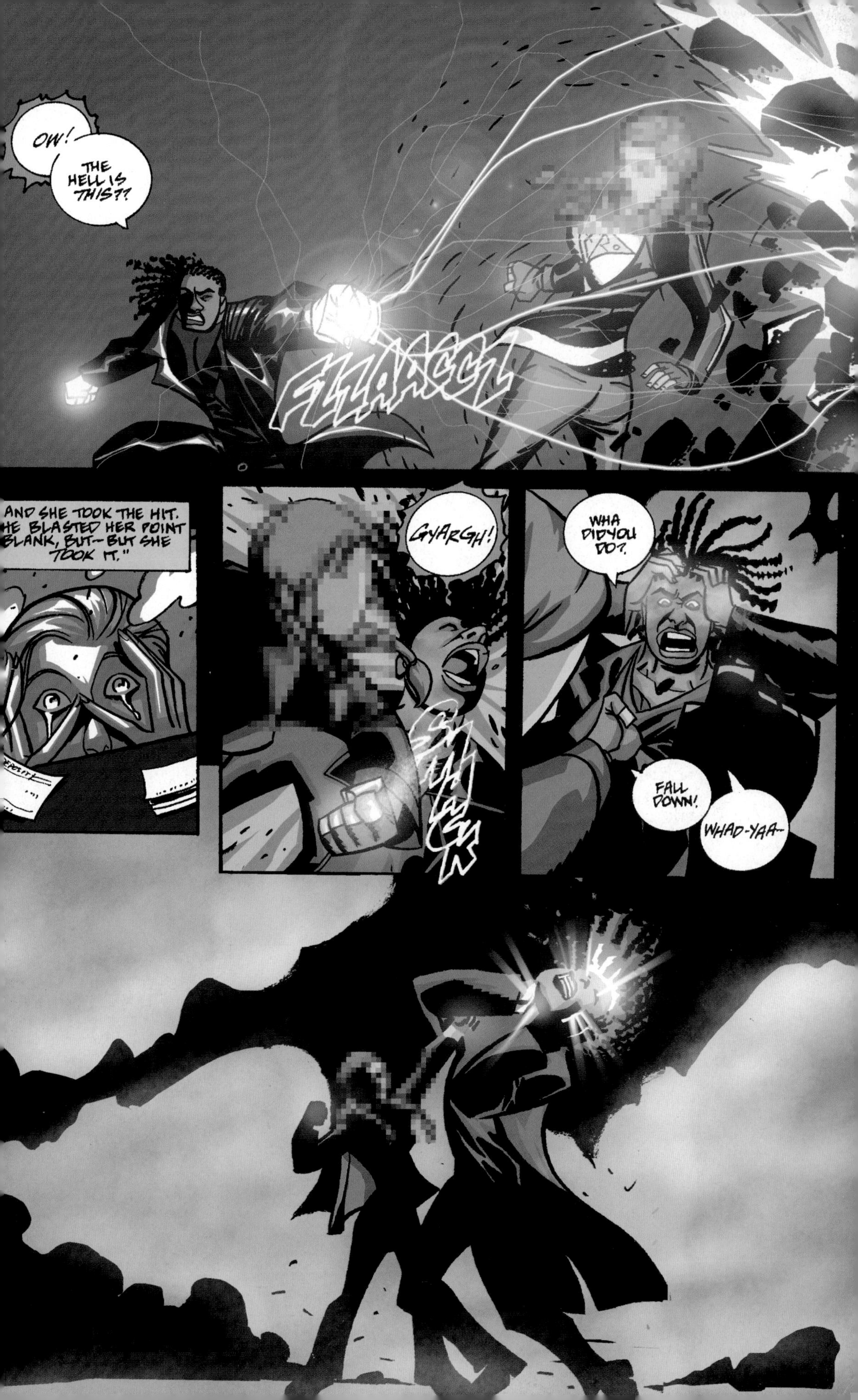
OW!
THE HELL IS THIS??
FZZAACCT
AND SHE TOOK THE HIT. HE BLASTED HER POINT BLANK, BUT-- BUT SHE TOOK IT."
GYARGH!
WHA DIDYOU DO?
FALL DOWN!
WHAD-YAA--

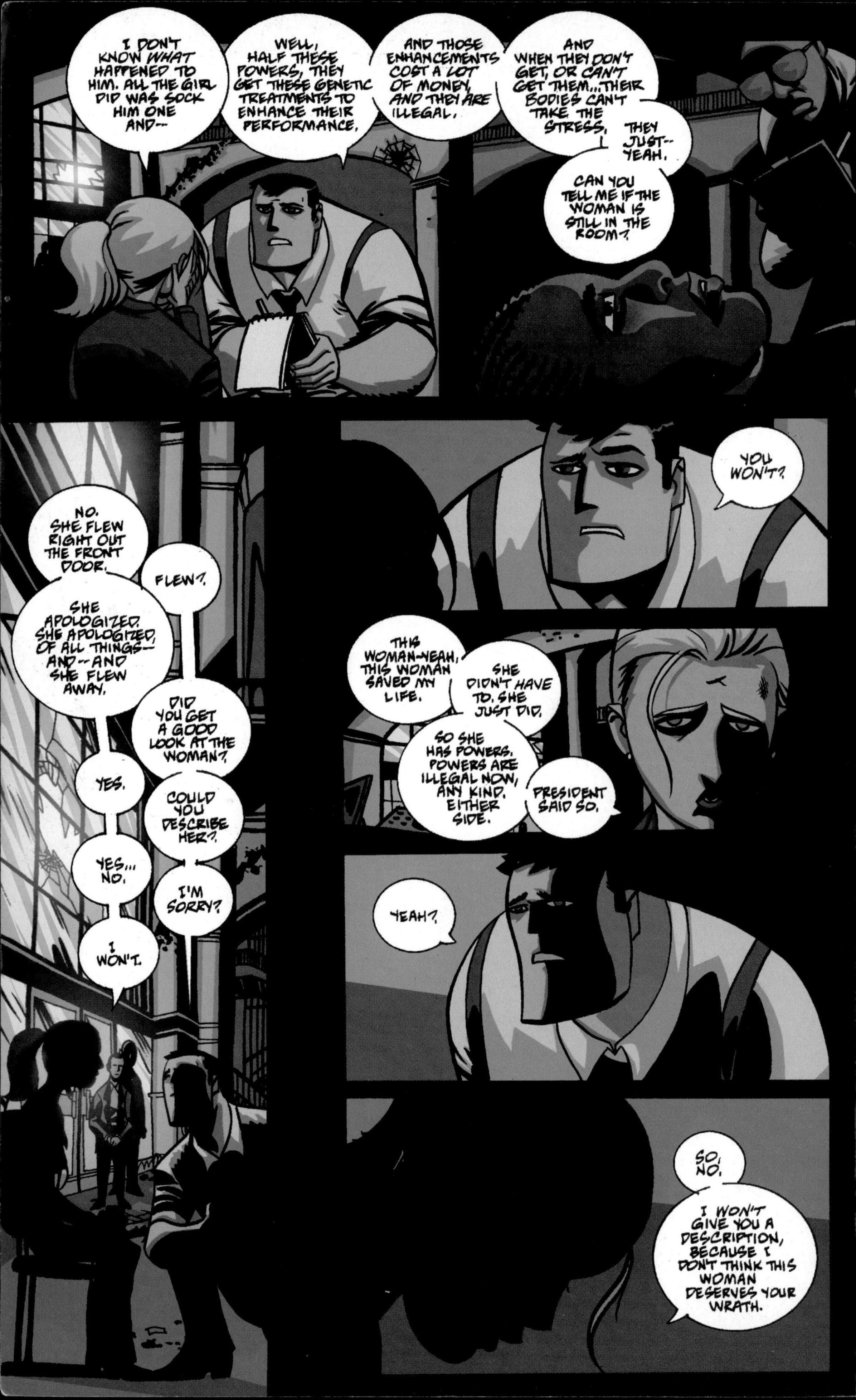
I DON'T KNOW WHAT HAPPENED TO HIM. ALL THE GIRL DID WAS SOCK HIM ONE AND--
WELL, HALF THESE POWERS, THEY GET THESE GENETIC TREATMENTS TO ENHANCE THEIR PERFORMANCE.
AND THOSE ENHANCEMENTS COST A LOT OF MONEY, AND THEY ARE ILLEGAL.
AND WHEN THEY DON'T GET, OR CAN'T GET THEM... THEIR BODIES CAN'T TAKE THE STRESS.
THEY JUST-- YEAH.
CAN YOU TELL ME IF THE WOMAN IS STILL IN THE ROOM?
NO. SHE FLEW RIGHT OUT THE FRONT DOOR.
FLEW?
SHE APOLOGIZED. SHE APOLOGIZED, OF ALL THINGS-- AND-- AND SHE FLEW AWAY.
DID YOU GET A GOOD LOOK AT THE WOMAN?
YES.
COULD YOU DESCRIBE HER?
YES... NO.
I'M SORRY?
I WON'T.
YOU WON'T?
THIS WOMAN--YEAH, THIS WOMAN SAVED MY LIFE.
SHE DIDN'T HAVE TO. SHE JUST DID.
SO SHE HAS POWERS. POWERS ARE ILLEGAL NOW, ANY KIND, EITHER SIDE.
PRESIDENT SAID SO.
YEAH?
SO, NO.
I WON'T GIVE YOU A DESCRIPTION, BECAUSE I DON'T THINK THIS WOMAN DESERVES YOUR WRATH.

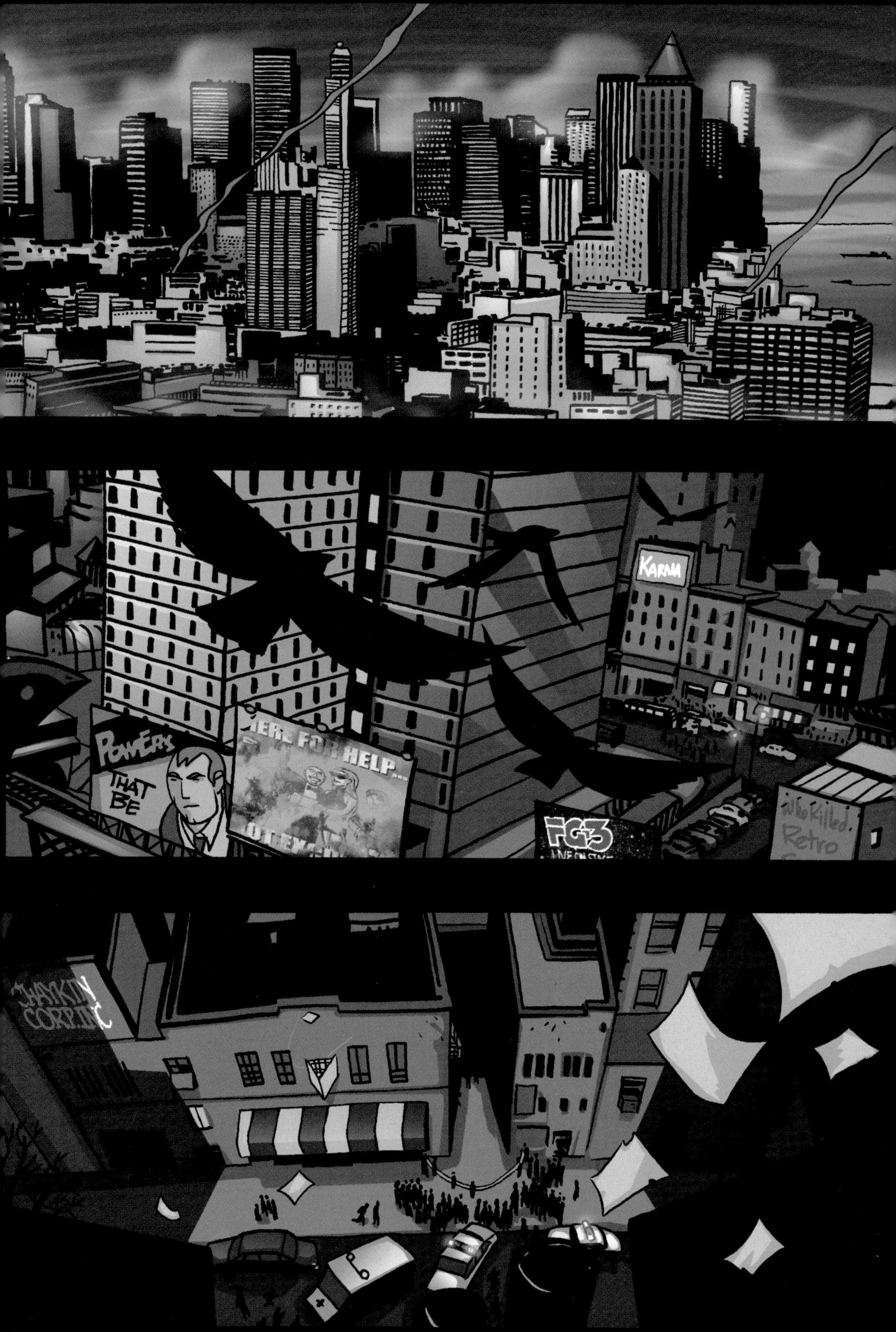
KARMA
POWERS THAT BE
FOR HELP...
FG3
Who Killed Retro

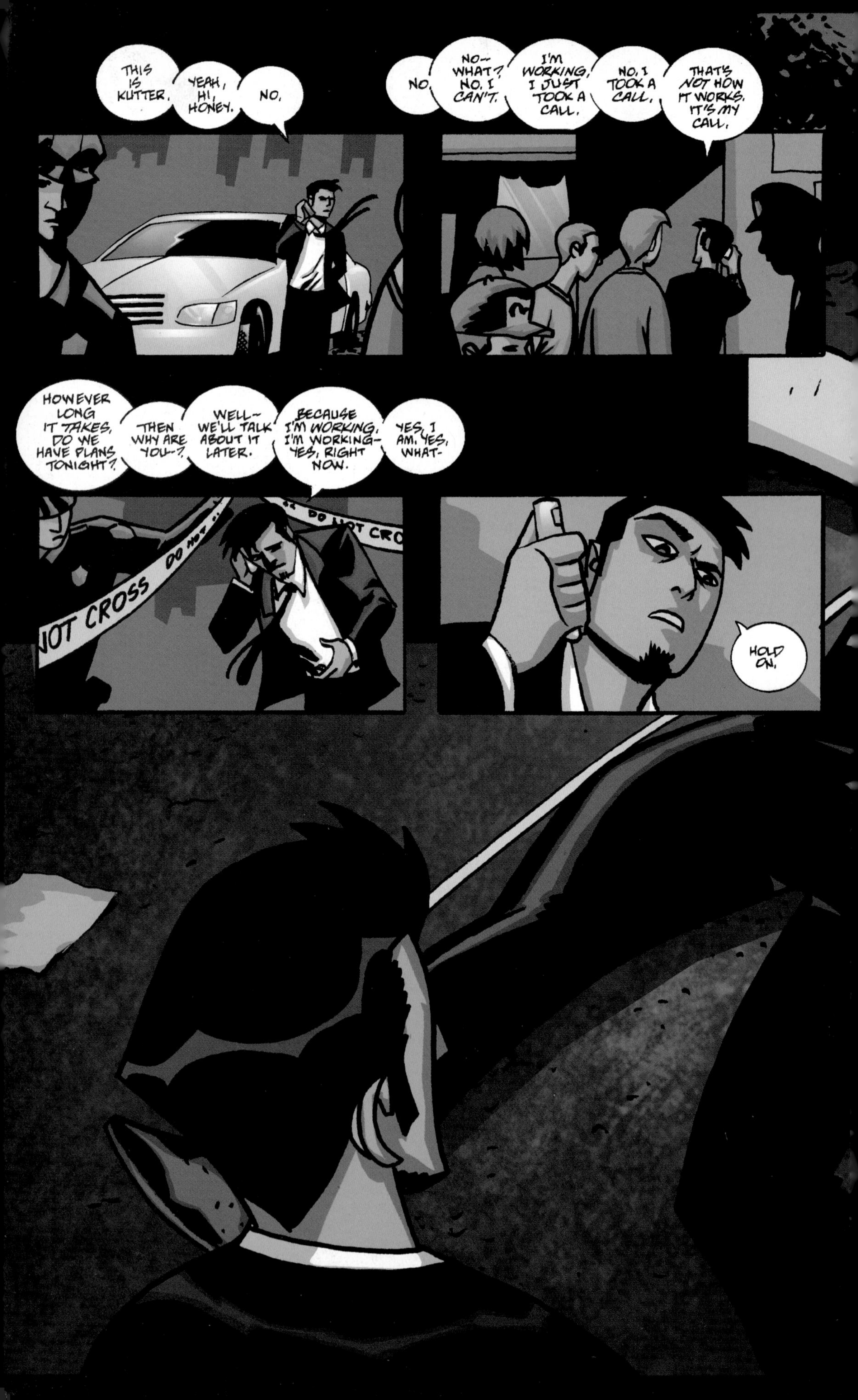

THIS IS KUTTER.
YEAH, HI, HONEY.
NO.
NO.
NO-- WHAT? NO, I CAN'T.
I'M WORKING, I JUST TOOK A CALL.
NO, I TOOK A CALL.
THAT'S NOT HOW IT WORKS. IT'S MY CALL.
HOWEVER LONG IT TAKES. DO WE HAVE PLANS TONIGHT?
THEN WHY ARE YOU--?
WELL-- WE'LL TALK ABOUT IT LATER.
BECAUSE I'M WORKING. I'M WORKING-- YES, RIGHT NOW.
YES, I AM. YES, WHAT--
DO NOT CROSS
NOT CROSS
HOLD ON.

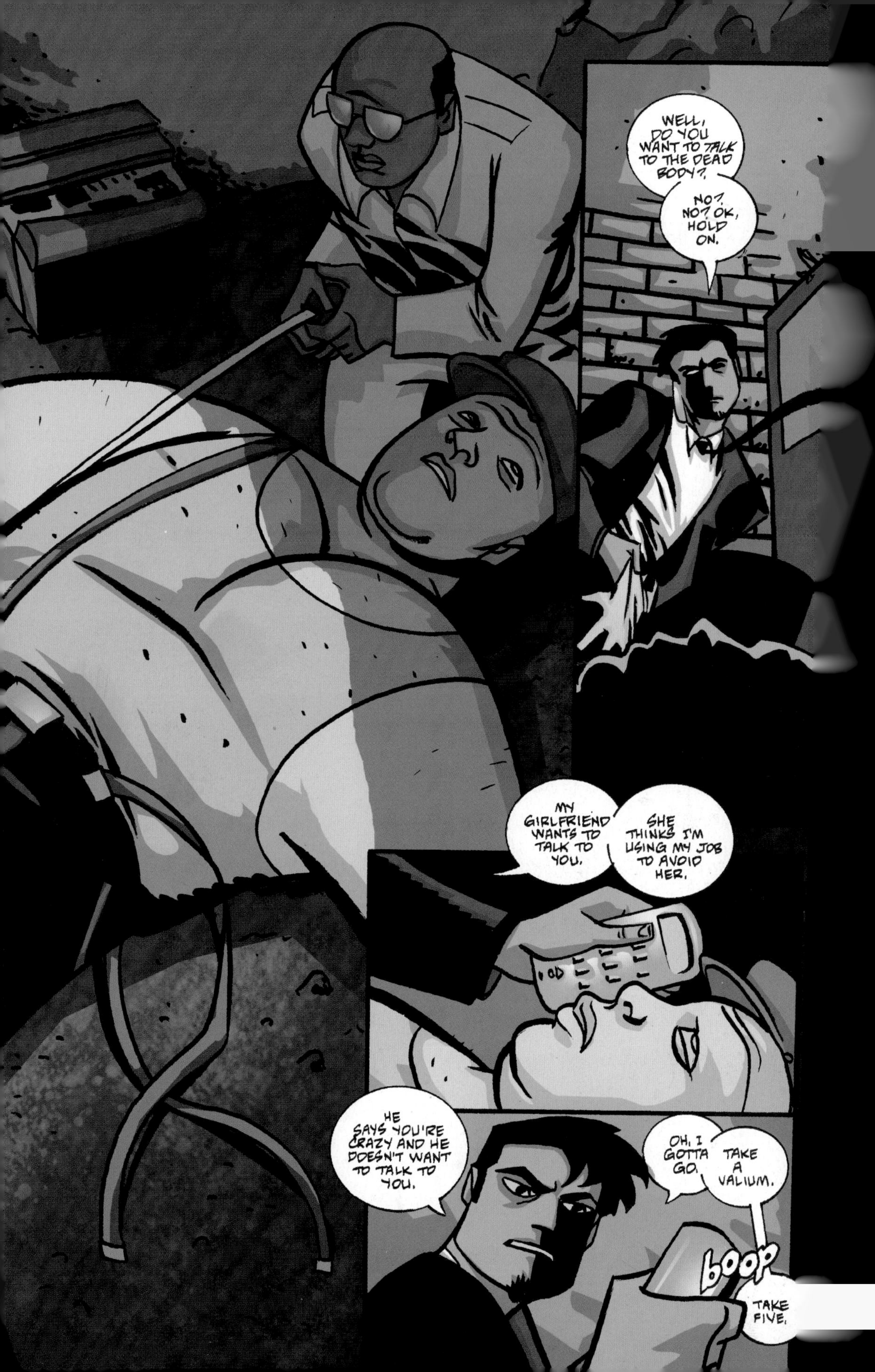
WELL, DO YOU WANT TO TALK TO THE DEAD BODY?
NO? NO? OK, HOLD ON.
MY GIRLFRIEND WANTS TO TALK TO YOU.
SHE THINKS I'M USING MY JOB TO AVOID HER.
HE SAYS YOU'RE CRAZY AND HE DOESN'T WANT TO TALK TO YOU.
OH, I GOTTA GO.
TAKE A VALIUM.
boop
TAKE FIVE.

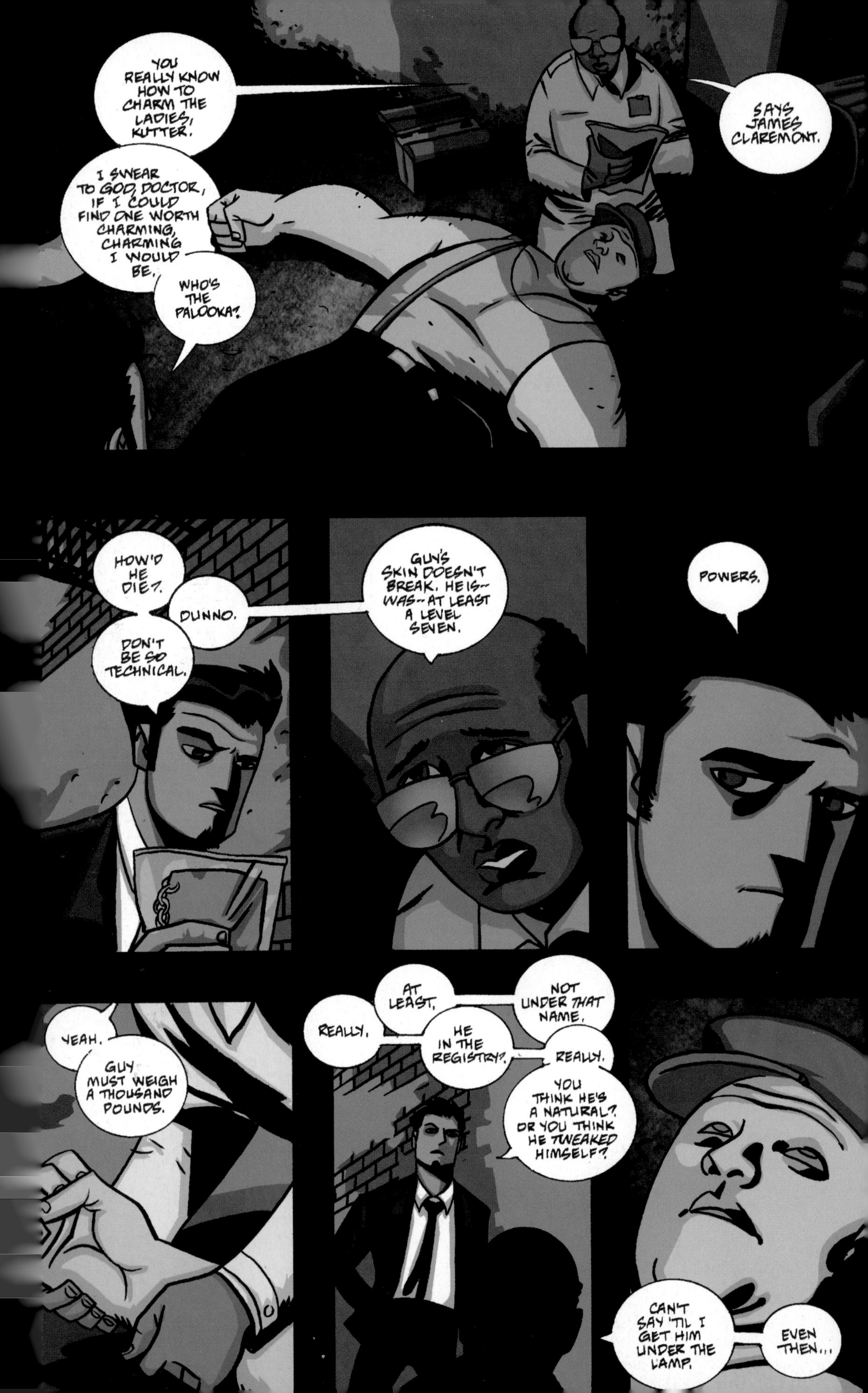
YOU REALLY KNOW HOW TO CHARM THE LADIES, KUTTER.
SAYS JAMES CLAREMONT.
I SWEAR TO GOD, DOCTOR, IF I COULD FIND ONE WORTH CHARMING, CHARMING I WOULD BE.
WHO'S THE PALOOKA?
HOW'D HE DIE?
DUNNO.
DON'T BE SO TECHNICAL.
GUY'S SKIN DOESN'T BREAK. HE IS-- WAS-- AT LEAST A LEVEL SEVEN.
POWERS.
YEAH.
GUY MUST WEIGH A THOUSAND POUNDS.
REALLY.
AT LEAST.
HE IN THE REGISTRY?
NOT UNDER THAT NAME.
REALLY.
YOU THINK HE'S A NATURAL? OR YOU THINK HE TWEAKED HIMSELF?
CAN'T SAY 'TIL I GET HIM UNDER THE LAMP.
EVEN THEN...

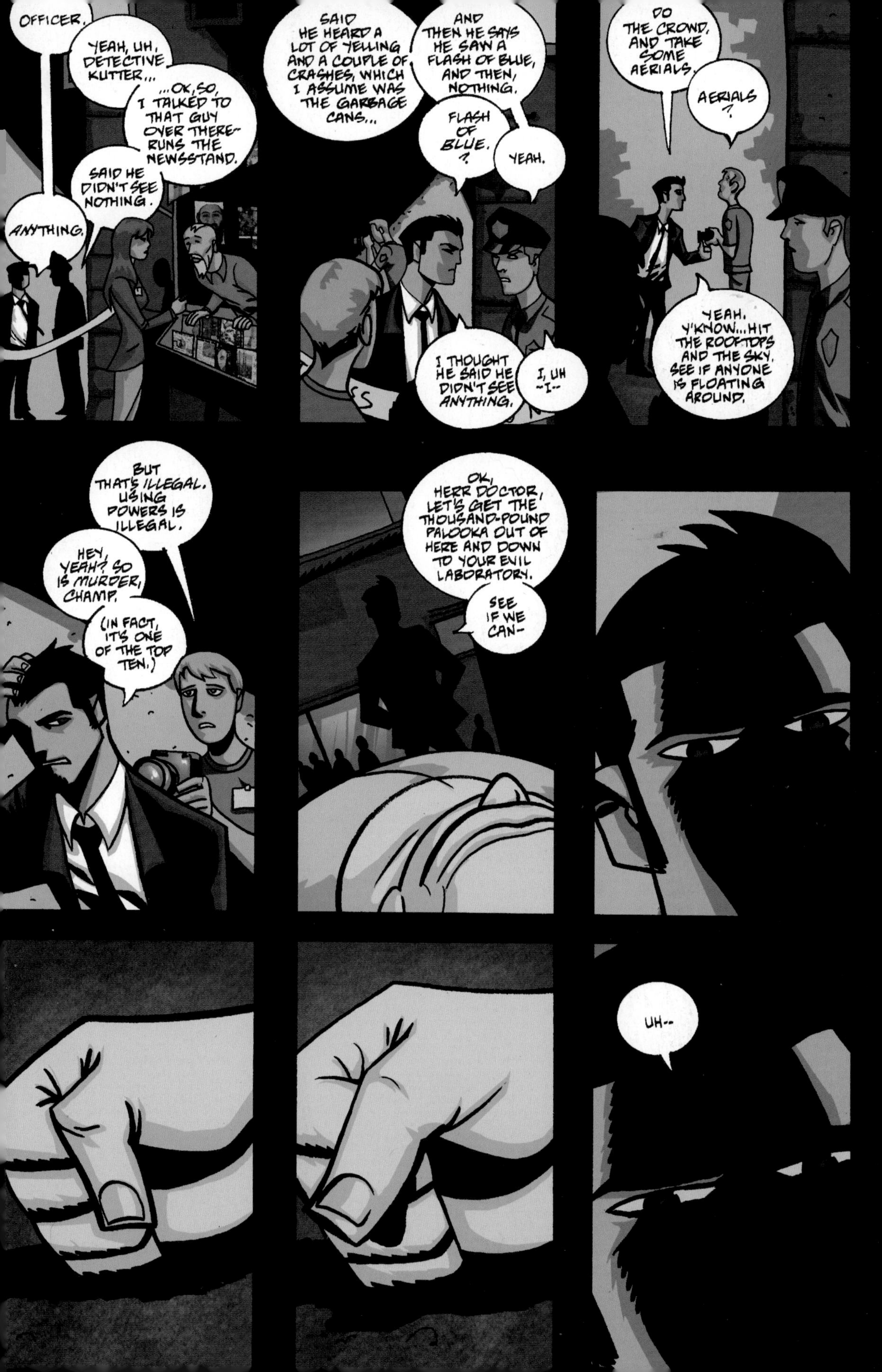
OFFICER.
YEAH, UH, DETECTIVE KUTTER...
...OK, SO, I TALKED TO THAT GUY OVER THERE-RUNS THE NEWSSTAND.
SAID HE DIDN'T SEE NOTHING.
ANYTHING.
SAID HE HEARD A LOT OF YELLING AND A COUPLE OF CRASHES, WHICH I ASSUME WAS THE GARBAGE CANS...
AND THEN HE SAYS HE SAW A FLASH OF BLUE, AND THEN, NOTHING.
FLASH OF BLUE. ?
YEAH.
I THOUGHT HE SAID HE DIDN'T SEE ANYTHING.
I, UH --I--
DO THE CROWD, AND TAKE SOME AERIALS.
AERIALS ?
YEAH. Y'KNOW...HIT THE ROOFTOPS AND THE SKY. SEE IF ANYONE IS FLOATING AROUND.
BUT THAT'S ILLEGAL. USING POWERS IS ILLEGAL.
HEY, YEAH? SO IS MURDER, CHAMP.
(IN FACT, IT'S ONE OF THE TOP TEN.)
OK, HERR DOCTOR, LET'S GET THE THOUSAND-POUND PALOOKA OUT OF HERE AND DOWN TO YOUR EVIL LABORATORY.
SEE IF WE CAN-
UH--

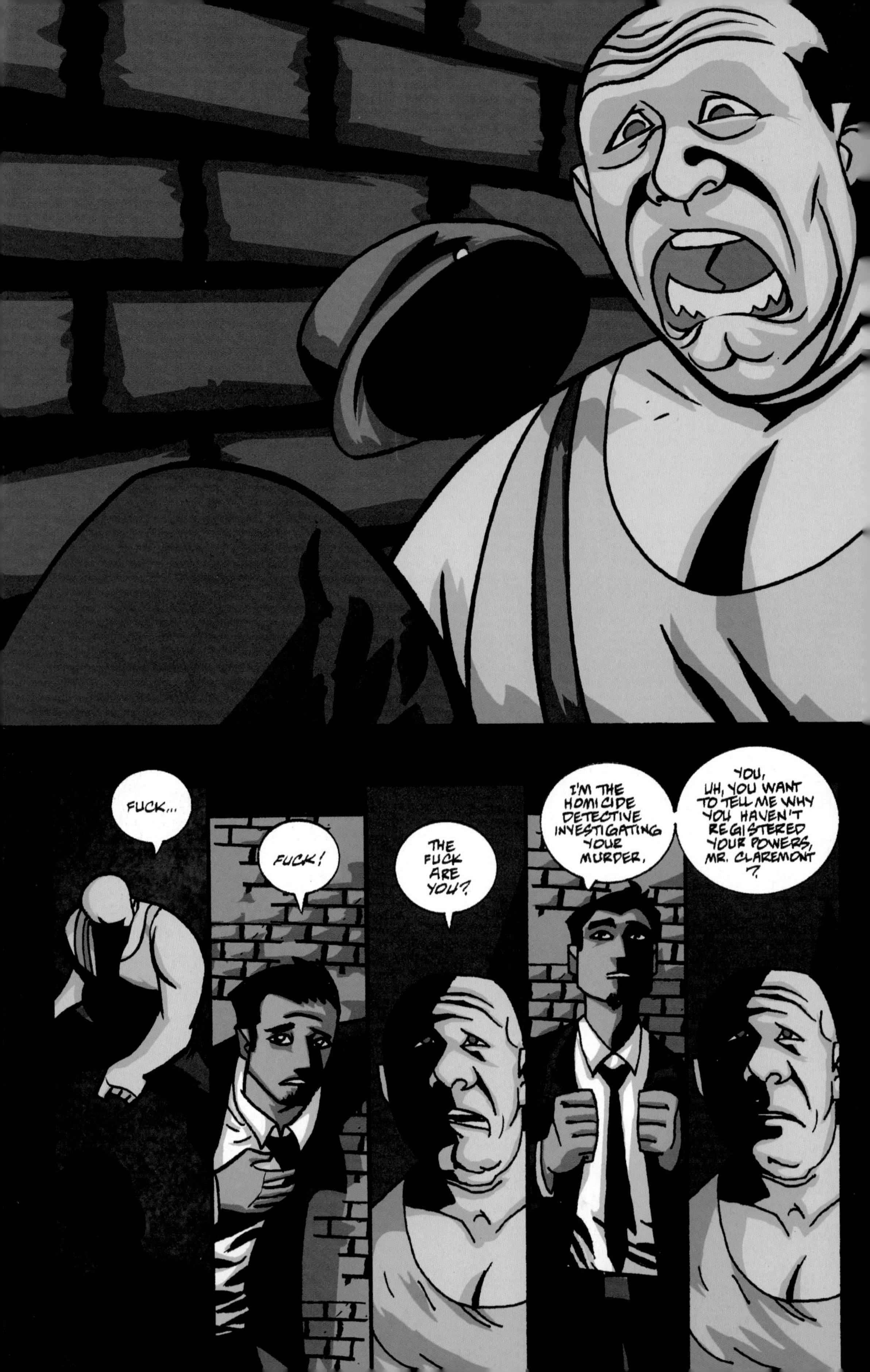
FUCK...
FUCK!
THE FUCK ARE YOU?
I'M THE HOMICIDE DETECTIVE INVESTIGATING YOUR MURDER.
YOU, UH, YOU WANT TO TELL ME WHY YOU HAVEN'T REGISTERED YOUR POWERS, MR. CLAREMONT?

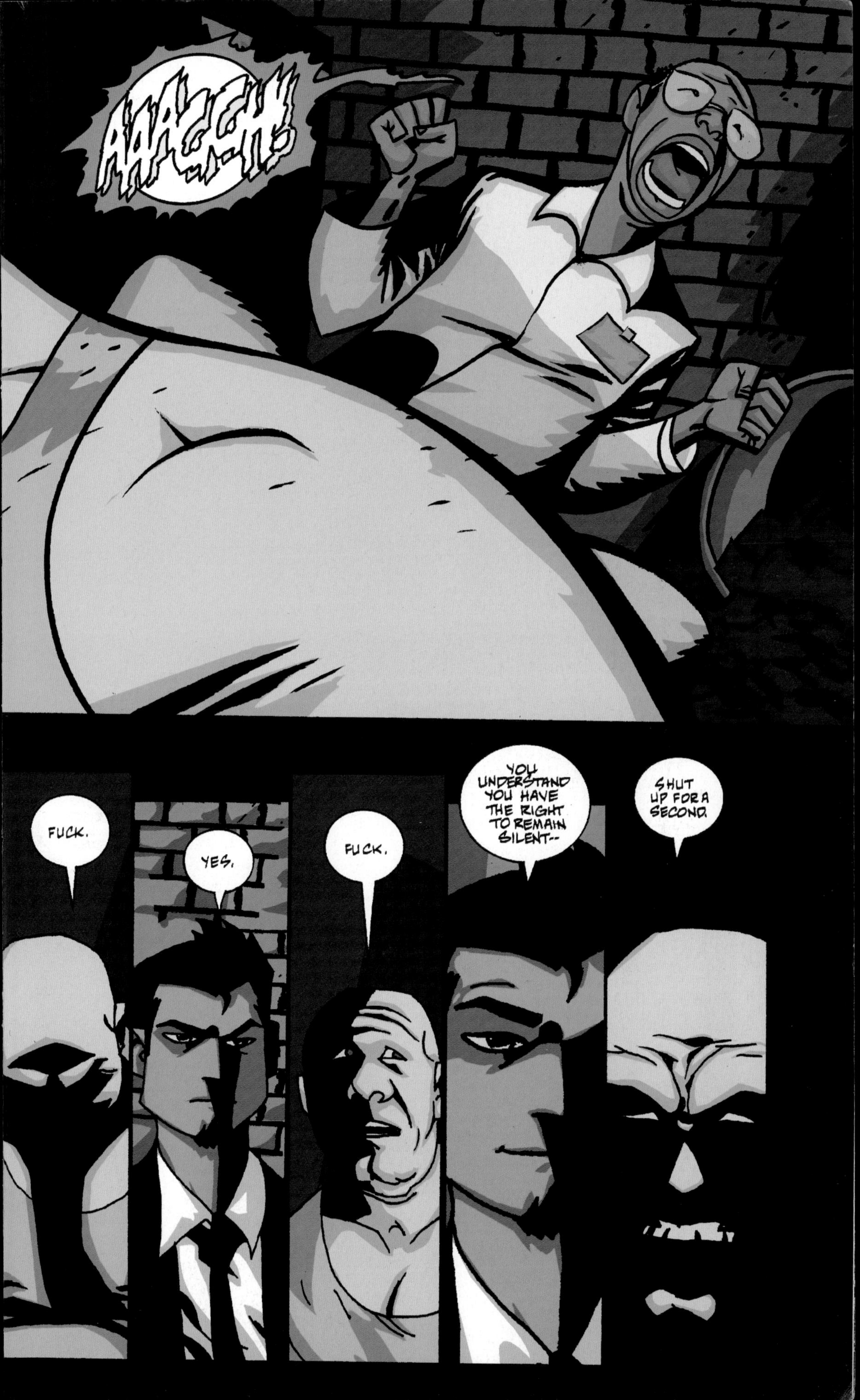
AAAGGH!
FUCK.
YES.
FUCK.
YOU UNDERSTAND YOU HAVE THE RIGHT TO REMAIN SILENT--
SHUT UP FOR A SECOND.

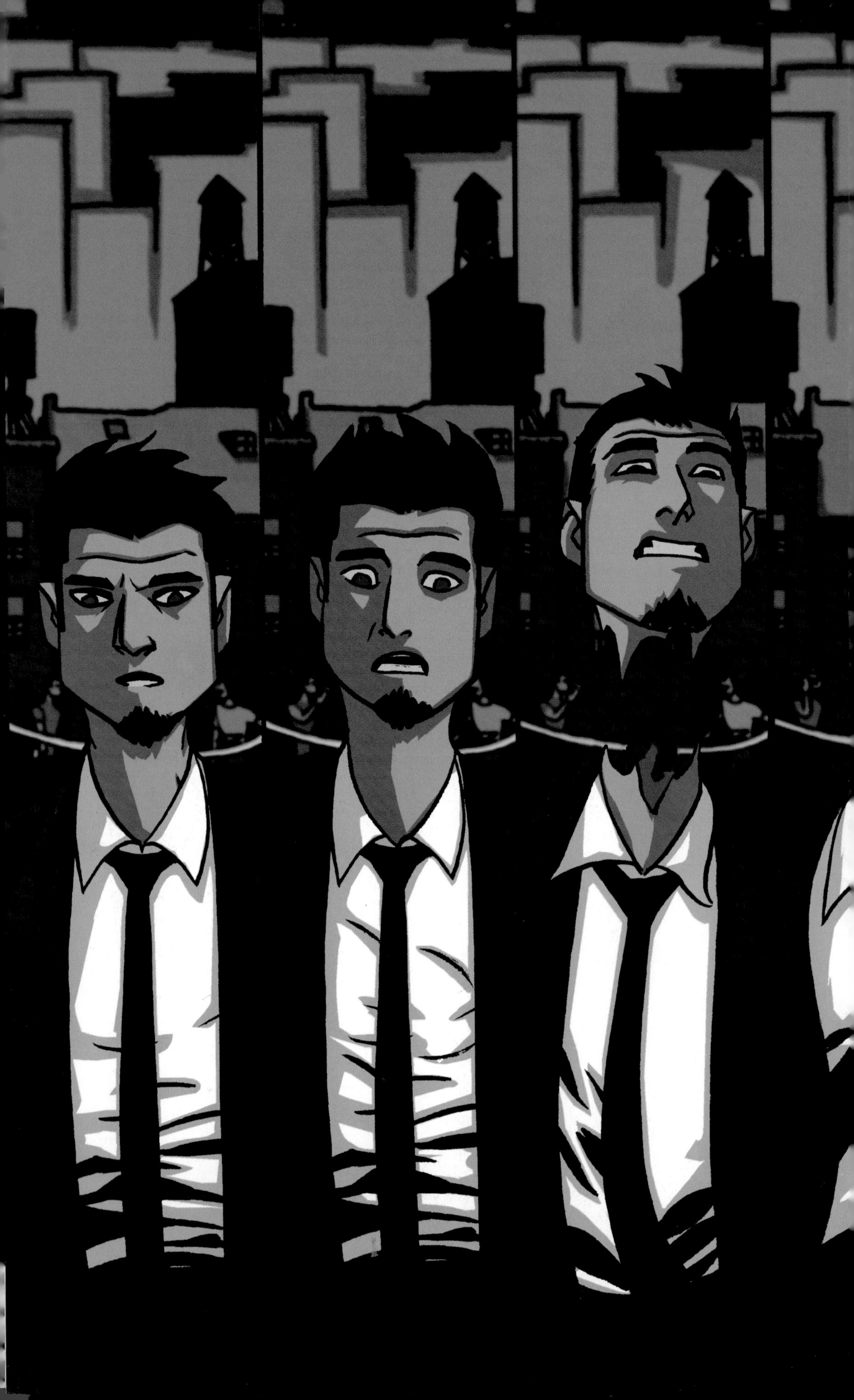

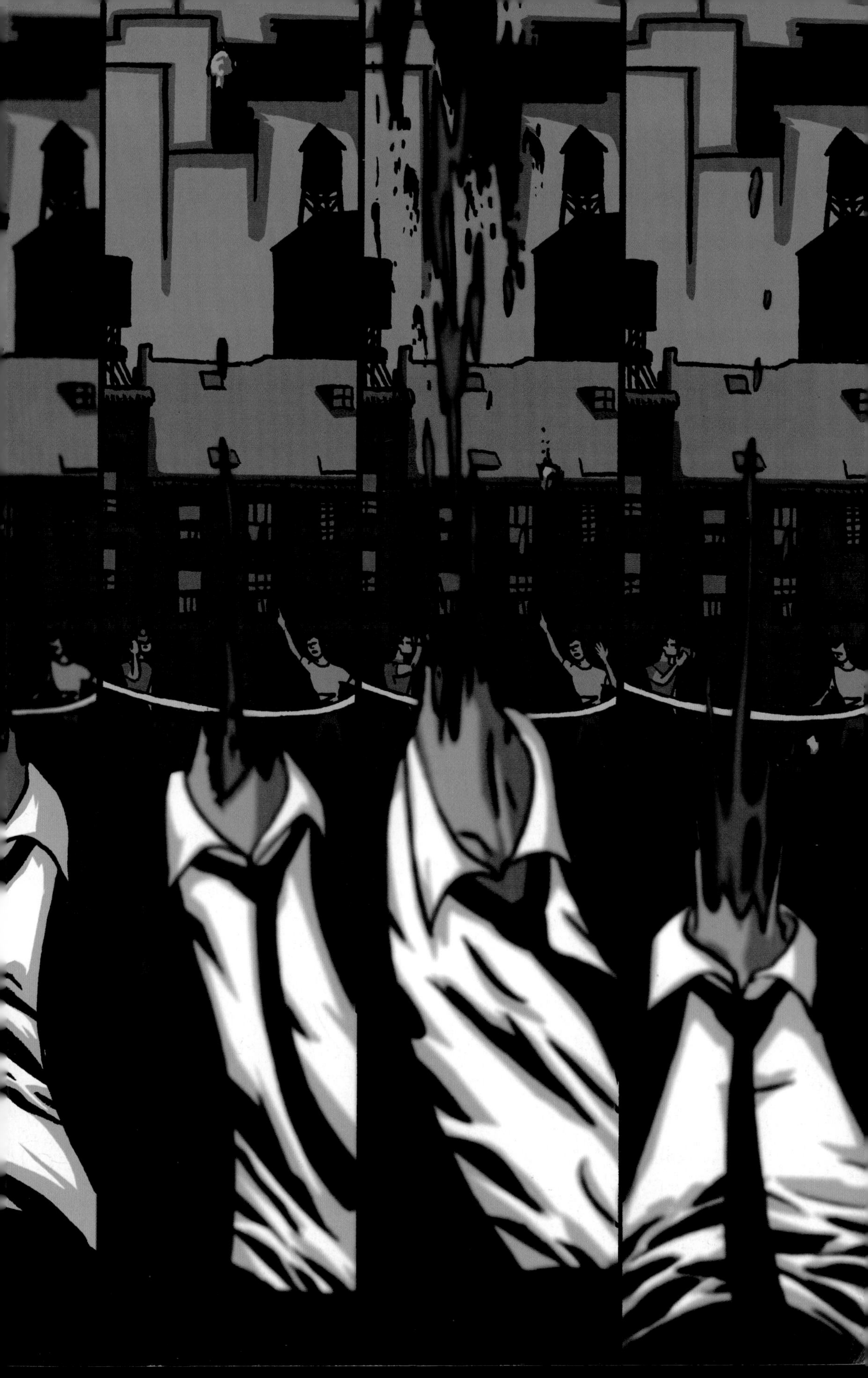

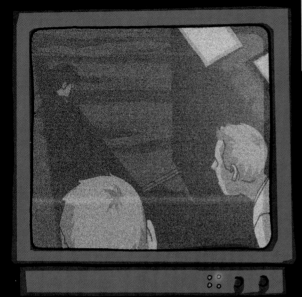

...17th POLICE OFFICER FELLED IN THE LINE OF DUTY IN UNDER TWO MONTHS.

AS THIS EXCLUSIVE FOOTAGE SHOWS...

THE ALLEGED ATTACKER IS STILL AT LARGE.

THIS POWERS-RELATED INCIDENT IS ONLY THE MOST RECENT TRAGEDY TO--

DIED ON TV.

I DON'T UNDERSTAND WHY YOU WOULD.

I KNOW.

WHAT? IT'S A "COP THING?" ONE OF THOSE THINGS ONLY A COP WOULD UNDER-STAND?

D'JA KNOW HIM?
YEAH, HE'S AN ASSHOLE.
YOU DON'T *HAVE* TO GO BACK, YOU KNOW.
DEENA?
I KNOW.
DO YOU?
TSK, THEY GONNA SHOW IT AGAIN?
OVER AND OVER TILL THE TAPE BREAKS.
IT'S DISGUSTING
WELCOME TO THE WORLD.

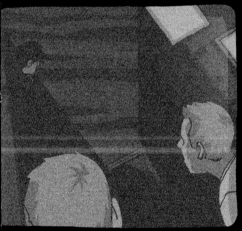

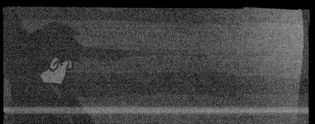

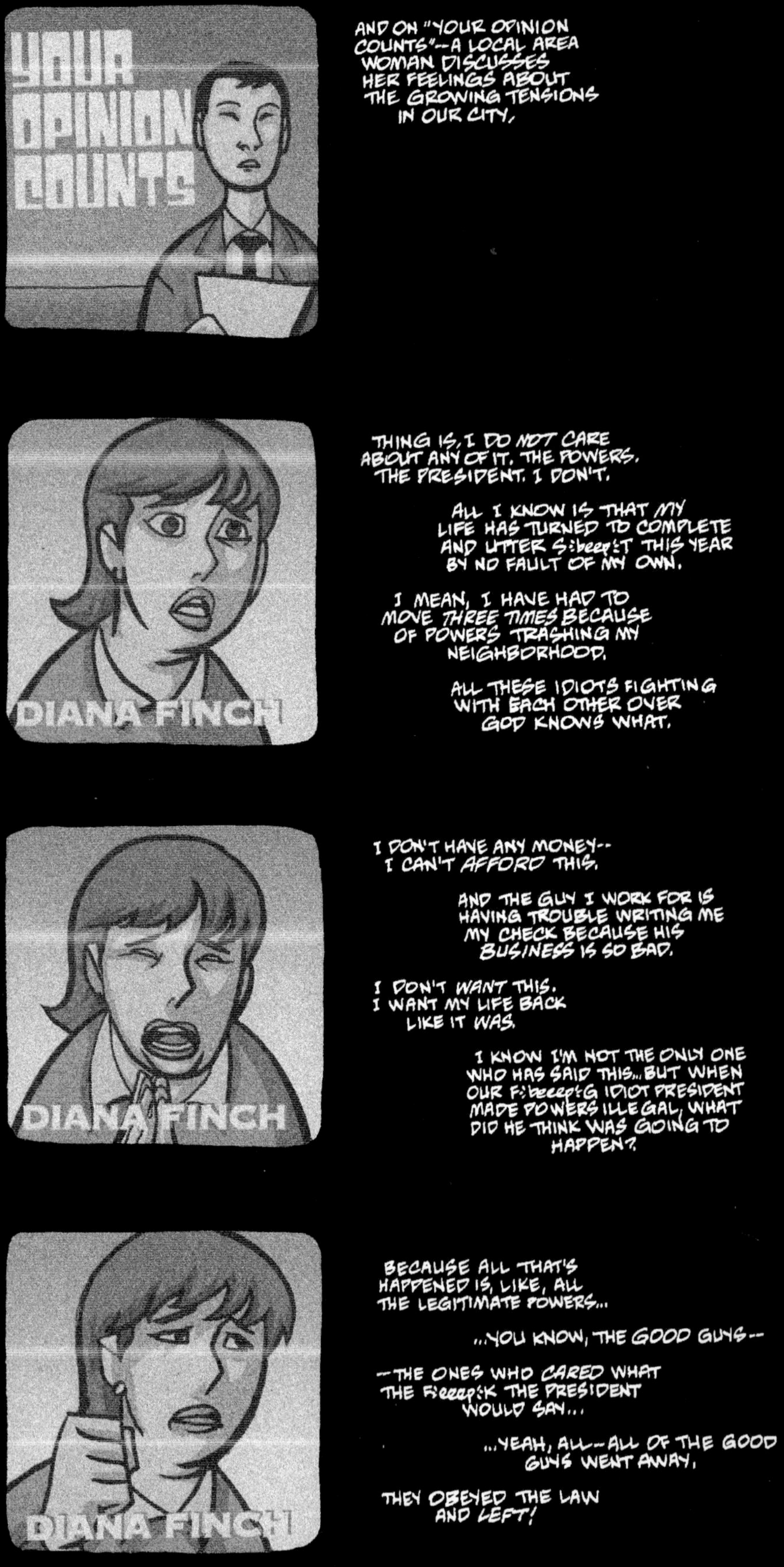
YOUR OPINION COUNTS
AND ON "YOUR OPINION COUNTS"--A LOCAL AREA WOMAN DISCUSSES HER FEELINGS ABOUT THE GROWING TENSIONS IN OUR CITY.
THING IS, I DO NOT CARE ABOUT ANY OF IT. THE POWERS. THE PRESIDENT. I DON'T.
ALL I KNOW IS THAT MY LIFE HAS TURNED TO COMPLETE AND UTTER S:beep:T THIS YEAR BY NO FAULT OF MY OWN.
I MEAN, I HAVE HAD TO MOVE THREE TIMES BECAUSE OF POWERS TRASHING MY NEIGHBORHOOD.
ALL THESE IDIOTS FIGHTING WITH EACH OTHER OVER GOD KNOWS WHAT.
DIANA FINCH
I DON'T HAVE ANY MONEY-- I CAN'T AFFORD THIS.
AND THE GUY I WORK FOR IS HAVING TROUBLE WRITING ME MY CHECK BECAUSE HIS BUSINESS IS SO BAD.
I DON'T WANT THIS. I WANT MY LIFE BACK LIKE IT WAS.
I KNOW I'M NOT THE ONLY ONE WHO HAS SAID THIS... BUT WHEN OUR F:beeep:G IDIOT PRESIDENT MADE POWERS ILLEGAL, WHAT DID HE THINK WAS GOING TO HAPPEN?
DIANA FINCH
BECAUSE ALL THAT'S HAPPENED IS, LIKE, ALL THE LEGITIMATE POWERS...
...YOU KNOW, THE GOOD GUYS--
--THE ONES WHO CARED WHAT THE F:eeeep:K THE PRESIDENT WOULD SAY...
...YEAH, ALL--ALL OF THE GOOD GUYS WENT AWAY.
THEY OBEYED THE LAW AND LEFT!
DIANA FINCH

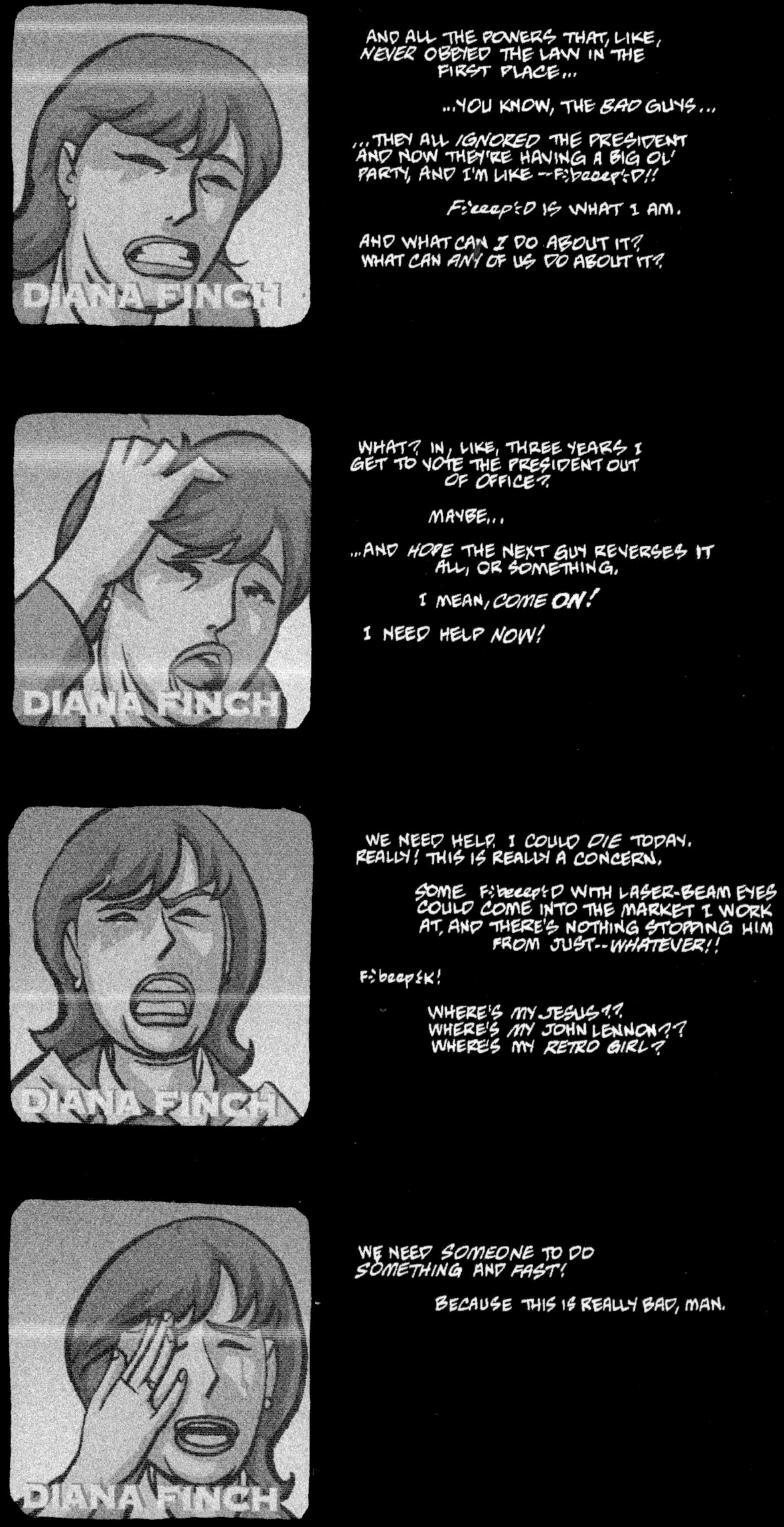
DIANA FINCH
AND ALL THE POWERS THAT, LIKE, NEVER OBEYED THE LAW IN THE FIRST PLACE...
...YOU KNOW, THE BAD GUYS...
...THEY ALL IGNORED THE PRESIDENT AND NOW THEY'RE HAVING A BIG OL' PARTY, AND I'M LIKE --F:beep:D!!
F:beep:D IS WHAT I AM.
AND WHAT CAN I DO ABOUT IT? WHAT CAN ANY OF US DO ABOUT IT?
DIANA FINCH
WHAT? IN, LIKE, THREE YEARS I GET TO VOTE THE PRESIDENT OUT OF OFFICE?
MAYBE...
...AND HOPE THE NEXT GUY REVERSES IT ALL, OR SOMETHING.
I MEAN, COME ON!
I NEED HELP NOW!
DIANA FINCH
WE NEED HELP. I COULD DIE TODAY. REALLY! THIS IS REALLY A CONCERN.
SOME F:beep:D WITH LASER-BEAM EYES COULD COME INTO THE MARKET I WORK AT, AND THERE'S NOTHING STOPPING HIM FROM JUST--WHATEVER!!
F:beep:K!
WHERE'S MY JESUS??
WHERE'S MY JOHN LENNON??
WHERE'S MY RETRO GIRL?
DIANA FINCH
WE NEED SOMEONE TO DO SOMETHING AND FAST!
BECAUSE THIS IS REALLY BAD, MAN.

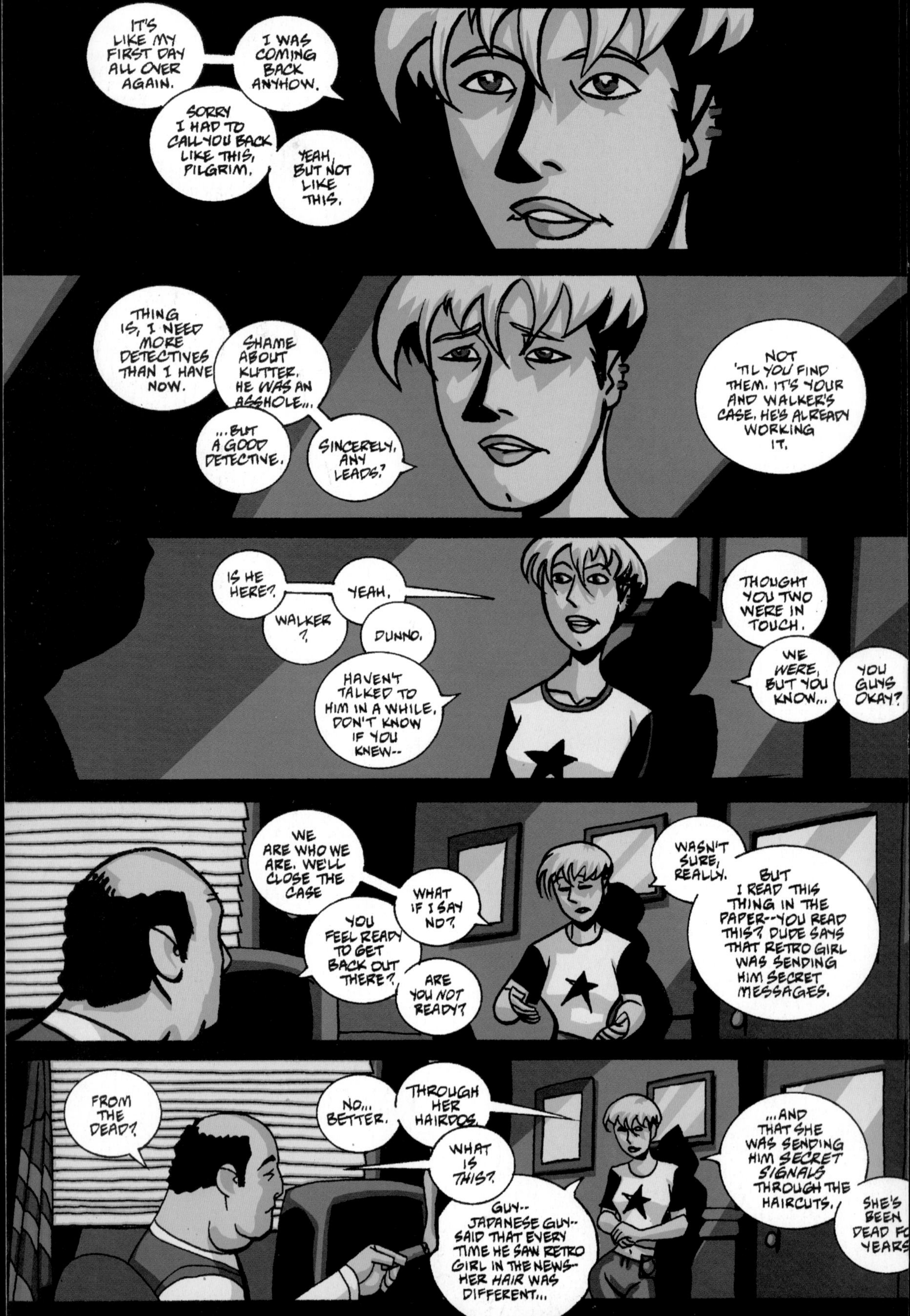

IT'S LIKE MY FIRST DAY ALL OVER AGAIN.
I WAS COMING BACK ANYHOW.
SORRY I HAD TO CALL YOU BACK LIKE THIS, PILGRIM.
YEAH, BUT NOT LIKE THIS.
THING IS, I NEED MORE DETECTIVES THAN I HAVE NOW.
SHAME ABOUT KUTTER. HE WAS AN ASSHOLE...
...BUT A GOOD DETECTIVE.
SINCERELY, ANY LEADS?
NOT 'TIL YOU FIND THEM. IT'S YOUR AND WALKER'S CASE. HE'S ALREADY WORKING IT.
IS HE HERE?
YEAH.
WALKER?
DUNNO.
HAVEN'T TALKED TO HIM IN A WHILE. DON'T KNOW IF YOU KNEW--
THOUGHT YOU TWO WERE IN TOUCH.
WE WERE, BUT YOU KNOW...
YOU GUYS OKAY?
WE ARE WHO WE ARE. WE'LL CLOSE THE CASE
WHAT IF I SAY NO?
YOU FEEL READY TO GET BACK OUT THERE?
ARE YOU NOT READY?
WASN'T SURE, REALLY.
BUT I READ THIS THING IN THE PAPER--YOU READ THIS? DUDE SAYS THAT RETRO GIRL WAS SENDING HIM SECRET MESSAGES.
FROM THE DEAD?
NO... BETTER.
THROUGH HER HAIRDOS.
WHAT IS THIS?
GUY-- JAPANESE GUY-- SAID THAT EVERY TIME HE SAW RETRO GIRL IN THE NEWS-- HER HAIR WAS DIFFERENT...
...AND THAT SHE WAS SENDING HIM SECRET SIGNALS THROUGH THE HAIRCUTS.
SHE'S BEEN DEAD FO YEARS

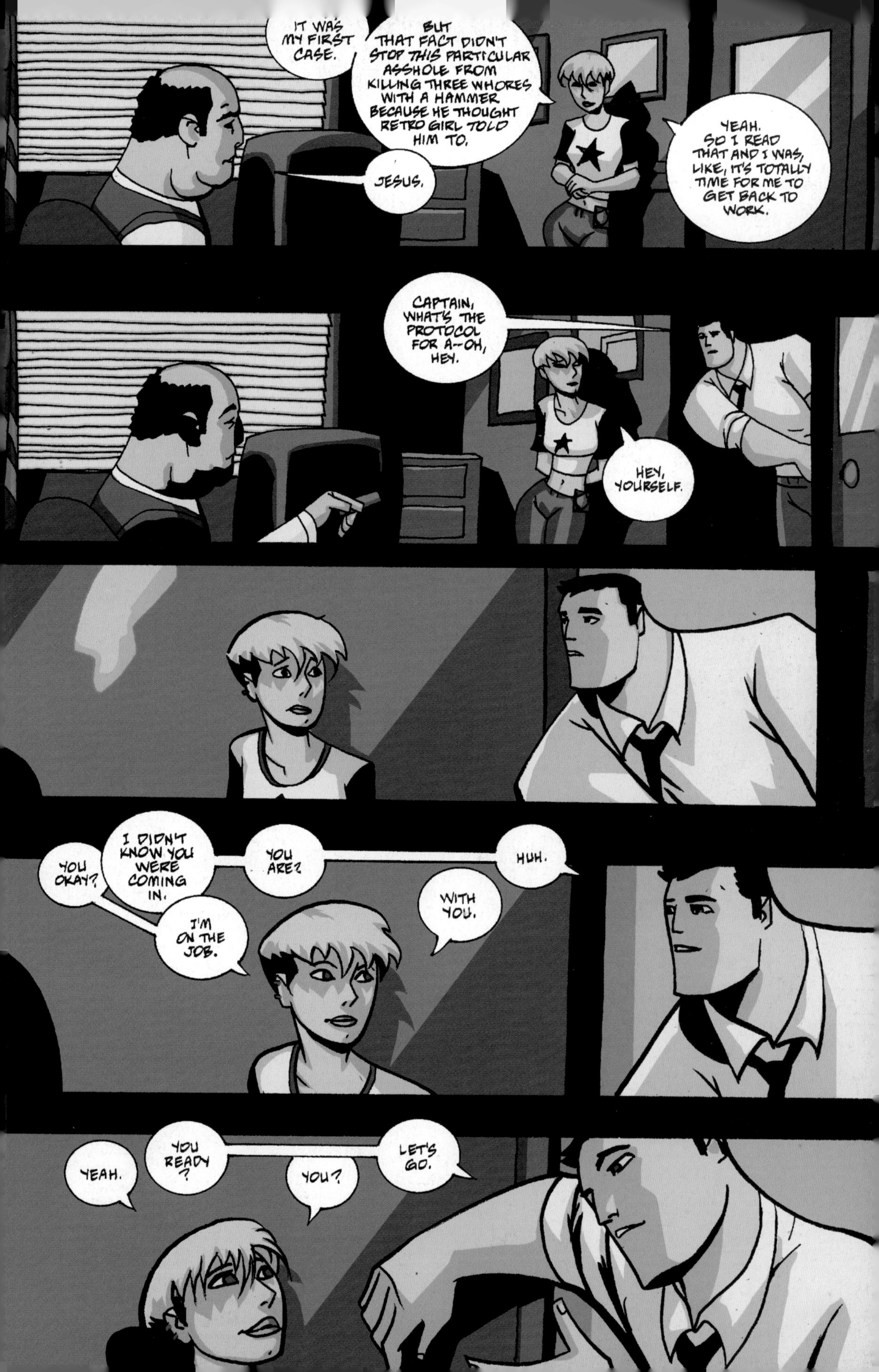
IT WAS MY FIRST CASE.
BUT THAT FACT DIDN'T STOP THIS PARTICULAR ASSHOLE FROM KILLING THREE WHORES WITH A HAMMER BECAUSE HE THOUGHT RETRO GIRL TOLD HIM TO.
JESUS.
YEAH. SO I READ THAT AND I WAS, LIKE, IT'S TOTALLY TIME FOR ME TO GET BACK TO WORK.
CAPTAIN, WHAT'S THE PROTOCOL FOR A--OH, HEY.
HEY, YOURSELF.
YOU OKAY?
I DIDN'T KNOW YOU WERE COMING IN.
I'M ON THE JOB.
YOU ARE?
WITH YOU.
HUH.
YEAH.
YOU READY?
YOU?
LET'S GO.

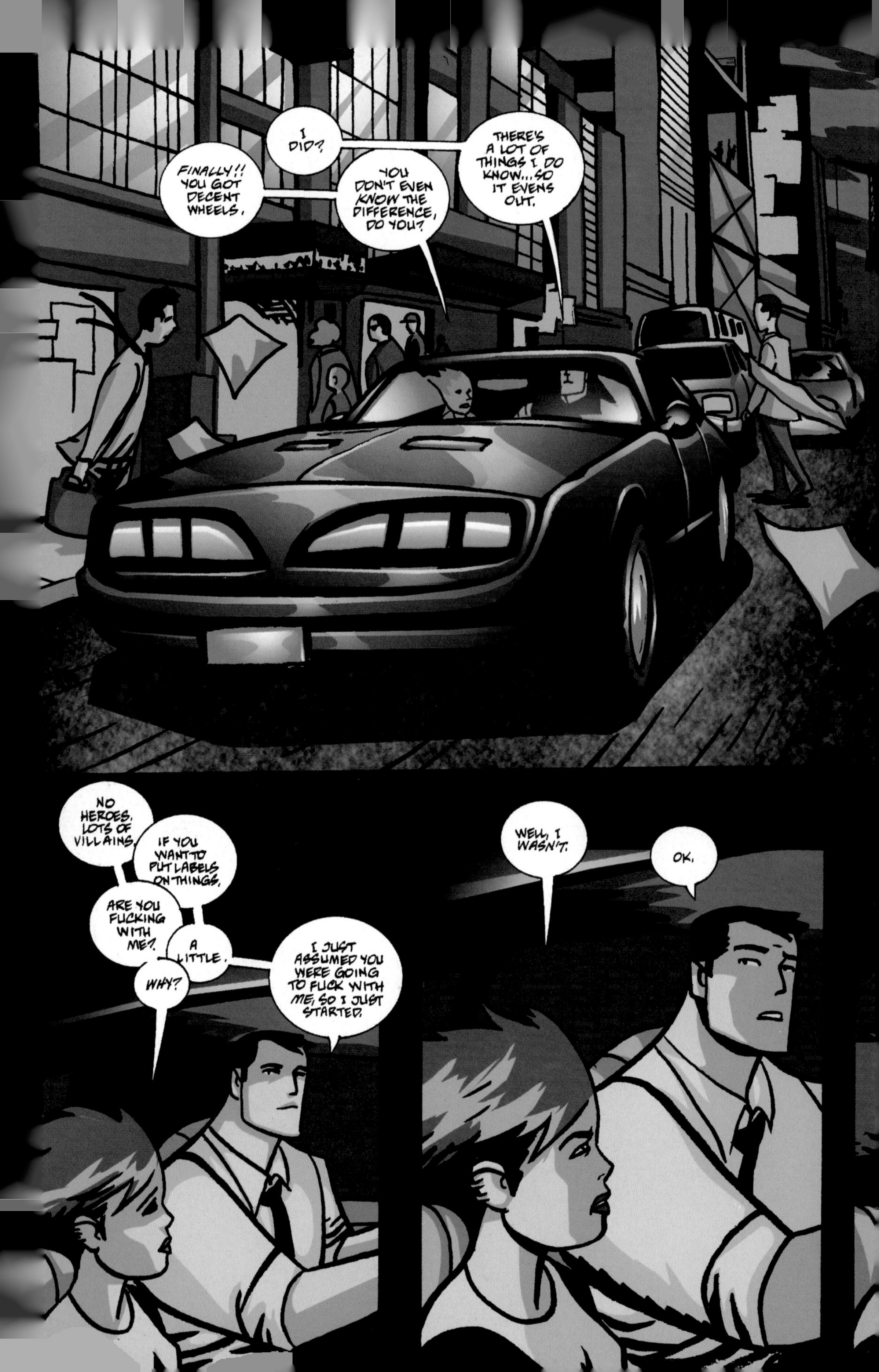
FINALLY!! YOU GOT DECENT WHEELS.
I DID?
YOU DON'T EVEN KNOW THE DIFFERENCE, DO YOU?
THERE'S A LOT OF THINGS I DO KNOW... SO IT EVENS OUT.
NO HEROES. LOTS OF VILLAINS.
IF YOU WANT TO PUT LABELS ON THINGS.
ARE YOU FUCKING WITH ME?
A LITTLE.
WHY?
I JUST ASSUMED YOU WERE GOING TO FUCK WITH ME, SO I JUST STARTED.
WELL, I WASN'T.
OK.

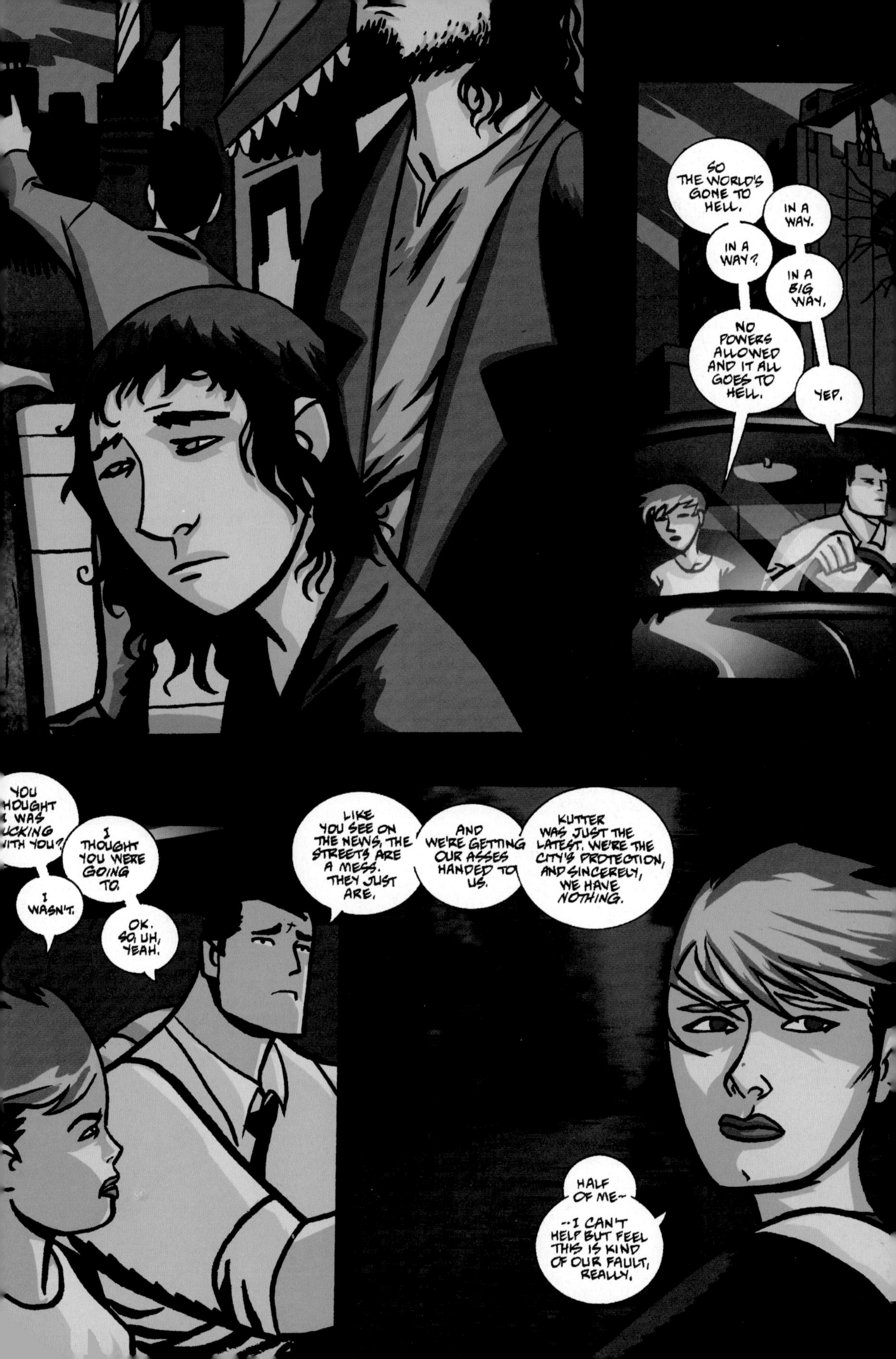
SO THE WORLD'S GONE TO HELL.
IN A WAY.
IN A WAY?
IN A BIG WAY.
NO POWERS ALLOWED AND IT ALL GOES TO HELL.
YEP.
YOU HOUGHT WAS UCKING ITH YOU?
I THOUGHT YOU WERE GOING TO.
I WASN'T.
OK. SO, UH, YEAH.
LIKE YOU SEE ON THE NEWS, THE STREETS ARE A MESS. THEY JUST ARE.
AND WE'RE GETTING OUR ASSES HANDED TO US.
KUTTER WAS JUST THE LATEST. WE'RE THE CITY'S PROTECTION, AND SINCERELY, WE HAVE *NOTHING*.
HALF OF ME--
--I CAN'T HELP BUT FEEL THIS IS KIND OF OUR FAULT, REALLY.

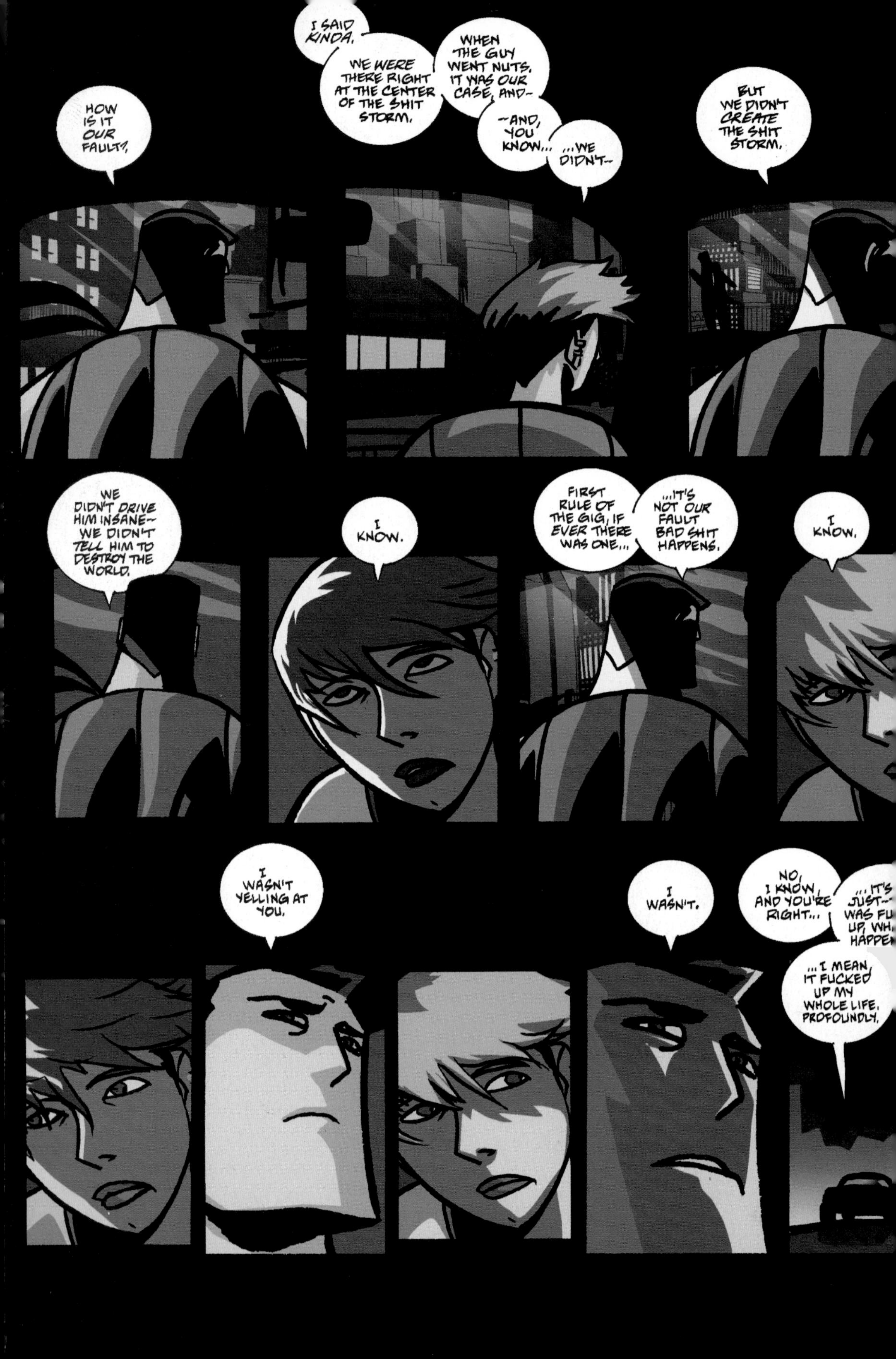
HOW IS IT OUR FAULT?,
I SAID KINDA.
WE WERE THERE RIGHT AT THE CENTER OF THE SHIT STORM.
WHEN THE GUY WENT NUTS, IT WAS OUR CASE, AND--
--AND, YOU KNOW...
...WE DIDN'T--
BUT WE DIDN'T CREATE THE SHIT STORM.
WE DIDN'T DRIVE HIM INSANE-- WE DIDN'T TELL HIM TO DESTROY THE WORLD.
I KNOW.
FIRST RULE OF THE GIG, IF EVER THERE WAS ONE...
...IT'S NOT OUR FAULT BAD SHIT HAPPENS.
I KNOW.
I WASN'T YELLING AT YOU.
I WASN'T.
NO, I KNOW, AND YOU'RE RIGHT...
...IT'S JUST--
...I MEAN, IT FUCKED UP MY WHOLE LIFE. PROFOUNDLY.

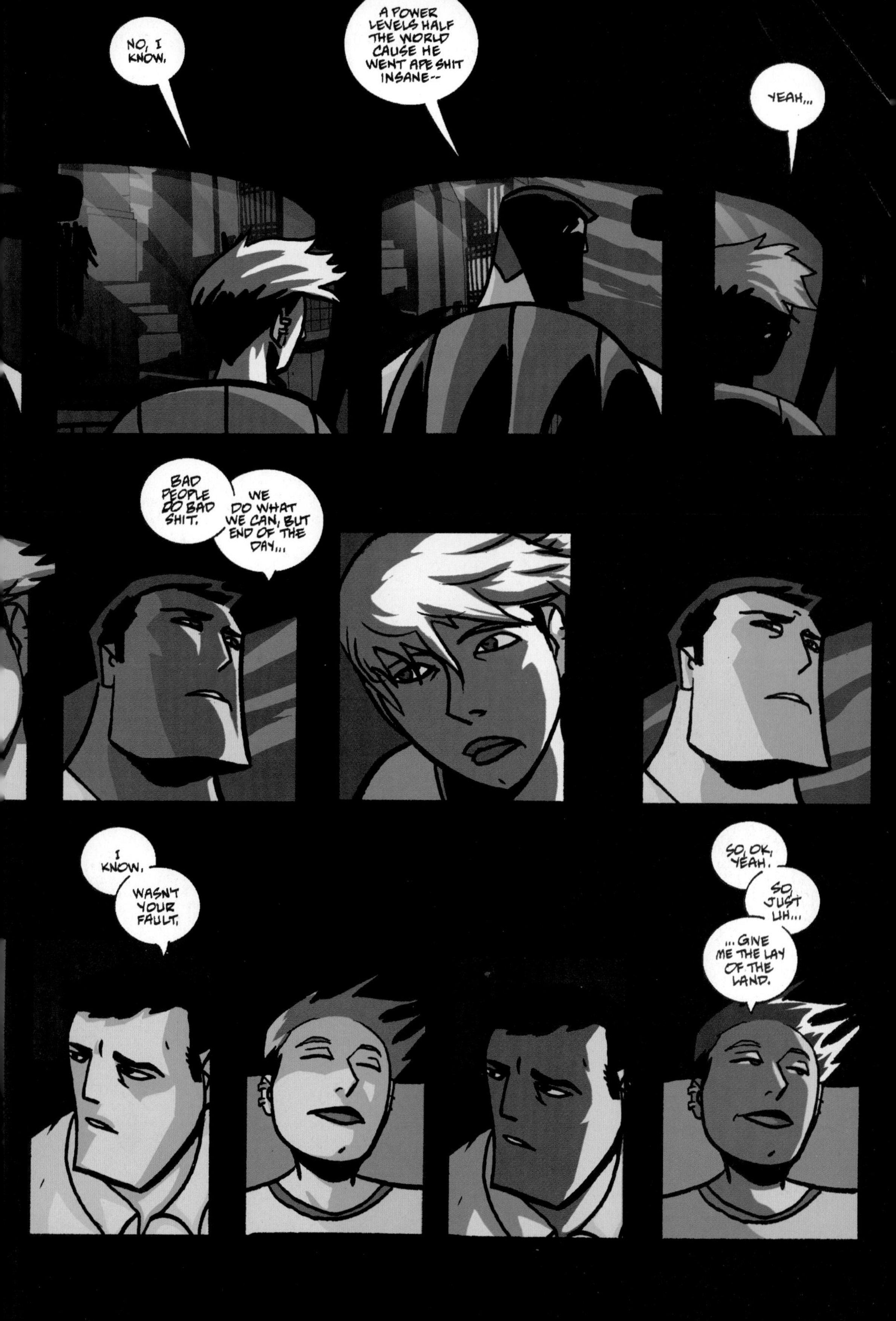
NO, I KNOW.
A POWER LEVELS HALF THE WORLD CAUSE HE WENT APE SHIT INSANE--
YEAH...
BAD PEOPLE DO BAD SHIT.
WE DO WHAT WE CAN, BUT END OF THE DAY...
I KNOW.
WASN'T YOUR FAULT.
SO, OK, YEAH.
SO, JUST UH...
...GIVE ME THE LAY OF THE LAND.

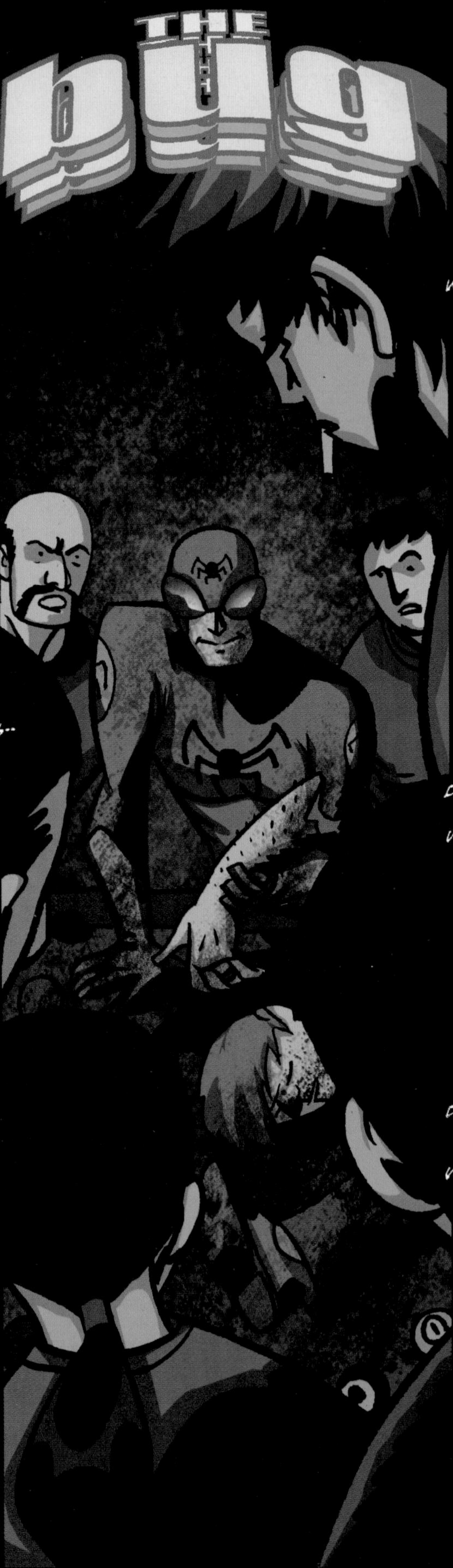
THE bug

WALKER:
AH, WELL...

IT'S NOT JUST THAT WE HAVE A BUNCH OF FUCKS WITH POWERS RUNNING AROUND BEING ASSHOLES.

...AND NO DECENT POWERS TO KEEP THEM IN LINE...

...IT'S THAT THEY'RE FIGHTING WITH *EACH OTHER.*

DEENA PILGRIM:
BIG SUPER-VILLAIN TURF WAR.

WALKER:
EXACTLY. BASICALLY WE HAVE THREE FAMILIES.

DEENA PILGRIM:
FAMILIES?

WALKER:
GANGS, SYNDICATES--THEY GOT TO CALLING THEM-SELVES FAMILIES, SO...

ONE IS LED BY "THE BUG."

DEENA PILGRIM:
NO.

WALKER:
YES.

DEENA PILGRIM:
THAT GUY?

WALKER:
YEAH.

DEENA PILGRIM:
I KNOW HIM. I PINCHED HIM WHEN I WAS WORKING VICE. GUY'S A LOW-RENT PIECE OF--

WALKER:
NO, YEAH, HE'S A FUCKING ASSHOLE. AND NOW--

DEENA PILGRIM:
AND NOW HE'S GOT A *CREW?* HOW DOES THAT HAPPEN EXACTLY?

WALKER:
HE'S *STEPPED UP* IN THE WORLD.

THERE WAS THIS GUY, ORLANDO. GUY COULD SPIN THIS COLOR STUFF OUT OF HIS FINGERS OR SOMETHING... JUST GOT OUT OF THE BIN FOR A B AND E.

THEY GOT INTO IT--IN PUBLIC--ORLANDO AND THE BUG.

(THIS WAS DOWN AT CHAYKIN'S, ON THE SQUARE.)

RUMOR IS--WORD IS--THAT THE BUG BEAT ORLANDO TO DEATH, AND RIGHT THERE--RIGHT IN FRONT OF EVERYBODY--HE *ATE* THE GUY.

DEENA PILGRIM:
WHAT?

WALKER:
OR *PART* OF THE GUY.

DON'T KNOW.

SCARED THE SHIT OUT OF *HALF* THE CITY, *IMPRESSED* THE SHIT OUT OF THE *OTHER* HALF.

HE GOT A LOT OF PEOPLE IN LINE--THIS BUG. GUY STEPPED UP. *ATE* A GUY.

DEENA PILGRIM:
THAT'LL DO IT. AND THAT'S...

WALKER:
THE NORTH SIDE.

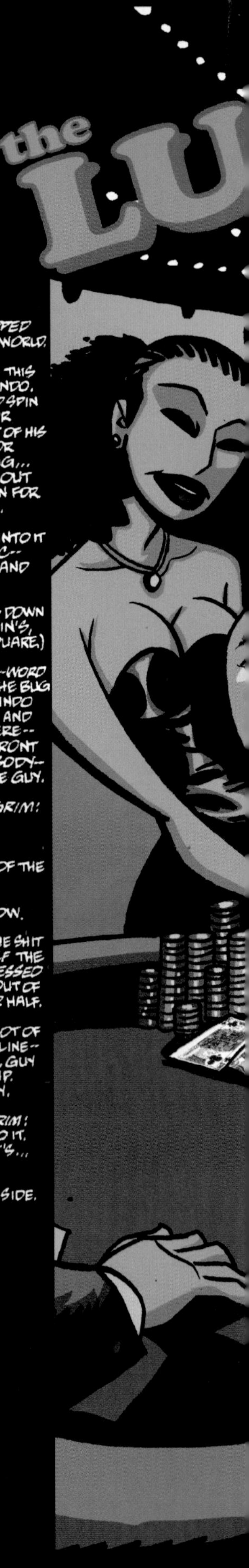
the LU

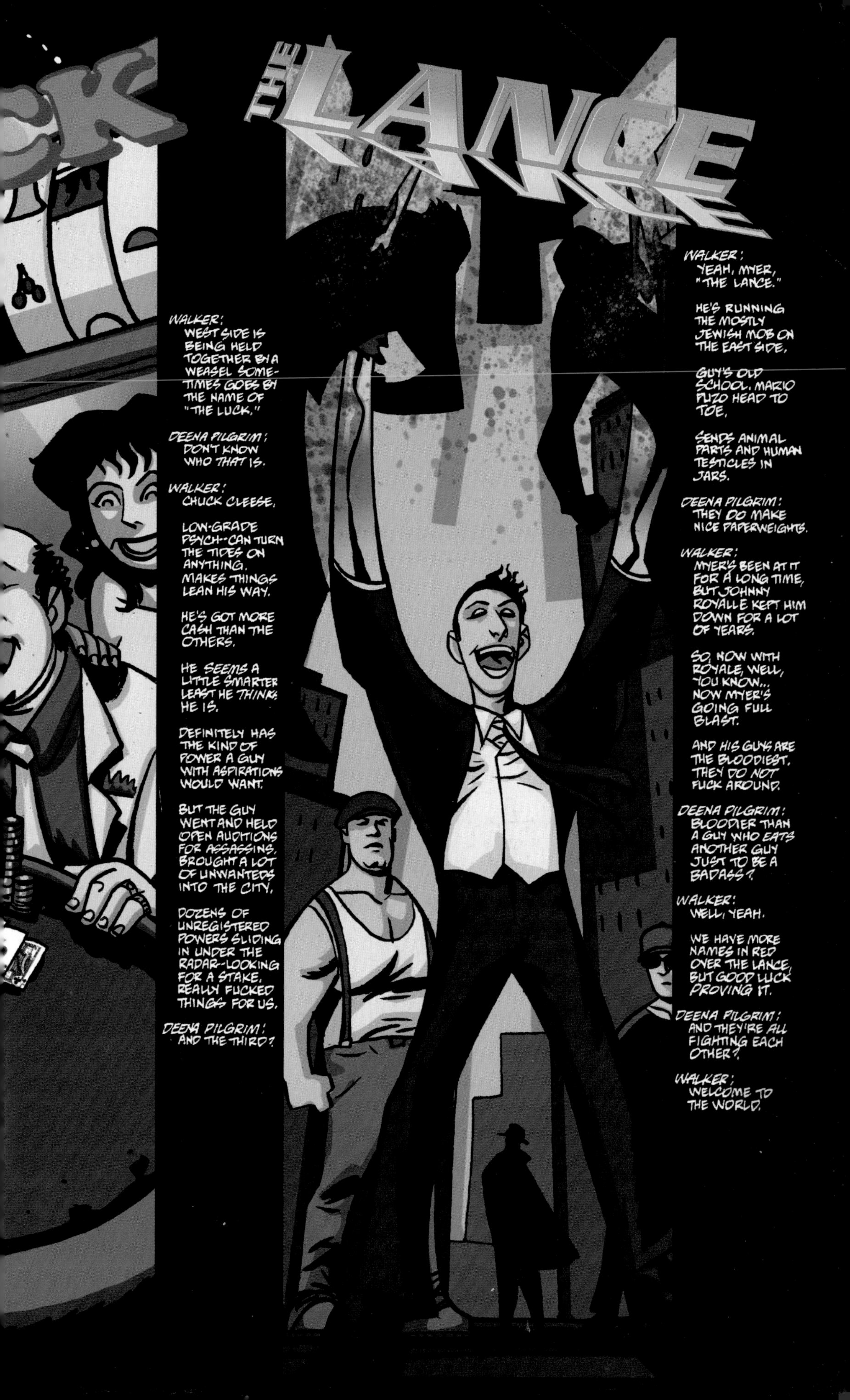
THE LANCE
WALKER:
WEST SIDE IS BEING HELD TOGETHER BY A WEASEL SOMETIMES GOES BY THE NAME OF "THE LUCK."
DEENA PILGRIM:
DON'T KNOW WHO THAT IS.
WALKER:
CHUCK CLEESE.
LOW-GRADE PSYCH--CAN TURN THE TIDES ON ANYTHING. MAKES THINGS LEAN HIS WAY.
HE'S GOT MORE CASH THAN THE OTHERS.
HE SEEMS A LITTLE SMARTER LEAST HE THINKS HE IS.
DEFINITELY HAS THE KIND OF POWER A GUY WITH ASPIRATIONS WOULD WANT.
BUT THE GUY WENT AND HELD OPEN AUDITIONS FOR ASSASSINS, BROUGHT A LOT OF UNWANTEDS INTO THE CITY.
DOZENS OF UNREGISTERED POWERS SLIDING IN UNDER THE RADAR--LOOKING FOR A STAKE. REALLY FUCKED THINGS FOR US.
DEENA PILGRIM:
AND THE THIRD?
WALKER:
YEAH, MYER, "THE LANCE."
HE'S RUNNING THE MOSTLY JEWISH MOB ON THE EAST SIDE.
GUY'S OLD SCHOOL. MARIO PUZO HEAD TO TOE.
SENDS ANIMAL PARTS AND HUMAN TESTICLES IN JARS.
DEENA PILGRIM:
THEY DO MAKE NICE PAPERWEIGHTS.
WALKER:
MYER'S BEEN AT IT FOR A LONG TIME, BUT JOHNNY ROYALLE KEPT HIM DOWN FOR A LOT OF YEARS.
SO, NOW WITH ROYALE, WELL, YOU KNOW... NOW MYER'S GOING FULL BLAST.
AND HIS GUYS ARE THE BLOODIEST. THEY DO NOT FUCK AROUND.
DEENA PILGRIM:
BLOODIER THAN A GUY WHO EATS ANOTHER GUY JUST TO BE A BADASS?
WALKER:
WELL, YEAH.
WE HAVE MORE NAMES IN RED OVER THE LANCE, BUT GOOD LUCK PROVING IT.
DEENA PILGRIM:
AND THEY'RE ALL FIGHTING EACH OTHER?
WALKER:
WELCOME TO THE WORLD.

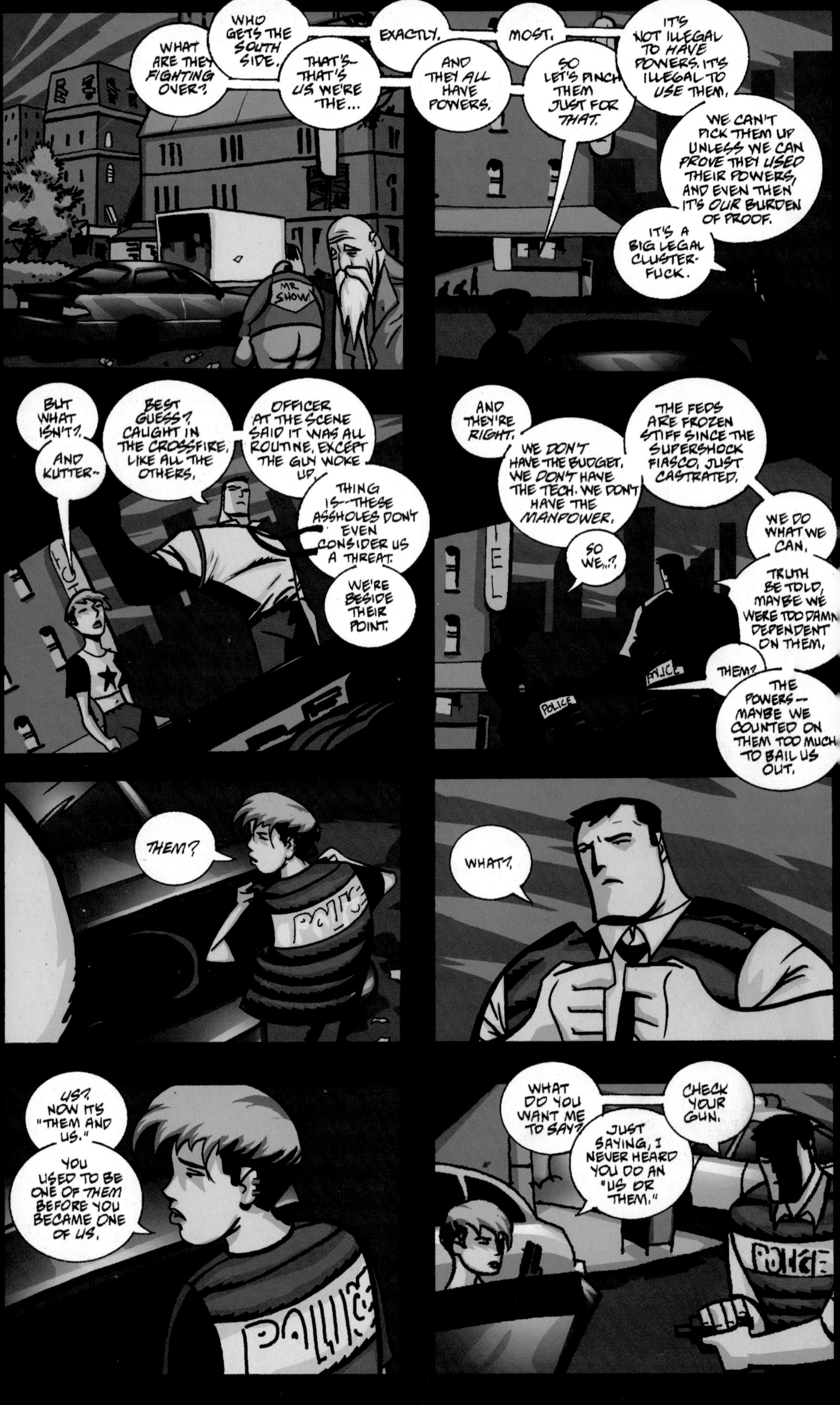
WHAT ARE THEY FIGHTING OVER?
WHO GETS THE SOUTH SIDE.
THAT'S-- THAT'S US WE'RE THE...
EXACTLY.
AND THEY ALL HAVE POWERS.
MOST.
SO LET'S PINCH THEM JUST FOR THAT.
IT'S NOT ILLEGAL TO HAVE POWERS. IT'S ILLEGAL TO USE THEM.
WE CAN'T PICK THEM UP UNLESS WE CAN PROVE THEY USED THEIR POWERS, AND EVEN THEN IT'S OUR BURDEN OF PROOF.
IT'S A BIG LEGAL CLUSTER-FUCK.
BUT WHAT ISN'T?
AND KUTTER--
BEST GUESS? CAUGHT IN THE CROSSFIRE, LIKE ALL THE OTHERS.
OFFICER AT THE SCENE SAID IT WAS ALL ROUTINE, EXCEPT THE GUY WOKE UP.
THING IS--THESE ASSHOLES DON'T EVEN CONSIDER US A THREAT.
WE'RE BESIDE THEIR POINT.
AND THEY'RE RIGHT.
WE DON'T HAVE THE BUDGET. WE DON'T HAVE THE TECH. WE DON'T HAVE THE MANPOWER.
THE FEDS ARE FROZEN STIFF SINCE THE SUPERSHOCK FIASCO. JUST CASTRATED.
SO WE...?
WE DO WHAT WE CAN.
TRUTH BE TOLD, MAYBE WE WERE TOO DAMN DEPENDENT ON THEM.
THEM?
THE POWERS-- MAYBE WE COUNTED ON THEM TOO MUCH TO BAIL US OUT.
THEM?
WHAT?
US? NOW IT'S "THEM AND US."
YOU USED TO BE ONE OF THEM BEFORE YOU BECAME ONE OF US.
WHAT DO YOU WANT ME TO SAY?
CHECK YOUR GUN.
JUST SAYING, I NEVER HEARD YOU DO AN "US OR THEM."

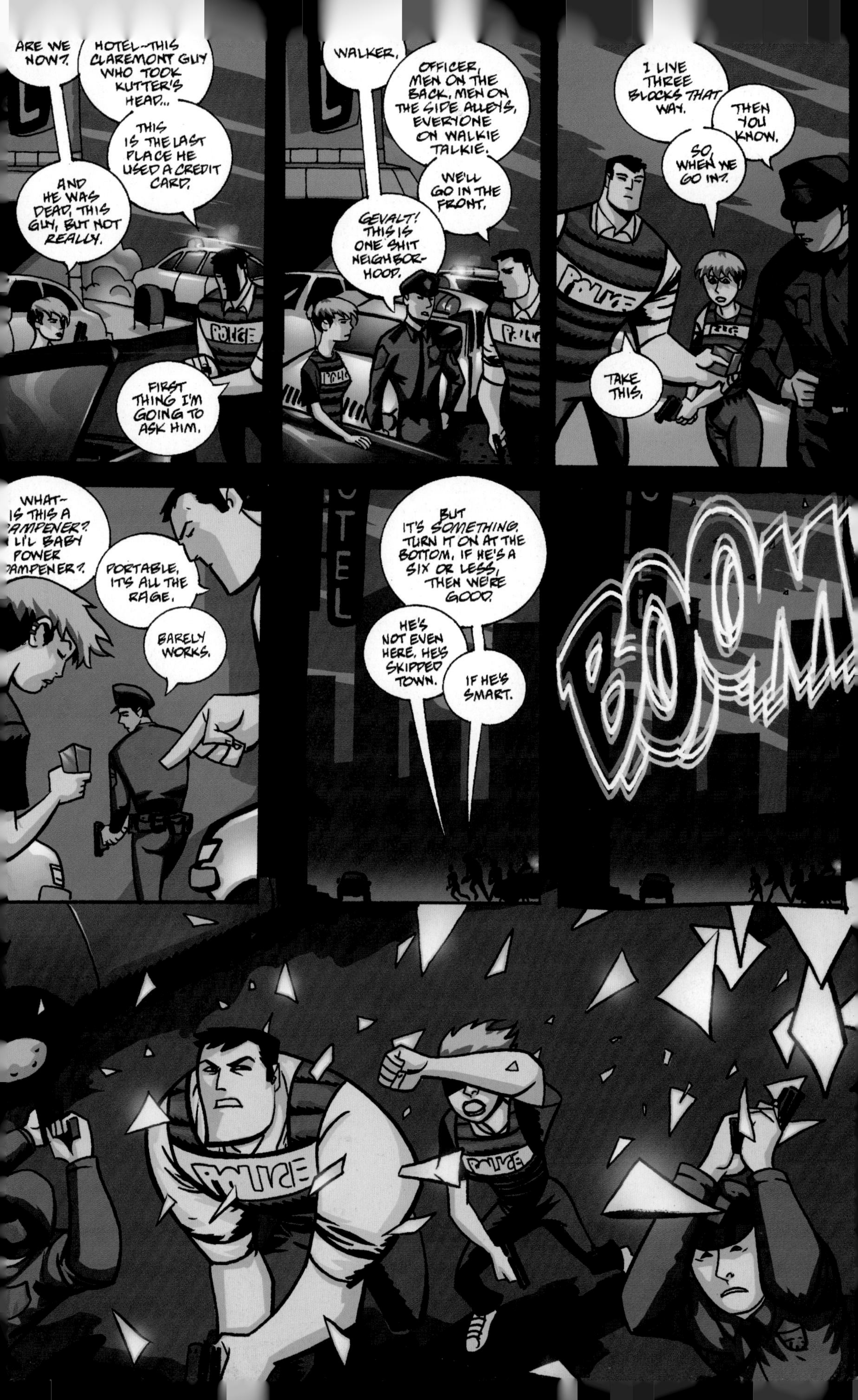
ARE WE NOW?
HOTEL--THIS CLAREMONT GUY WHO TOOK KUTTER'S HEAD...
THIS IS THE LAST PLACE HE USED A CREDIT CARD.
AND HE WAS DEAD, THIS GUY, BUT NOT REALLY.
FIRST THING I'M GOING TO ASK HIM.
WALKER.
OFFICER, MEN ON THE BACK, MEN ON THE SIDE ALLEYS, EVERYONE ON WALKIE TALKIE.
WE'LL GO IN THE FRONT.
GEVALT! THIS IS ONE SHIT NEIGHBORHOOD.
I LIVE THREE BLOCKS THAT WAY.
THEN YOU KNOW.
SO, WHEN WE GO IN?
TAKE THIS.
WHAT-- IS THIS A DAMPENER? LI'L BABY POWER DAMPENER?
PORTABLE, IT'S ALL THE RAGE.
BARELY WORKS.
BUT IT'S SOMETHING. TURN IT ON AT THE BOTTOM. IF HE'S A SIX OR LESS, THEN WE'RE GOOD.
HE'S NOT EVEN HERE. HE'S SKIPPED TOWN.
IF HE'S SMART.
BOOM
POLICE
POLICE

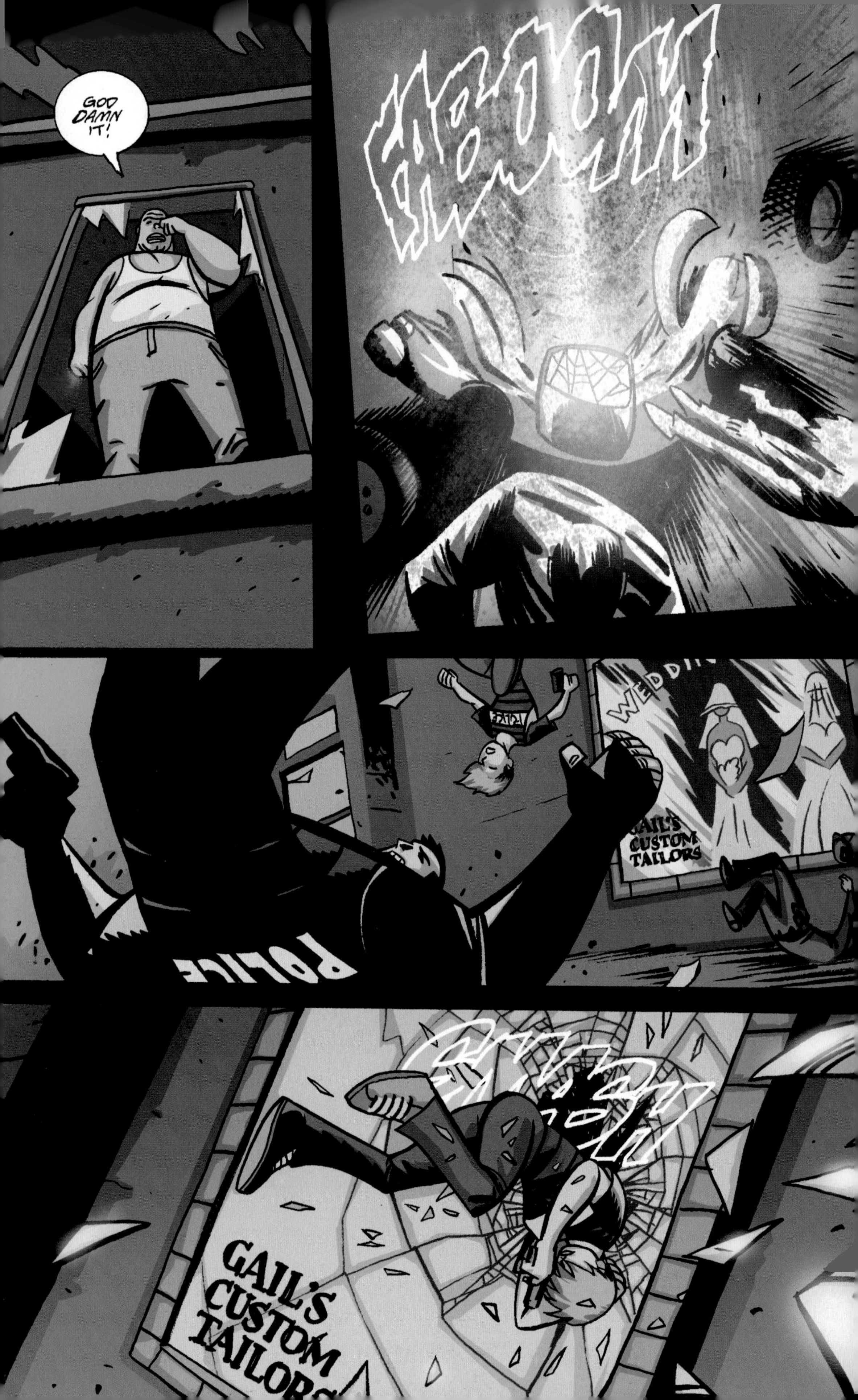

GOD DAMN IT!
GAIL'S CUSTOM TAILORS
GAIL'S CUSTOM TAILORS

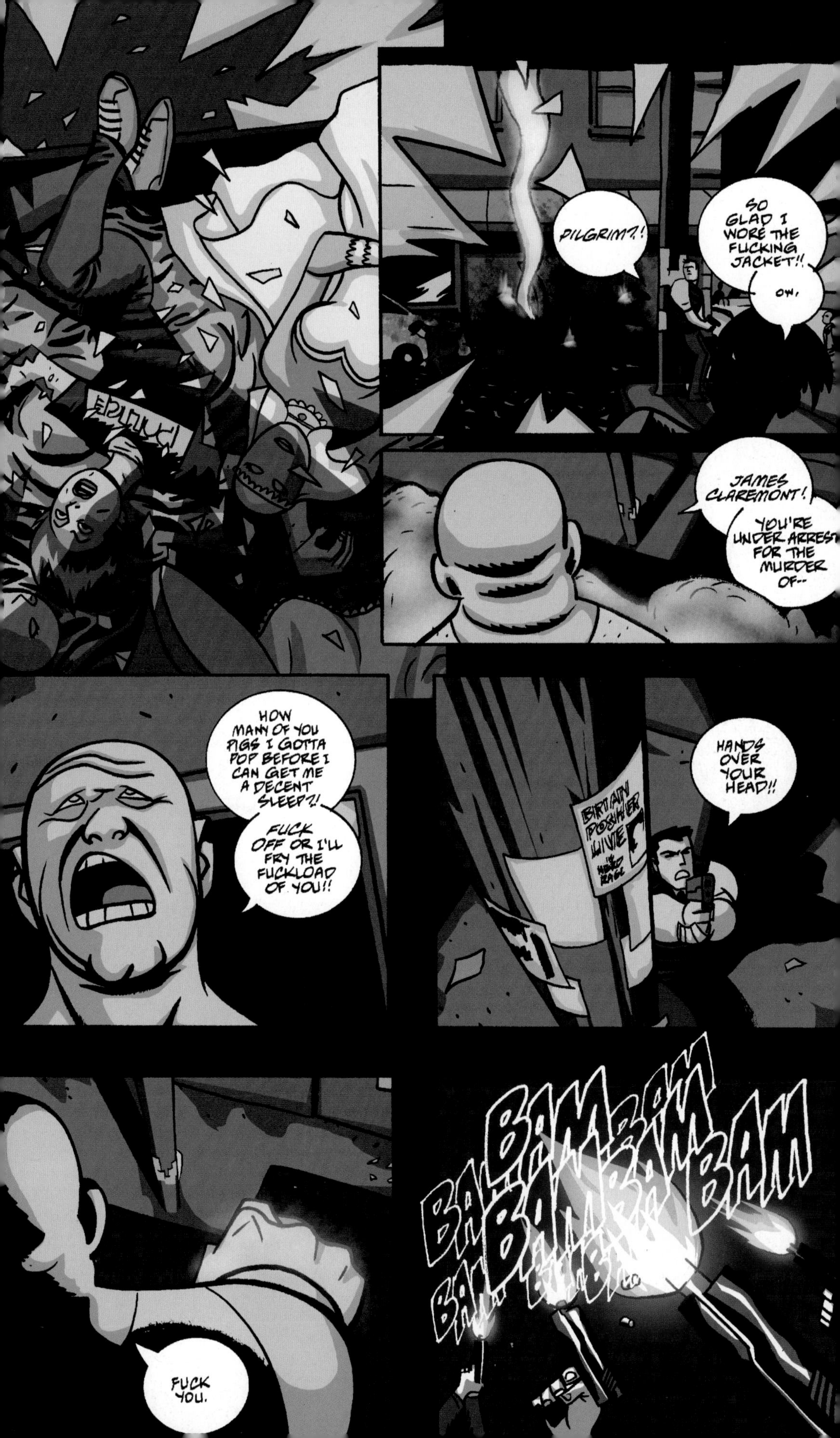
PILGRIM?!
SO GLAD I WORE THE FUCKING JACKET!!
OW.
JAMES CLAREMONT!
YOU'RE UNDER ARREST FOR THE MURDER OF--
HOW MANY OF YOU PIGS I GOTTA POP BEFORE I CAN GET ME A DECENT SLEEP?!
FUCK OFF OR I'LL FRY THE FUCKLOAD OF YOU!!
HANDS OVER YOUR HEAD!!
FUCK YOU.
BAM BAM BAM BAM BAM BAM

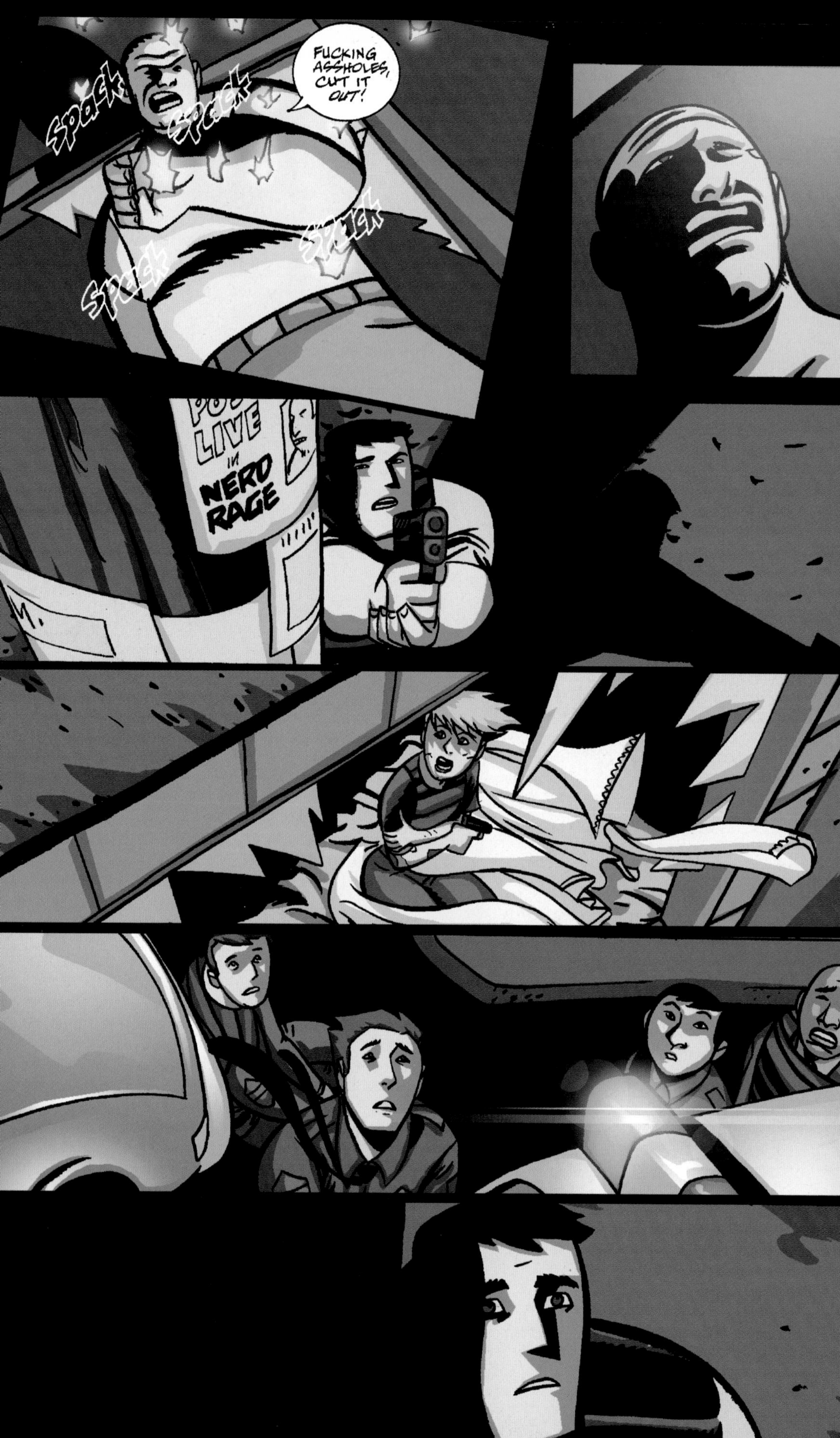
Spack Spack
FUCKING ASSHOLES, CUT IT OUT!
Spack Spack
LIVE IN NERD RAGE

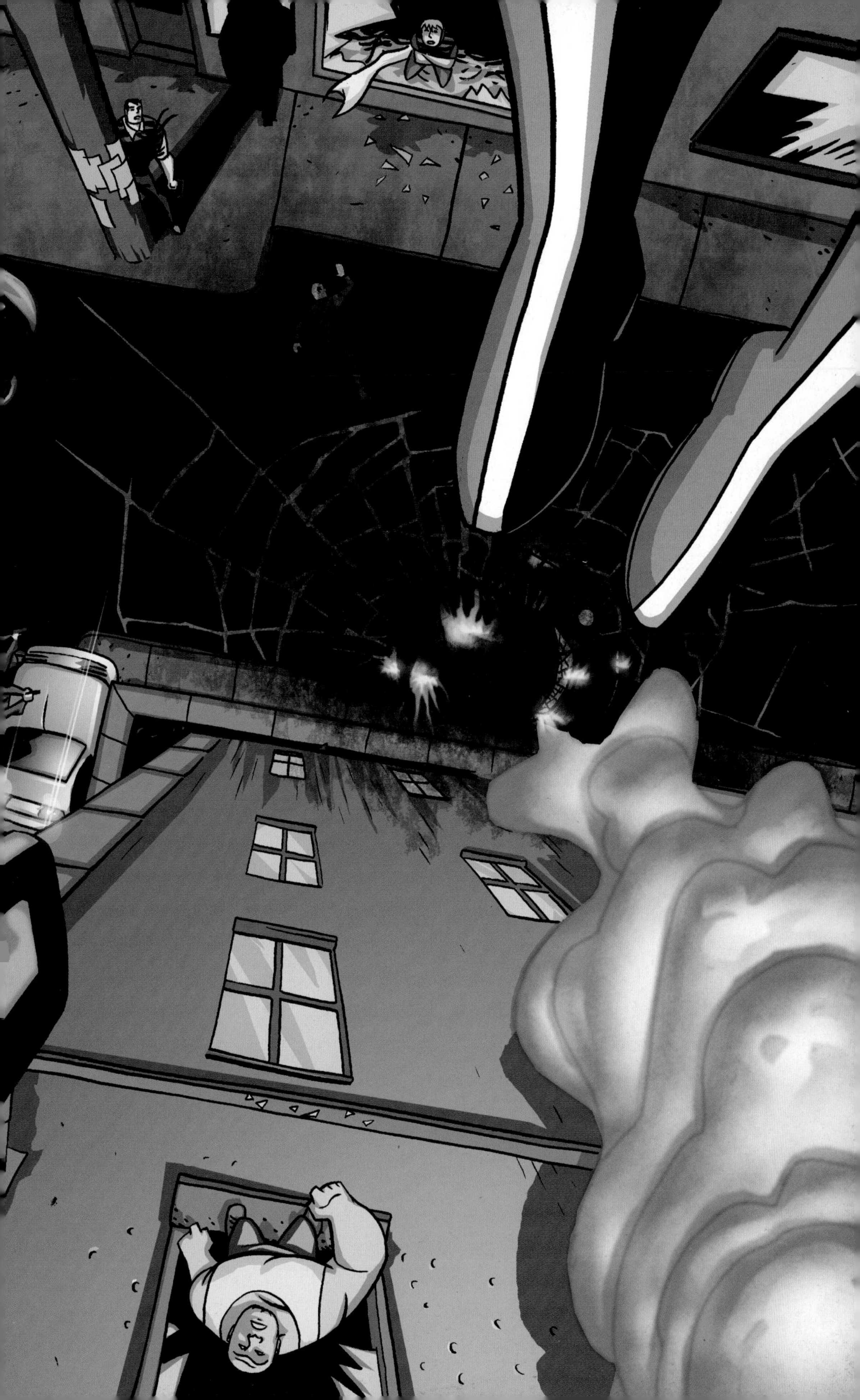

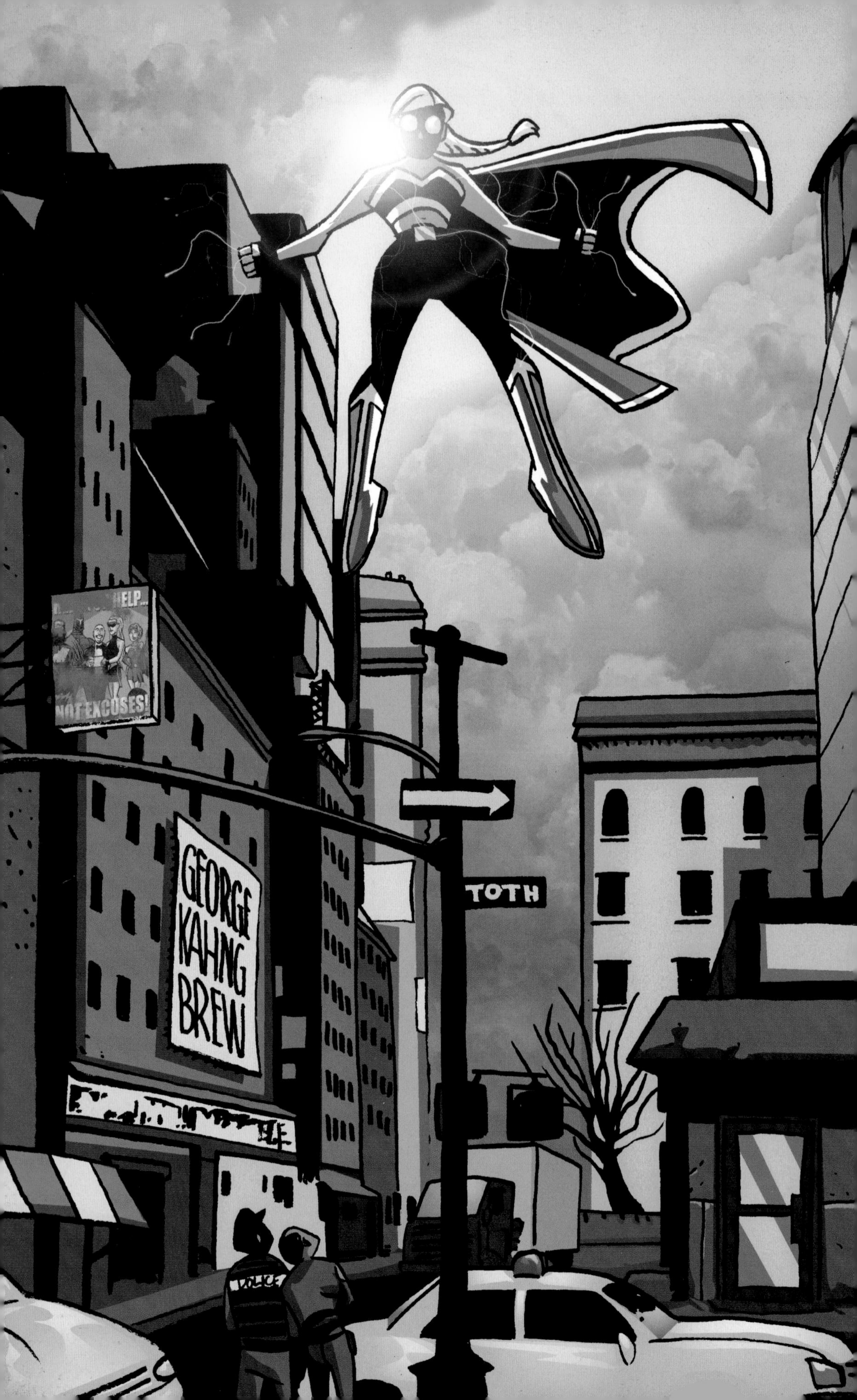
HELP...
NOT EXCUSES!
GEORGE KAHNG BREW
TOTH
POLICE

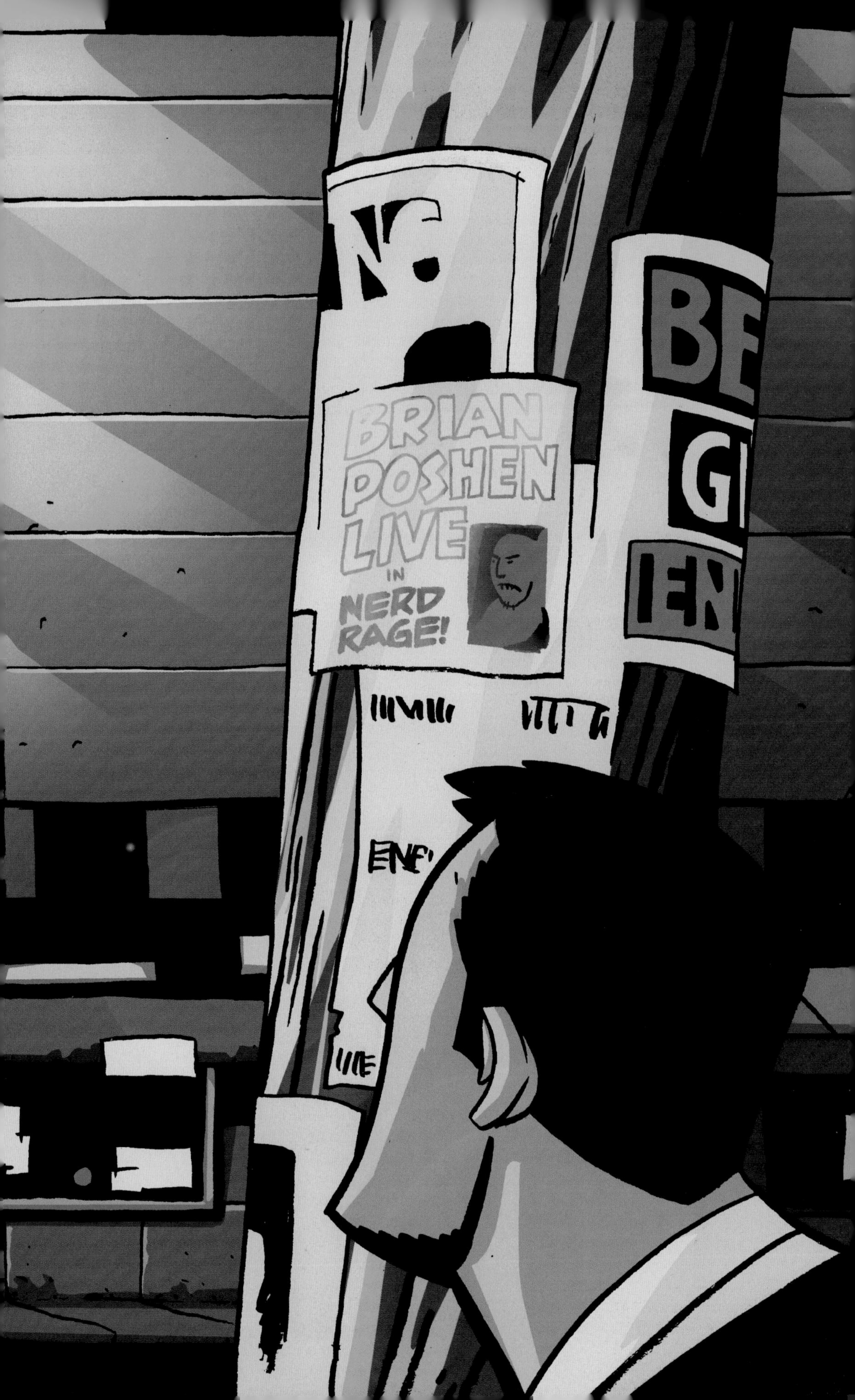
BRIAN POSHEN LIVE IN NERD RAGE!

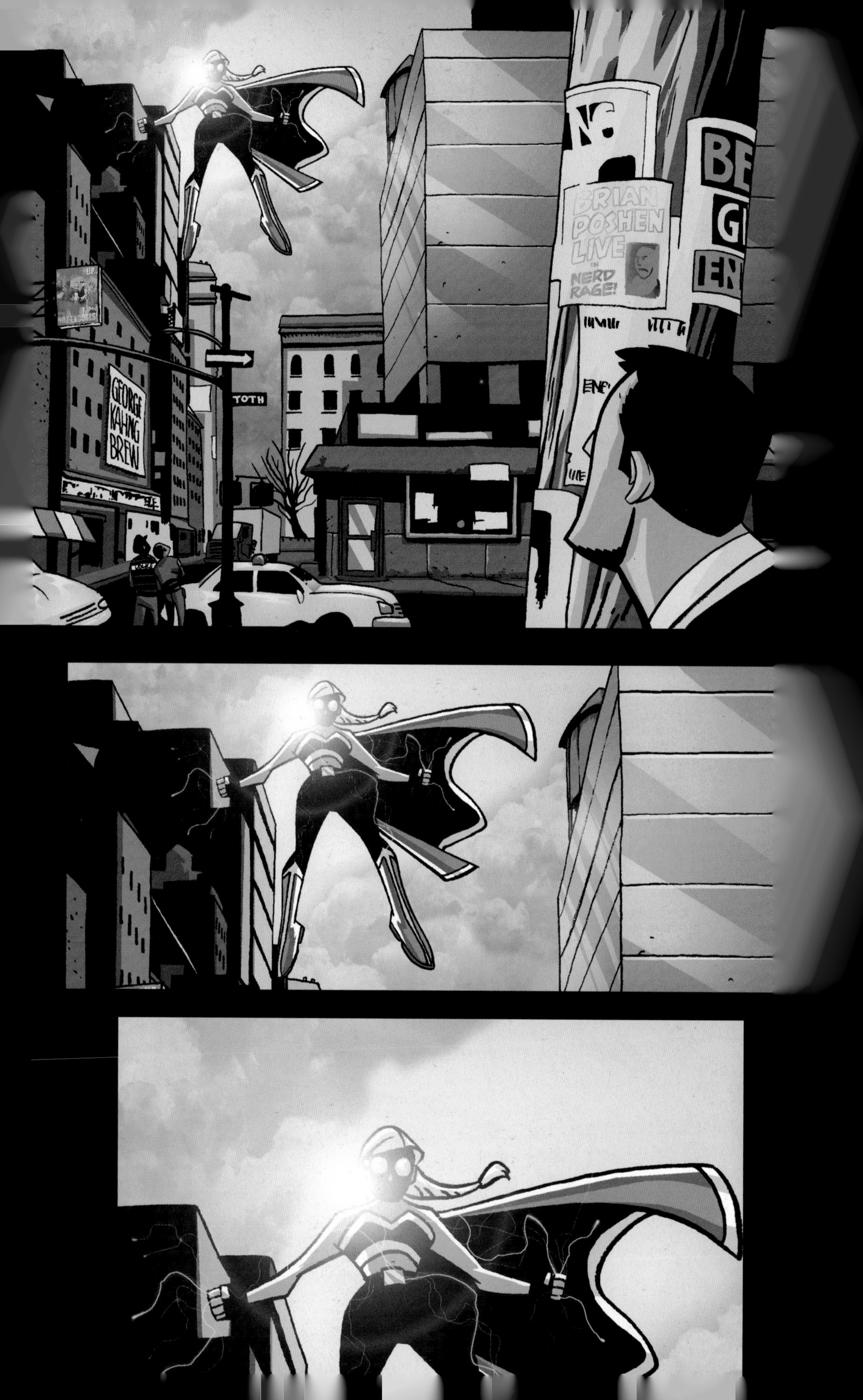
GEORGE KAHNG BREW
TOTH
BRIAN POSHEN LIVE IN NERD RAGE!

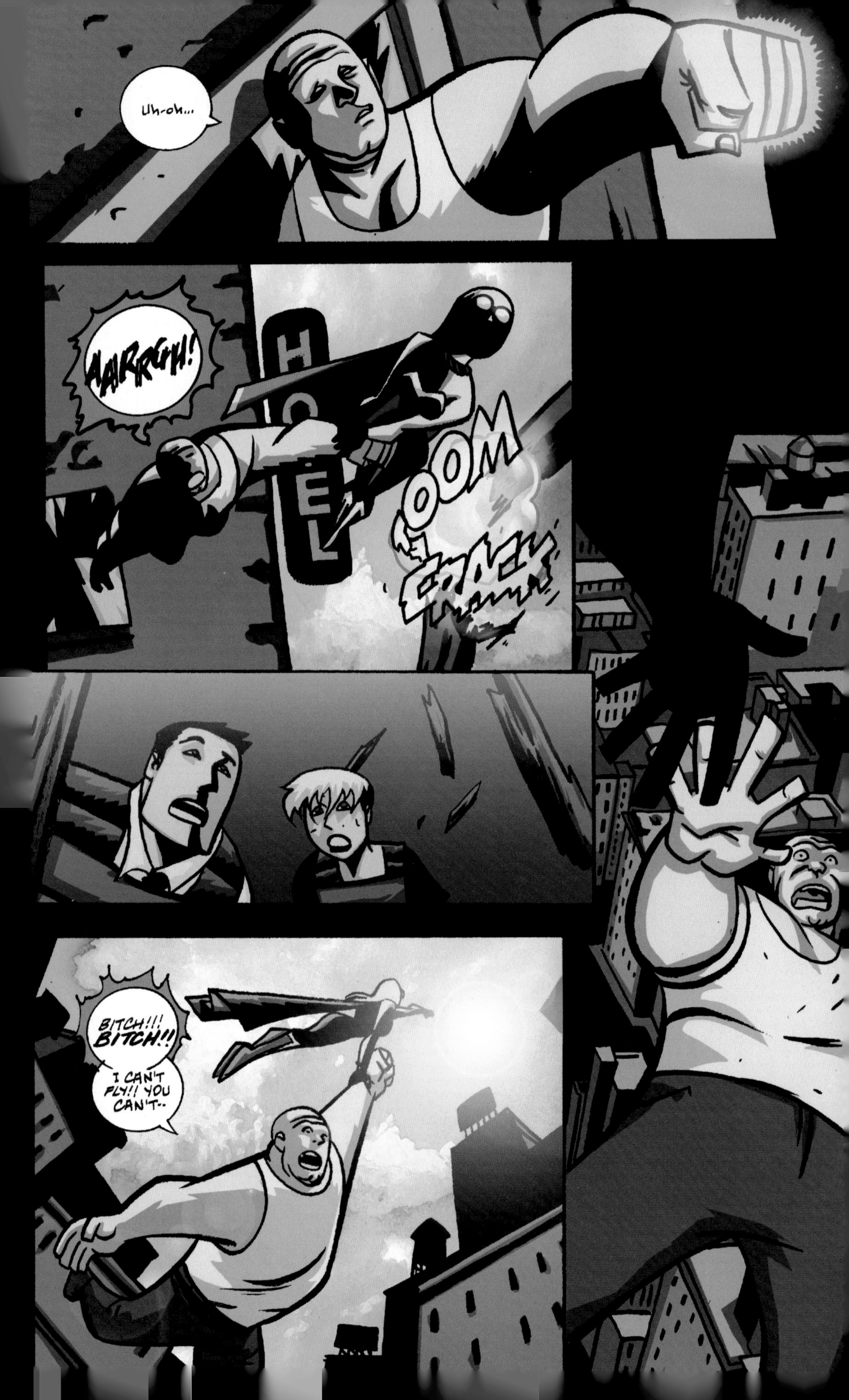
Uh-oh...
AARRGH!
HOTEL
FOOOM
CRACK
BITCH!!! BITCH!!
I CAN'T FLY!! YOU CAN'T..

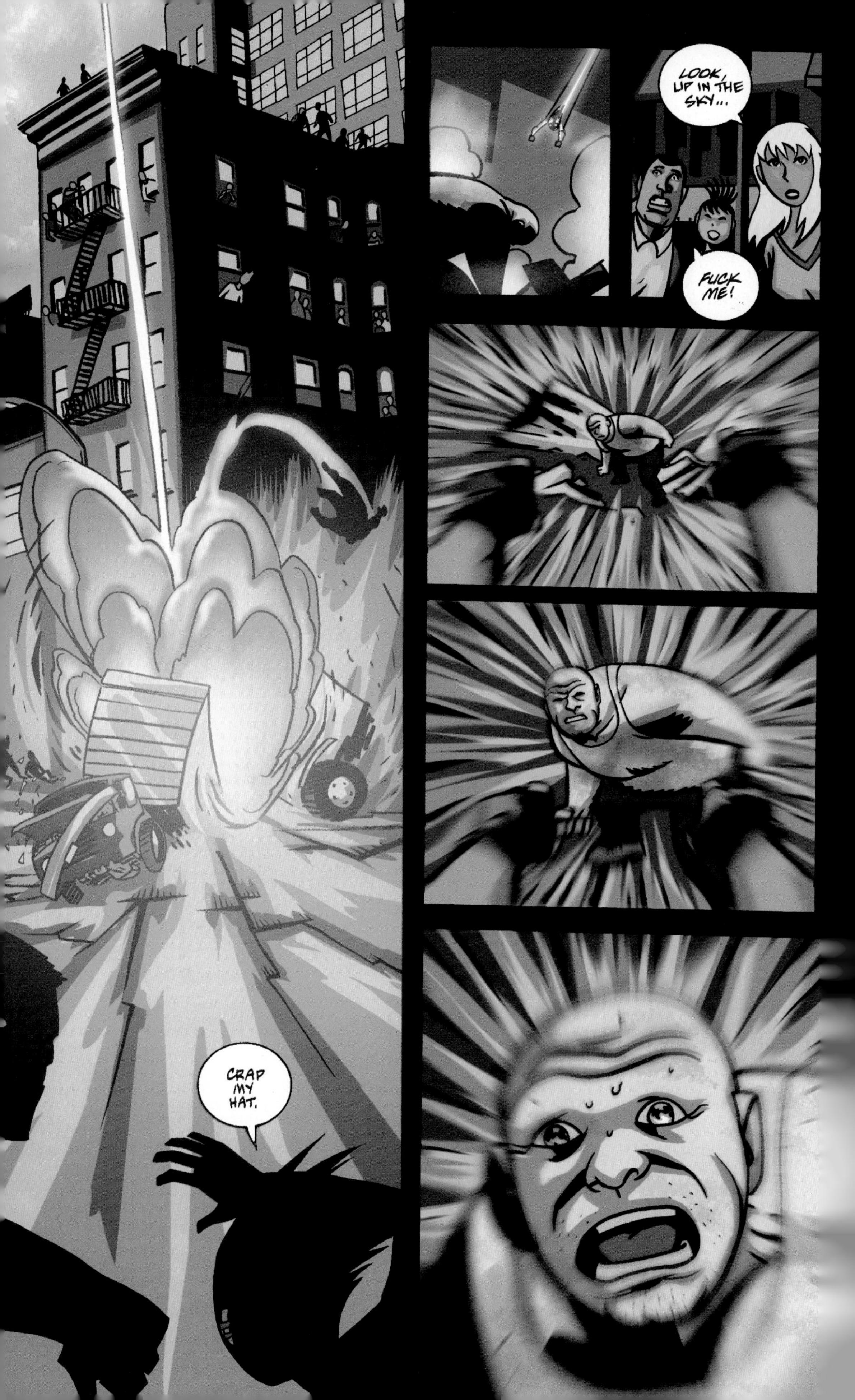

CRAP MY HAT.
LOOK, UP IN THE SKY...
FUCK ME!

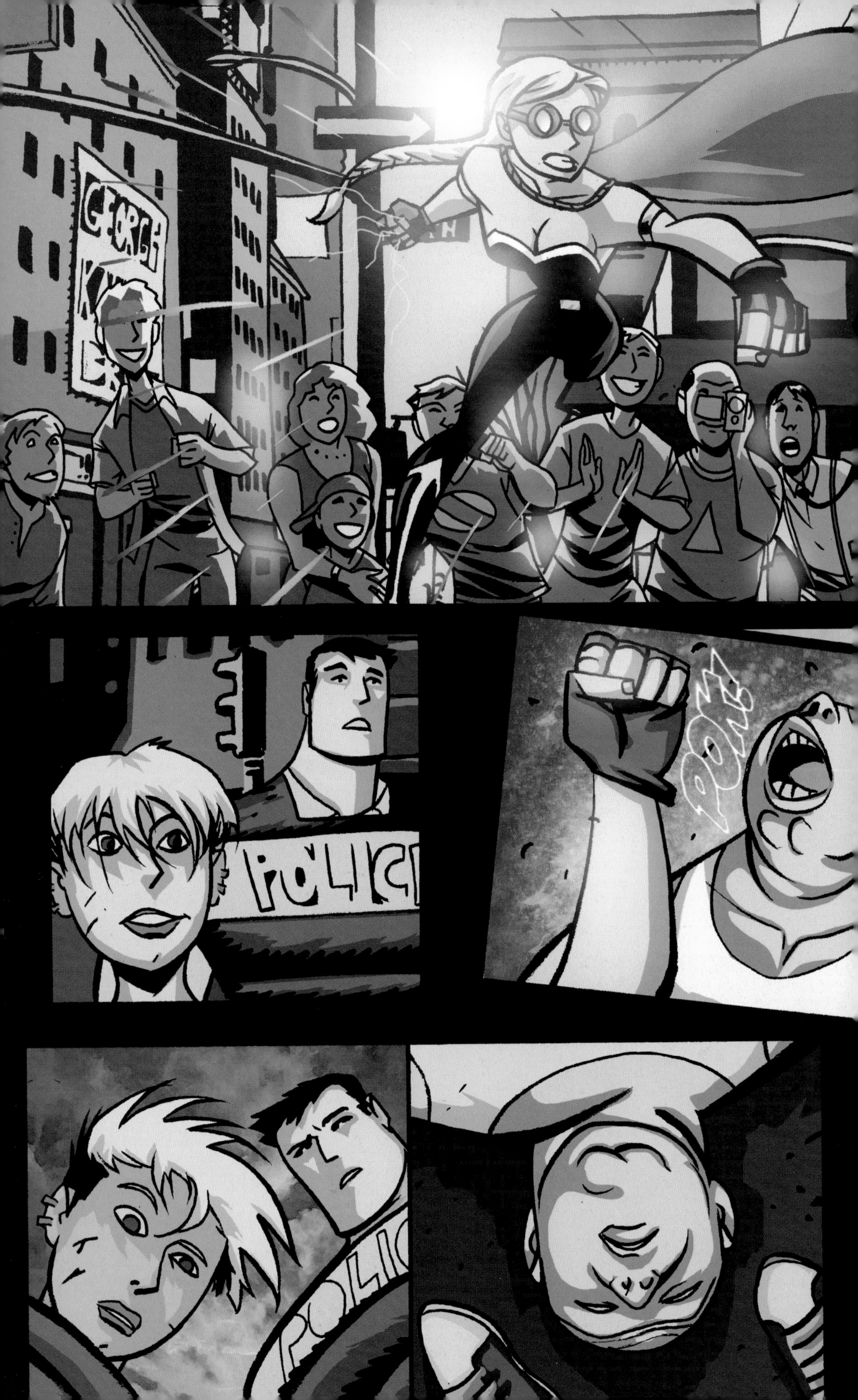
POLIC

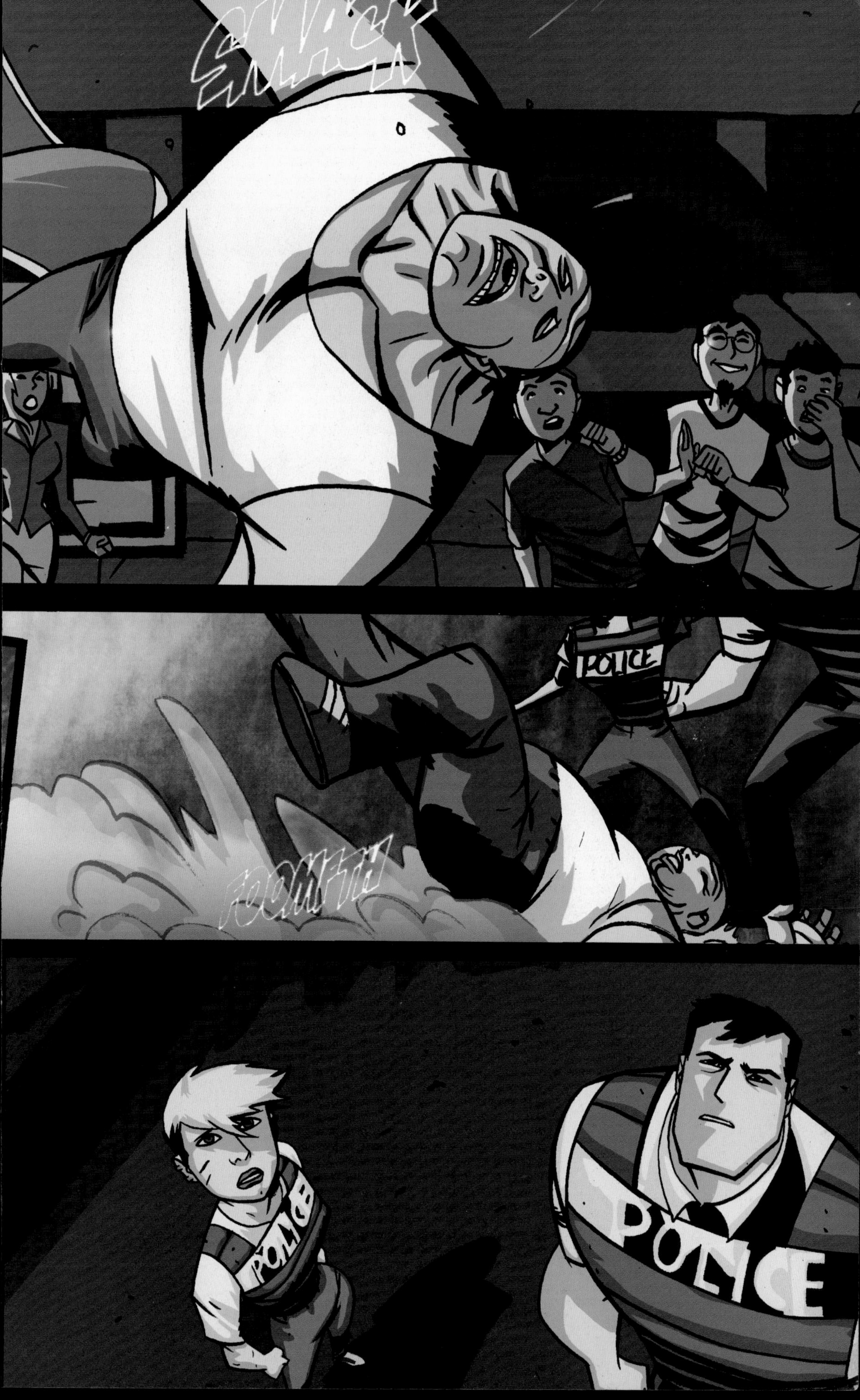
SMACK
POLICE
POLICE
POLICE

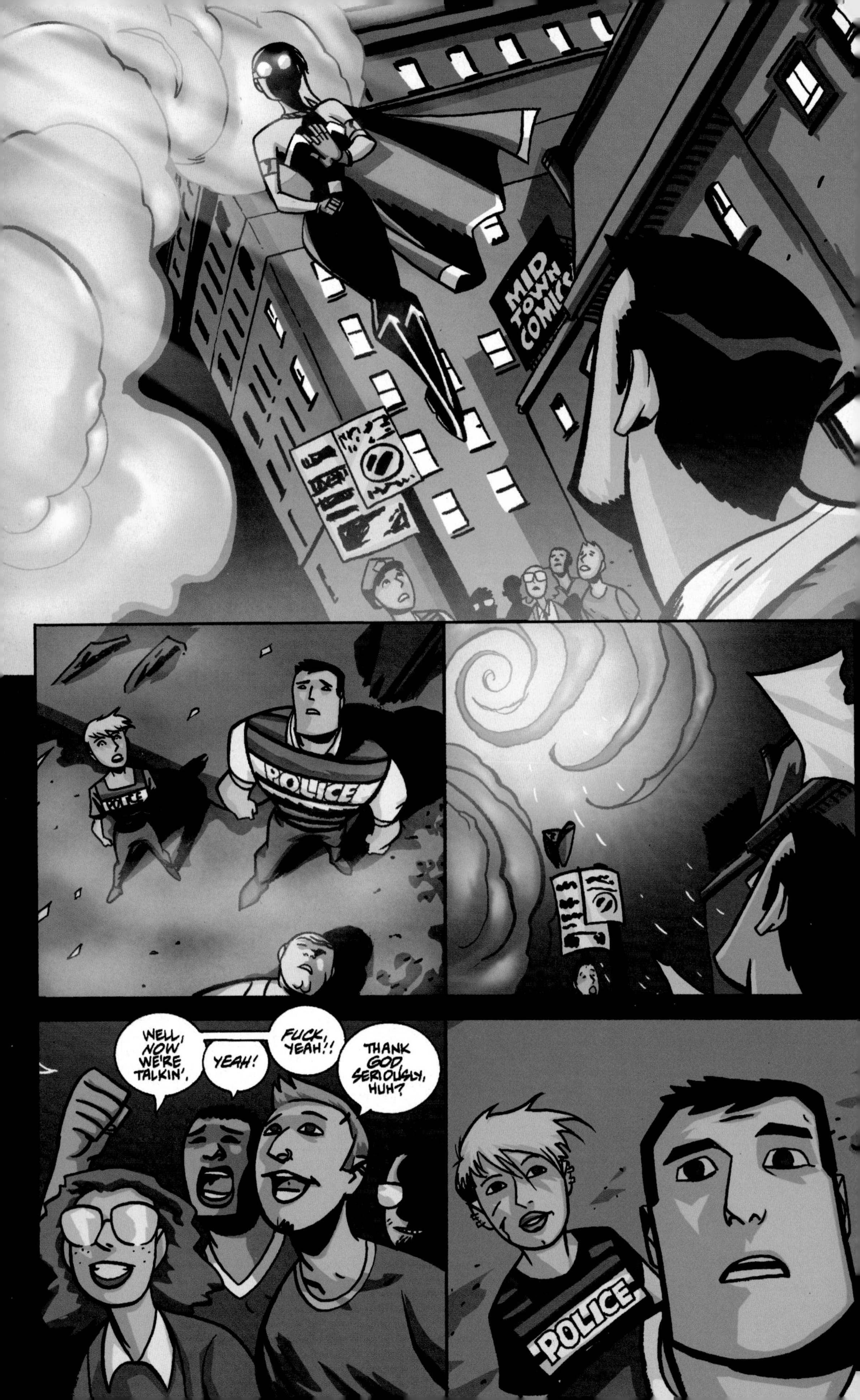
MID TOWN COMICS
POLICE
POLICE
WELL, NOW WE'RE TALKIN'.
YEAH!
FUCK, YEAH!!
THANK GOD. SERIOUSLY, HUH?
POLICE

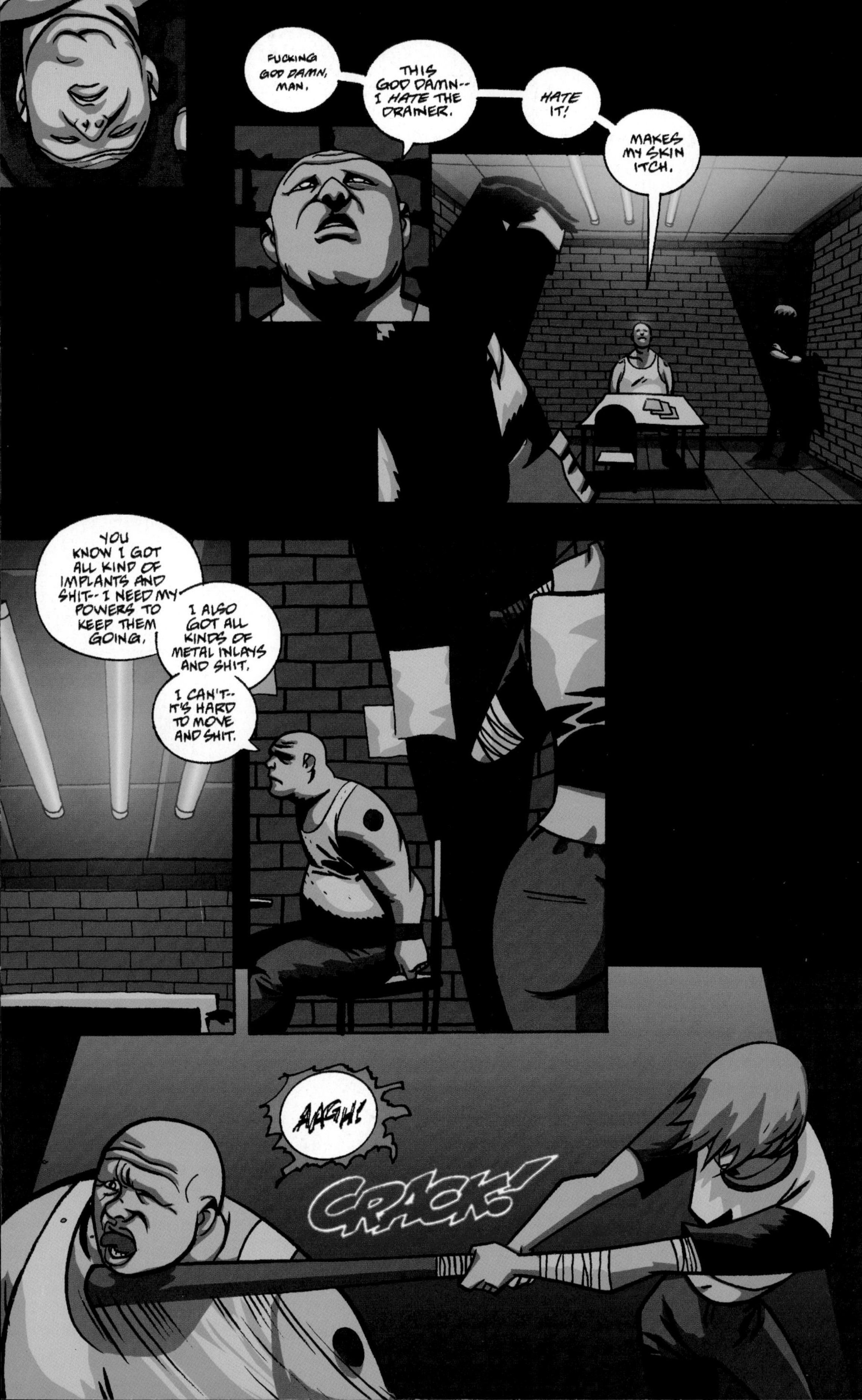
FUCKING GOD DAMN, MAN.
THIS GOD DAMN-- I HATE THE DRAINER.
HATE IT!
MAKES MY SKIN ITCH.
YOU KNOW I GOT ALL KIND OF IMPLANTS AND SHIT-- I NEED MY POWERS TO KEEP THEM GOING.
I ALSO GOT ALL KINDS OF METAL INLAYS AND SHIT.
I CAN'T-- IT'S HARD TO MOVE AND SHIT.
AAGH!
CRACK!

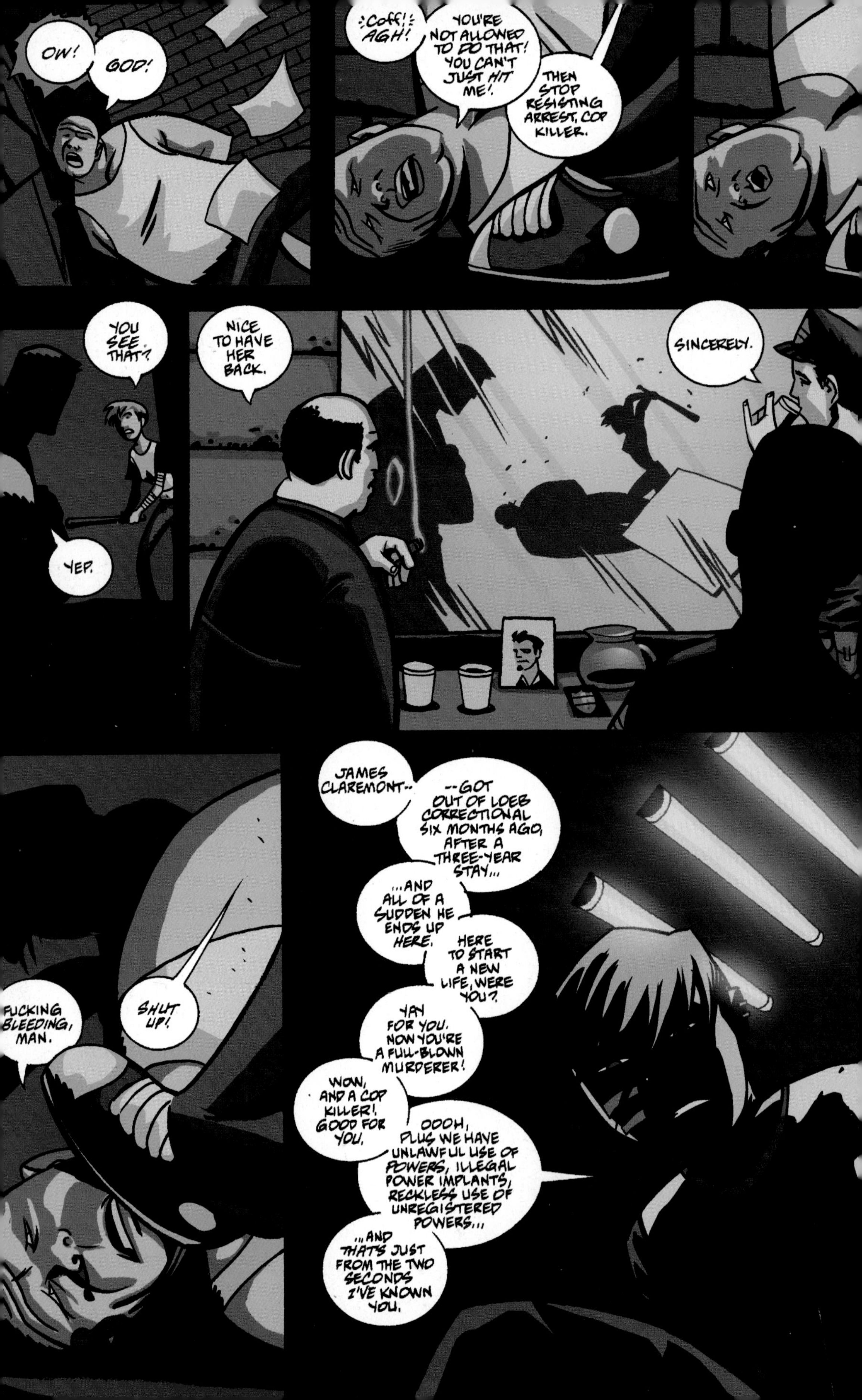
OW!
GOD!
COFF! AGH!
YOU'RE NOT ALLOWED TO DO THAT! YOU CAN'T JUST HIT ME!
THEN STOP RESISTING ARREST, COP KILLER.
YOU SEE THAT?
YEP.
NICE TO HAVE HER BACK.
SINCERELY.
JAMES CLAREMONT--
--GOT OUT OF LOEB CORRECTIONAL SIX MONTHS AGO, AFTER A THREE-YEAR STAY...
...AND ALL OF A SUDDEN HE ENDS UP HERE.
HERE TO START A NEW LIFE, WERE YOU?
YAY FOR YOU. NOW YOU'RE A FULL-BLOWN MURDERER!
WOW, AND A COP KILLER! GOOD FOR YOU.
OOOH, PLUS WE HAVE UNLAWFUL USE OF POWERS, ILLEGAL POWER IMPLANTS, RECKLESS USE OF UNREGISTERED POWERS...
...AND THAT'S JUST FROM THE TWO SECONDS I'VE KNOWN YOU.
FUCKING BLEEDING, MAN.
SHUT UP!

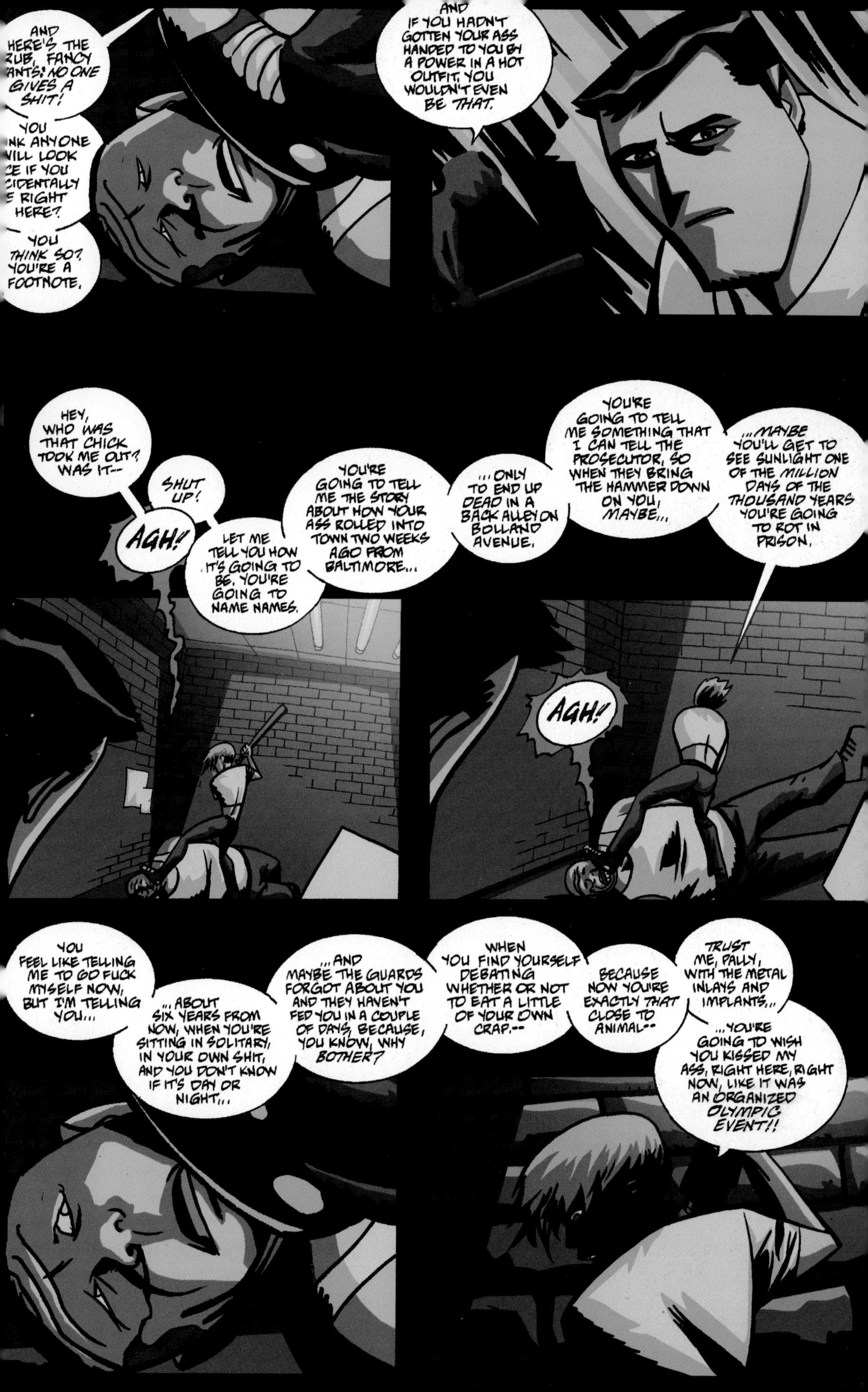
AND HERE'S THE RUB, FANCY PANTS: NO ONE GIVES A SHIT!
YOU THINK ANYONE WILL LOOK TWICE IF YOU ACCIDENTALLY DIE RIGHT HERE?
YOU THINK SO? YOU'RE A FOOTNOTE.
AND IF YOU HADN'T GOTTEN YOUR ASS HANDED TO YOU BY A POWER IN A HOT OUTFIT, YOU WOULDN'T EVEN BE THAT.
HEY, WHO WAS THAT CHICK TOOK ME OUT? WAS IT--
SHUT UP!
AGH!
LET ME TELL YOU HOW IT'S GOING TO BE. YOU'RE GOING TO NAME NAMES.
YOU'RE GOING TO TELL ME THE STORY ABOUT HOW YOUR ASS ROLLED INTO TOWN TWO WEEKS AGO FROM BALTIMORE...
...ONLY TO END UP DEAD IN A BACK ALLEY ON BOLLAND AVENUE.
YOU'RE GOING TO TELL ME SOMETHING THAT I CAN TELL THE PROSECUTOR, SO WHEN THEY BRING THE HAMMER DOWN ON YOU, MAYBE...
...MAYBE YOU'LL GET TO SEE SUNLIGHT ONE OF THE MILLION DAYS OF THE THOUSAND YEARS YOU'RE GOING TO ROT IN PRISON.
AGH!
YOU FEEL LIKE TELLING ME TO GO FUCK MYSELF NOW, BUT I'M TELLING YOU...
...ABOUT SIX YEARS FROM NOW, WHEN YOU'RE SITTING IN SOLITARY, IN YOUR OWN SHIT, AND YOU DON'T KNOW IF IT'S DAY OR NIGHT...
...AND MAYBE THE GUARDS FORGOT ABOUT YOU AND THEY HAVEN'T FED YOU IN A COUPLE OF DAYS, BECAUSE, YOU KNOW, WHY BOTHER?
WHEN YOU FIND YOURSELF DEBATING WHETHER OR NOT TO EAT A LITTLE OF YOUR OWN CRAP--
BECAUSE NOW YOU'RE EXACTLY THAT CLOSE TO ANIMAL--
TRUST ME, PALLY, WITH THE METAL INLAYS AND IMPLANTS...
...YOU'RE GOING TO WISH YOU KISSED MY ASS, RIGHT HERE, RIGHT NOW, LIKE IT WAS AN ORGANIZED OLYMPIC EVENT!!

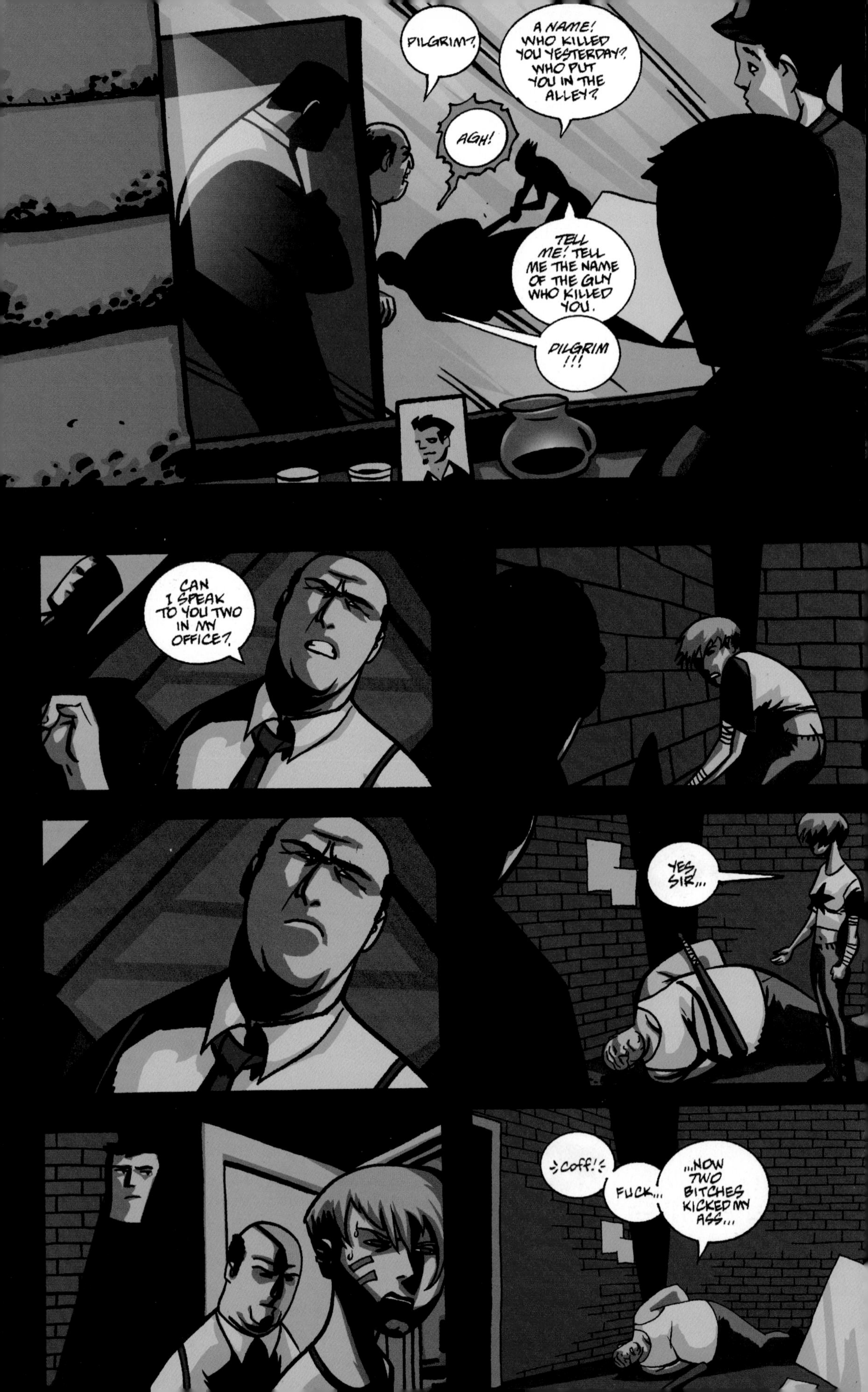
PILGRIM?
A NAME! WHO KILLED YOU YESTERDAY? WHO PUT YOU IN THE ALLEY?
AGH!
TELL ME! TELL ME THE NAME OF THE GUY WHO KILLED YOU.
PILGRIM !!!
CAN I SPEAK TO YOU TWO IN MY OFFICE?
YES, SIR...
coff!
FUCK...
...NOW TWO BITCHES KICKED MY ASS...

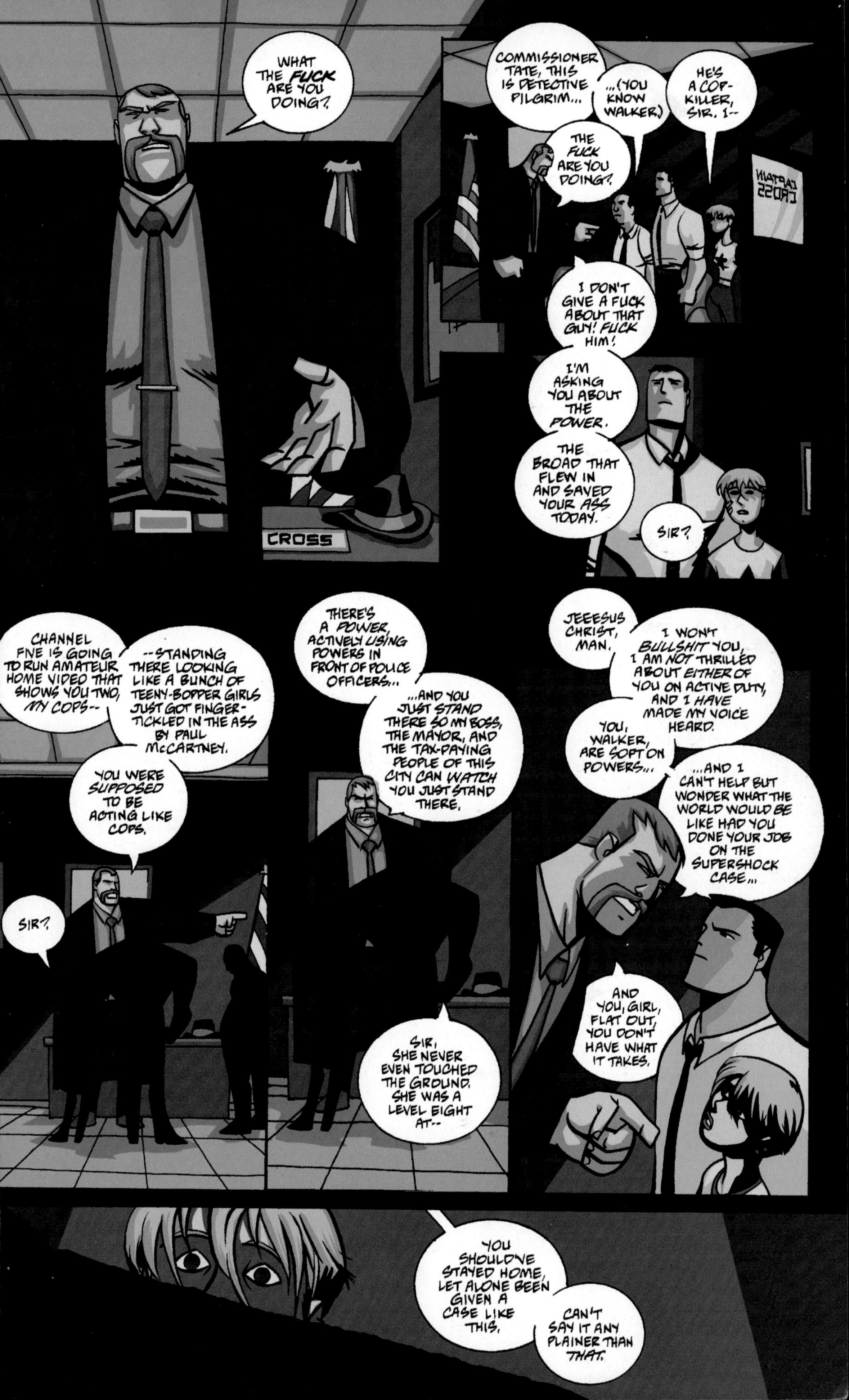

WHAT THE FUCK ARE YOU DOING?
COMMISSIONER TATE, THIS IS DETECTIVE PILGRIM...
...(YOU KNOW WALKER.)
HE'S A COP-KILLER, SIR. I--
THE FUCK ARE YOU DOING?
CAPTAIN CROSS
I DON'T GIVE A FUCK ABOUT THAT GUY! FUCK HIM!
I'M ASKING YOU ABOUT THE POWER.
THE BROAD THAT FLEW IN AND SAVED YOUR ASS TODAY.
SIR?
CROSS
CHANNEL FIVE IS GOING TO RUN AMATEUR HOME VIDEO THAT SHOWS YOU TWO, MY COPS--
--STANDING THERE LOOKING LIKE A BUNCH OF TEENY-BOPPER GIRLS JUST GOT FINGER-TICKLED IN THE ASS BY PAUL McCARTNEY.
YOU WERE SUPPOSED TO BE ACTING LIKE COPS.
SIR?
THERE'S A POWER, ACTIVELY USING POWERS IN FRONT OF POLICE OFFICERS...
...AND YOU JUST STAND THERE SO MY BOSS, THE MAYOR, AND THE TAX-PAYING PEOPLE OF THIS CITY CAN WATCH YOU JUST STAND THERE.
SIR, SHE NEVER EVEN TOUCHED THE GROUND. SHE WAS A LEVEL EIGHT AT--
JEEEESUS CHRIST, MAN.
I WON'T BULLSHIT YOU, I AM NOT THRILLED ABOUT EITHER OF YOU ON ACTIVE DUTY, AND I HAVE MADE MY VOICE HEARD.
YOU, WALKER, ARE SOFT ON POWERS...
...AND I CAN'T HELP BUT WONDER WHAT THE WORLD WOULD BE LIKE HAD YOU DONE YOUR JOB ON THE SUPERSHOCK CASE...
AND YOU, GIRL, FLAT OUT, YOU DON'T HAVE WHAT IT TAKES.
YOU SHOULD'VE STAYED HOME, LET ALONE BEEN GIVEN A CASE LIKE THIS.
CAN'T SAY IT ANY PLAINER THAN THAT.

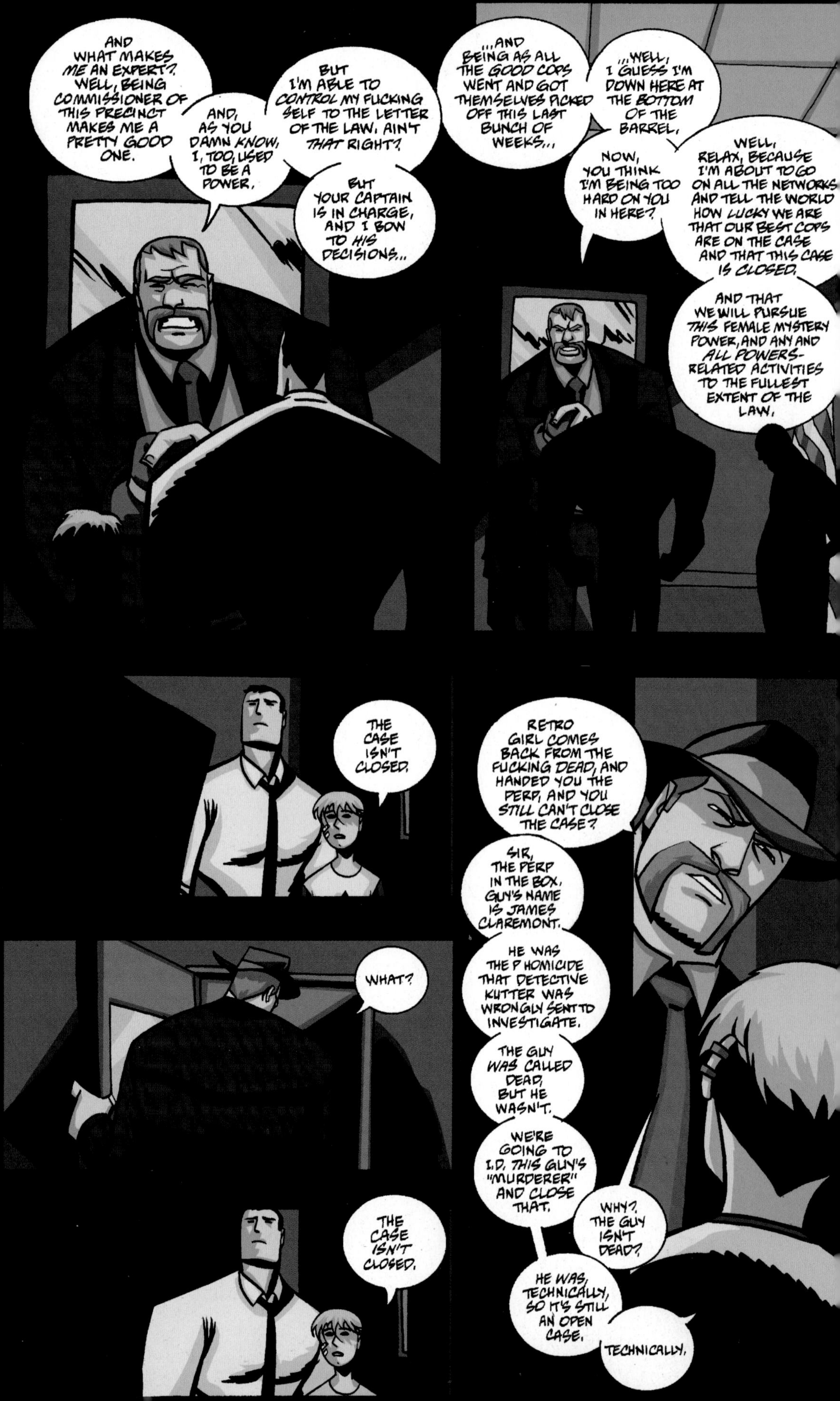
AND WHAT MAKES ME AN EXPERT? WELL, BEING COMMISSIONER OF THIS PRECINCT MAKES ME A PRETTY GOOD ONE.
AND, AS YOU DAMN KNOW, I, TOO, USED TO BE A POWER.
BUT I'M ABLE TO CONTROL MY FUCKING SELF TO THE LETTER OF THE LAW. AIN'T THAT RIGHT?
BUT YOUR CAPTAIN IS IN CHARGE, AND I BOW TO HIS DECISIONS...
...AND BEING AS ALL THE GOOD COPS WENT AND GOT THEMSELVES PICKED OFF THIS LAST BUNCH OF WEEKS...
...WELL, I GUESS I'M DOWN HERE AT THE BOTTOM OF THE BARREL.
NOW, YOU THINK I'M BEING TOO HARD ON YOU IN HERE?
WELL, RELAX, BECAUSE I'M ABOUT TO GO ON ALL THE NETWORKS AND TELL THE WORLD HOW LUCKY WE ARE THAT OUR BEST COPS ARE ON THE CASE AND THAT THIS CASE IS CLOSED.
AND THAT WE WILL PURSUE THIS FEMALE MYSTERY POWER, AND ANY AND ALL POWERS-RELATED ACTIVITIES TO THE FULLEST EXTENT OF THE LAW.
THE CASE ISN'T CLOSED.
WHAT?
THE CASE ISN'T CLOSED.
RETRO GIRL COMES BACK FROM THE FUCKING DEAD, AND HANDED YOU THE PERP, AND YOU STILL CAN'T CLOSE THE CASE?
SIR, THE PERP IN THE BOX, GUY'S NAME IS JAMES CLAREMONT.
HE WAS THE P HOMICIDE THAT DETECTIVE KUTTER WAS WRONGLY SENT TO INVESTIGATE.
THE GUY WAS CALLED DEAD, BUT HE WASN'T.
WE'RE GOING TO I.D. THIS GUY'S "MURDERER" AND CLOSE THAT.
WHY? THE GUY ISN'T DEAD?
HE WAS, TECHNICALLY, SO IT'S STILL AN OPEN CASE.
TECHNICALLY.

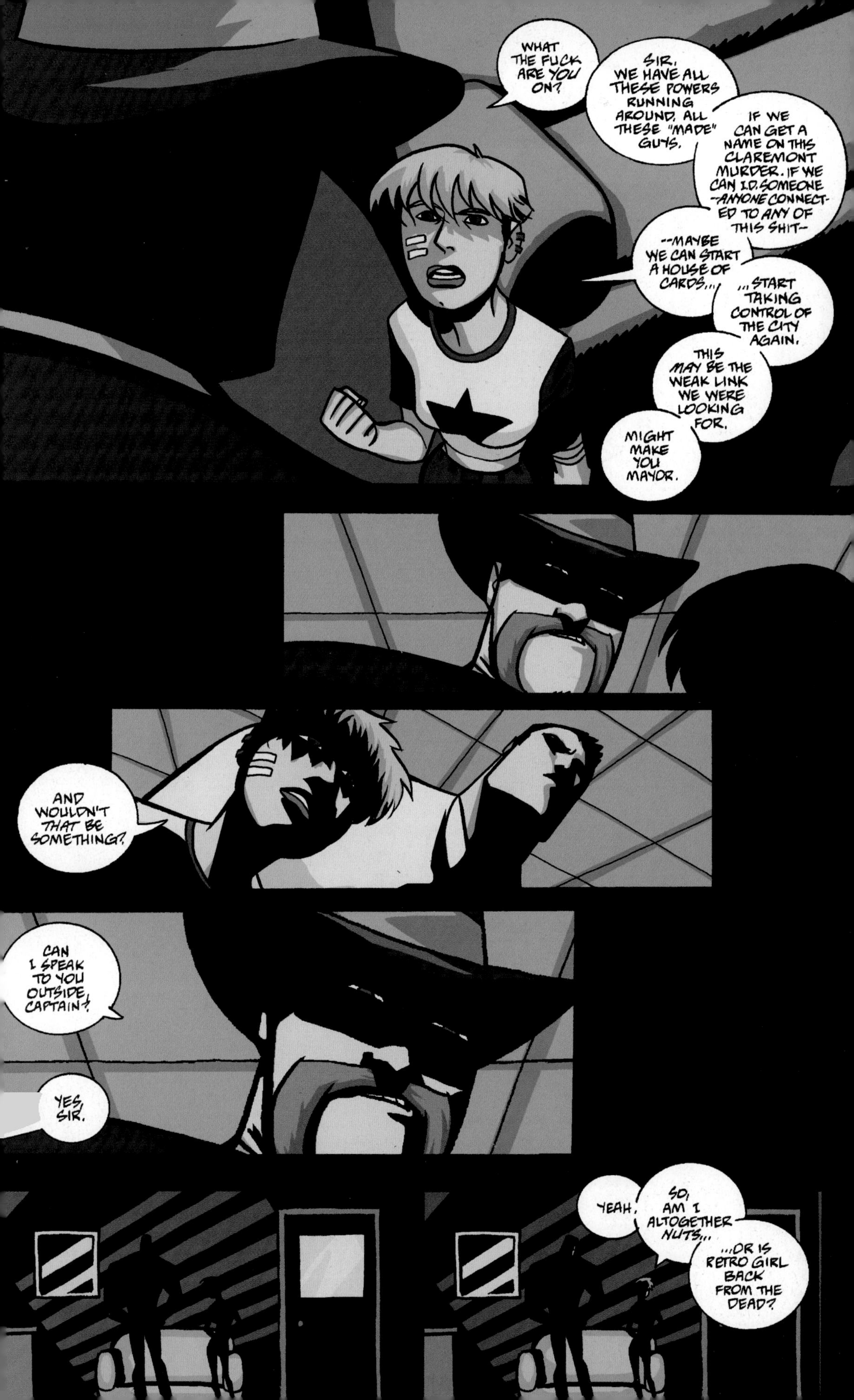
WHAT THE FUCK ARE YOU ON?
SIR. WE HAVE ALL THESE POWERS RUNNING AROUND. ALL THESE "MADE" GUYS.
IF WE CAN GET A NAME ON THIS CLAREMONT MURDER. IF WE CAN I.D. SOMEONE --ANYONE CONNECTED TO ANY OF THIS SHIT--
--MAYBE WE CAN START A HOUSE OF CARDS...
...START TAKING CONTROL OF THE CITY AGAIN.
THIS MAY BE THE WEAK LINK WE WERE LOOKING FOR.
MIGHT MAKE YOU MAYOR.
AND WOULDN'T THAT BE SOMETHING?
CAN I SPEAK TO YOU OUTSIDE, CAPTAIN?
YES, SIR.
YEAH.
SO, AM I ALTOGETHER NUTS...
...OR IS RETRO GIRL BACK FROM THE DEAD?

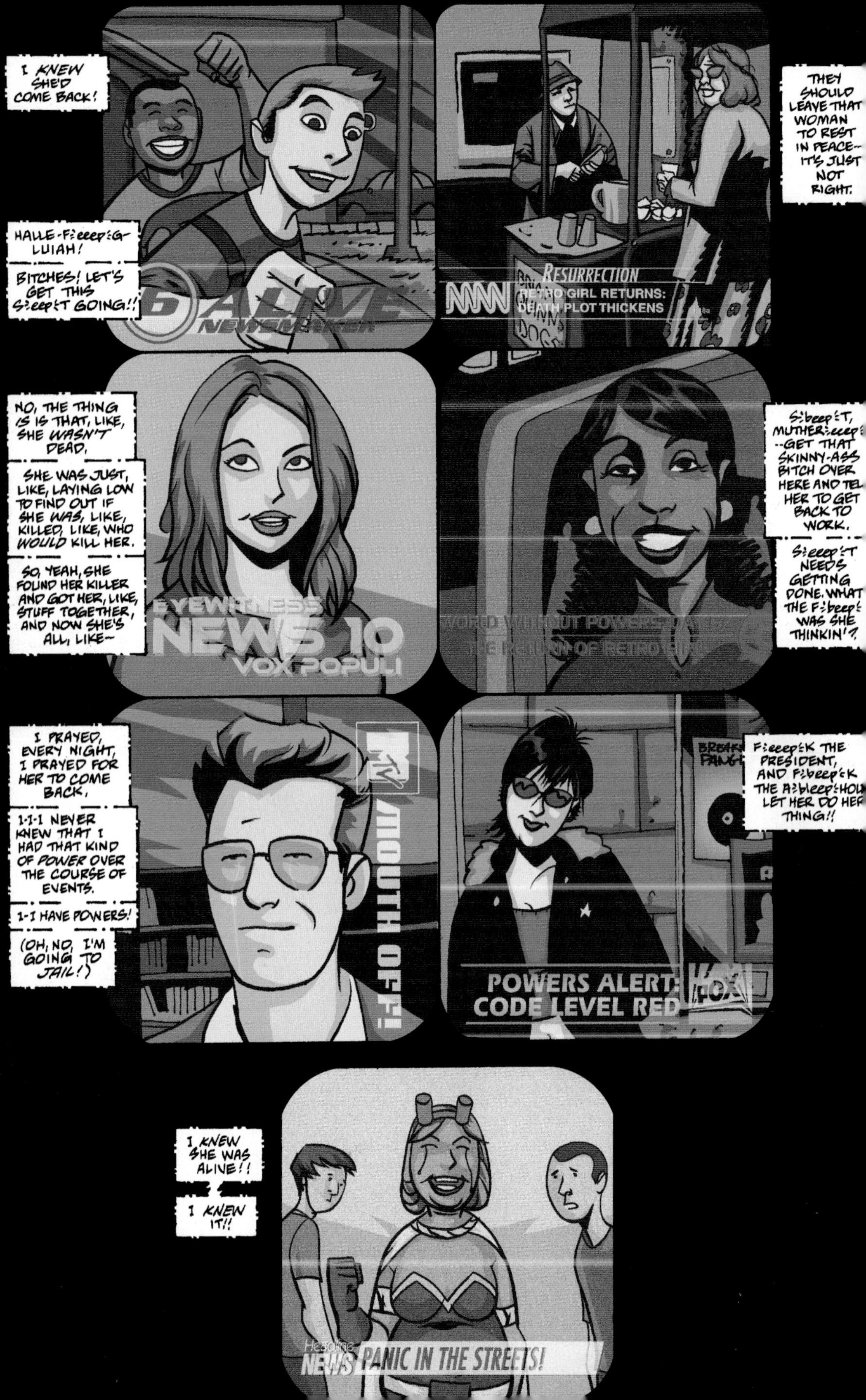
I KNEW SHE'D COME BACK!
HALLE-F:beep:G-LUIAH!
BITCHES! LET'S GET THIS S:beep:T GOING!!
6 ALIVE NEWSMAKER
THEY SHOULD LEAVE THAT WOMAN TO REST IN PEACE-- IT'S JUST NOT RIGHT.
RESURRECTION
RETRO GIRL RETURNS: DEATH PLOT THICKENS
NO, THE THING IS IS THAT, LIKE, SHE WASN'T DEAD.
SHE WAS JUST, LIKE, LAYING LOW TO FIND OUT IF SHE WAS, LIKE, KILLED, LIKE, WHO WOULD KILL HER.
SO, YEAH, SHE FOUND HER KILLER AND GOT HER, LIKE, STUFF TOGETHER, AND NOW SHE'S ALL, LIKE--
EYEWITNESS NEWS 10 VOX POPULI
S:beep:T, MUTHER:eeep: --GET THAT SKINNY-ASS BITCH OVER HERE AND TEL HER TO GET BACK TO WORK.
S:eeep:T NEEDS GETTING DONE. WHAT THE F:beep: WAS SHE THINKIN'?
WORLD WITHOUT POWERS
THE RETURN OF RETRO GIRL
I PRAYED, EVERY NIGHT, I PRAYED FOR HER TO COME BACK.
I-I-I NEVER KNEW THAT I HAD THAT KIND OF POWER OVER THE COURSE OF EVENTS.
I-I HAVE POWERS!
(OH, NO, I'M GOING TO JAIL!)
MOUTH OFF!
F:eeep:K THE PRESIDENT, AND F:beep:K THE A:bleep:HOL LET HER DO HER THING!!
POWERS ALERT: CODE LEVEL RED
I KNEW SHE WAS ALIVE!!
I KNEW IT!!
Headline NEWS PANIC IN THE STREETS!

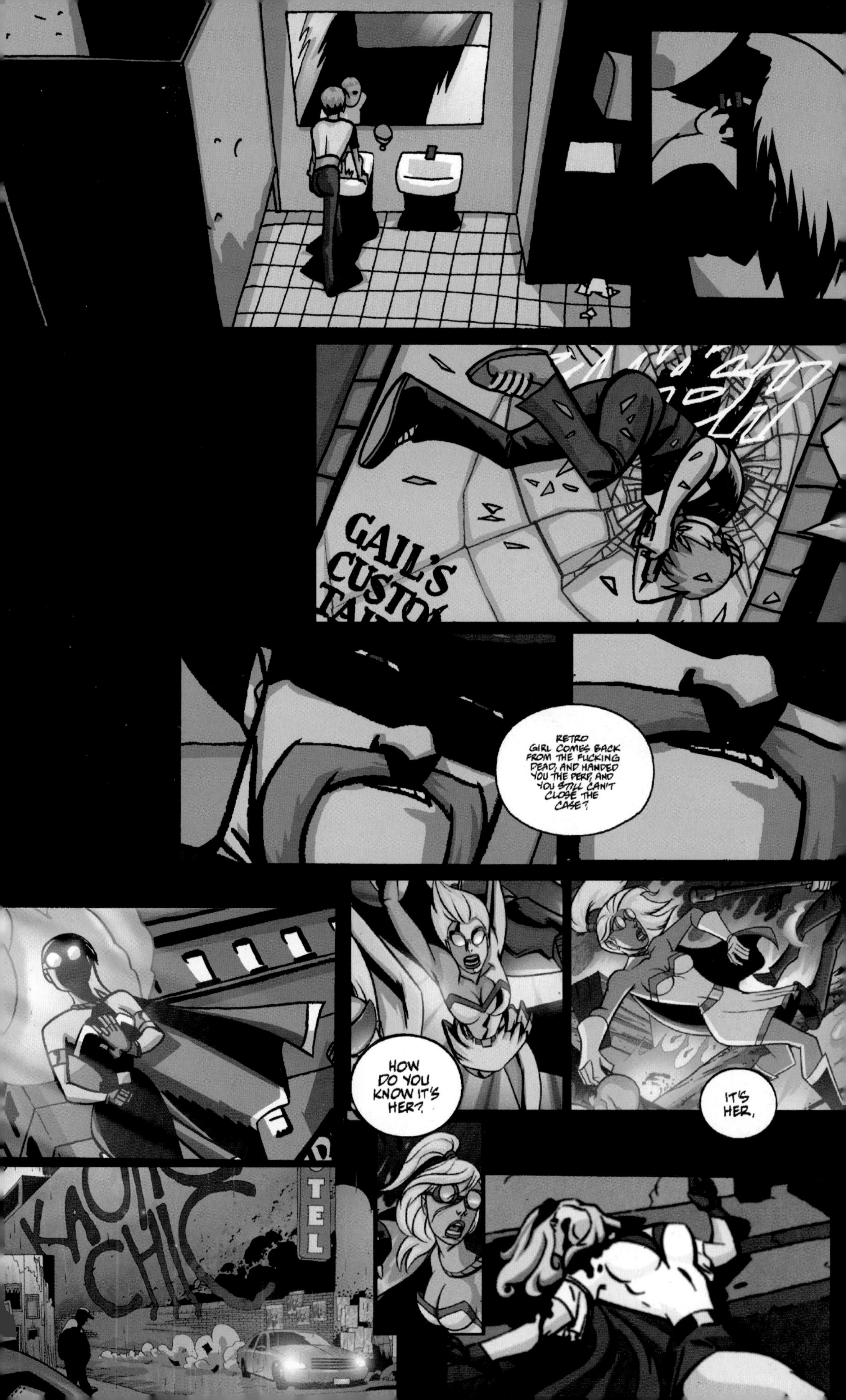

GAIL'S
CUSTO
RETRO GIRL COMES BACK FROM THE FUCKING DEAD, AND HANDED YOU THE PERP, AND YOU STILL CAN'T CLOSE THE CASE?
HOW DO YOU KNOW IT'S HER?
IT'S HER.
TEL

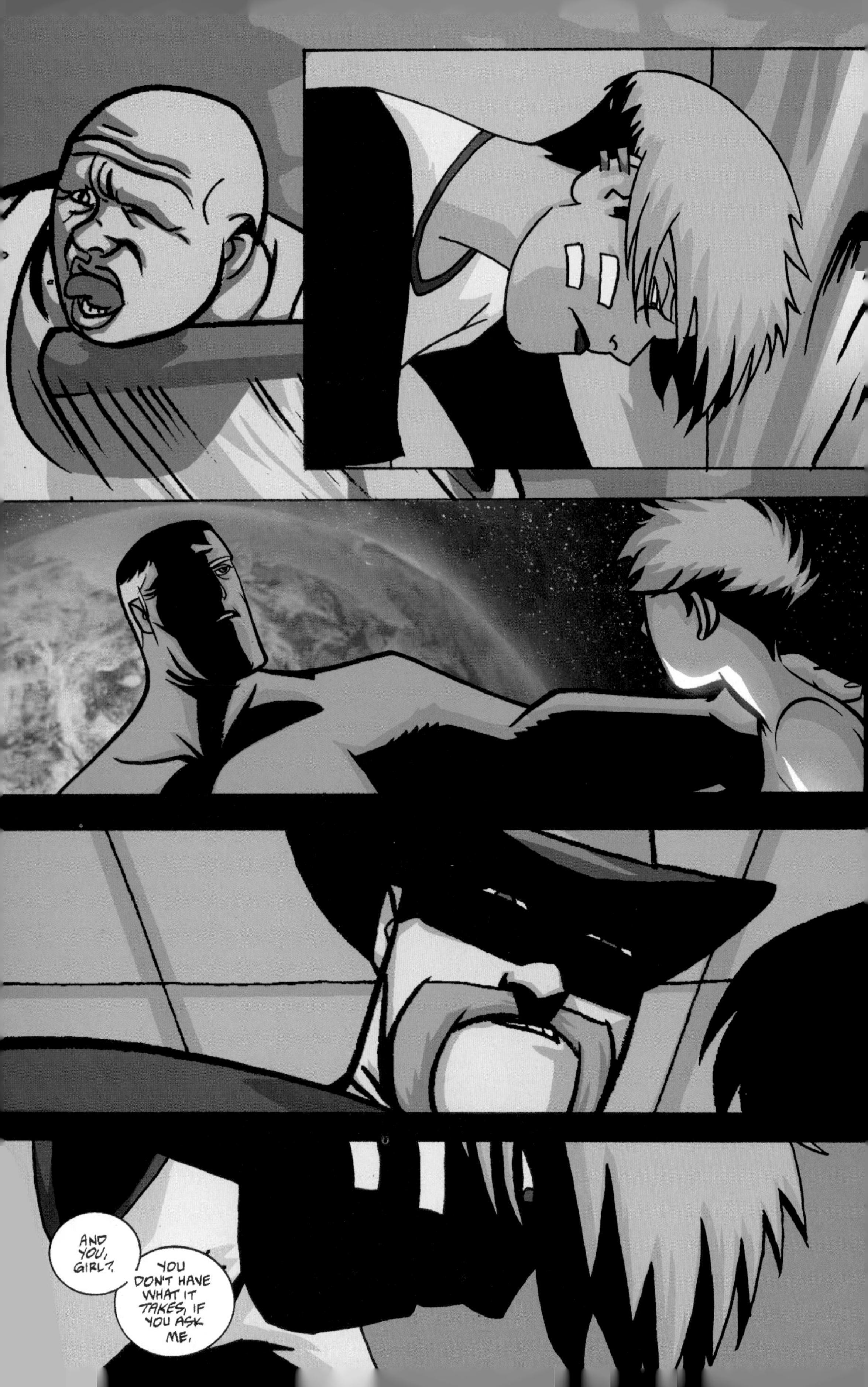
AND YOU, GIRL?
YOU DON'T HAVE WHAT IT TAKES, IF YOU ASK ME.

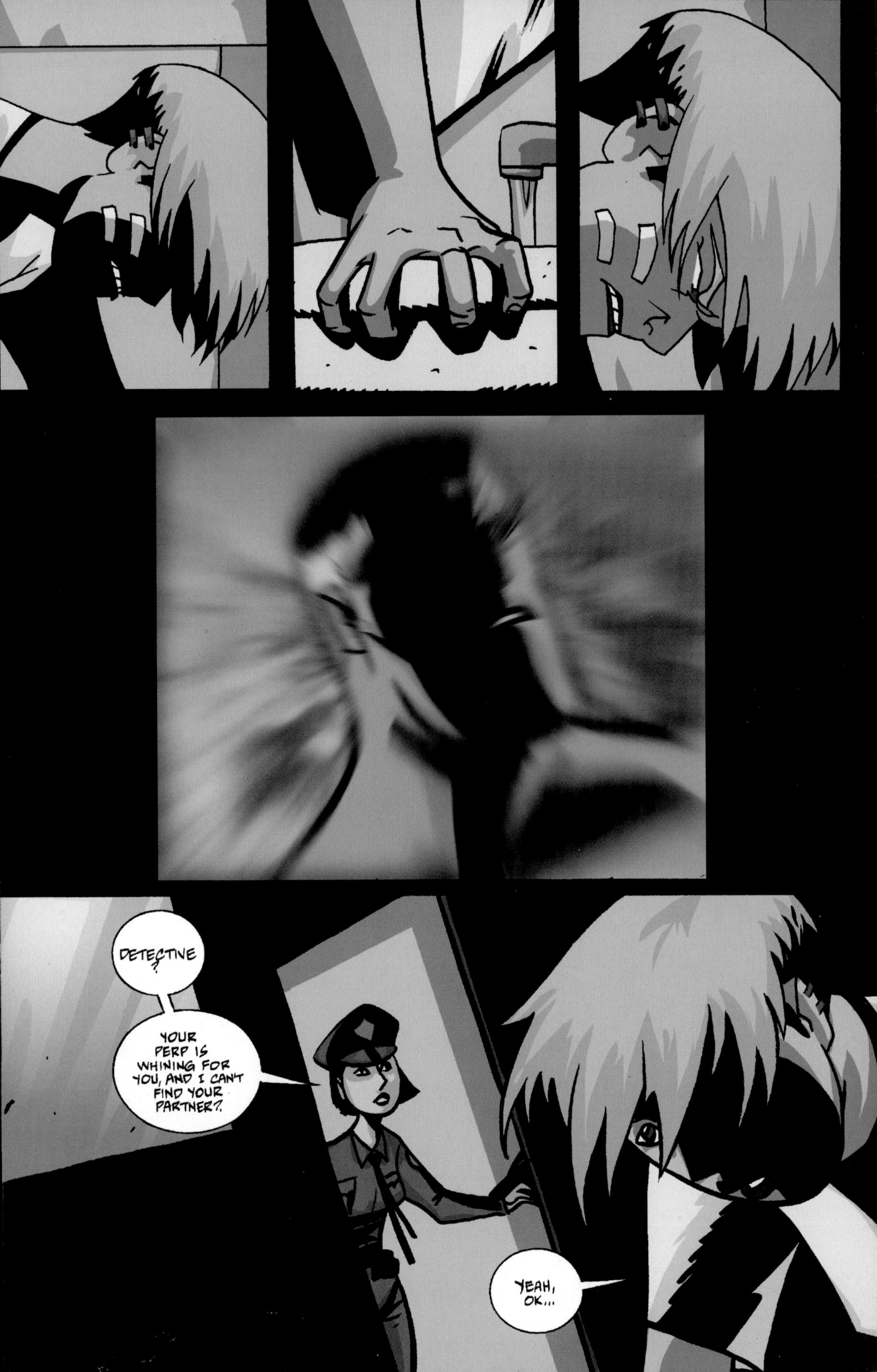
DETECTIVE?
YOUR PERP IS WHINING FOR YOU, AND I CAN'T FIND YOUR PARTNER?.
YEAH, OK...

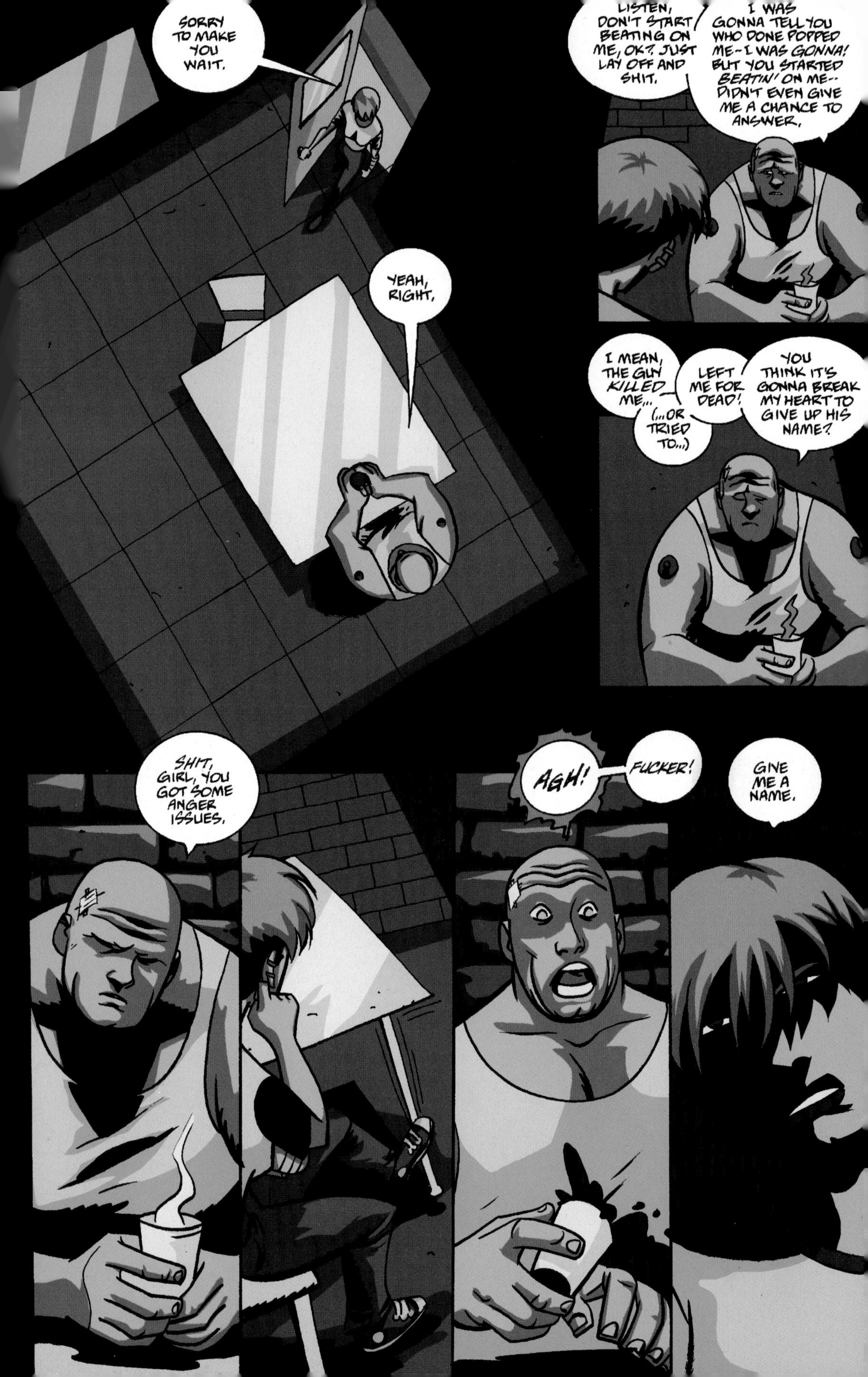
SORRY TO MAKE YOU WAIT.
YEAH, RIGHT.
LISTEN, DON'T START BEATING ON ME, OK? JUST LAY OFF AND SHIT.
I WAS GONNA TELL YOU WHO DONE POPPED ME-- I WAS GONNA! BUT YOU STARTED BEATIN' ON ME-- DIDN'T EVEN GIVE ME A CHANCE TO ANSWER.
I MEAN, THE GUY KILLED ME...
(...OR TRIED TO...)
LEFT ME FOR DEAD!
YOU THINK IT'S GONNA BREAK MY HEART TO GIVE UP HIS NAME?
SHIT, GIRL, YOU GOT SOME ANGER ISSUES.
AGH!
FUCKER!
GIVE ME A NAME.

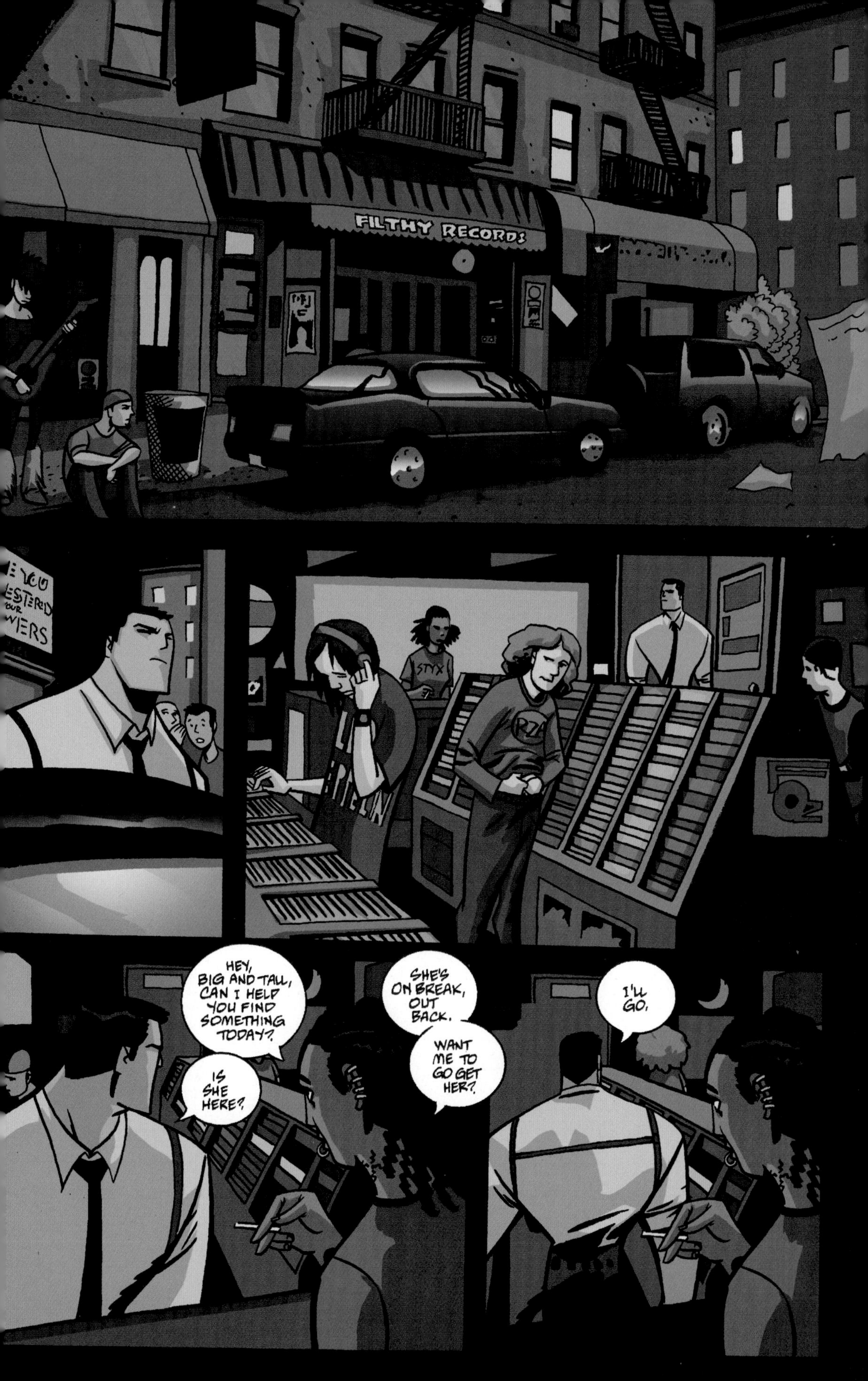
FILTHY RECORDS
STYX
RZA
HEY, BIG AND TALL, CAN I HELP YOU FIND SOMETHING TODAY?
IS SHE HERE?
SHE'S ON BREAK, OUT BACK.
WANT ME TO GO GET HER?
I'LL GO.

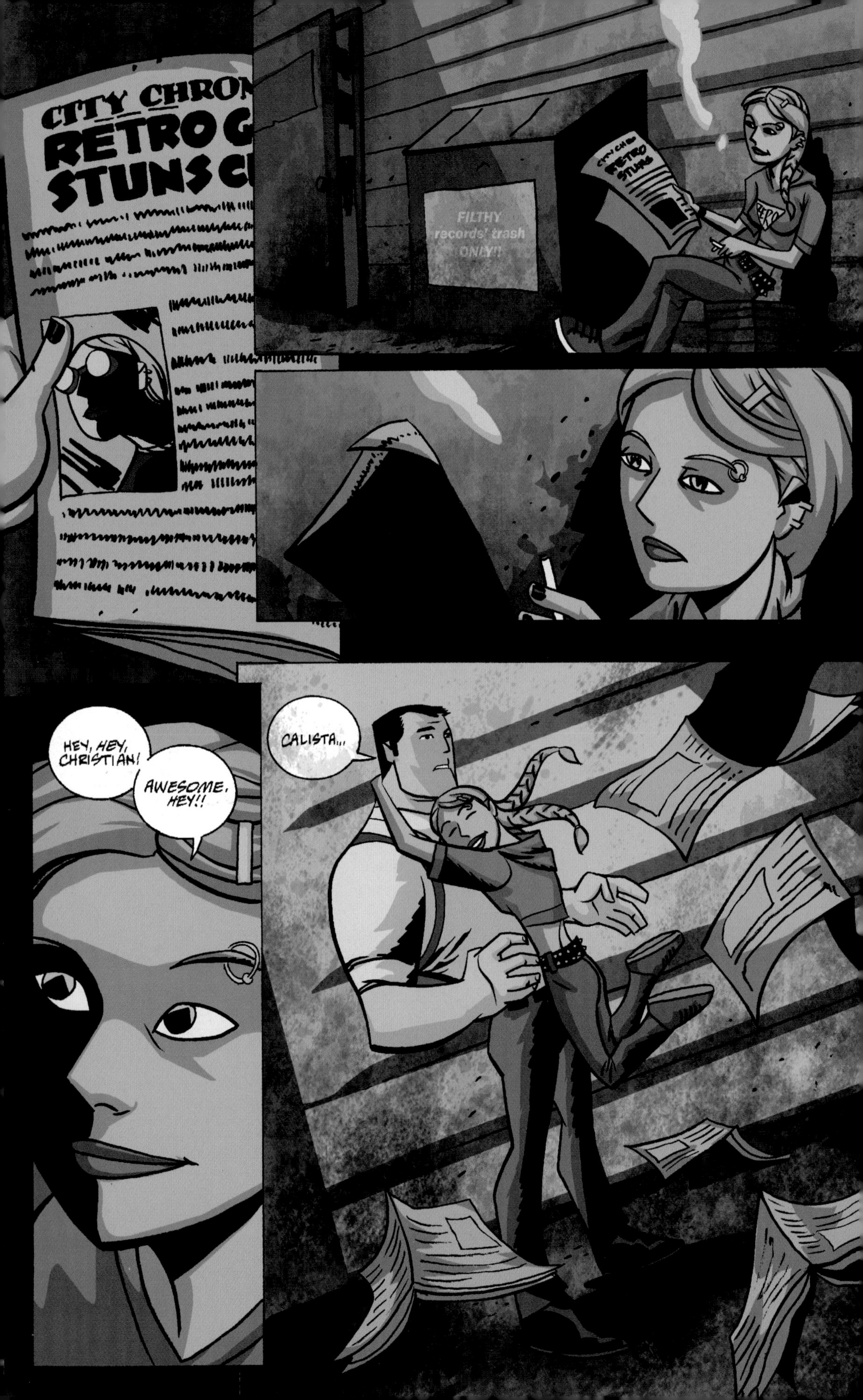
CITY CHRON
RETRO G
STUNS C
FILTHY records' trash ONLY!!
HEY, HEY, CHRISTIAN!
AWESOME. HEY!!
CALISTA...

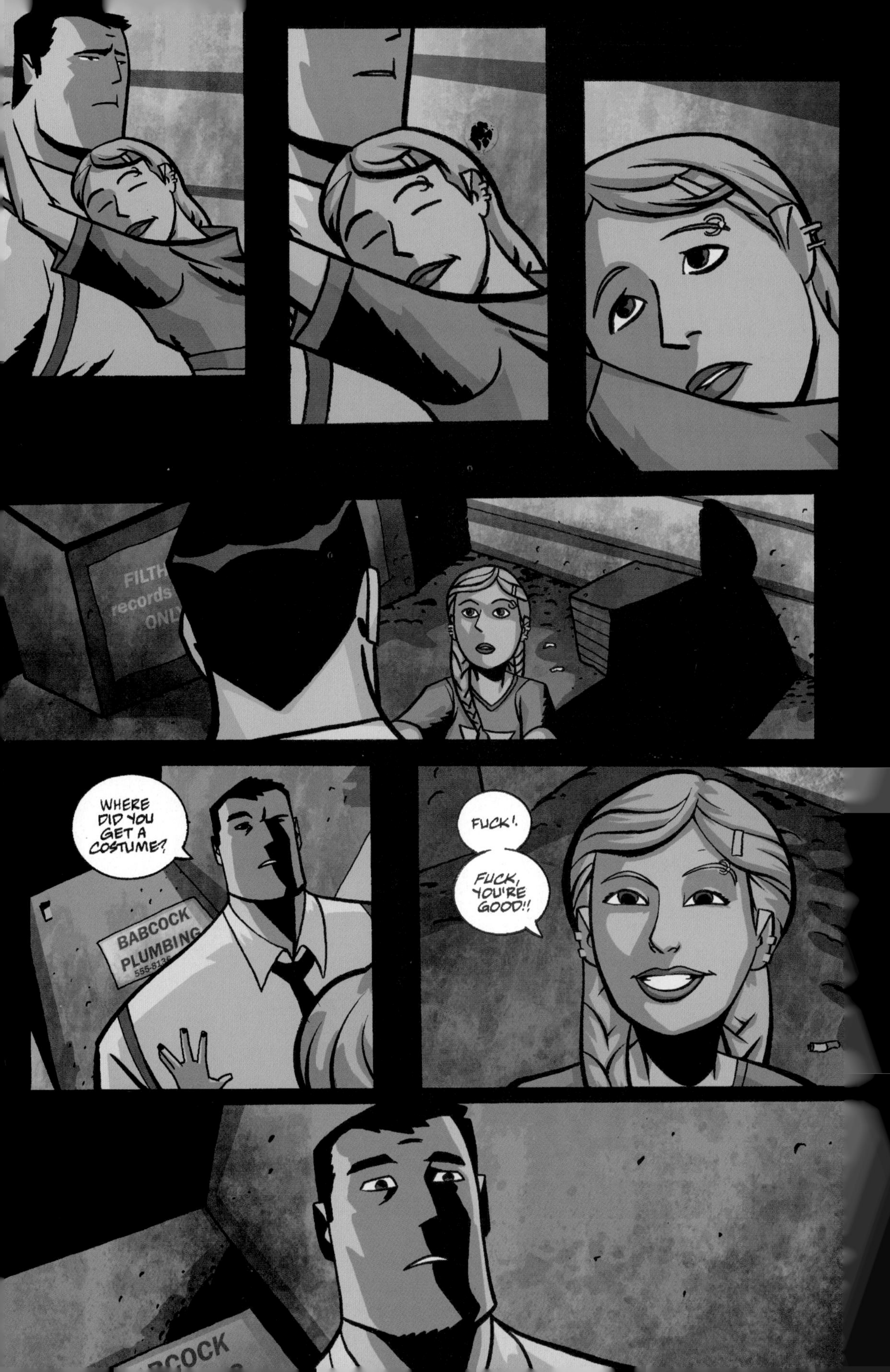
FILTH
records
ONLY
WHERE DID YOU GET A COSTUME?
BABCOCK
PLUMBING
FUCK!
FUCK, YOU'RE GOOD!!
BCOCK

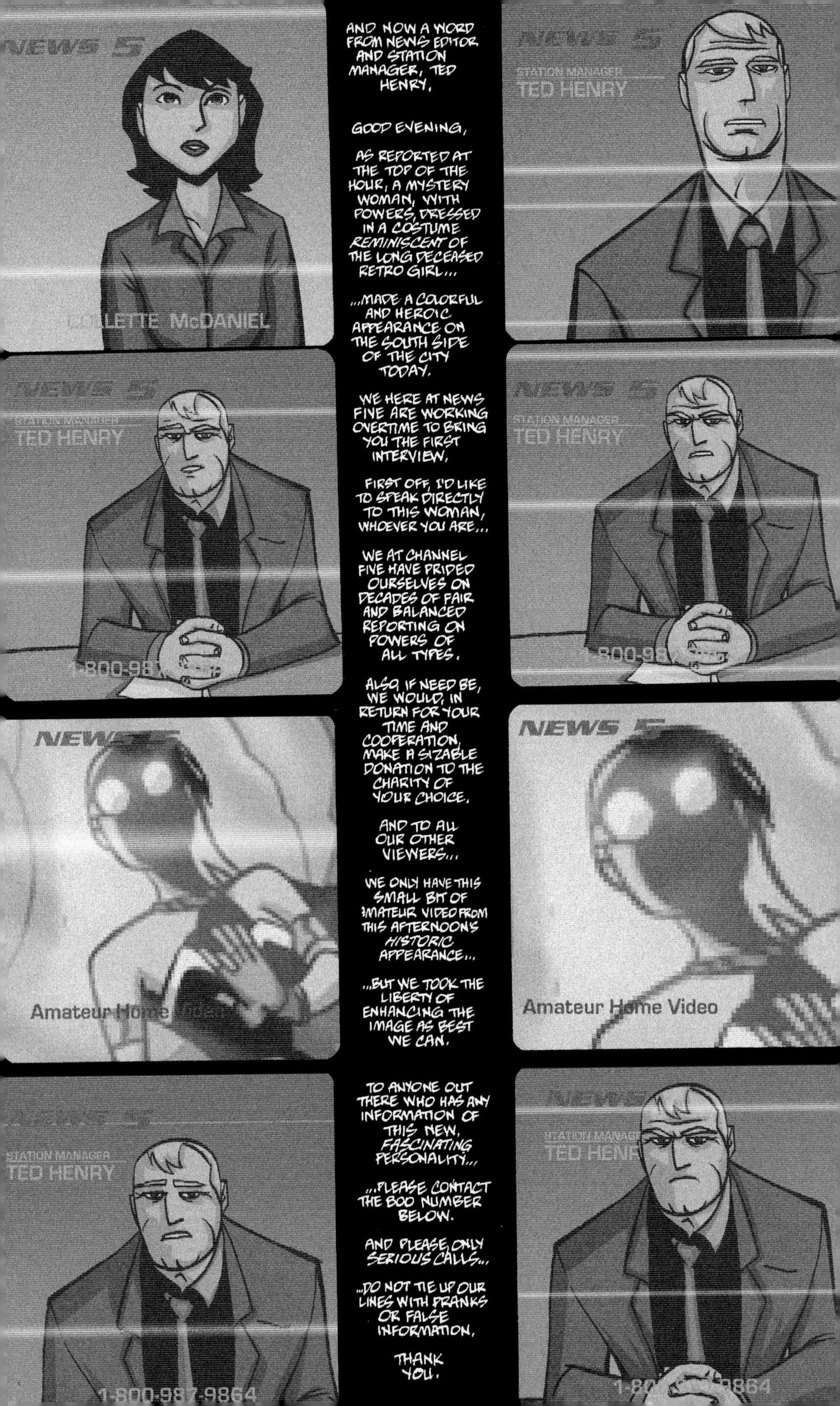

NEWS 5
COLLETTE McDANIEL
AND NOW A WORD FROM NEWS EDITOR AND STATION MANAGER, TED HENRY.
NEWS 5
STATION MANAGER
TED HENRY
GOOD EVENING.
AS REPORTED AT THE TOP OF THE HOUR, A MYSTERY WOMAN, WITH POWERS, DRESSED IN A COSTUME *REMINISCENT* OF THE LONG DECEASED RETRO GIRL...
...MADE A COLORFUL AND HEROIC APPEARANCE ON THE SOUTH SIDE OF THE CITY TODAY.
NEWS 5
STATION MANAGER
TED HENRY
WE HERE AT NEWS FIVE ARE WORKING OVERTIME TO BRING YOU THE FIRST INTERVIEW.
FIRST OFF, I'D LIKE TO SPEAK DIRECTLY TO THIS WOMAN, WHOEVER YOU ARE...
WE AT CHANNEL FIVE HAVE PRIDED OURSELVES ON DECADES OF FAIR AND BALANCED REPORTING ON POWERS OF ALL TYPES.
NEWS 5
STATION MANAGER
TED HENRY
ALSO, IF NEED BE, WE WOULD, IN RETURN FOR YOUR TIME AND COOPERATION, MAKE A SIZABLE DONATION TO THE CHARITY OF YOUR CHOICE.
AND TO ALL OUR OTHER VIEWERS...
Amateur Home Video
WE ONLY HAVE THIS SMALL BIT OF AMATEUR VIDEO FROM THIS AFTERNOON'S *HISTORIC* APPEARANCE...
...BUT WE TOOK THE LIBERTY OF ENHANCING THE IMAGE AS BEST WE CAN.
NEWS 5
Amateur Home Video
STATION MANAGER
TED HENRY
TO ANYONE OUT THERE WHO HAS ANY INFORMATION OF THIS NEW, *FASCINATING* PERSONALITY...
...PLEASE CONTACT THE 800 NUMBER BELOW.
AND PLEASE, ONLY *SERIOUS* CALLS...
...DO NOT TIE UP OUR LINES WITH PRANKS OR FALSE INFORMATION.
1-800-987-9864
THANK YOU.

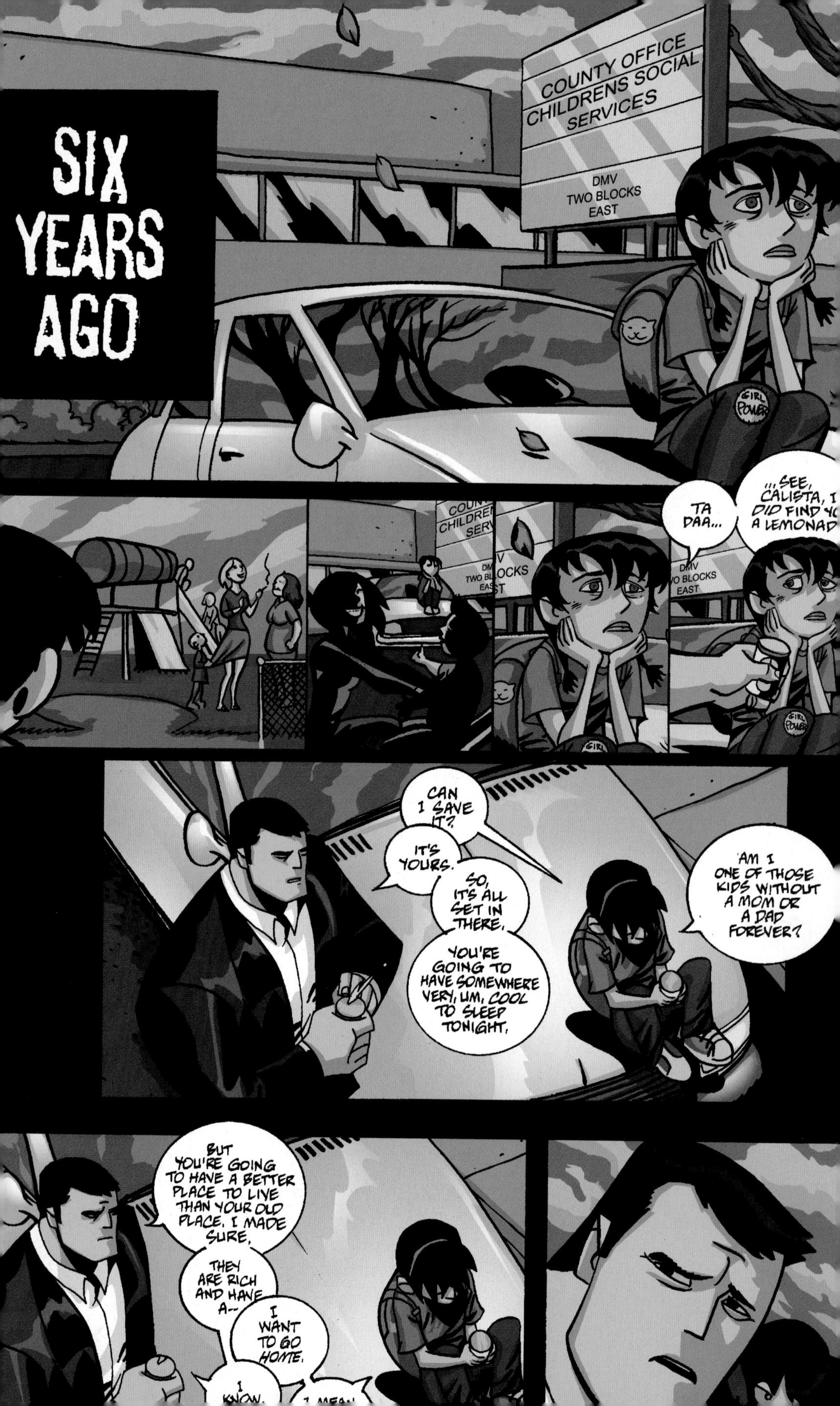
SIX YEARS AGO
COUNTY OFFICE CHILDRENS SOCIAL SERVICES
DMV TWO BLOCKS EAST
GIRL POWER
TA DAA...
...SEE, CALISTA, I DID FIND YO A LEMONAD
CAN I SAVE IT?
IT'S YOURS.
SO, IT'S ALL SET IN THERE.
YOU'RE GOING TO HAVE SOMEWHERE VERY, UM, COOL TO SLEEP TONIGHT.
AM I ONE OF THOSE KIDS WITHOUT A MOM OR A DAD FOREVER?
BUT YOU'RE GOING TO HAVE A BETTER PLACE TO LIVE THAN YOUR OLD PLACE. I MADE SURE.
THEY ARE RICH AND HAVE A--
I WANT TO GO HOME.

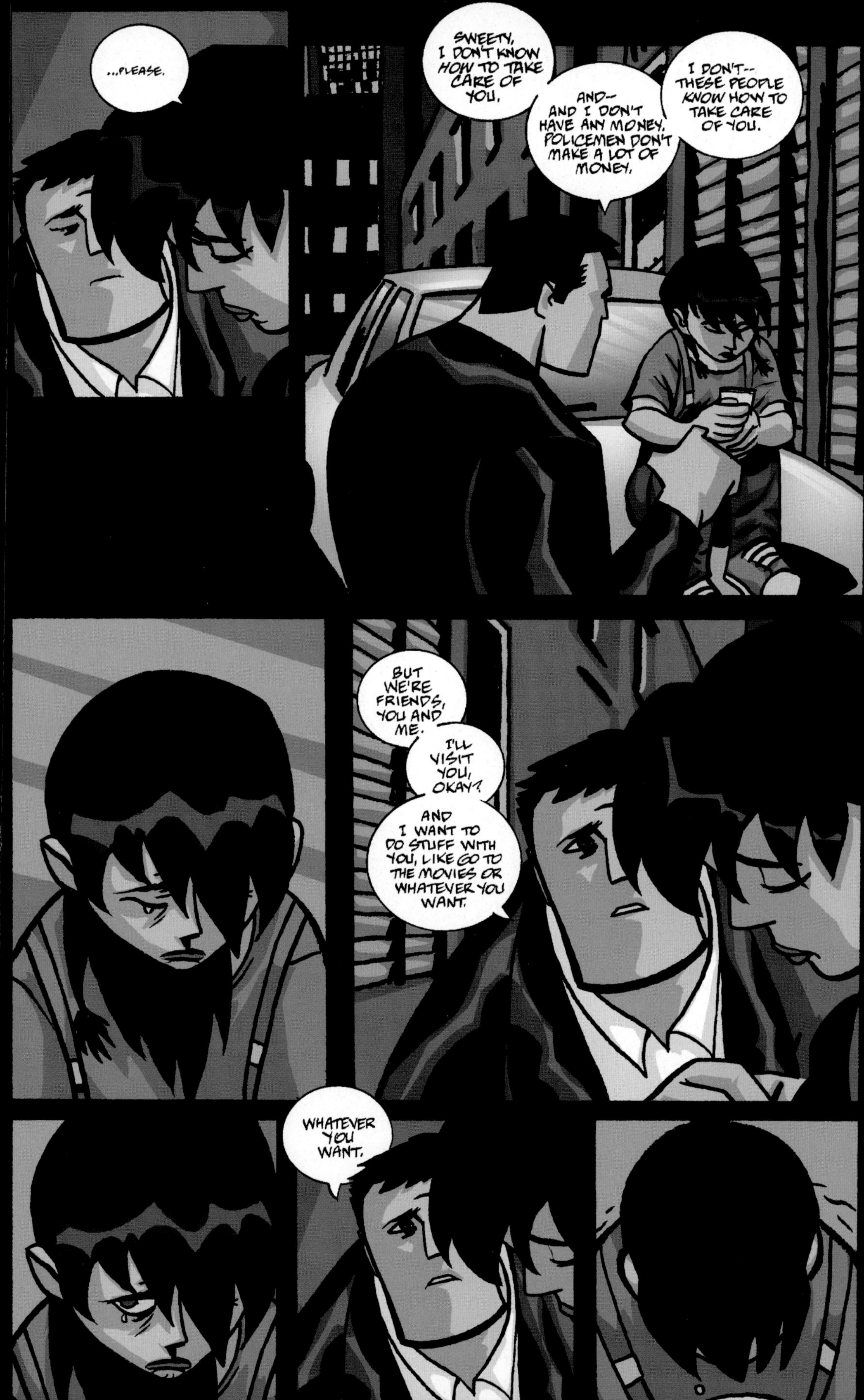

...PLEASE.
SWEETY, I DON'T KNOW HOW TO TAKE CARE OF YOU.
AND-- AND I DON'T HAVE ANY MONEY. POLICEMEN DON'T MAKE A LOT OF MONEY.
I DON'T-- THESE PEOPLE KNOW HOW TO TAKE CARE OF YOU.
BUT WE'RE FRIENDS, YOU AND ME.
I'LL VISIT YOU, OKAY?
AND I WANT TO DO STUFF WITH YOU, LIKE GO TO THE MOVIES OR WHATEVER YOU WANT.
WHATEVER YOU WANT.

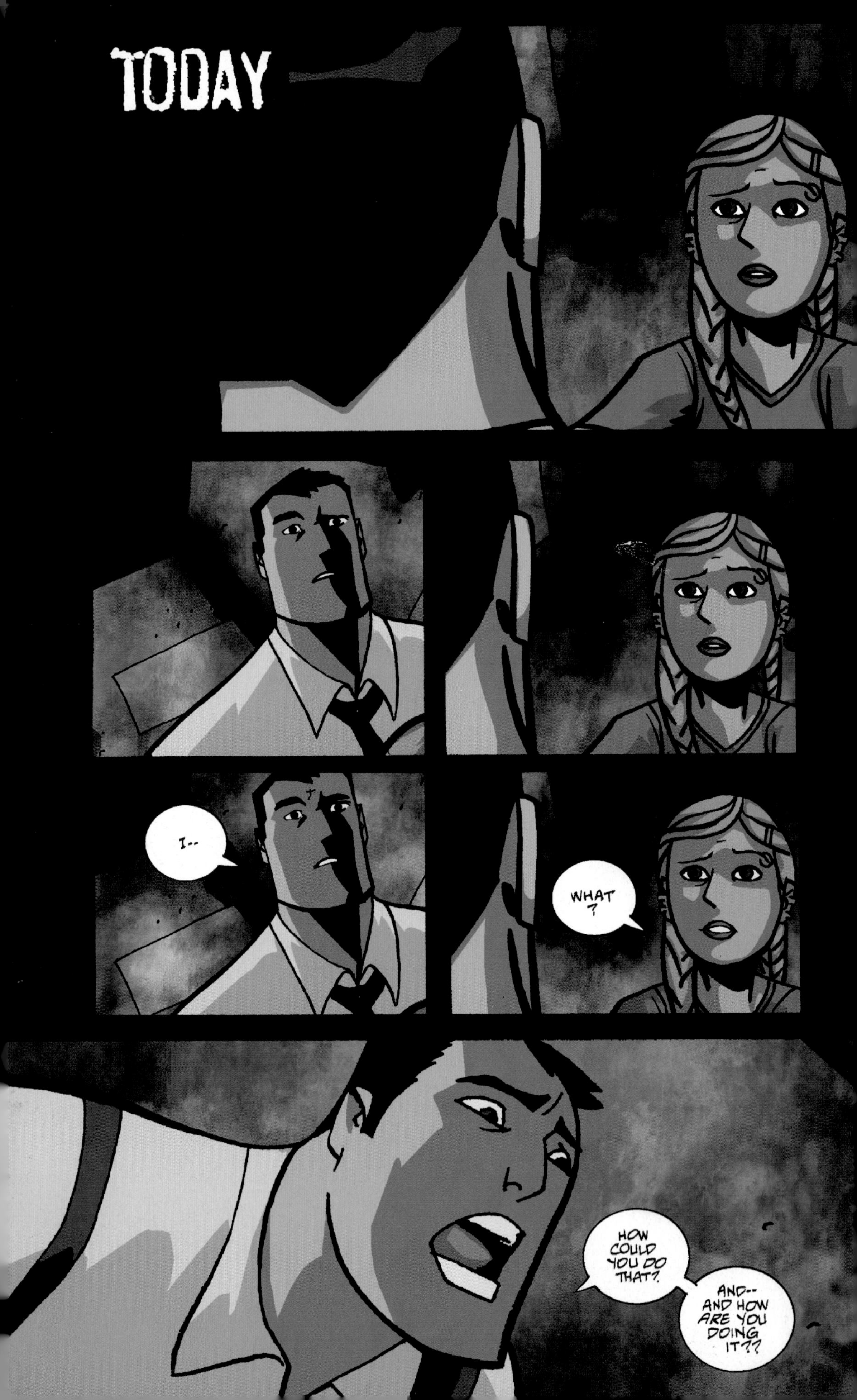
TODAY
I--
WHAT?
HOW COULD YOU DO THAT?
AND-- AND HOW ARE YOU DOING IT??

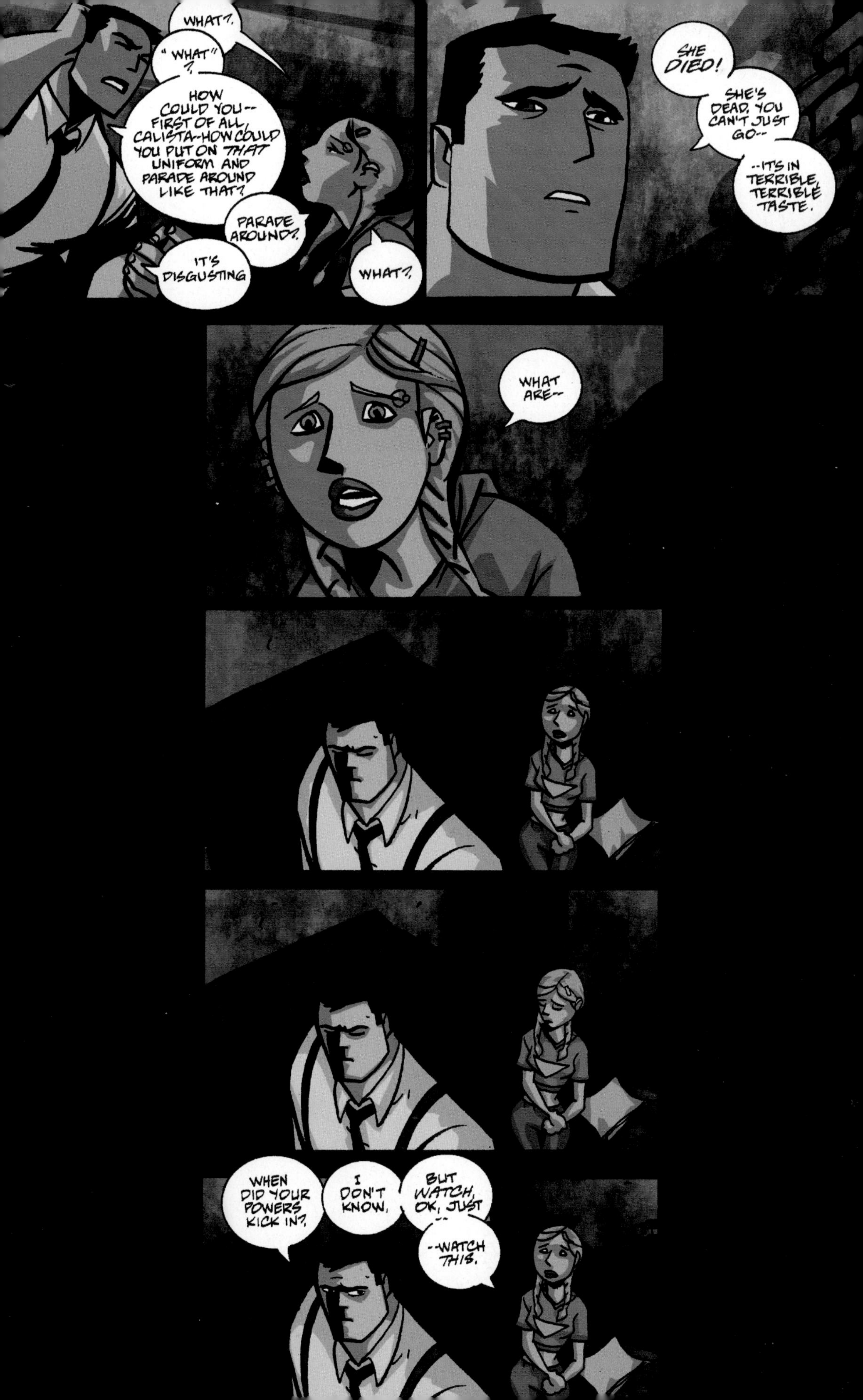
WHAT?
"WHAT"?
HOW COULD YOU-- FIRST OF ALL, CALISTA--HOW COULD YOU PUT ON *THAT* UNIFORM AND PARADE AROUND LIKE THAT?
PARADE AROUND?
IT'S DISGUSTING
WHAT?
SHE *DIED*!
SHE'S DEAD, YOU CAN'T JUST GO--
--IT'S IN TERRIBLE, TERRIBLE TASTE.
WHAT ARE--
WHEN DID YOUR POWERS KICK IN?
I DON'T KNOW.
BUT *WATCH*, OK, JUST --
--WATCH *THIS*.

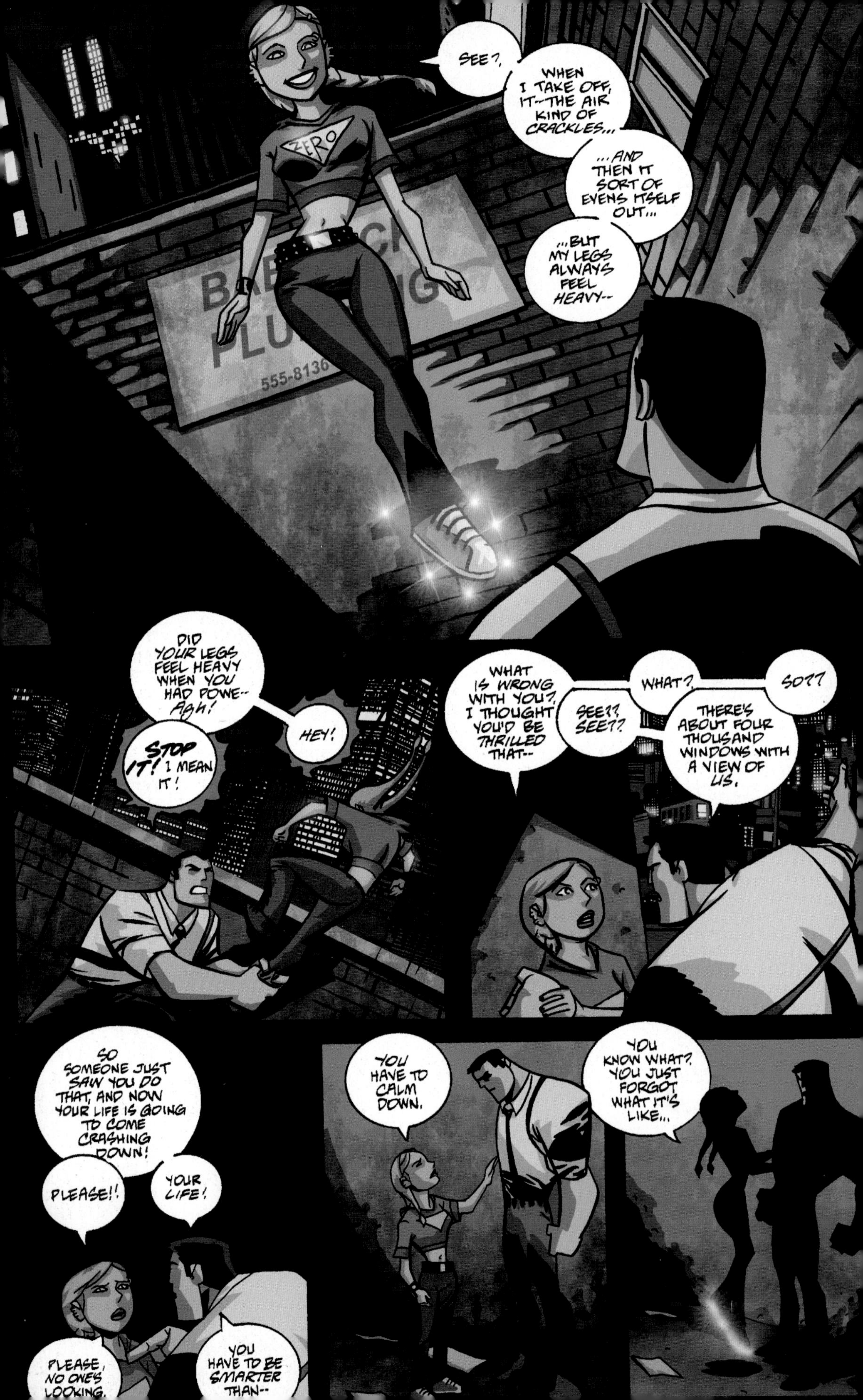
SEE?,
WHEN I TAKE OFF, IT--THE AIR KIND OF CRACKLES...
...AND THEN IT SORT OF EVENS ITSELF OUT...
...BUT MY LEGS ALWAYS FEEL HEAVY--
ZERO
555-8136
DID YOUR LEGS FEEL HEAVY WHEN YOU HAD POWE-- Agh!
HEY!
STOP IT! I MEAN IT!
WHAT IS WRONG WITH YOU?, I THOUGHT YOU'D BE THRILLED THAT--
WHAT?,
SO??
SEE??, SEE??
THERE'S ABOUT FOUR THOUSAND WINDOWS WITH A VIEW OF US.
SO SOMEONE JUST SAW YOU DO THAT, AND NOW YOUR LIFE IS GOING TO COME CRASHING DOWN!
PLEASE!!
YOUR LIFE!
PLEASE, NO ONE'S LOOKING.
YOU HAVE TO BE SMARTER THAN--
YOU HAVE TO CALM DOWN.
YOU KNOW WHAT?, YOU JUST FORGOT WHAT IT'S LIKE...

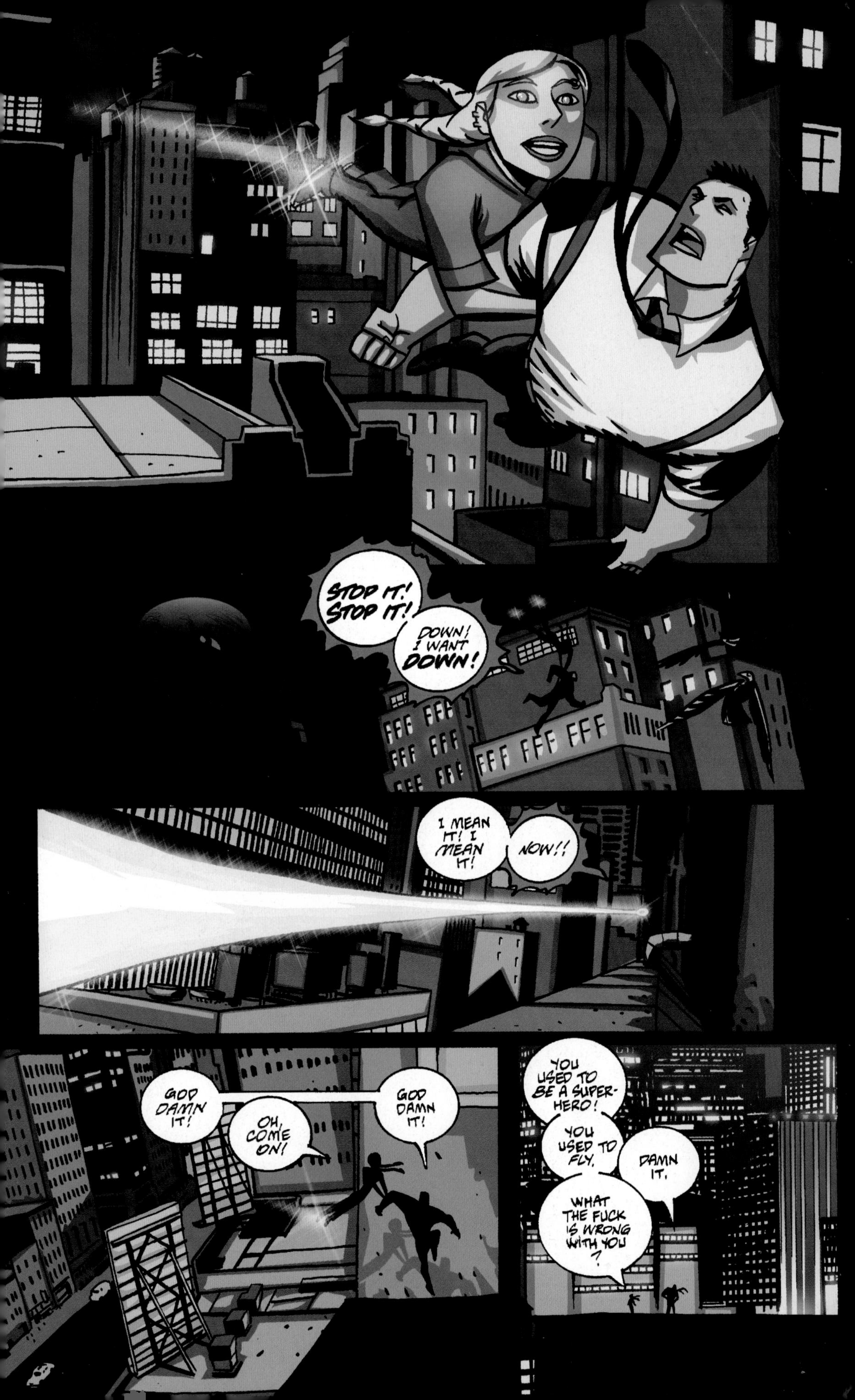
STOP IT! STOP IT!
DOWN! I WANT DOWN!
I MEAN IT! I MEAN IT!
NOW!!
GOD DAMN IT!
OH, COME ON!
GOD DAMN IT!
YOU USED TO BE A SUPER-HERO!
YOU USED TO FLY.
DAMN IT.
WHAT THE FUCK IS WRONG WITH YOU?

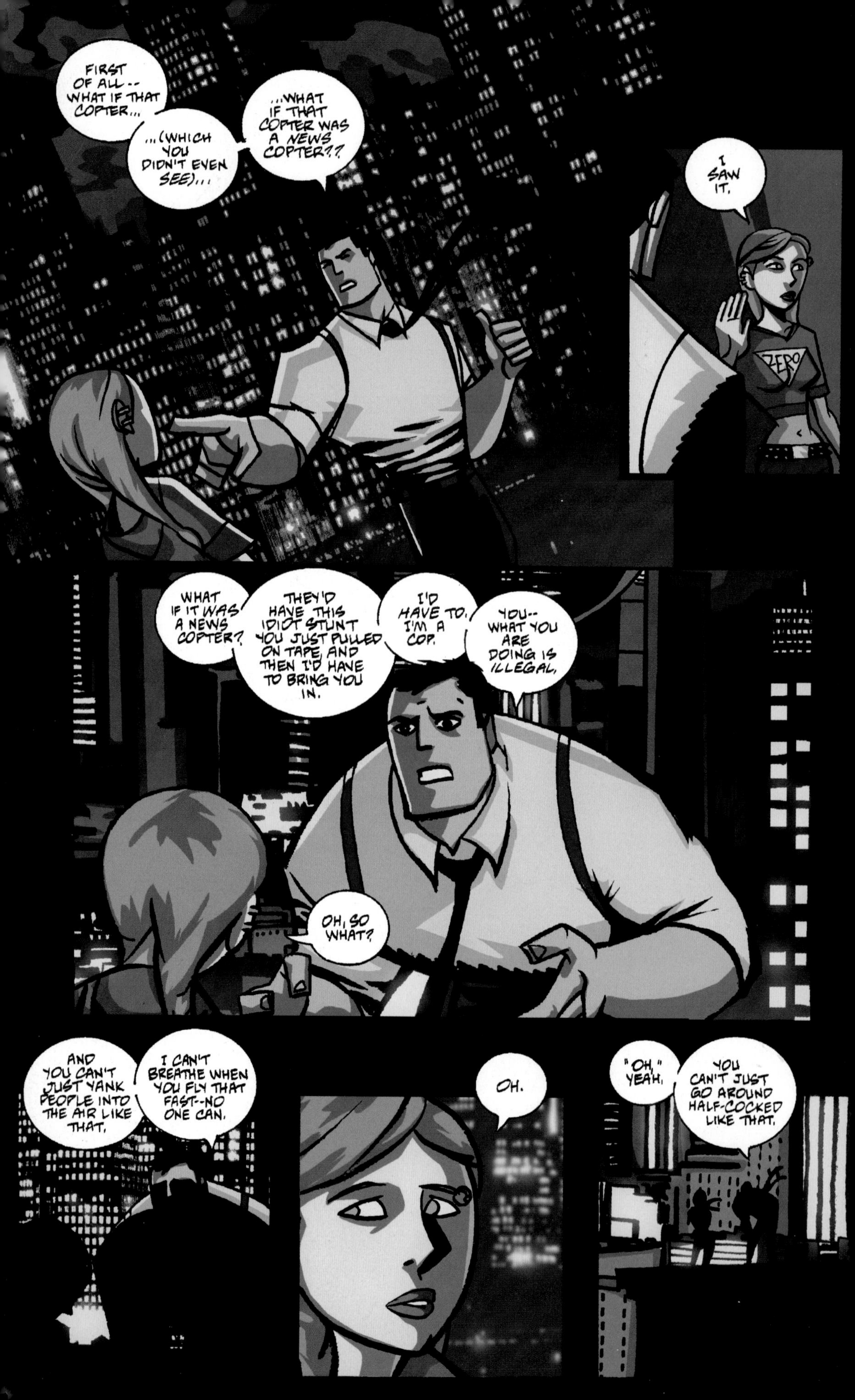
FIRST OF ALL-- WHAT IF THAT COPTER...
...(WHICH YOU DIDN'T EVEN SEE)...
...WHAT IF THAT COPTER WAS A NEWS COPTER??
I SAW IT.
WHAT IF IT WAS A NEWS COPTER?
THEY'D HAVE THIS IDIOT STUNT YOU JUST PULLED ON TAPE, AND THEN I'D HAVE TO BRING YOU IN.
I'D HAVE TO. I'M A COP.
YOU-- WHAT YOU ARE DOING IS ILLEGAL.
OH, SO WHAT?
AND YOU CAN'T JUST YANK PEOPLE INTO THE AIR LIKE THAT.
I CAN'T BREATHE WHEN YOU FLY THAT FAST--NO ONE CAN.
OH.
"OH," YEAH.
YOU CAN'T JUST GO AROUND HALF-COCKED LIKE THAT.

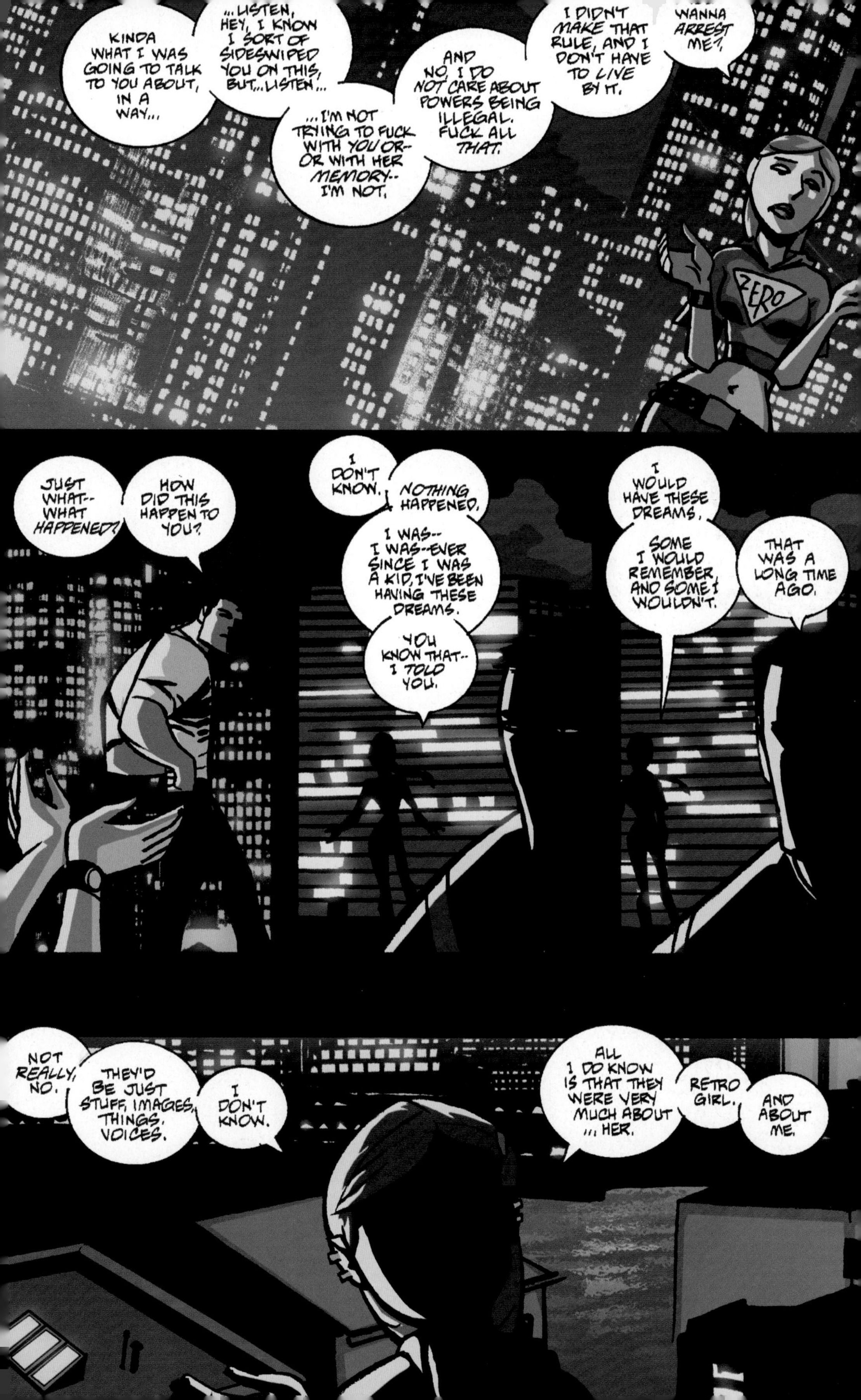
KINDA WHAT I WAS GOING TO TALK TO YOU ABOUT, IN A WAY...
...LISTEN, HEY, I KNOW I SORT OF SIDESWIPED YOU ON THIS, BUT... LISTEN...
...I'M NOT TRYING TO FUCK WITH YOU OR-- OR WITH HER MEMORY-- I'M NOT.
AND NO, I DO NOT CARE ABOUT POWERS BEING ILLEGAL. FUCK ALL THAT.
I DIDN'T MAKE THAT RULE, AND I DON'T HAVE TO LIVE BY IT.
WANNA ARREST ME?
JUST WHAT-- WHAT HAPPENED?
HOW DID THIS HAPPEN TO YOU?
I DON'T KNOW.
NOTHING HAPPENED.
I WAS-- I WAS--EVER SINCE I WAS A KID, I'VE BEEN HAVING THESE DREAMS.
YOU KNOW THAT-- I TOLD YOU.
I WOULD HAVE THESE DREAMS.
SOME I WOULD REMEMBER, AND SOME I WOULDN'T.
THAT WAS A LONG TIME AGO.
NOT REALLY, NO.
THEY'D BE JUST STUFF, IMAGES, THINGS, VOICES.
I DON'T KNOW.
ALL I DO KNOW IS THAT THEY WERE VERY MUCH ABOUT ... HER.
RETRO GIRL.
AND ABOUT ME.

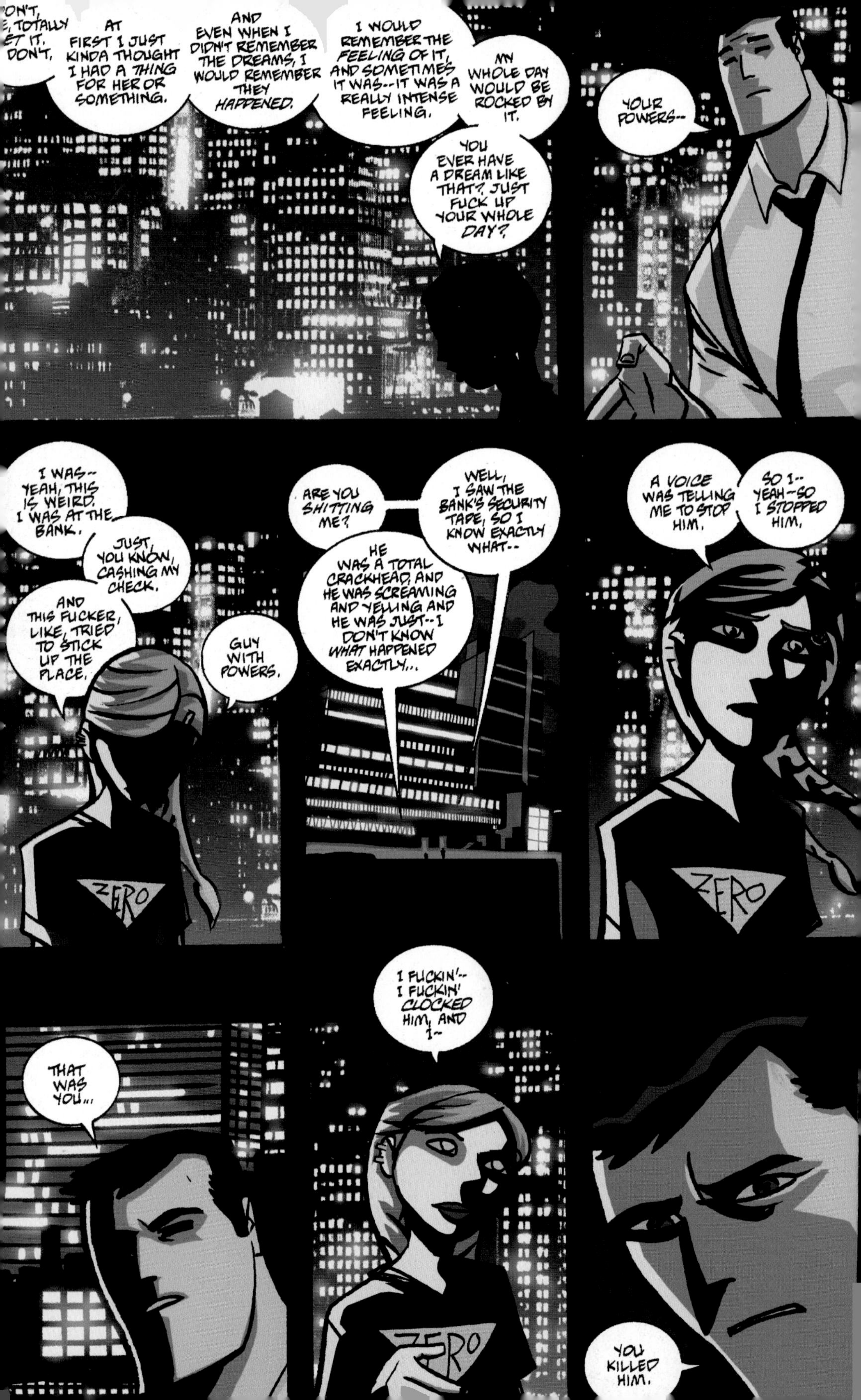
TOTALLY DON'T.
AT FIRST I JUST KINDA THOUGHT I HAD A *THING* FOR HER OR SOMETHING.
AND EVEN WHEN I DIDN'T REMEMBER THE DREAMS, I WOULD REMEMBER THEY *HAPPENED.*
I WOULD REMEMBER THE *FEELING* OF IT, AND SOMETIMES IT WAS-- IT WAS A REALLY INTENSE FEELING.
MY WHOLE DAY WOULD BE ROCKED BY IT.
YOU EVER HAVE A DREAM LIKE THAT? JUST FUCK UP YOUR WHOLE *DAY?*
YOUR POWERS--
I WAS-- YEAH, THIS IS WEIRD. I WAS AT THE BANK.
JUST, YOU KNOW, CASHING MY CHECK.
AND THIS FUCKER, LIKE, TRIED TO STICK UP THE PLACE.
GUY WITH POWERS.
ARE YOU *SHITTING* ME?
WELL, I SAW THE BANK'S SECURITY TAPE, SO I KNOW EXACTLY WHAT--
HE WAS A TOTAL CRACKHEAD, AND HE WAS SCREAMING AND YELLING AND HE WAS JUST-- I DON'T KNOW *WHAT* HAPPENED EXACTLY...
A VOICE WAS TELLING ME TO STOP HIM.
SO I-- YEAH-- SO I STOPPED HIM.
THAT WAS YOU...
I FUCKIN'-- I FUCKIN' *CLOCKED* HIM, AND I--
YOU KILLED HIM.
ZERO

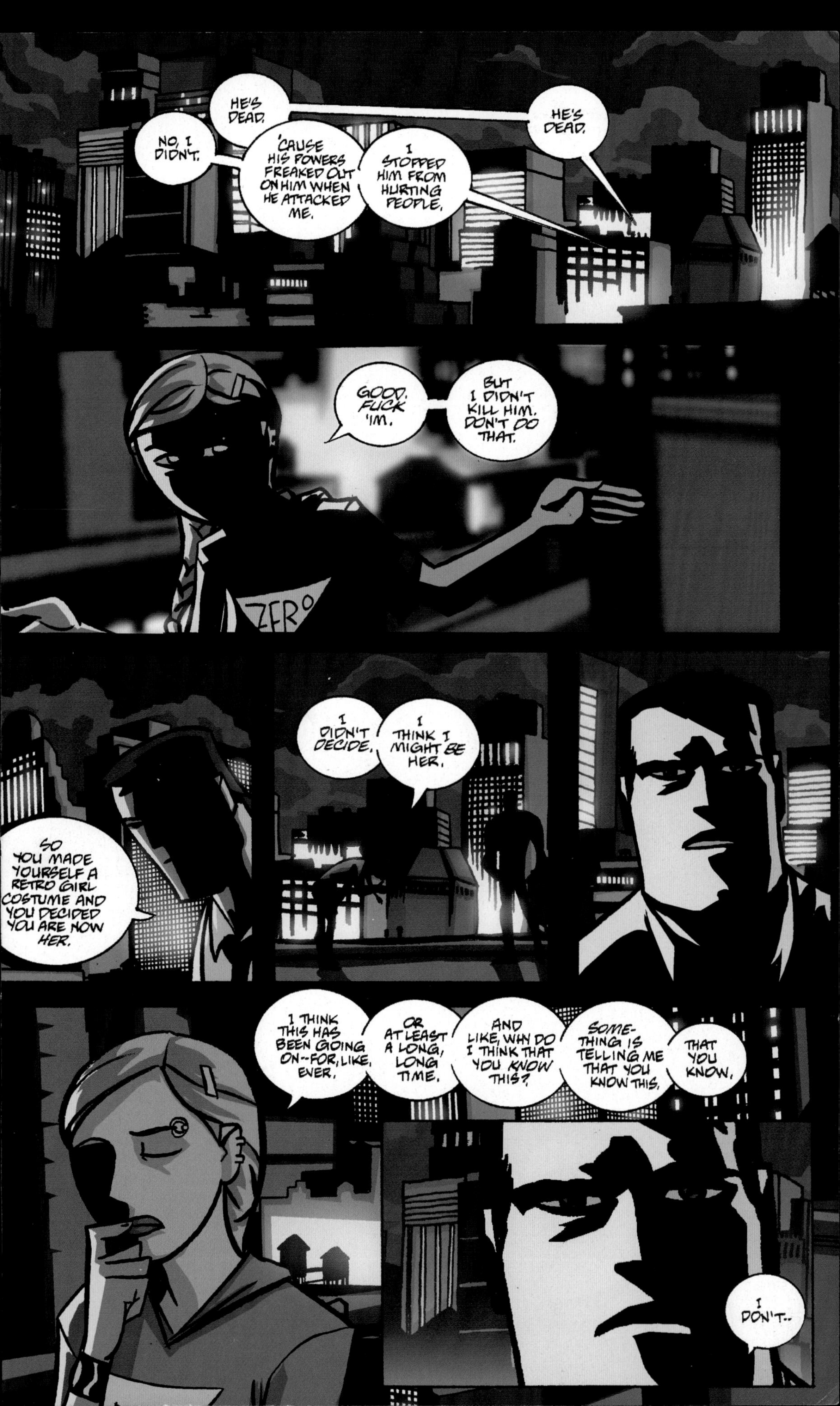

HE'S DEAD.
NO, I DIDN'T.
'CAUSE HIS POWERS FREAKED OUT ON HIM WHEN HE ATTACKED ME.
I STOPPED HIM FROM HURTING PEOPLE.
HE'S DEAD.
GOOD. FUCK 'IM.
BUT I DIDN'T KILL HIM. DON'T DO THAT.
ZERO
SO YOU MADE YOURSELF A RETRO GIRL COSTUME AND YOU DECIDED YOU ARE NOW HER.
I DIDN'T DECIDE.
I THINK I MIGHT BE HER.
I THINK THIS HAS BEEN GOING ON--FOR, LIKE, EVER.
OR AT LEAST A LONG, LONG TIME.
AND LIKE, WHY DO I THINK THAT YOU KNOW THIS?
SOME-THING IS TELLING ME THAT YOU KNOW THIS,
THAT YOU KNOW.
I DON'T..

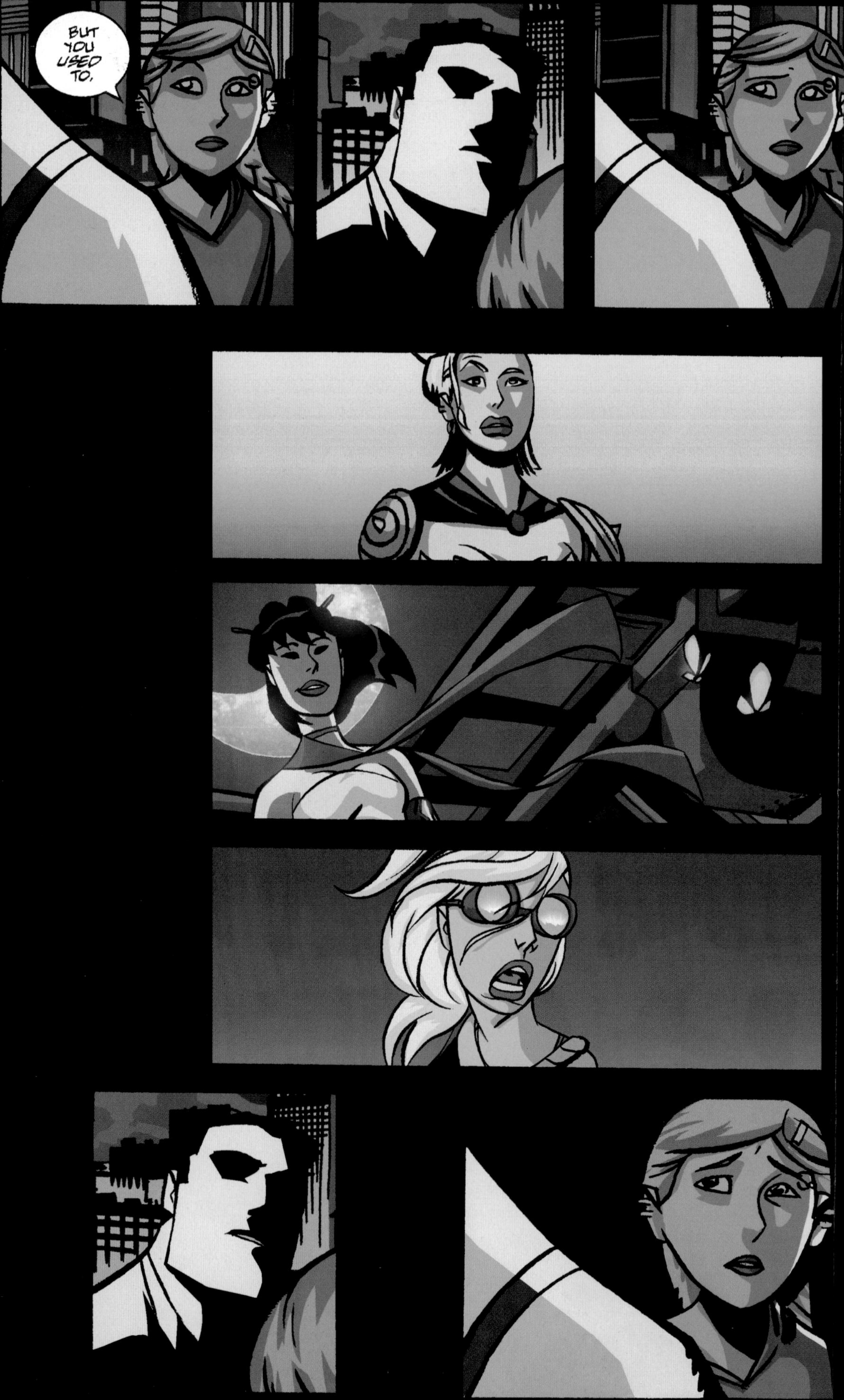
BUT YOU USED TO.

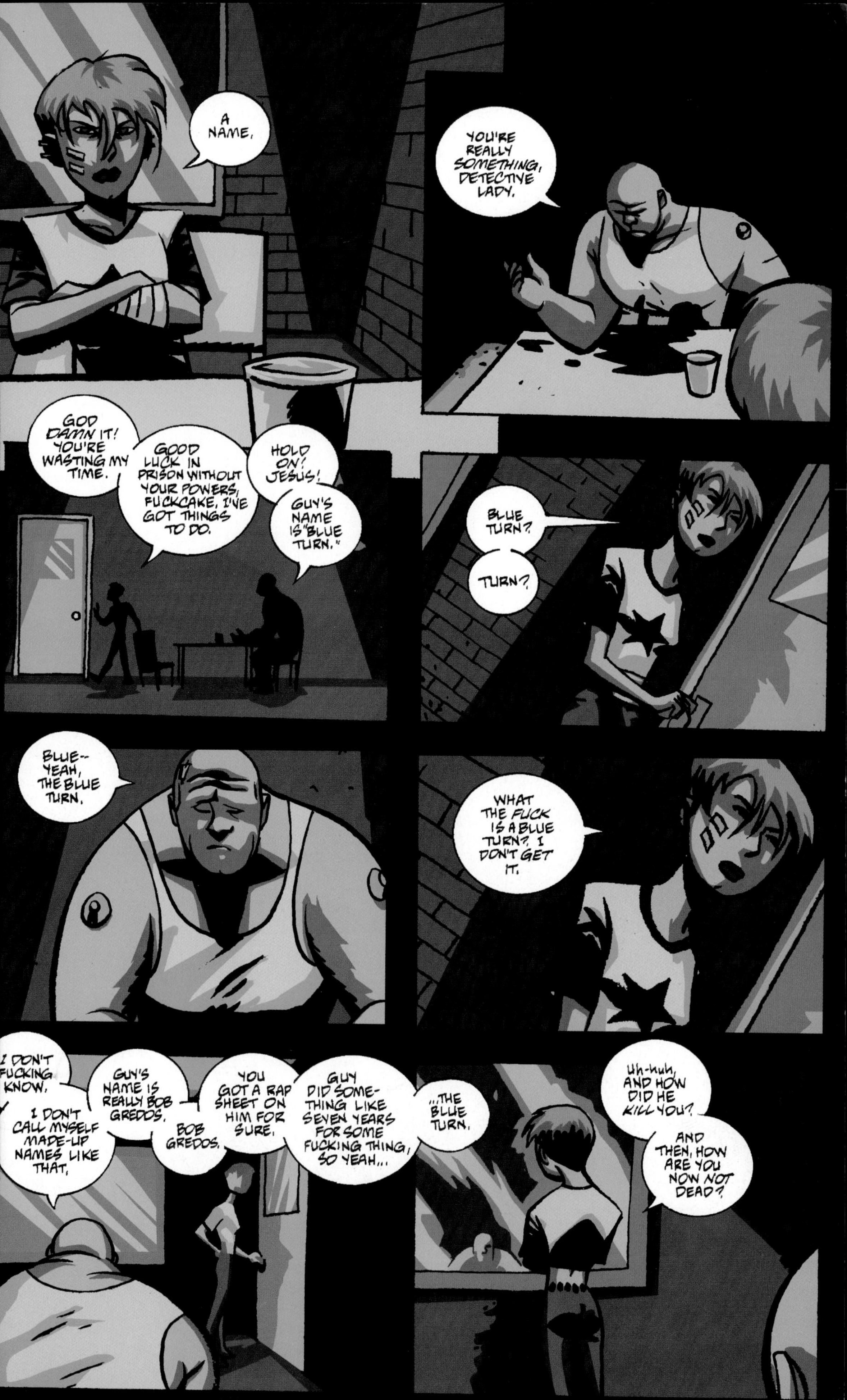
A NAME.
YOU'RE REALLY SOMETHING, DETECTIVE LADY.
GOD DAMN IT! YOU'RE WASTING MY TIME.
GOOD LUCK IN PRISON WITHOUT YOUR POWERS, FUCKCAKE, I'VE GOT THINGS TO DO.
HOLD ON! JESUS!
GUY'S NAME IS "BLUE TURN."
BLUE TURN?
TURN?
BLUE-- YEAH, THE BLUE TURN.
WHAT THE FUCK IS A BLUE TURN? I DON'T GET IT.
I DON'T FUCKING KNOW.
I DON'T CALL MYSELF MADE-UP NAMES LIKE THAT.
GUY'S NAME IS REALLY BOB GREDOS.
BOB GREDOS.
YOU GOT A RAP SHEET ON HIM FOR SURE.
GUY DID SOME-THING LIKE SEVEN YEARS FOR SOME FUCKING THING, SO YEAH...
...THE BLUE TURN.
UH-HUH, AND HOW DID HE KILL YOU?
AND THEN, HOW ARE YOU NOW NOT DEAD?

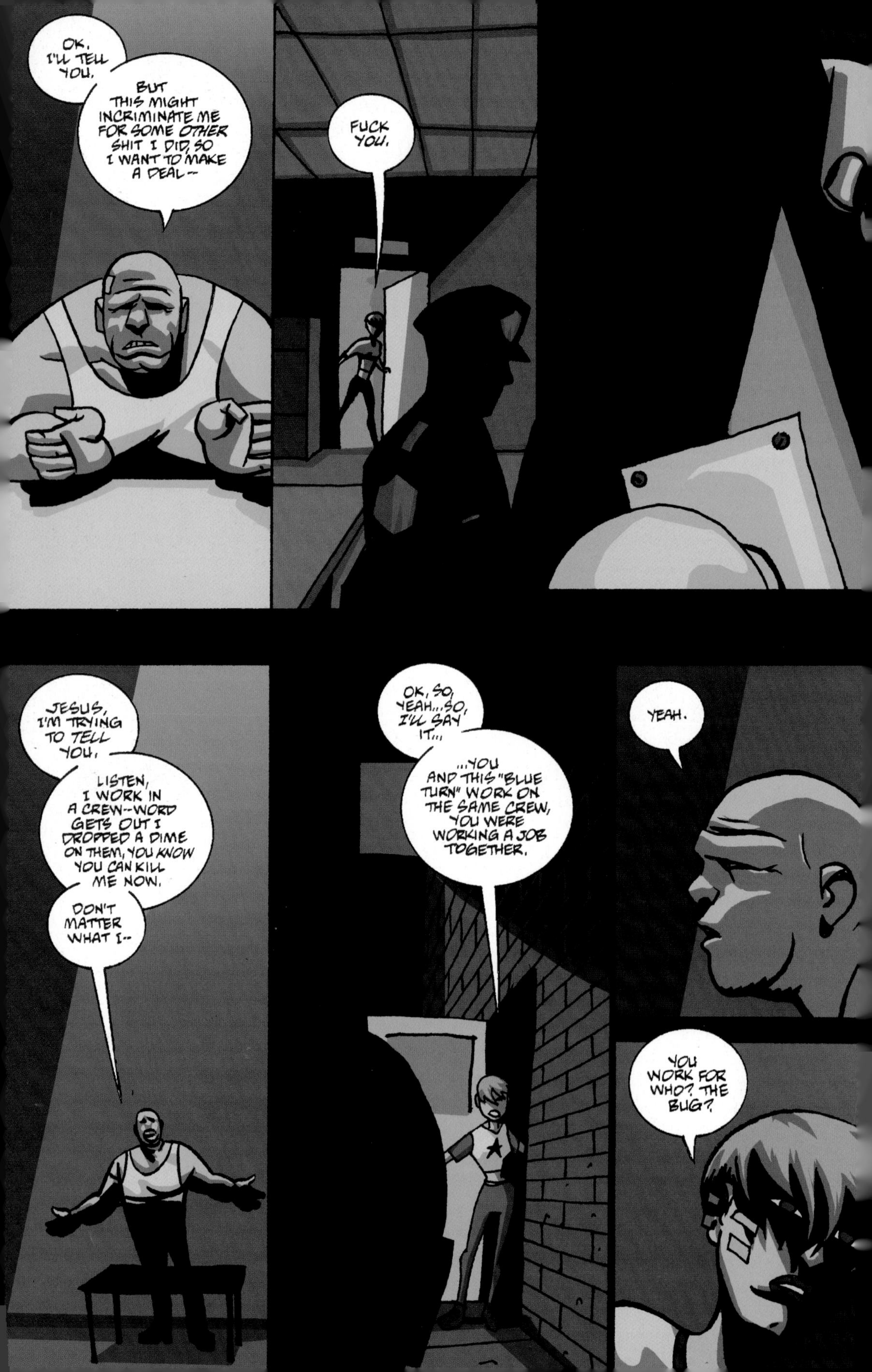
OK, I'LL TELL YOU.
BUT THIS MIGHT INCRIMINATE ME FOR SOME OTHER SHIT I DID, SO I WANT TO MAKE A DEAL--
FUCK YOU.
JESUS, I'M TRYING TO TELL YOU.
LISTEN, I WORK IN A CREW--WORD GETS OUT I DROPPED A DIME ON THEM, YOU KNOW YOU CAN KILL ME NOW.
DON'T MATTER WHAT I--
OK, SO, YEAH...SO, I'LL SAY IT...
...YOU AND THIS "BLUE TURN" WORK ON THE SAME CREW, YOU WERE WORKING A JOB TOGETHER.
YEAH.
YOU WORK FOR WHO? THE BUG?

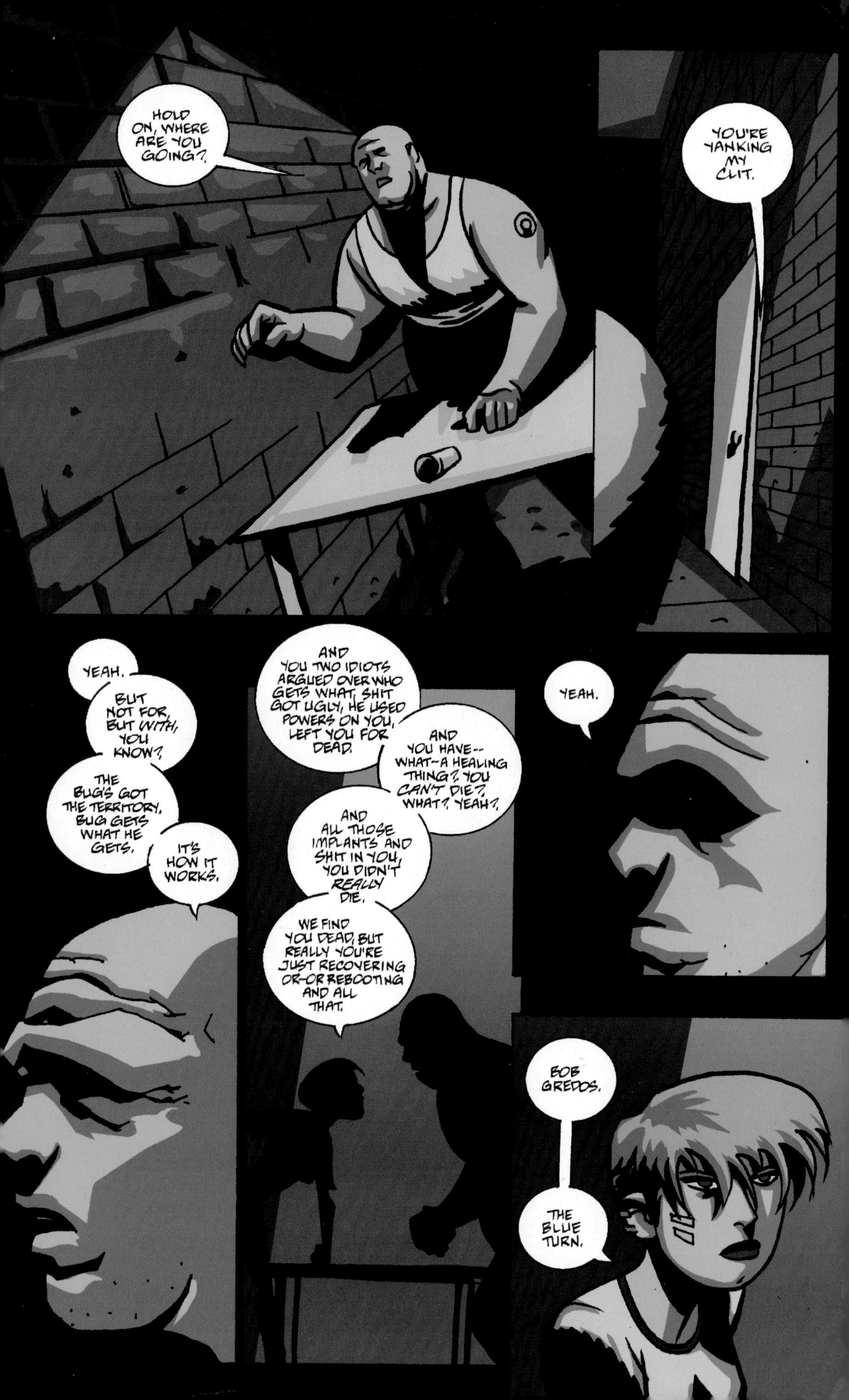
HOLD ON, WHERE ARE YOU GOING?
YOU'RE YANKING MY CLIT.
YEAH.
BUT NOT FOR, BUT WITH, YOU KNOW?
THE BUG'S GOT THE TERRITORY, BUG GETS WHAT HE GETS.
IT'S HOW IT WORKS.
AND YOU TWO IDIOTS ARGUED OVER WHO GETS WHAT, SHIT GOT UGLY, HE USED POWERS ON YOU, LEFT YOU FOR DEAD.
AND YOU HAVE-- WHAT--A HEALING THING? YOU CAN'T DIE? WHAT? YEAH?
AND ALL THOSE IMPLANTS AND SHIT IN YOU, YOU DIDN'T REALLY DIE.
WE FIND YOU DEAD, BUT REALLY YOU'RE JUST RECOVERING OR-OR REBOOTING AND ALL THAT.
YEAH.
BOB GREDOS.
THE BLUE TURN.

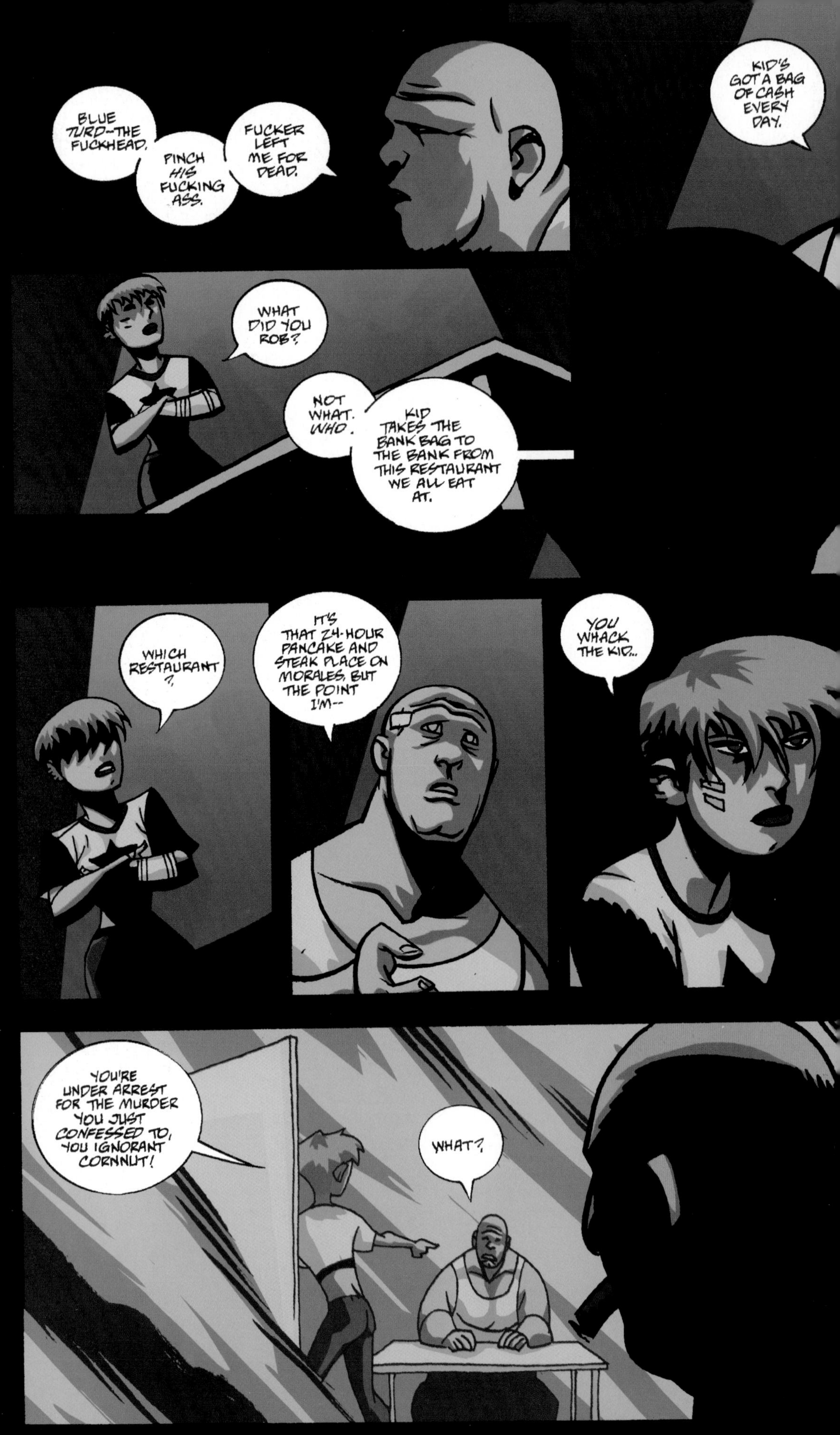
BLUE TURD--THE FUCKHEAD.
PINCH HIS FUCKING ASS.
FUCKER LEFT ME FOR DEAD.
KID'S GOT A BAG OF CASH EVERY DAY.
WHAT DID YOU ROB?
NOT WHAT. WHO.
KID TAKES THE BANK BAG TO THE BANK FROM THIS RESTAURANT WE ALL EAT AT.
WHICH RESTAURANT?
IT'S THAT 24-HOUR PANCAKE AND STEAK PLACE ON MORALES, BUT THE POINT I'M--
YOU WHACK THE KID...
YOU'RE UNDER ARREST FOR THE MURDER YOU JUST CONFESSED TO, YOU IGNORANT CORNNUT!
WHAT?

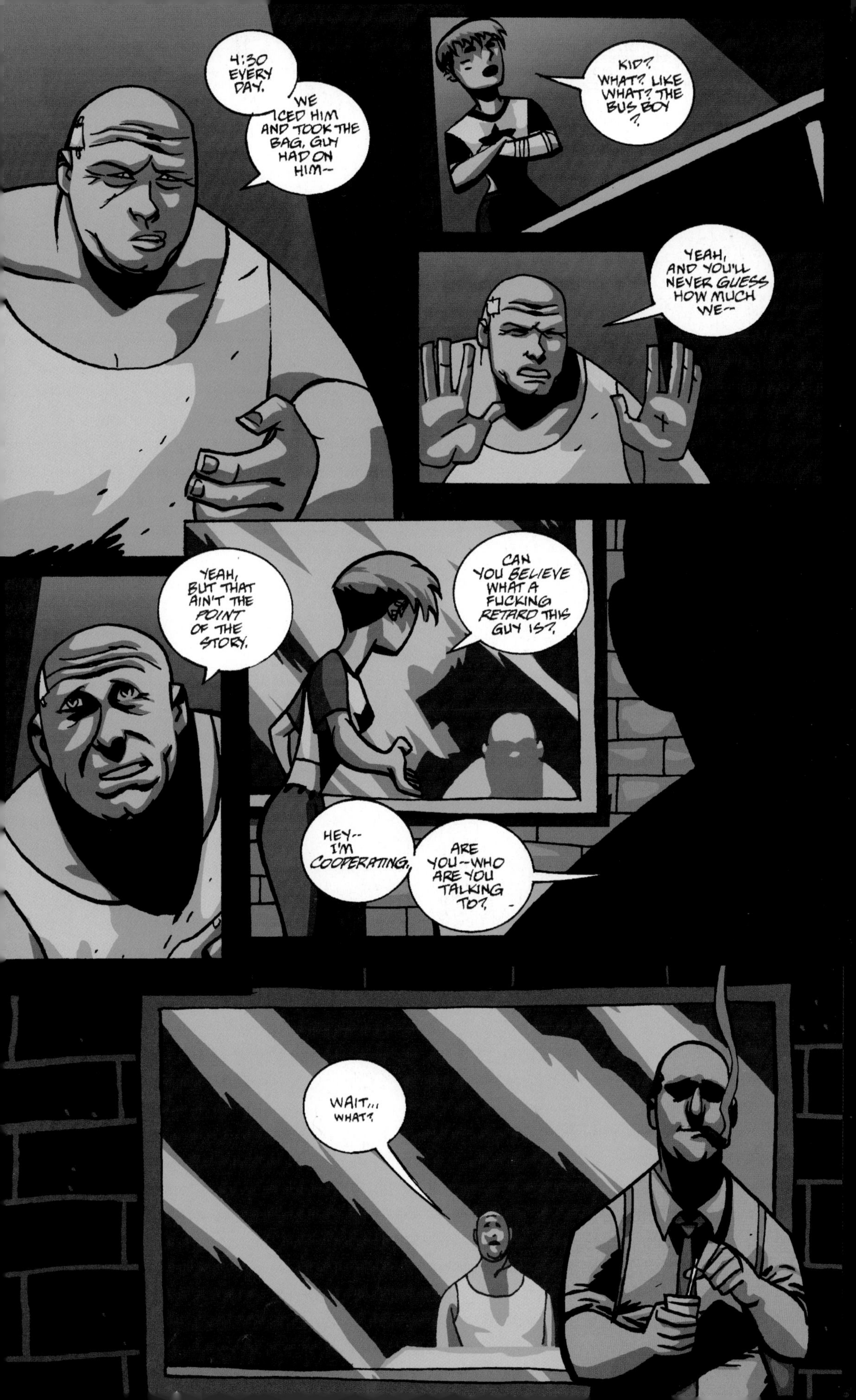
4:30 EVERY DAY.
WE ICED HIM AND TOOK THE BAG, GUY HAD ON HIM--
KID? WHAT? LIKE WHAT? THE BUS BOY?
YEAH, AND YOU'LL NEVER GUESS HOW MUCH WE--
YEAH, BUT THAT AIN'T THE POINT OF THE STORY.
CAN YOU BELIEVE WHAT A FUCKING RETARD THIS GUY IS?
HEY-- I'M COOPERATING.
ARE YOU--WHO ARE YOU TALKING TO?
WAIT... WHAT?

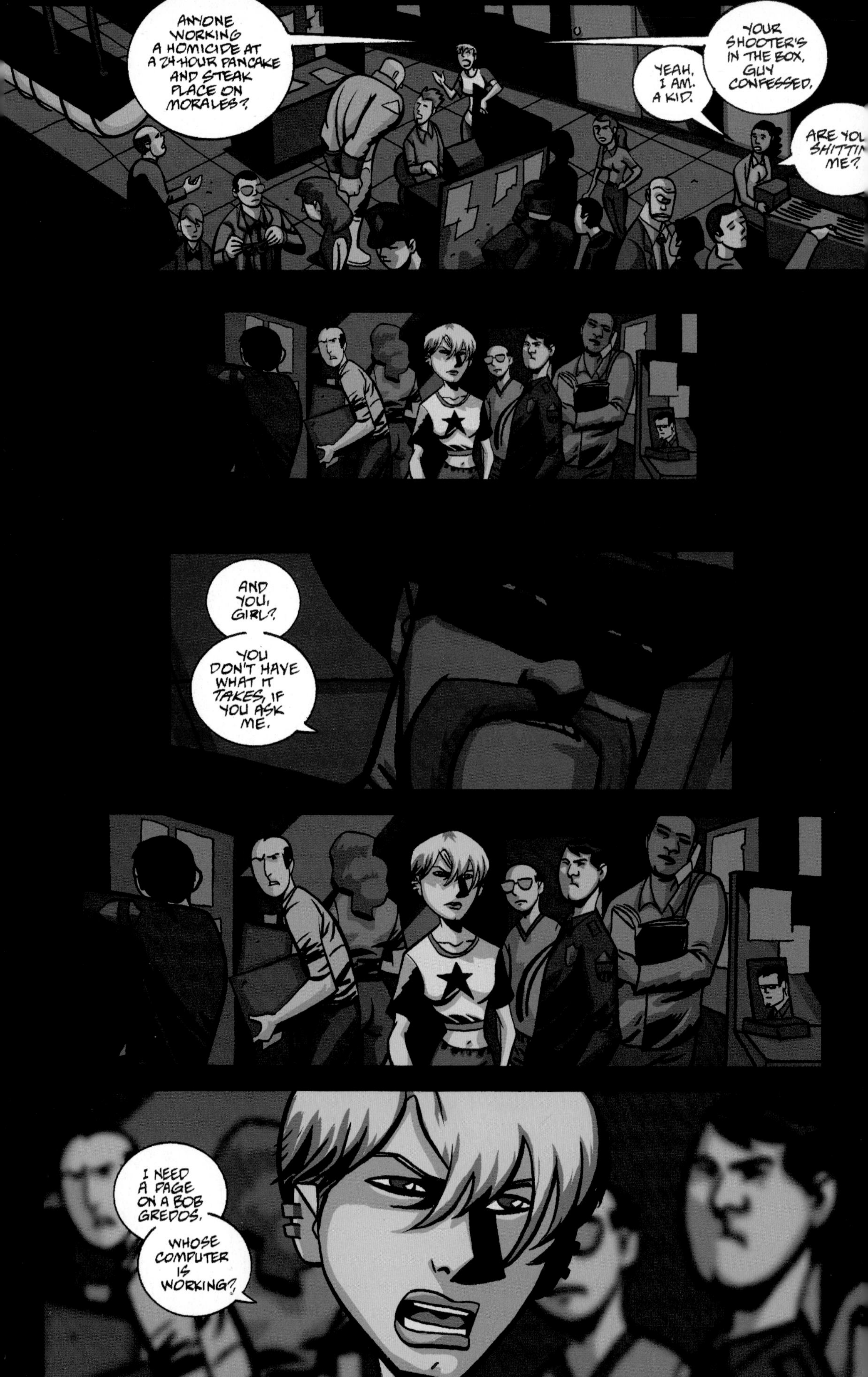
ANYONE WORKING A HOMICIDE AT A 24-HOUR PANCAKE AND STEAK PLACE ON MORALES?
YOUR SHOOTER'S IN THE BOX, GUY CONFESSED.
YEAH, I AM. A KID.
AND YOU, GIRL?
YOU DON'T HAVE WHAT IT TAKES, IF YOU ASK ME.
I NEED A PAGE ON A BOB GREDOS.
WHOSE COMPUTER IS WORKING?

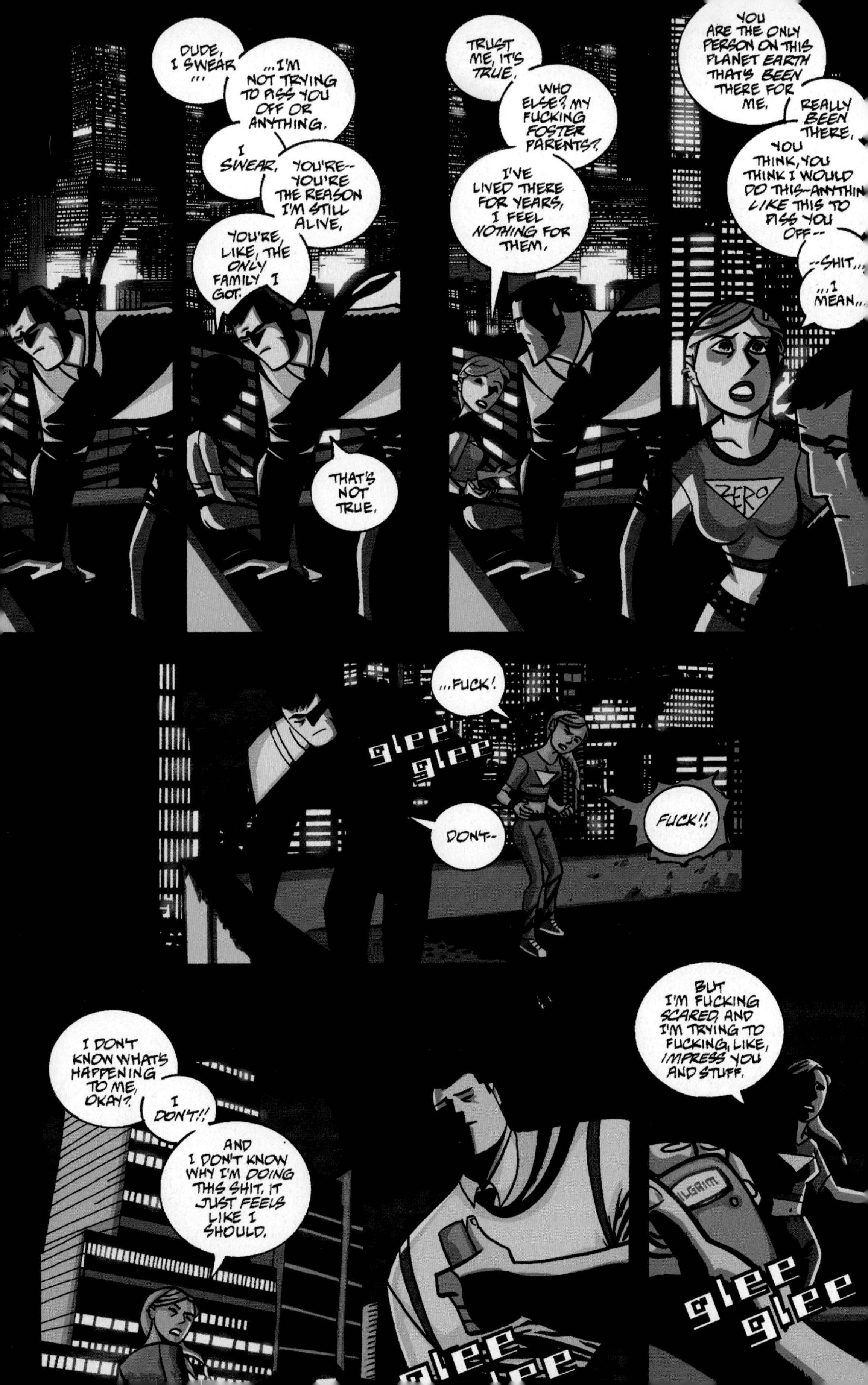
DUDE, I SWEAR ...
...I'M NOT TRYING TO PISS YOU OFF OR ANYTHING.
I SWEAR.
YOU'RE-- YOU'RE THE REASON I'M STILL ALIVE.
YOU'RE, LIKE, THE ONLY FAMILY I GOT.
THAT'S NOT TRUE.
TRUST ME, IT'S TRUE.
WHO ELSE? MY FUCKING FOSTER PARENTS?
I'VE LIVED THERE FOR YEARS, I FEEL NOTHING FOR THEM.
YOU ARE THE ONLY PERSON ON THIS PLANET EARTH THAT'S BEEN THERE FOR ME.
REALLY BEEN THERE.
YOU THINK, YOU THINK I WOULD DO THIS--ANYTHIN LIKE THIS TO PISS YOU OFF--
--SHIT...
...I MEAN...
...FUCK!
glee glee
DON'T--
FUCK!!
I DON'T KNOW WHAT'S HAPPENING TO ME, OKAY?
I DON'T!!
AND I DON'T KNOW WHY I'M DOING THIS SHIT. IT JUST FEELS LIKE I SHOULD.
BUT I'M FUCKING SCARED, AND I'M TRYING TO FUCKING, LIKE, IMPRESS YOU AND STUFF.
PILGRIM
glee glee
glee glee

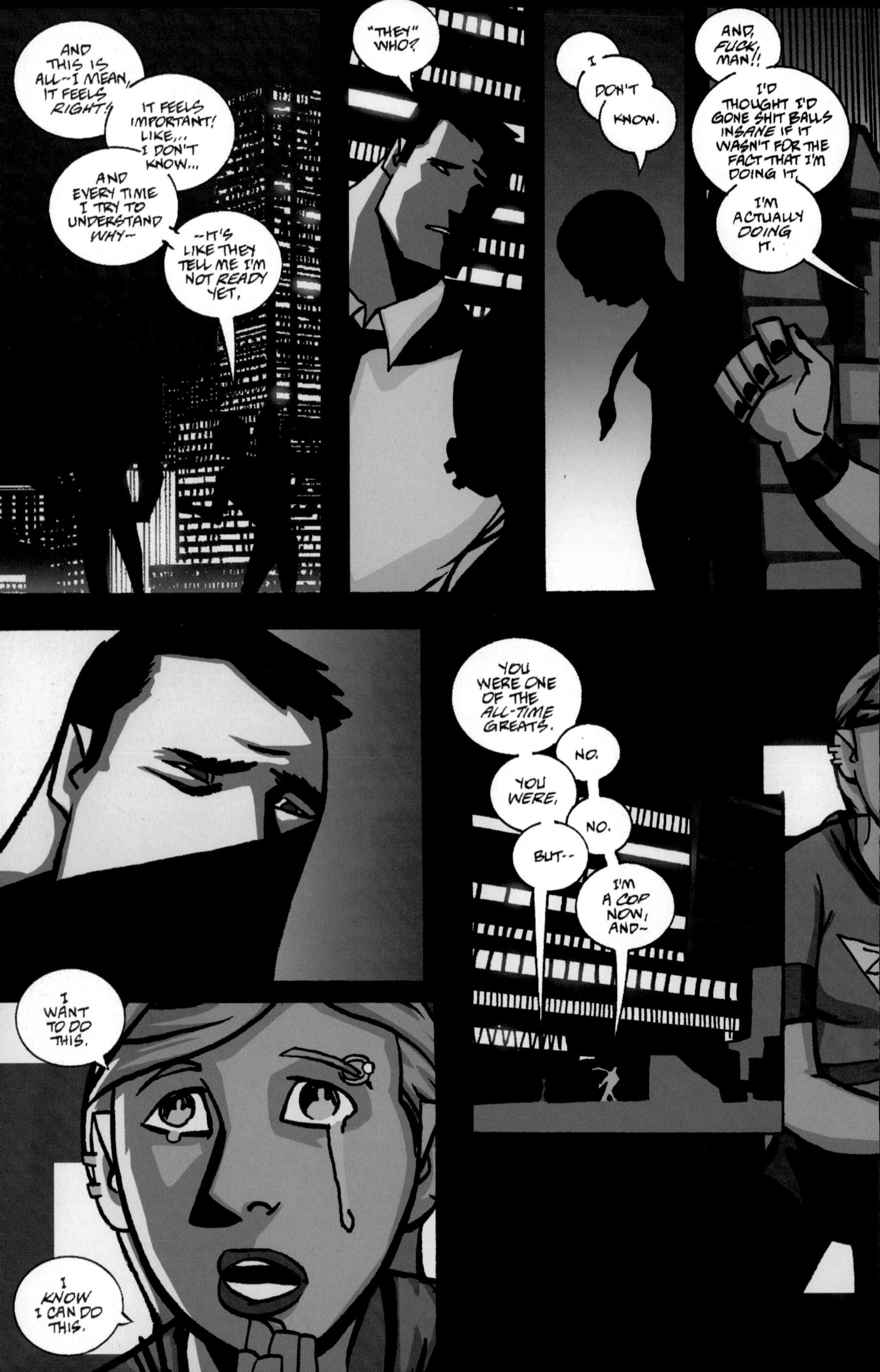
AND THIS IS ALL--I MEAN, IT FEELS RIGHT!
IT FEELS IMPORTANT! LIKE,... I DON'T KNOW...
AND EVERY TIME I TRY TO UNDERSTAND WHY--
--IT'S LIKE THEY TELL ME I'M NOT READY YET.
"THEY" WHO?
I
DON'T
KNOW.
AND, FUCK, MAN!!
I'D THOUGHT I'D GONE SHIT BALLS INSANE IF IT WASN'T FOR THE FACT THAT I'M DOING IT.
I'M ACTUALLY DOING IT.
YOU WERE ONE OF THE ALL-TIME GREATS.
NO.
YOU WERE.
NO.
BUT--
I'M A COP NOW, AND--
I WANT TO DO THIS.
I KNOW I CAN DO THIS.

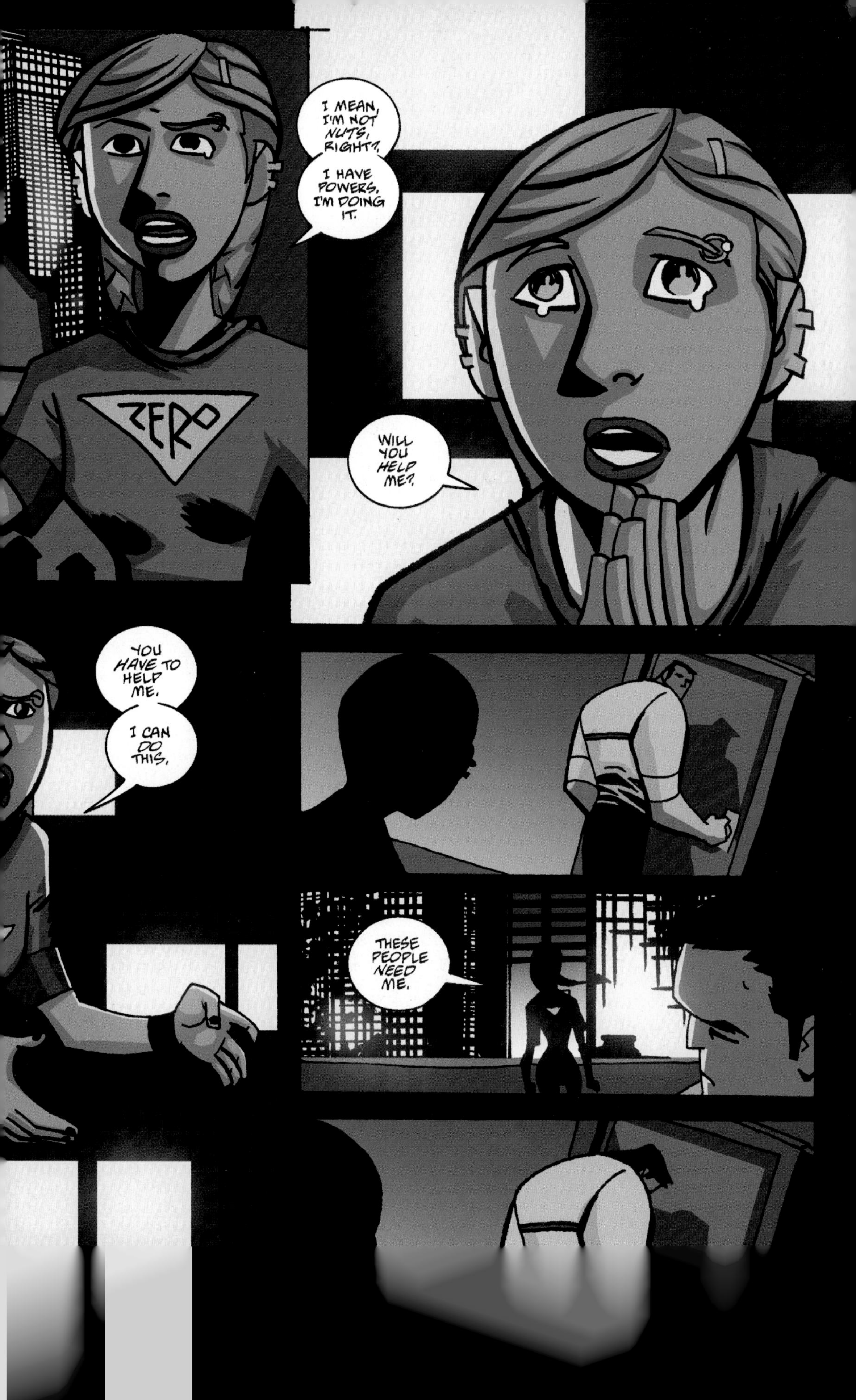
I MEAN, I'M NOT NUTS, RIGHT?
I HAVE POWERS. I'M DOING IT.
ZERO
WILL YOU HELP ME?
YOU HAVE TO HELP ME.
I CAN DO THIS.
THESE PEOPLE NEED ME.

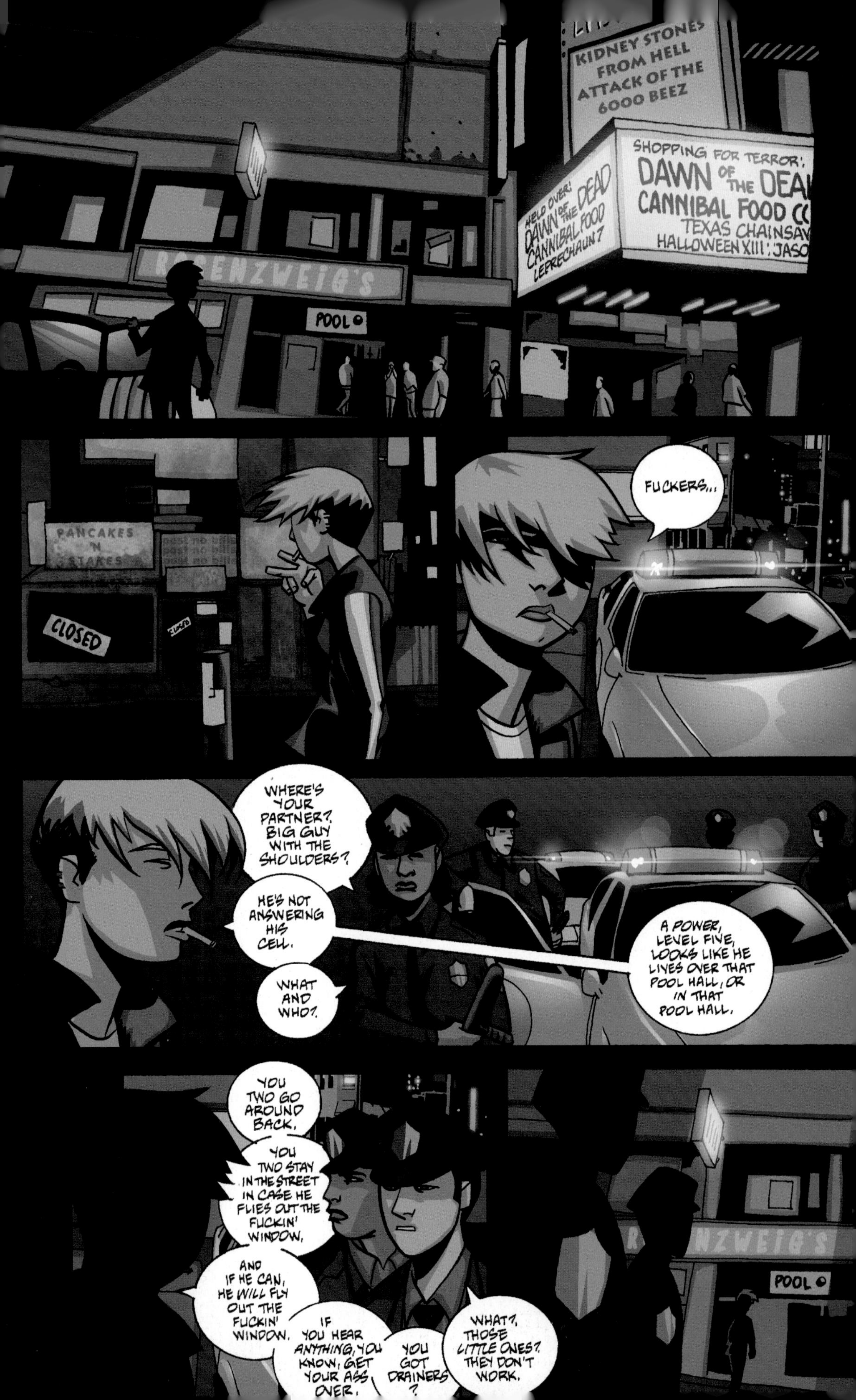
KIDNEY STONES FROM HELL
ATTACK OF THE 6000 BEEZ
SHOPPING FOR TERROR: DAWN OF THE DEA
CANNIBAL FOOD C
TEXAS CHAINSAV
HALLOWEEN XIII: JASO
HELD OVER! DAWN OF THE DEAD
CANNIBAL FOOD
LEPRECHAUN 7
POOL
PANCAKES 'N STAKES
CLOSED
FUCKERS...
WHERE'S YOUR PARTNER? BIG GUY WITH THE SHOULDERS?
HE'S NOT ANSWERING HIS CELL.
WHAT AND WHO?
A POWER, LEVEL FIVE, LOOKS LIKE HE LIVES OVER THAT POOL HALL, OR IN THAT POOL HALL.
YOU TWO GO AROUND BACK.
YOU TWO STAY IN THE STREET IN CASE HE FLIES OUT THE FUCKIN' WINDOW.
AND IF HE CAN, HE WILL FLY OUT THE FUCKIN' WINDOW.
IF YOU HEAR ANYTHING, YOU KNOW, GET YOUR ASS OVER.
YOU GOT DRAINERS?
WHAT?, THOSE LITTLE ONES? THEY DON'T WORK.
POOL

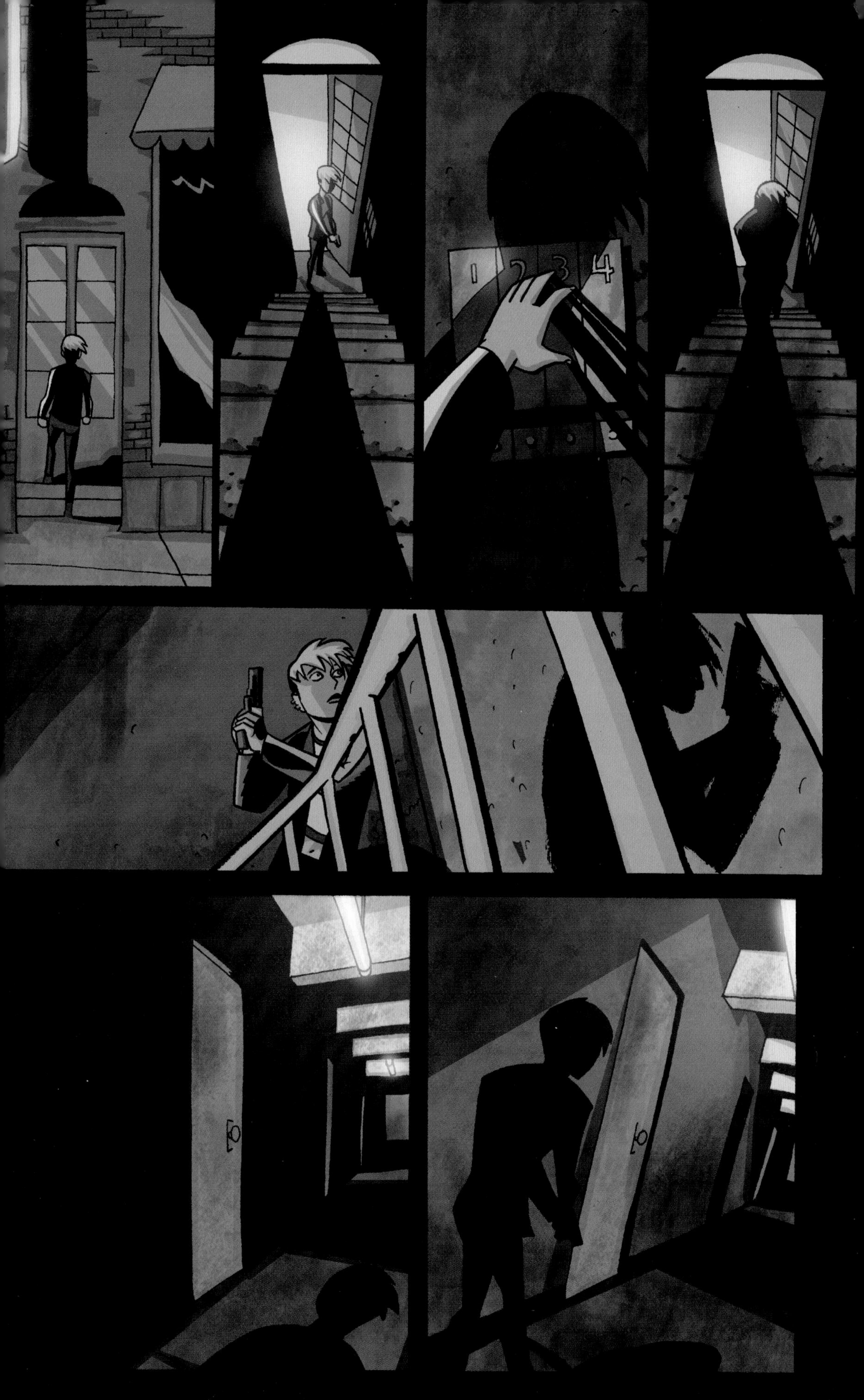
1 2 3 4

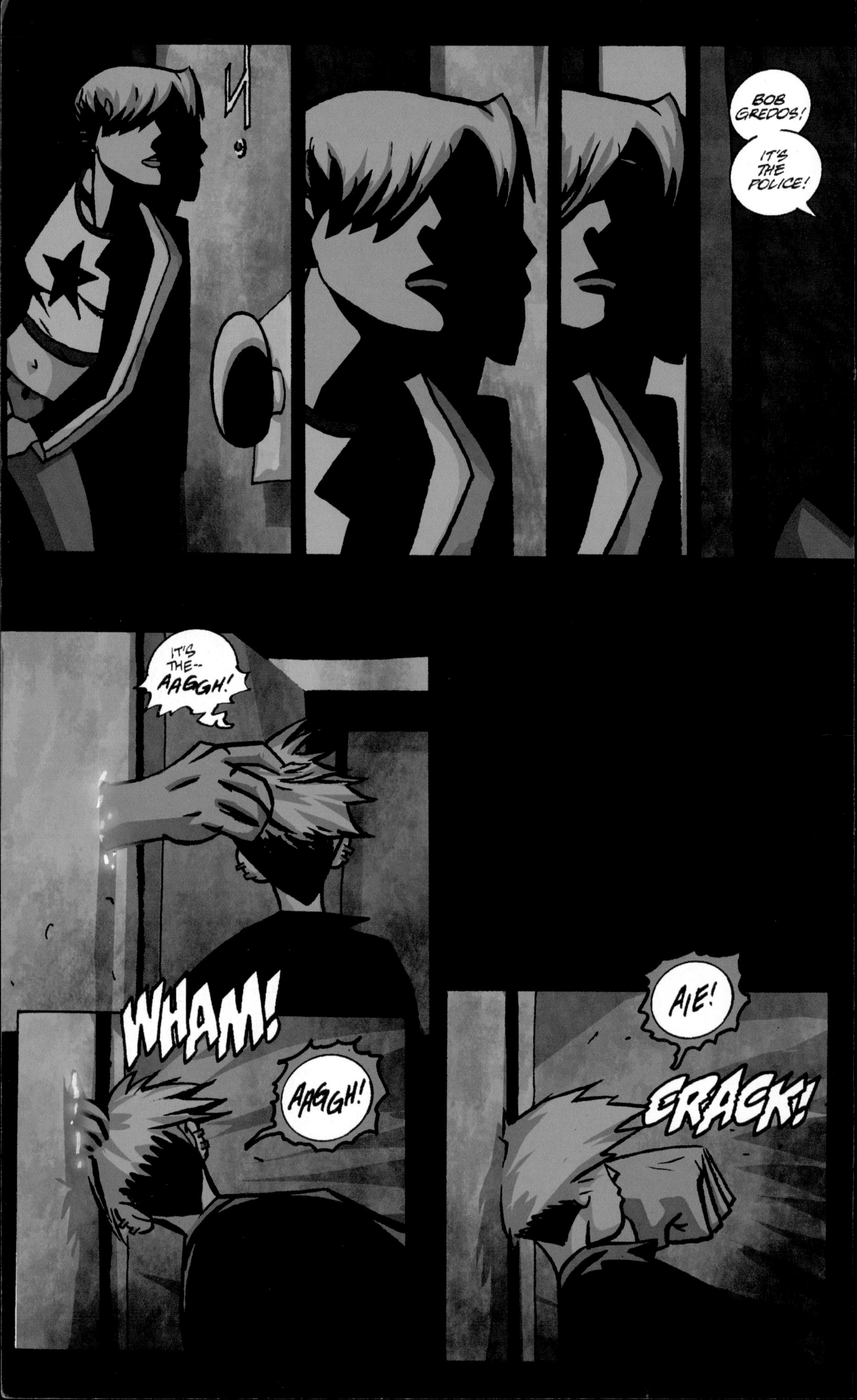
BOB GREDOS!
IT'S THE POLICE!
IT'S THE-- AAGGH!
WHAM!
AAGGH!
AIE!
CRACK!

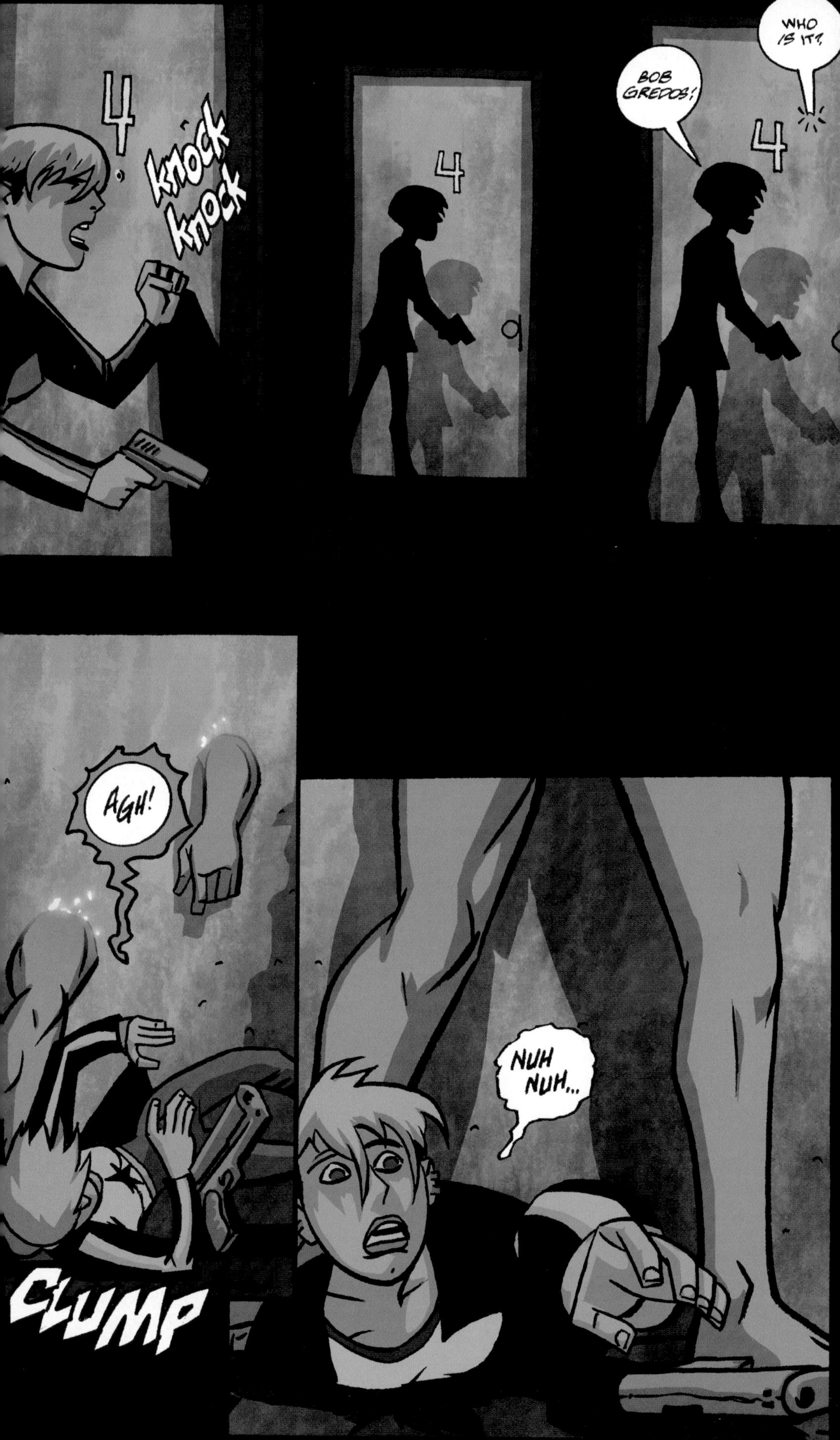
4
knock knock
4
BOB GREDOS!
WHO IS IT?
4
AGH!
CLUMP
NUH NUH...

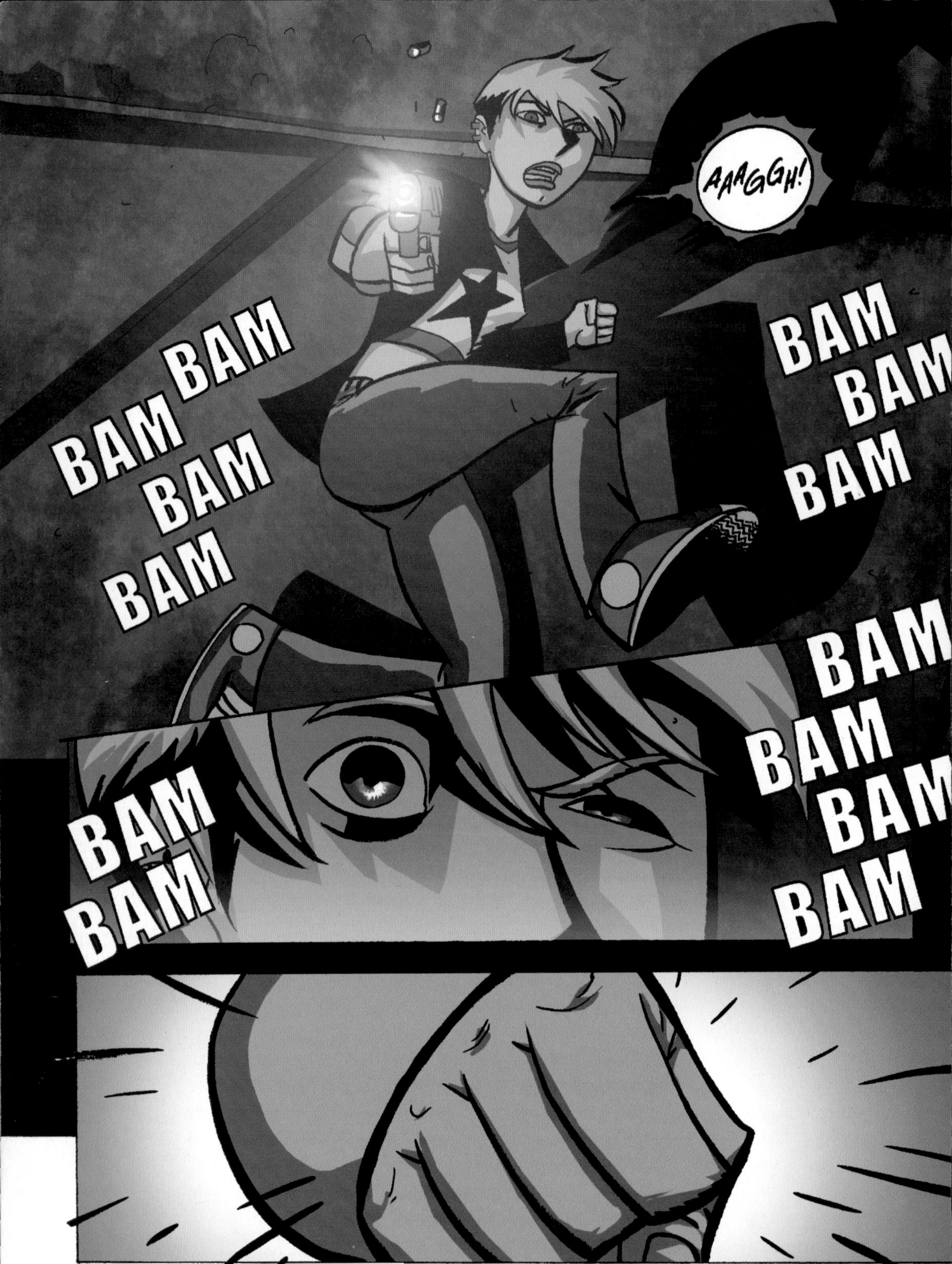
AAAGGH!
BAM BAM
BAM
BAM
BAM
BAM
BAM
BAM
BAM
BAM
BAM
BAM
BAM
BAM

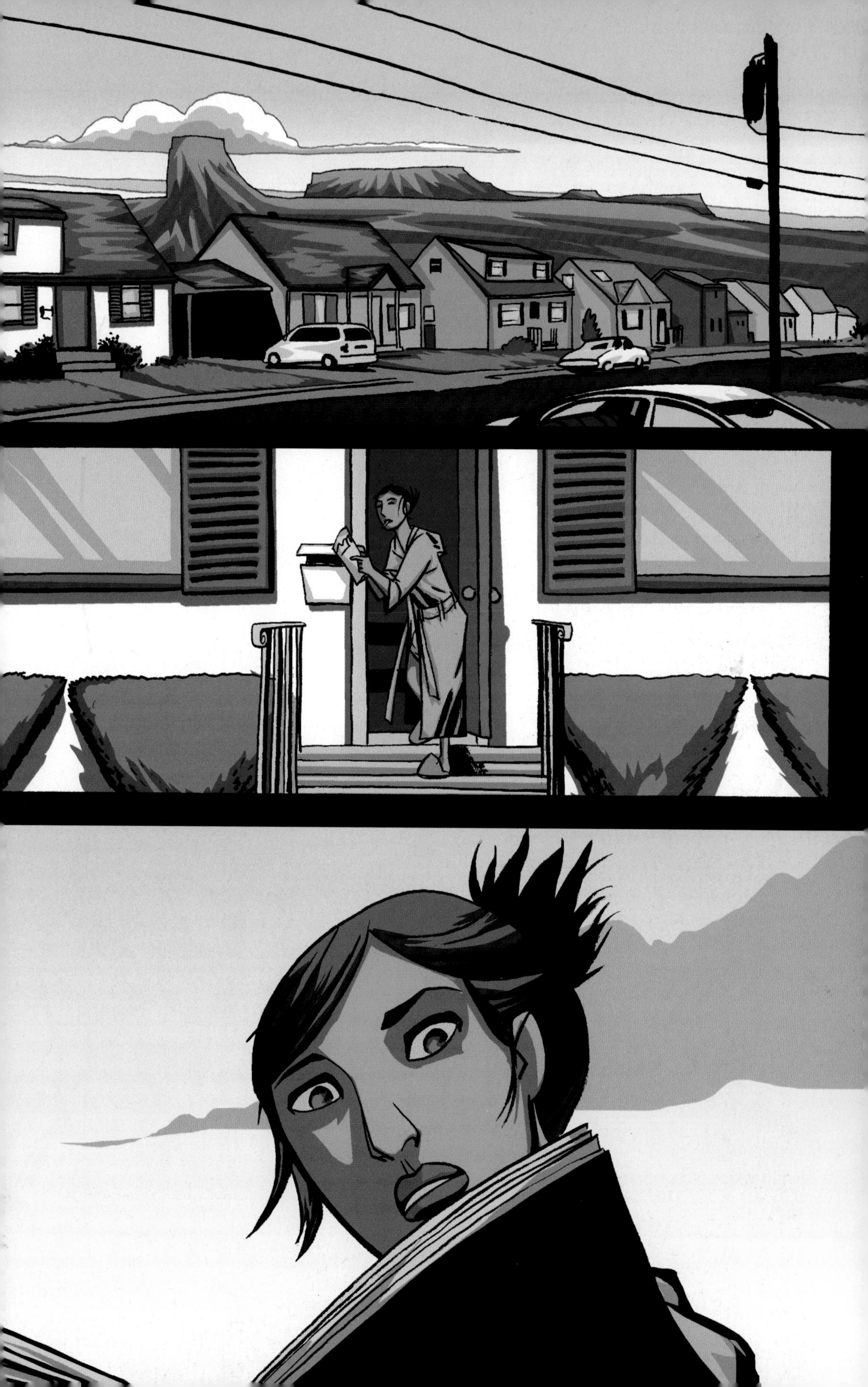

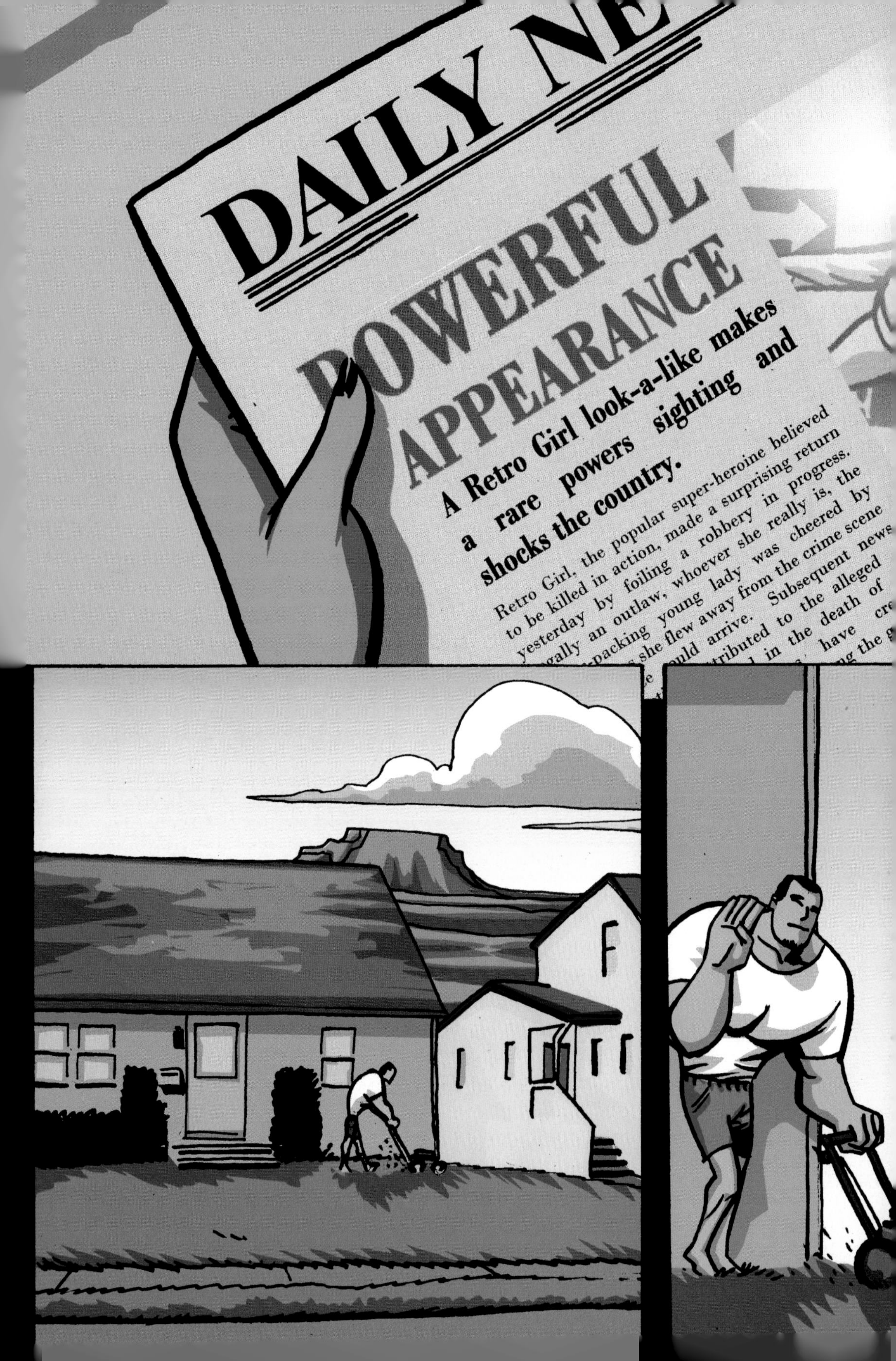
DAILY NE
POWERFUL APPEARANCE
A Retro Girl look-a-like makes a rare powers sighting and shocks the country.
Retro Girl, the popular super-heroine believed to be killed in action, made a surprising return yesterday by foiling a robbery in progress.
whoever she really is, the
young lady was cheered by
she flew away from the crime scene
arrive. Subsequent news
to the alleged
in the death of

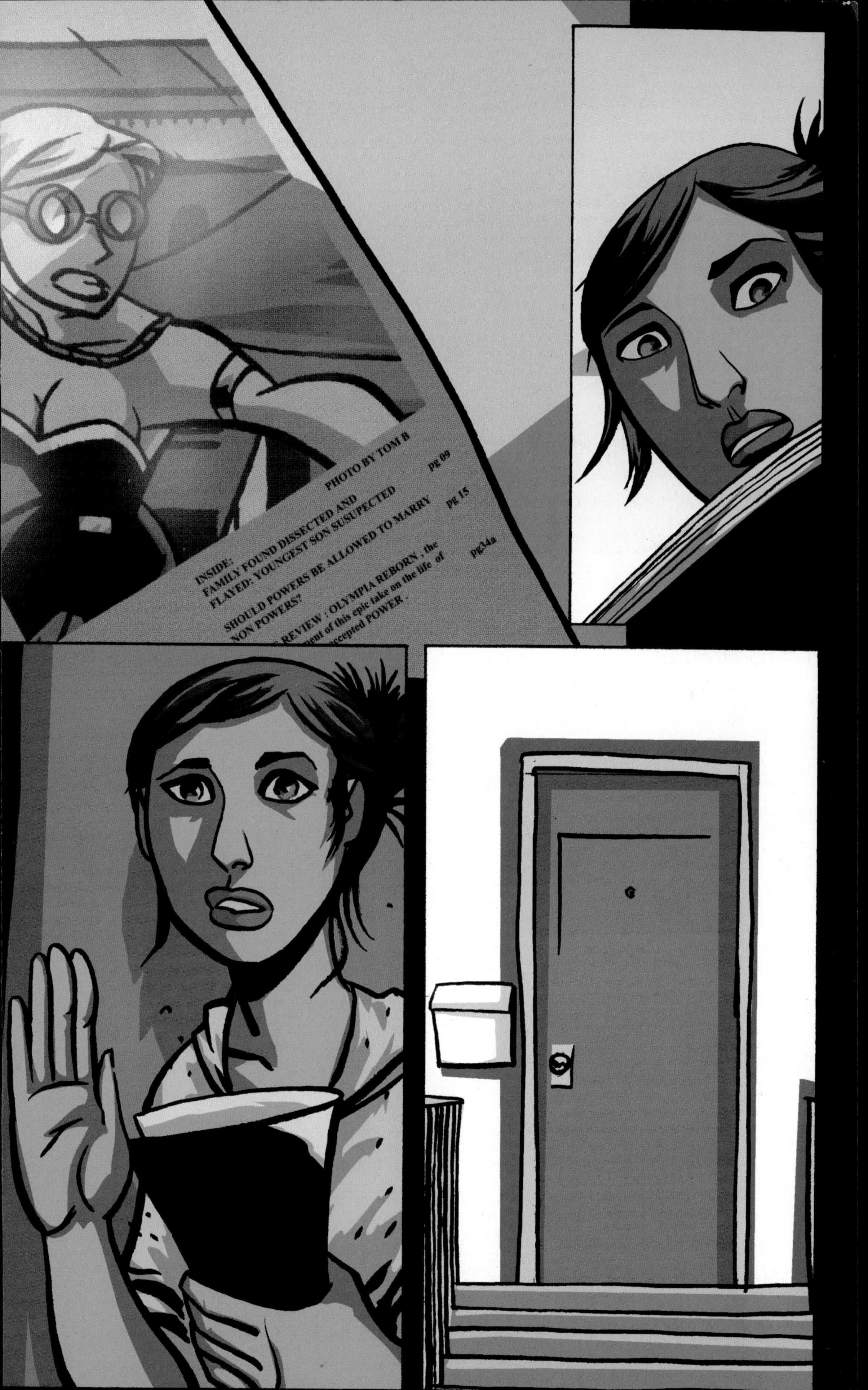
PHOTO BY TOM B
INSIDE:
FAMILY FOUND DISSECTED AND
FLAYED: YOUNGEST SON SUSUPECTED pg 09
SHOULD POWERS BE ALLOWED TO MARRY
NON POWERS? pg 15
REVIEW : OLYMPIA REBORN , the
of this epic take on the life of
POWER . Pg34a

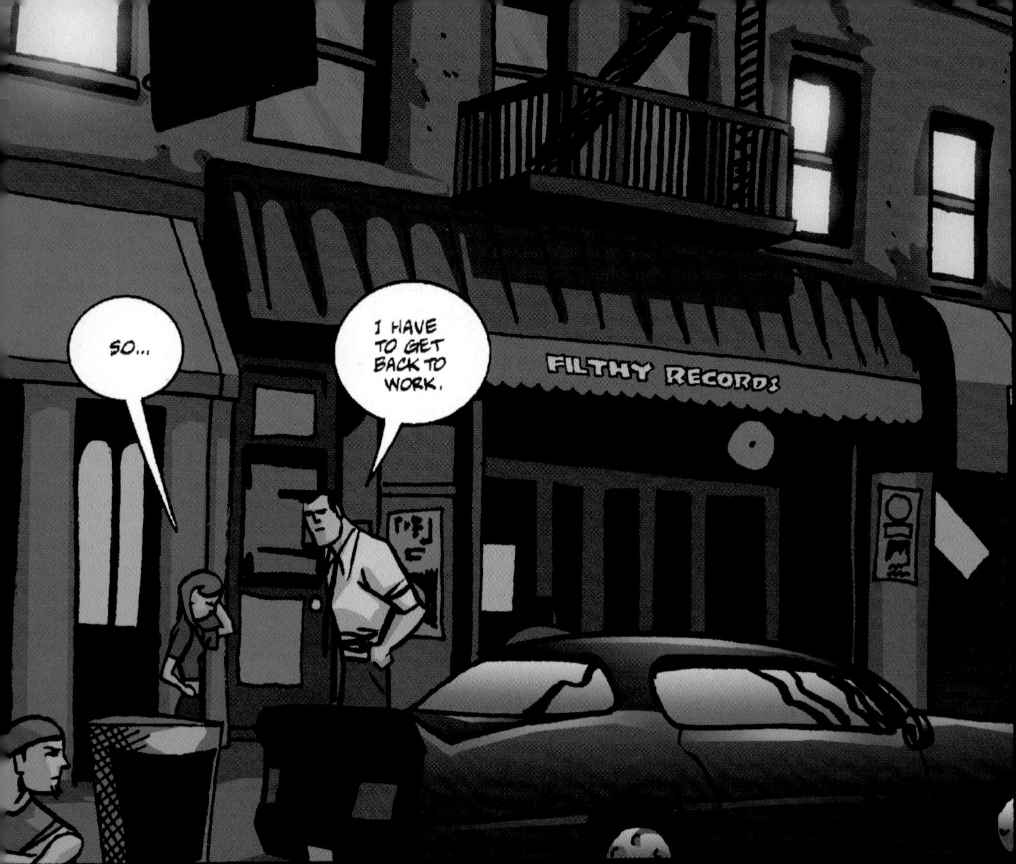
FILTHY RECORDS
SO...
I HAVE TO GET BACK TO WORK.

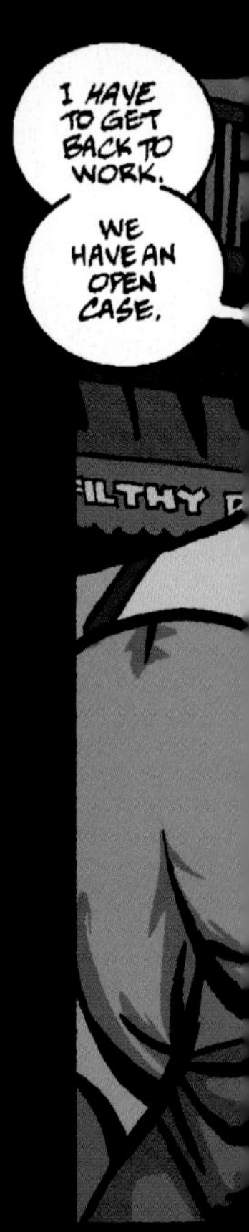
I HAVE TO GET BACK TO WORK.
WE HAVE AN OPEN CASE.

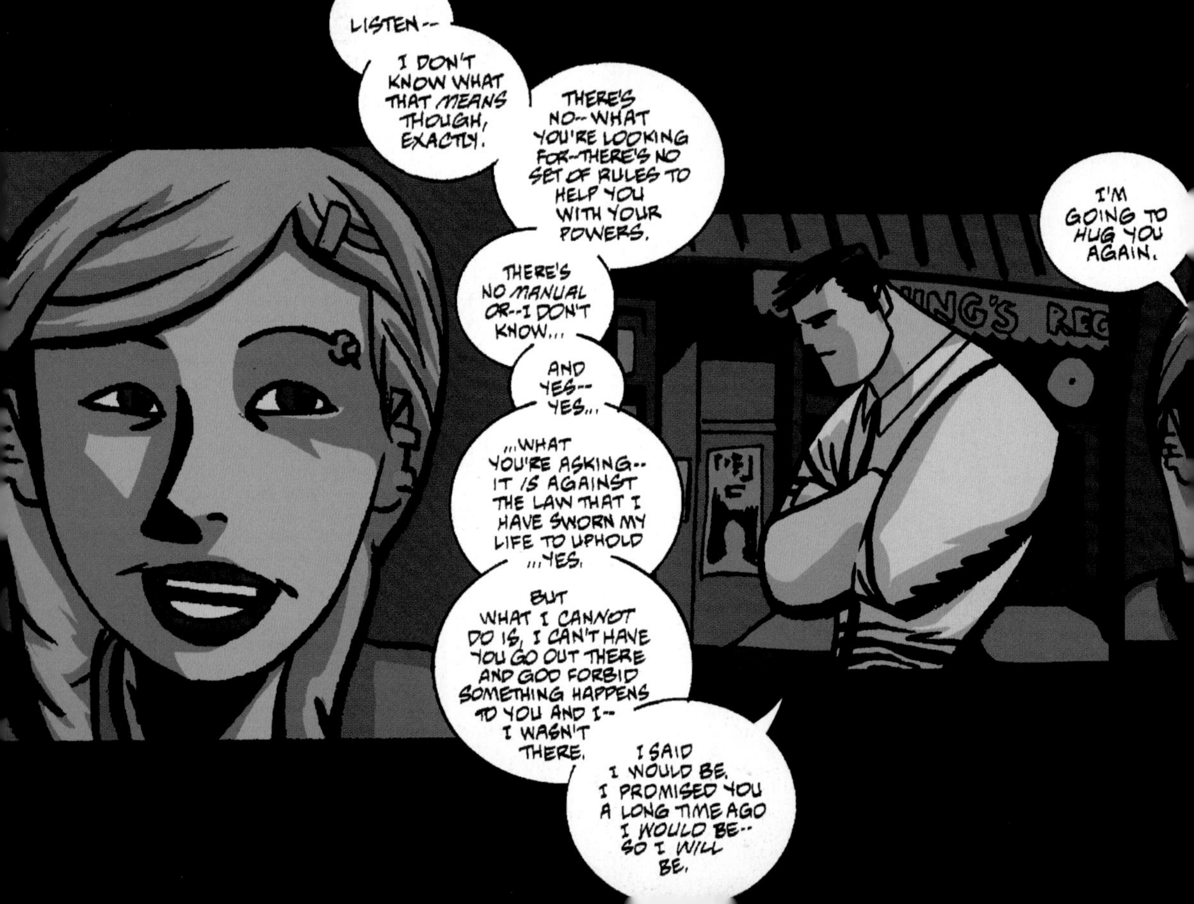
LISTEN--
I DON'T KNOW WHAT THAT MEANS THOUGH, EXACTLY.
THERE'S NO-- WHAT YOU'RE LOOKING FOR--THERE'S NO SET OF RULES TO HELP YOU WITH YOUR POWERS.
THERE'S NO MANUAL OR--I DON'T KNOW...
AND YES-- YES...
...WHAT YOU'RE ASKING-- IT IS AGAINST THE LAW THAT I HAVE SWORN MY LIFE TO UPHOLD ...YES.
BUT WHAT I CANNOT DO IS, I CAN'T HAVE YOU GO OUT THERE AND GOD FORBID SOMETHING HAPPENS TO YOU AND I-- I WASN'T THERE.
I SAID I WOULD BE. I PROMISED YOU A LONG TIME AGO I WOULD BE-- SO I WILL BE.
I'M GOING TO HUG YOU AGAIN.

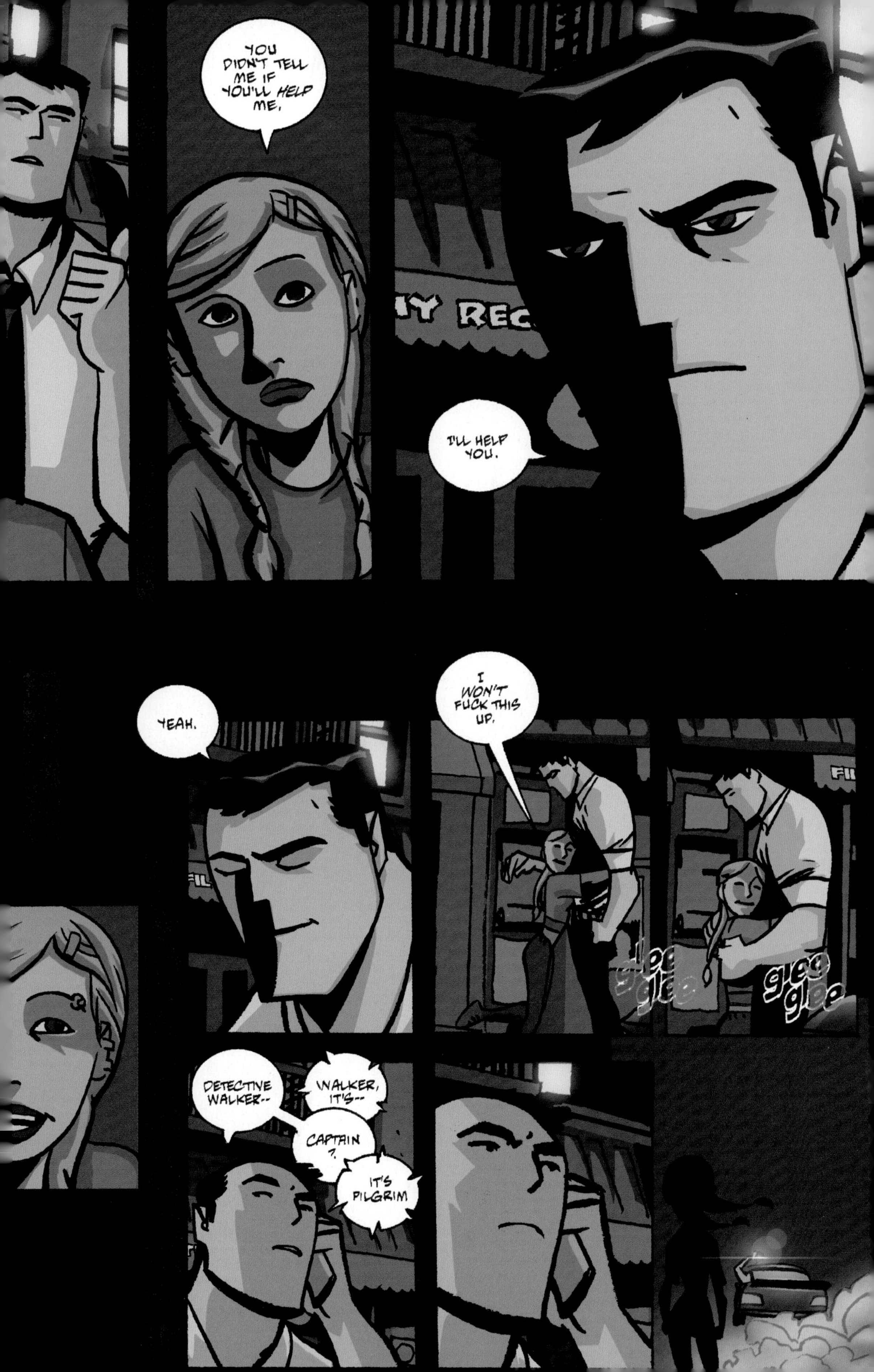
YOU DIDN'T TELL ME IF YOU'LL HELP ME.
I'LL HELP YOU.
YEAH.
I WON'T FUCK THIS UP.
DETECTIVE WALKER--
WALKER, IT'S--
CAPTAIN?
IT'S PILGRIM

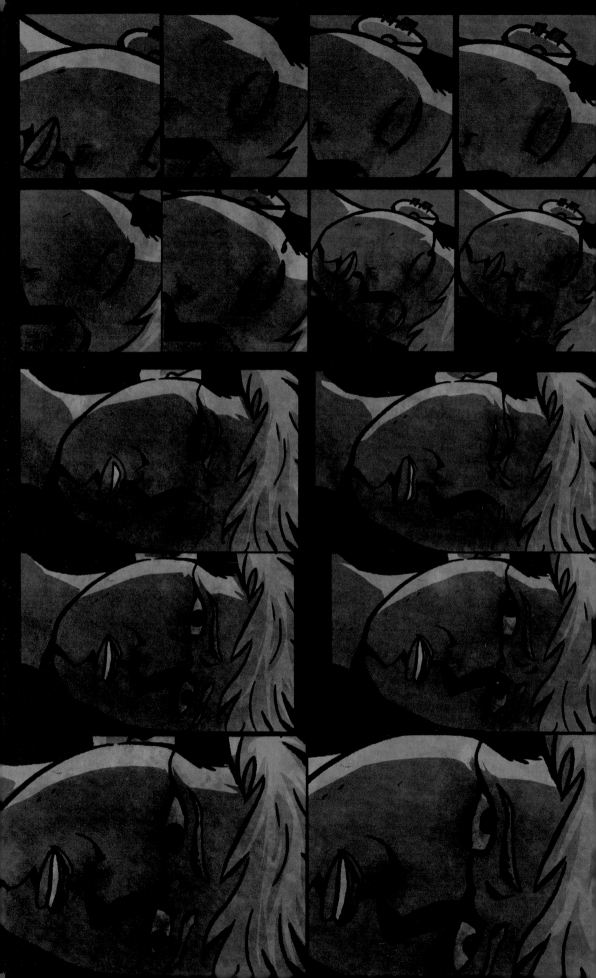

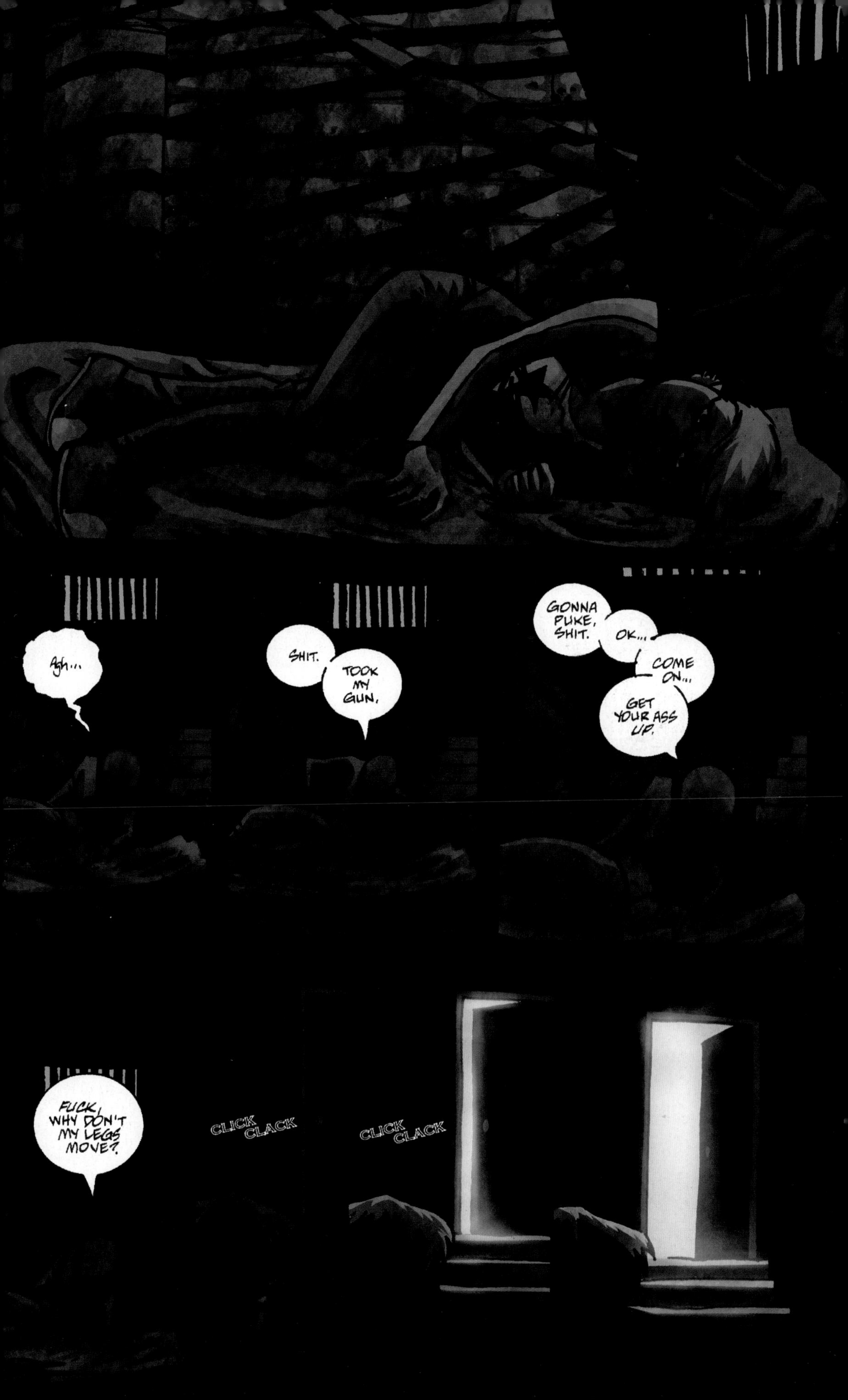
Agh...
SHIT.
TOOK MY GUN.
GONNA PUKE, SHIT.
OK...
COME ON...
GET YOUR ASS UP.
FUCK, WHY DON'T MY LEGS MOVE?
CLICK CLACK
CLICK CLACK

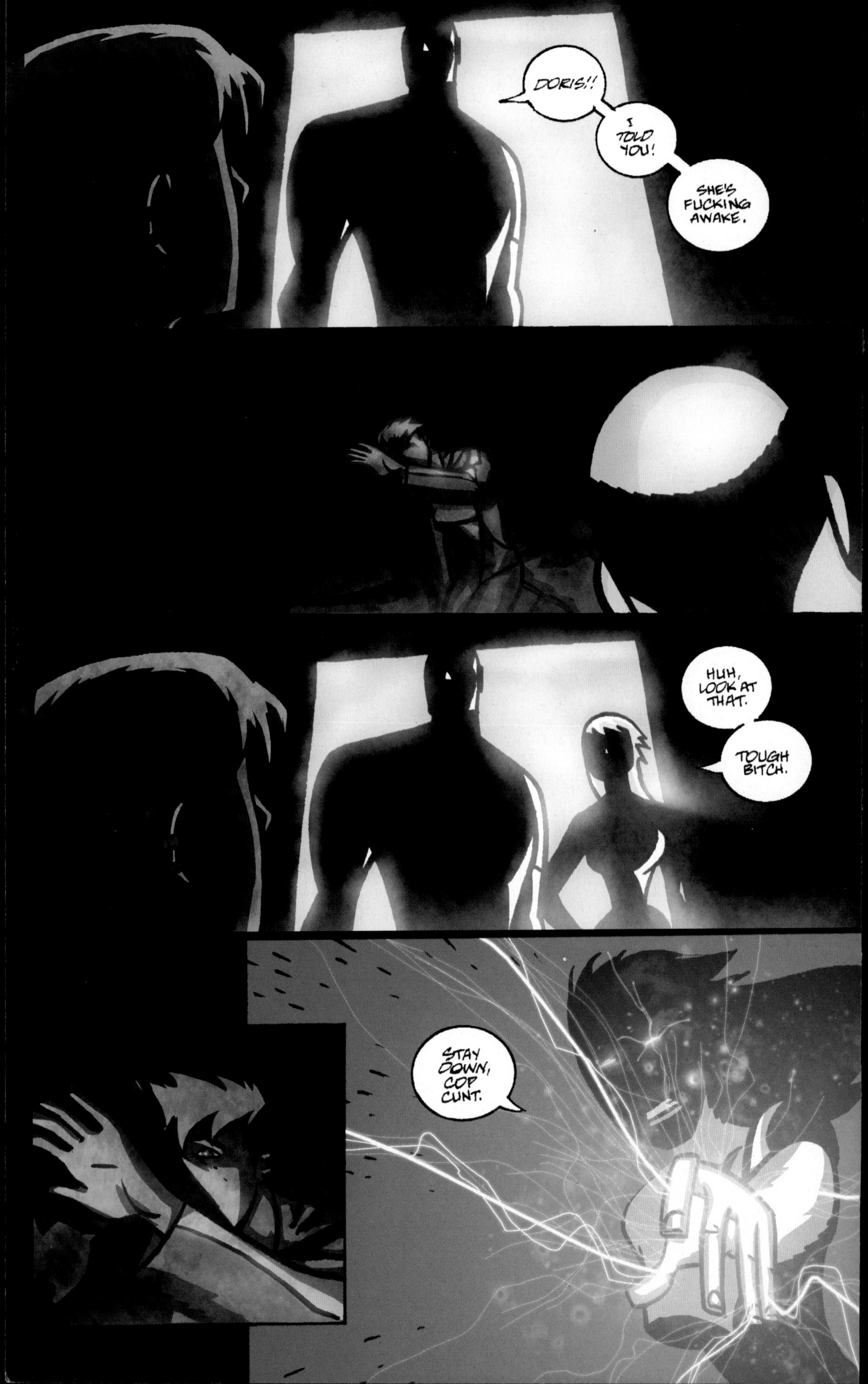
DORIS!!
I TOLD YOU!
SHE'S FUCKING AWAKE.
HUH, LOOK AT THAT.
TOUGH BITCH.
STAY DOWN, COP CUNT.

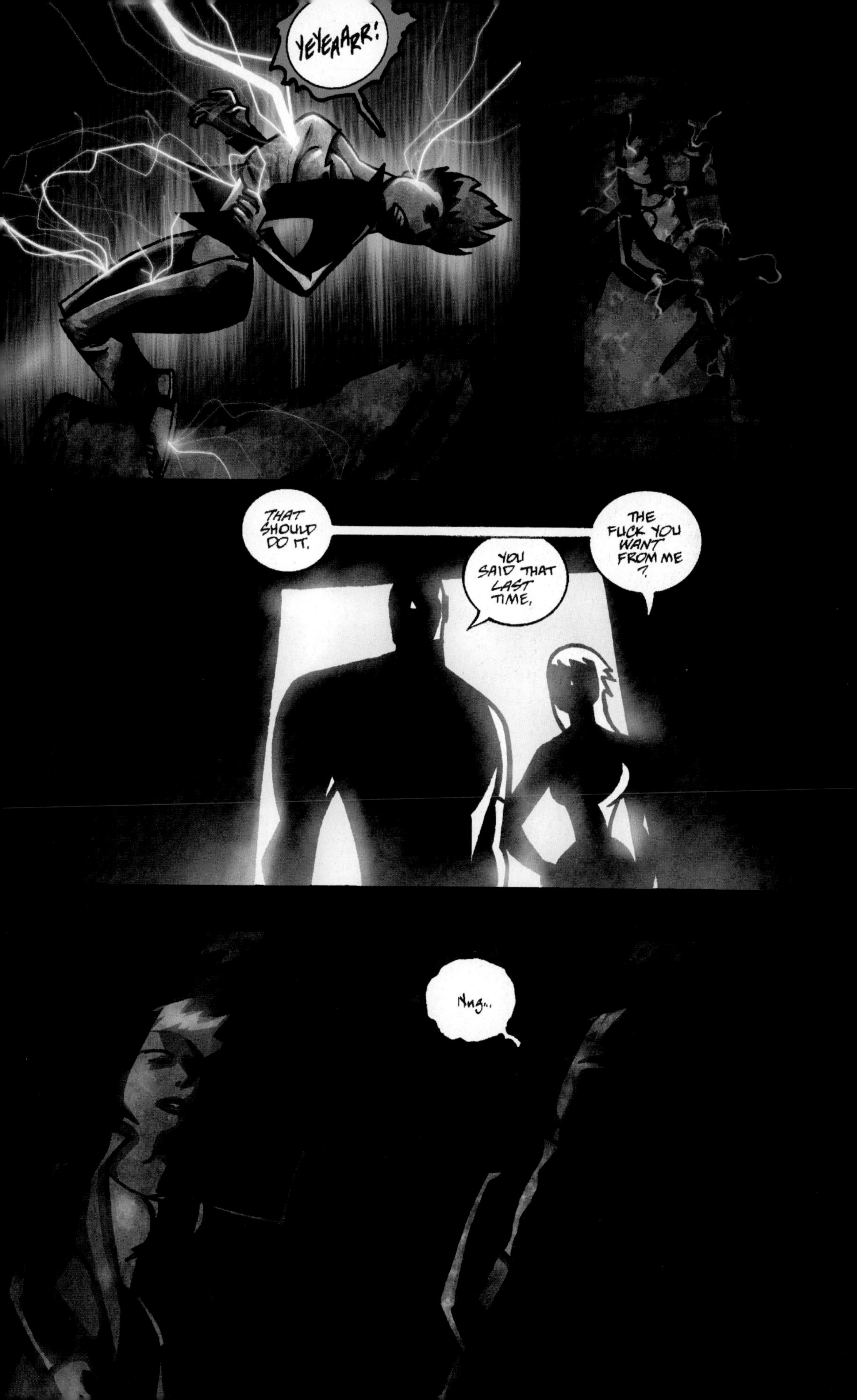
YEYEAARR!
THAT SHOULD DO IT.
THE FUCK YOU WANT FROM ME?
YOU SAID THAT LAST TIME.
Nng...

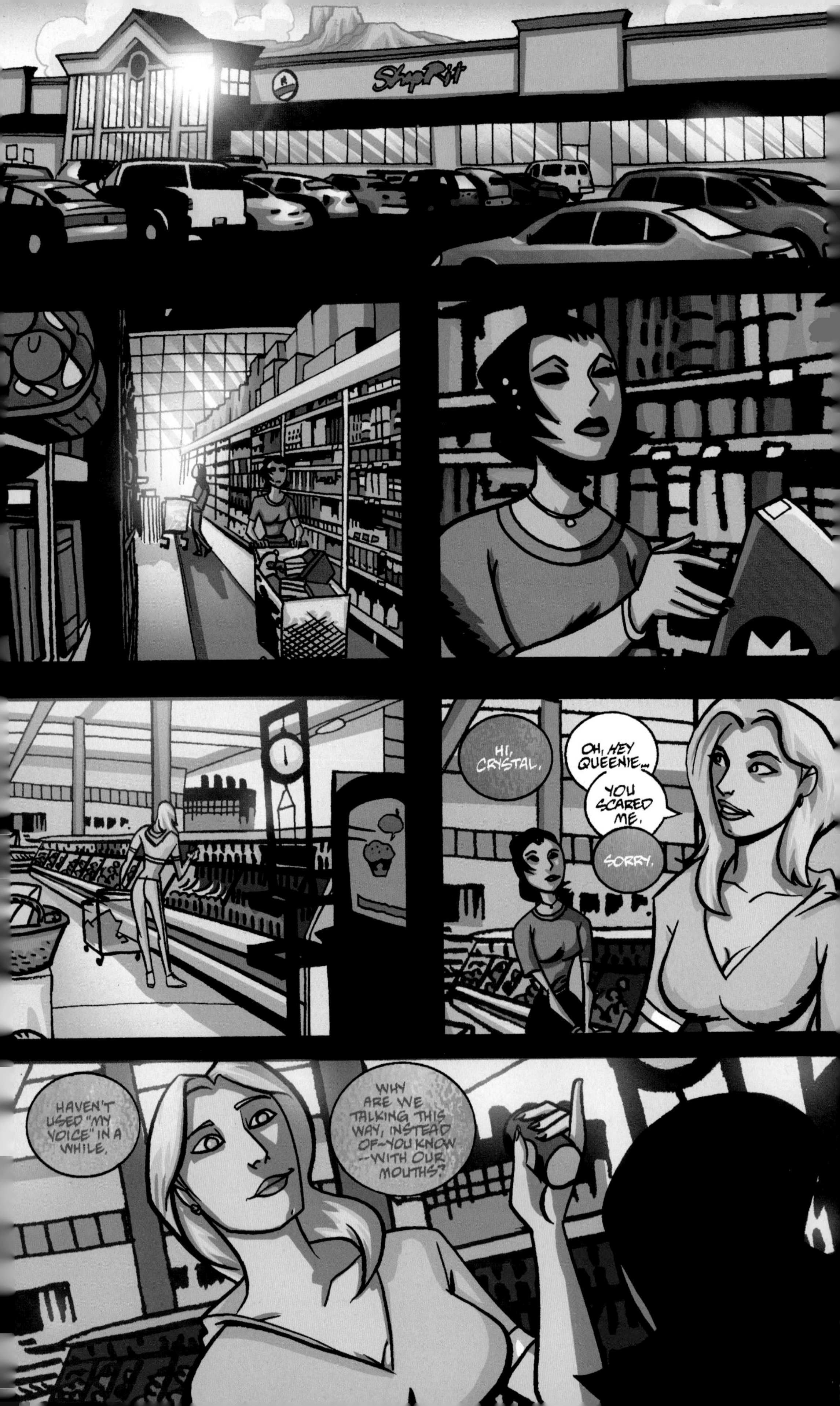
ShopRite
HI, CRYSTAL.
OH, HEY QUEENIE...
YOU SCARED ME.
SORRY.
HAVEN'T USED "MY VOICE" IN A WHILE.
WHY ARE WE TALKING THIS WAY, INSTEAD OF--YOU KNOW --WITH OUR MOUTHS?

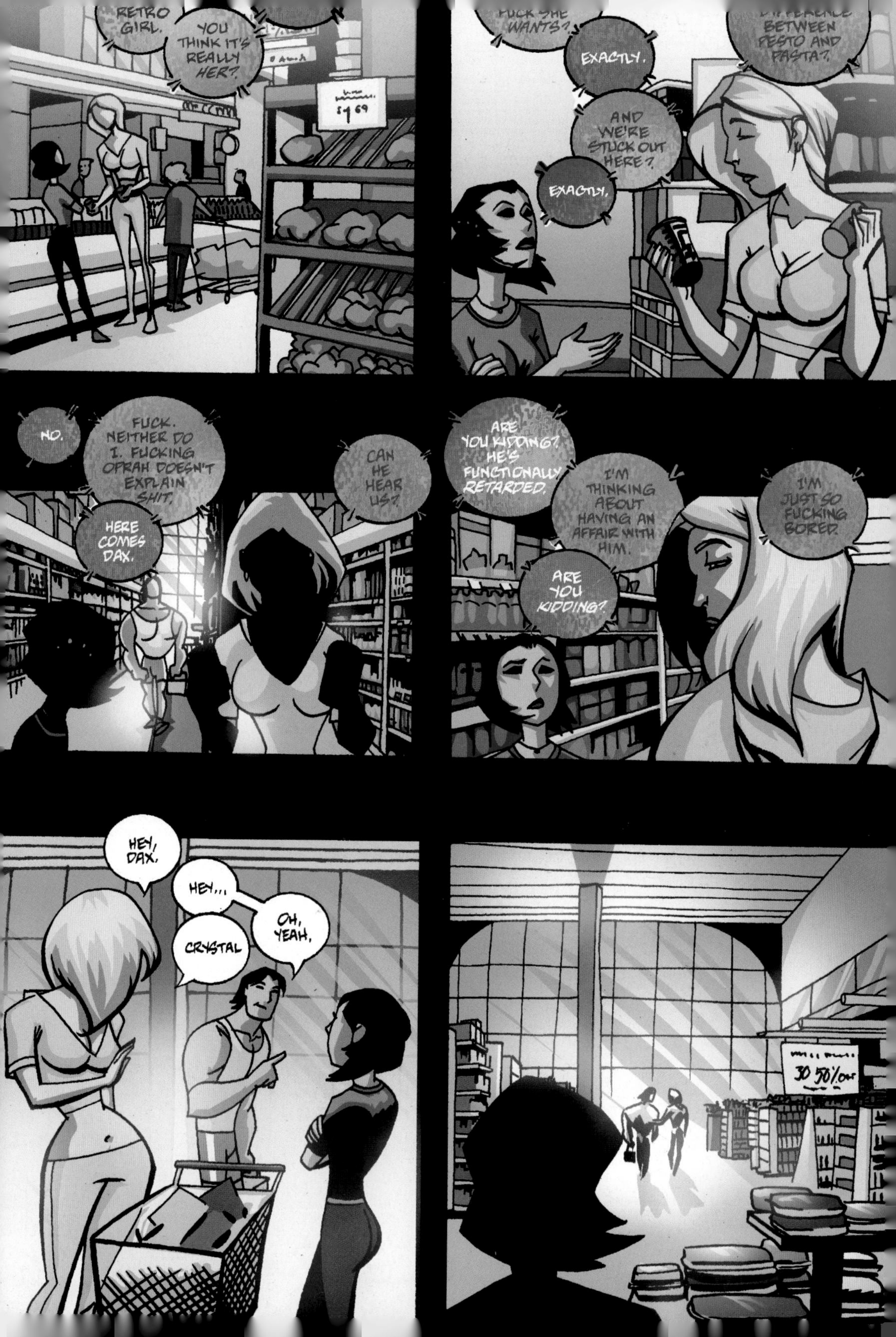
RETRO GIRL.
YOU THINK IT'S REALLY HER?
FUCK SHE WANTS?
EXACTLY.
BETWEEN PESTO AND PASTA?
AND WE'RE STUCK OUT HERE?
EXACTLY.
NO.
FUCK. NEITHER DO I. FUCKING OPRAH DOESN'T EXPLAIN SHIT.
HERE COMES DAX.
CAN HE HEAR US?
ARE YOU KIDDING? HE'S FUNCTIONALLY RETARDED.
I'M THINKING ABOUT HAVING AN AFFAIR WITH HIM.
ARE YOU KIDDING?
I'M JUST SO FUCKING BORED.
HEY, DAX.
HEY...
CRYSTAL
OH, YEAH.

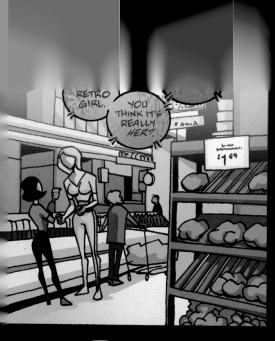

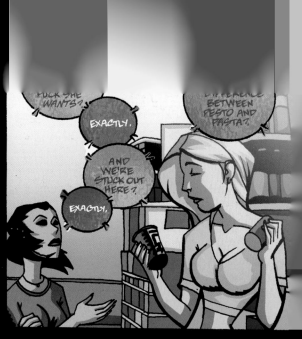

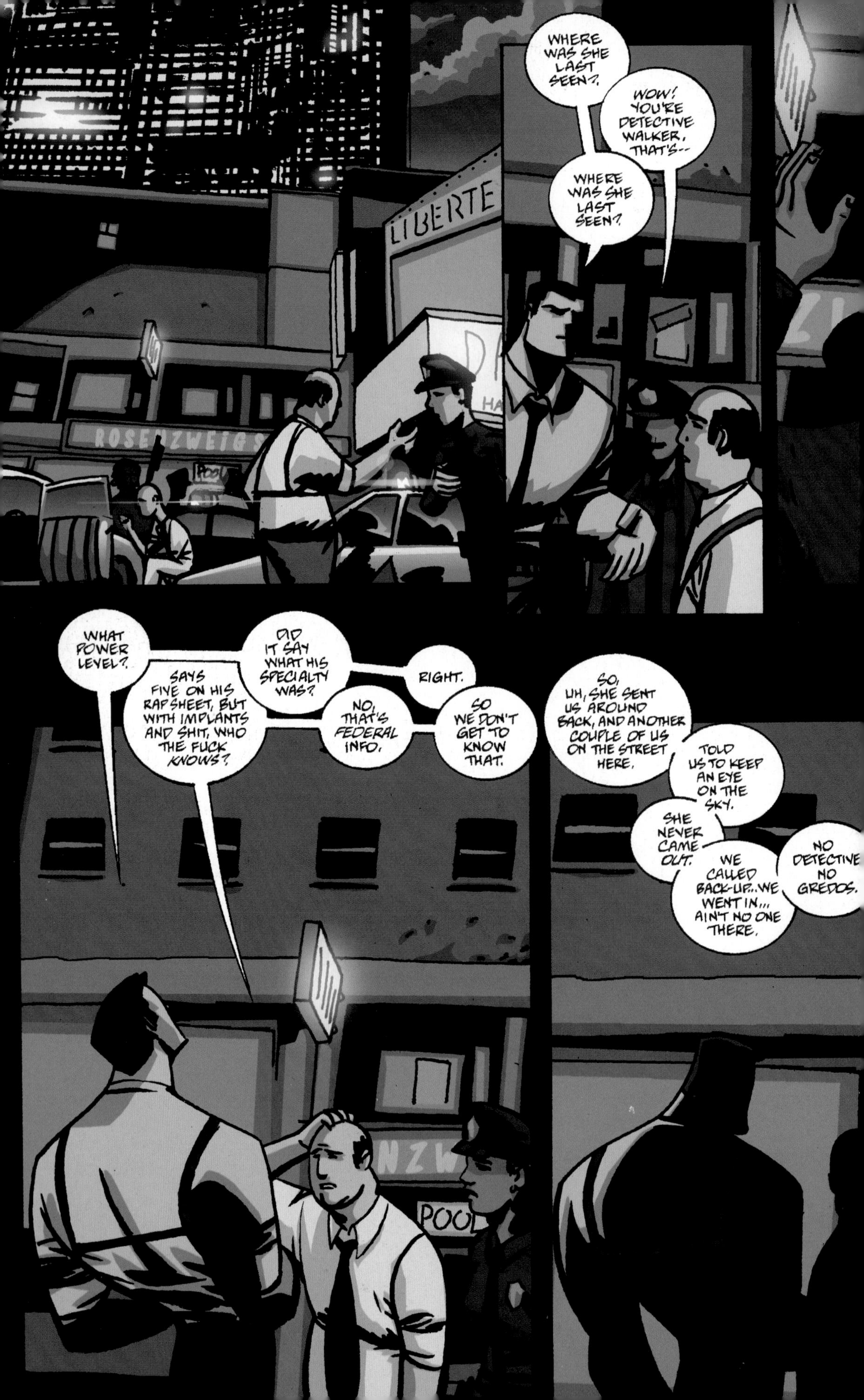
LIBERTE
ROSENZWEIGS
WHERE WAS SHE LAST SEEN?
WOW! YOU'RE DETECTIVE WALKER. THAT'S--
WHERE WAS SHE LAST SEEN?
WHAT POWER LEVEL?
SAYS FIVE ON HIS RAP SHEET, BUT WITH IMPLANTS AND SHIT, WHO THE FUCK KNOWS?
DID IT SAY WHAT HIS SPECIALTY WAS?
NO, THAT'S FEDERAL INFO.
RIGHT.
SO WE DON'T GET TO KNOW THAT.
SO, UH, SHE SENT US AROUND BACK, AND ANOTHER COUPLE OF US ON THE STREET HERE.
TOLD US TO KEEP AN EYE ON THE SKY.
SHE NEVER CAME OUT.
WE CALLED BACK-UP...WE WENT IN... AIN'T NO ONE THERE.
NO DETECTIVE NO GREDOS.

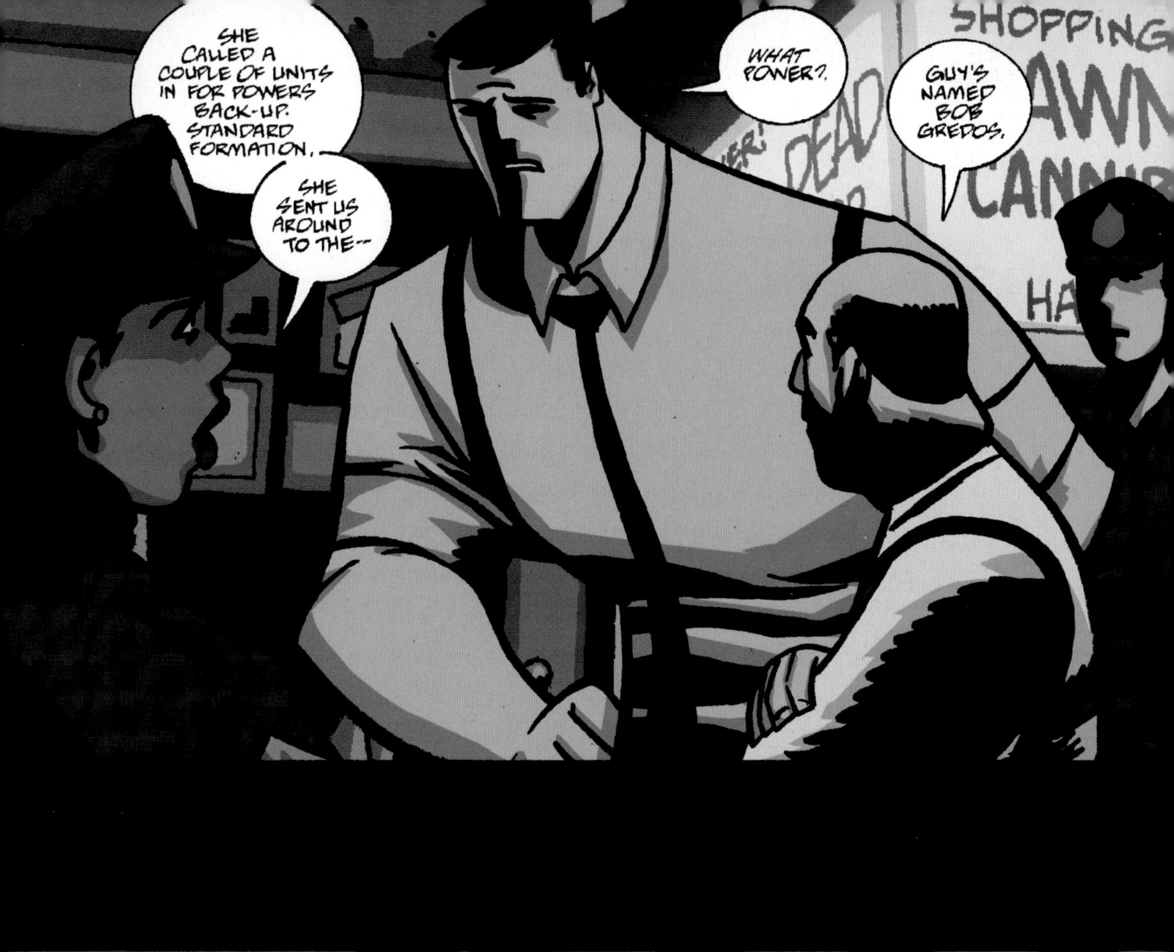
SHE CALLED A COUPLE OF UNITS IN FOR POWERS BACK-UP. STANDARD FORMATION.
SHE SENT US AROUND TO THE--
WHAT POWER?
GUY'S NAMED BOB GREDOS.
SHOPPING
DEAD
CANN
HA

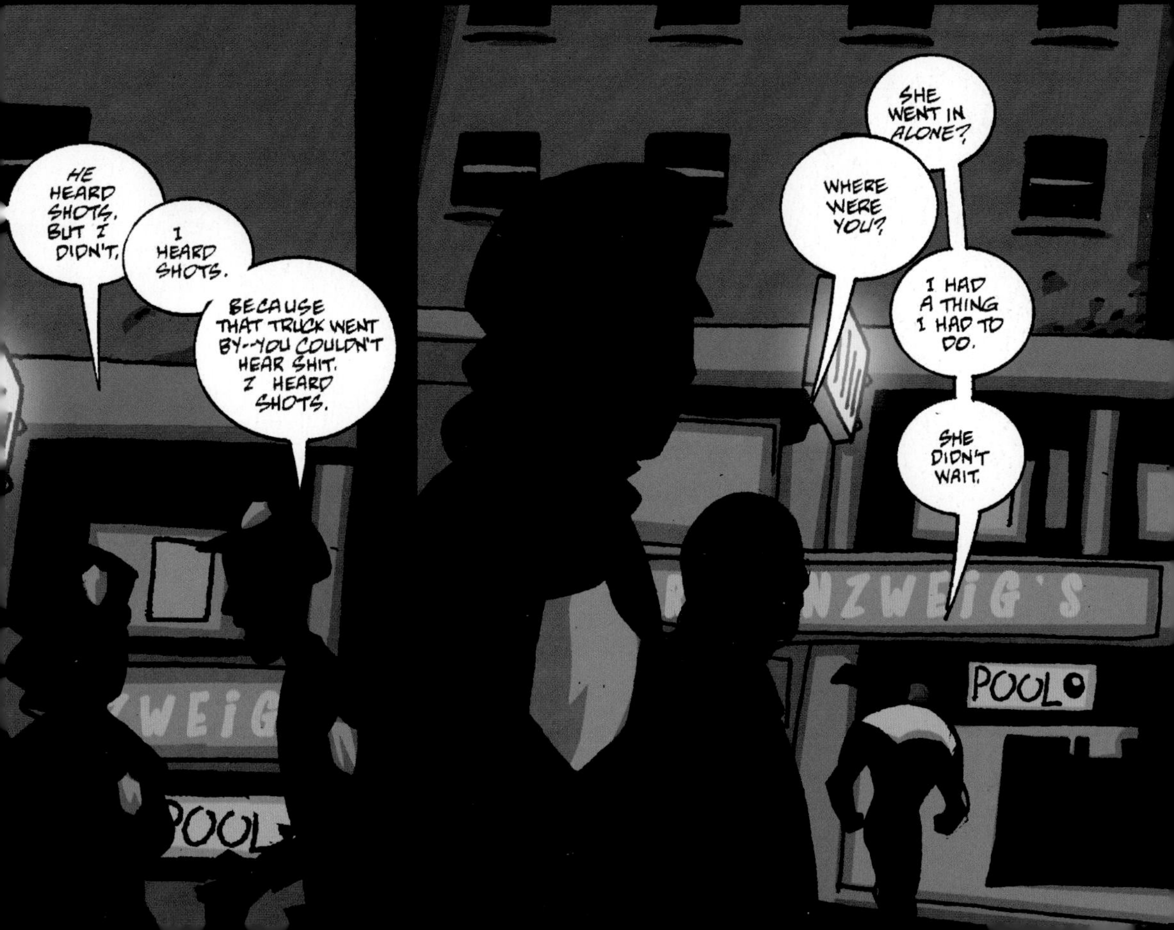
HE HEARD SHOTS, BUT I DIDN'T.
I HEARD SHOTS.
BECAUSE THAT TRUCK WENT BY--YOU COULDN'T HEAR SHIT. I HEARD SHOTS.
SHE WENT IN ALONE?
WHERE WERE YOU?
I HAD A THING I HAD TO DO.
SHE DIDN'T WAIT.
NZWEIG'S
POOL
WEIG
POOL

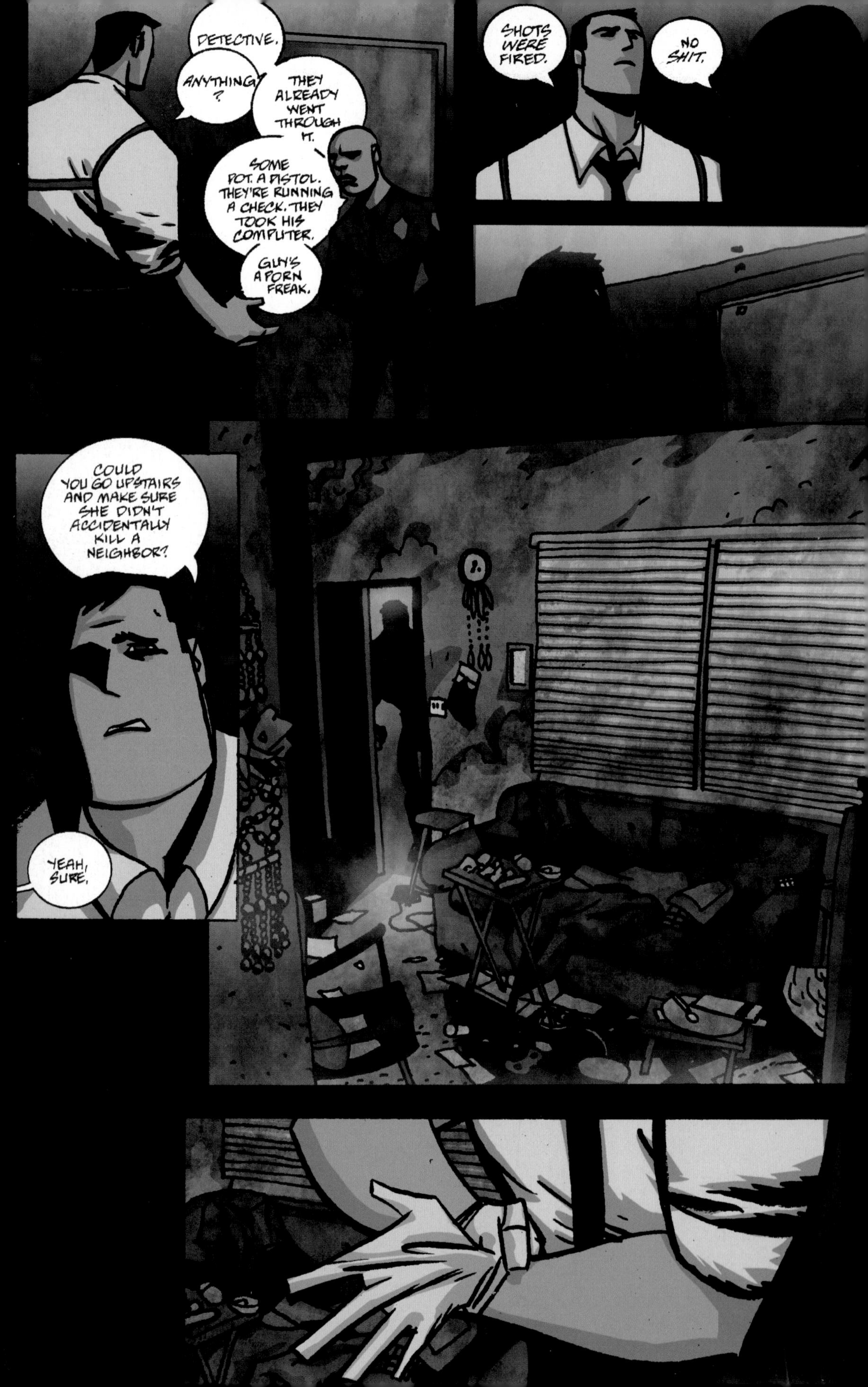
DETECTIVE.
ANYTHING?
THEY ALREADY WENT THROUGH IT.
SOME POT. A PISTOL. THEY'RE RUNNING A CHECK. THEY TOOK HIS COMPUTER.
GUY'S A PORN FREAK.
SHOTS WERE FIRED.
NO SHIT.
COULD YOU GO UPSTAIRS AND MAKE SURE SHE DIDN'T ACCIDENTALLY KILL A NEIGHBOR?
YEAH, SURE.

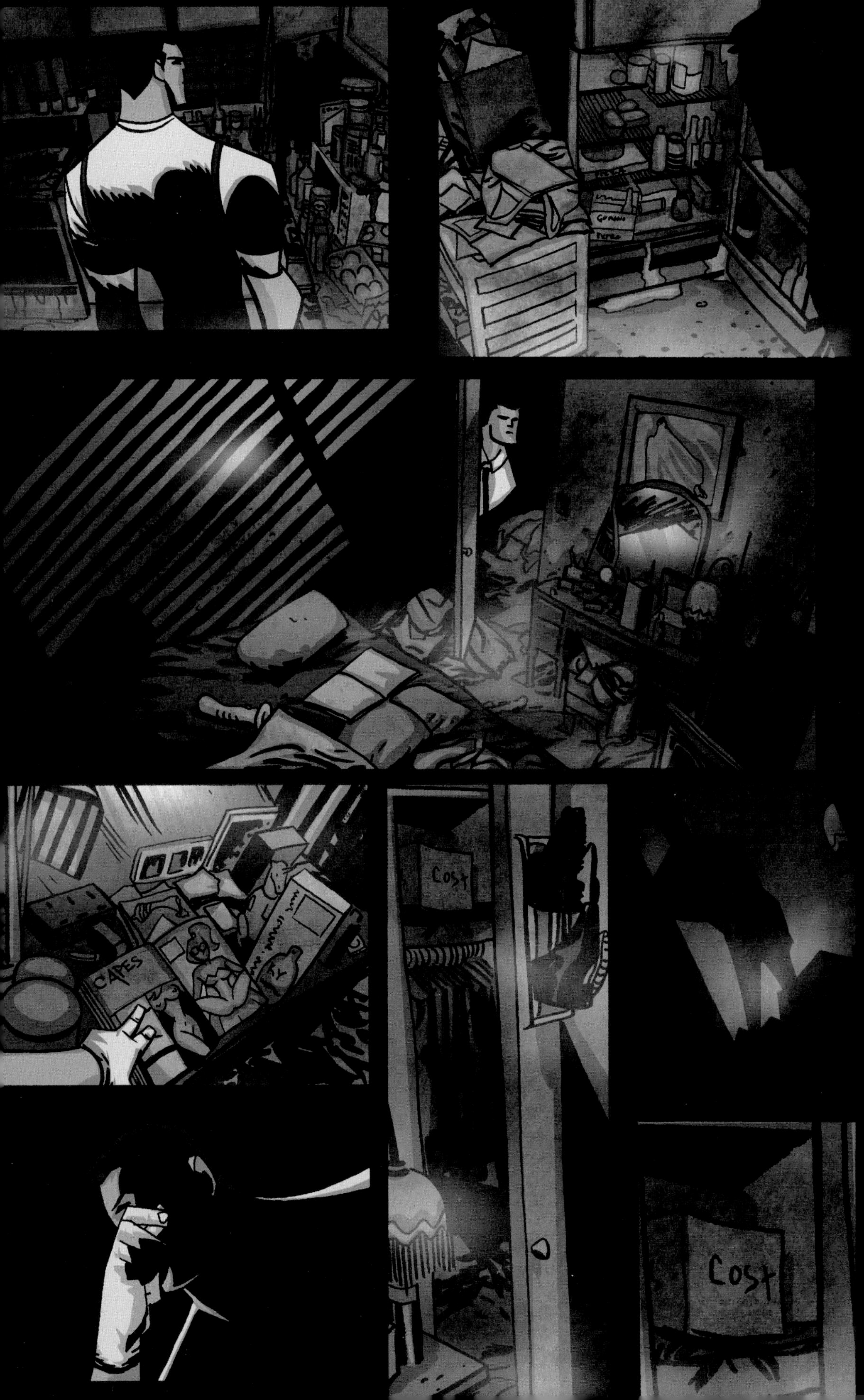
CAPES
Cost
Cost

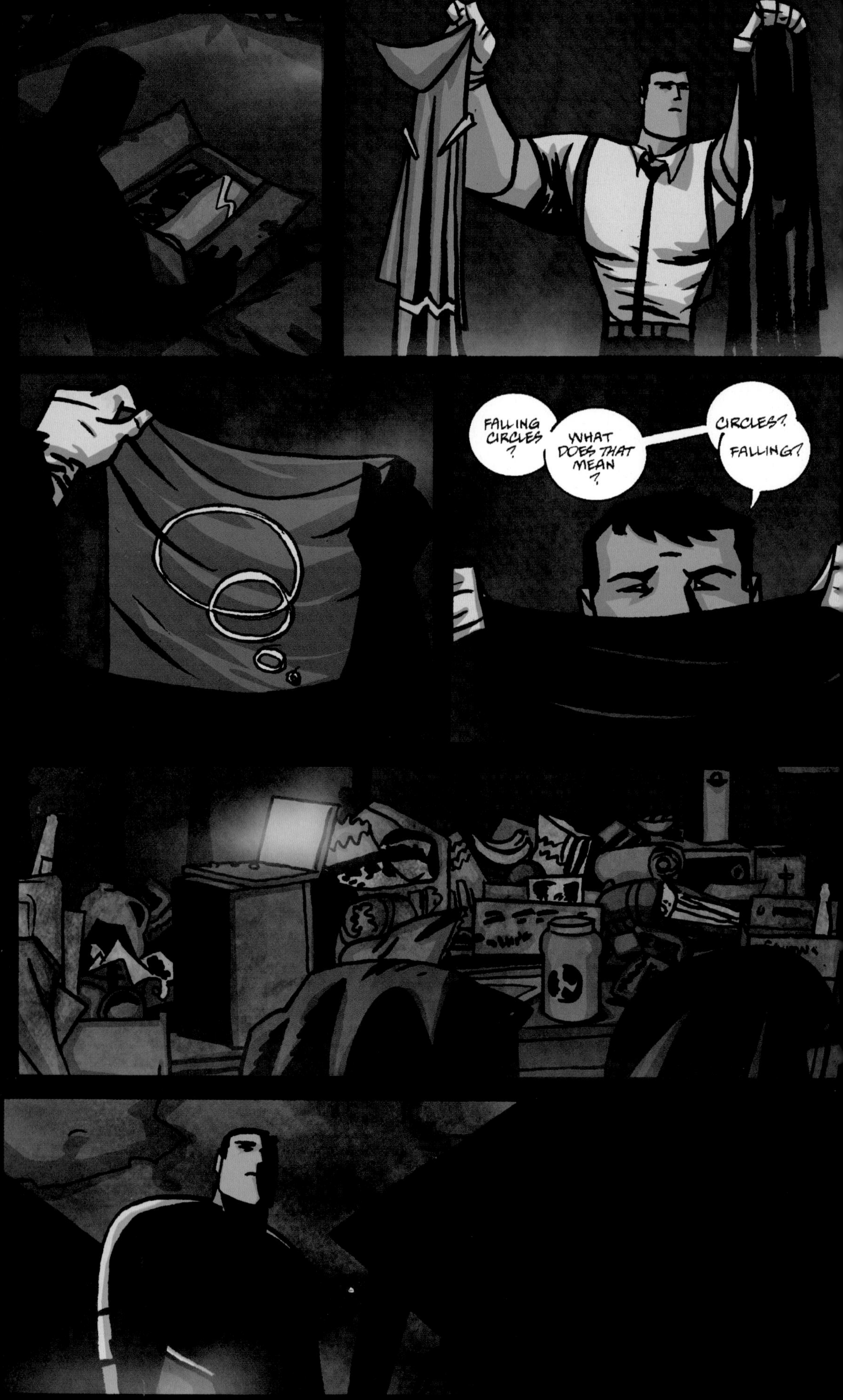
FALLING CIRCLES ?
WHAT DOES THAT MEAN ?
CIRCLES?
FALLING?

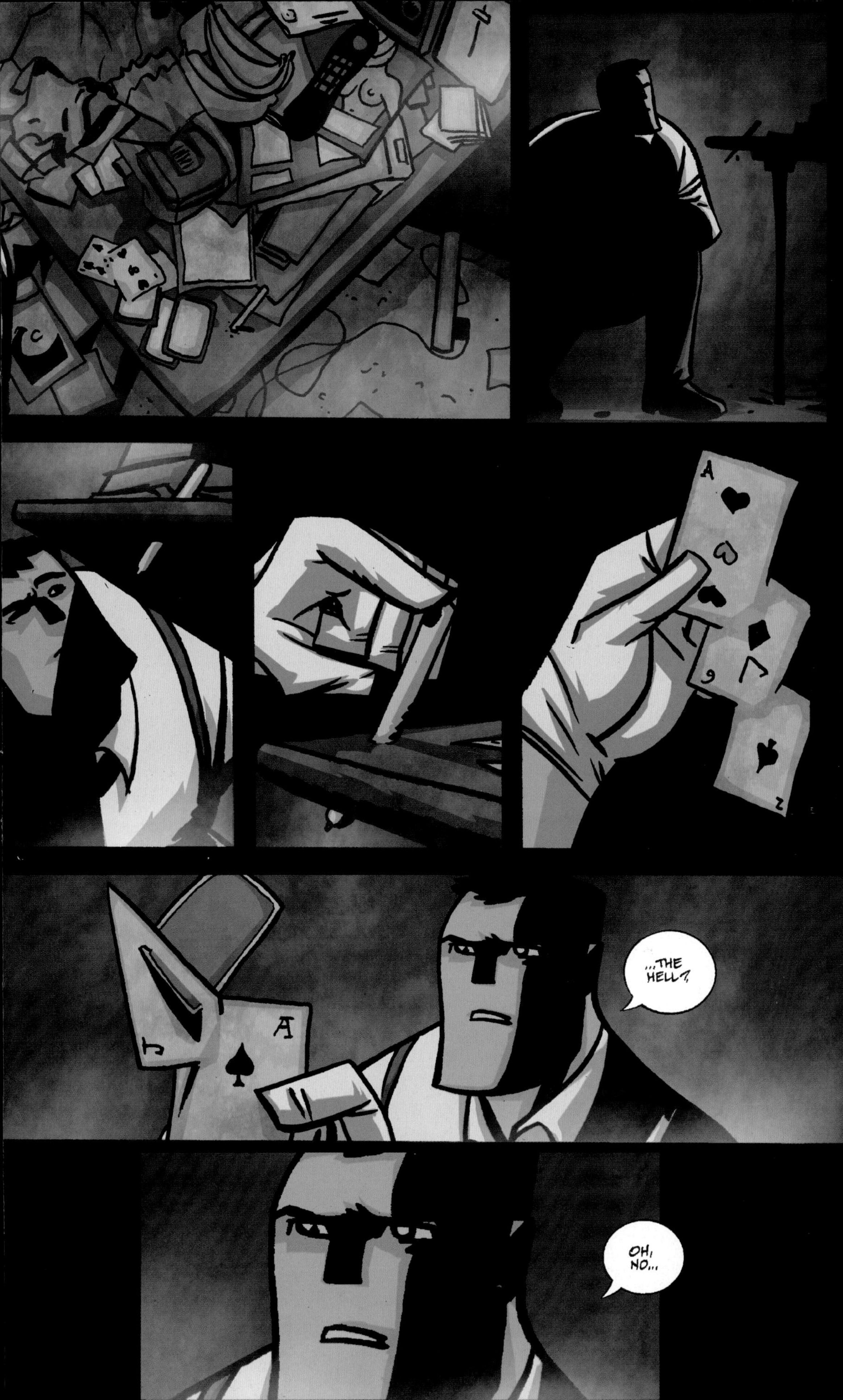
...THE HELL?
OH, NO...

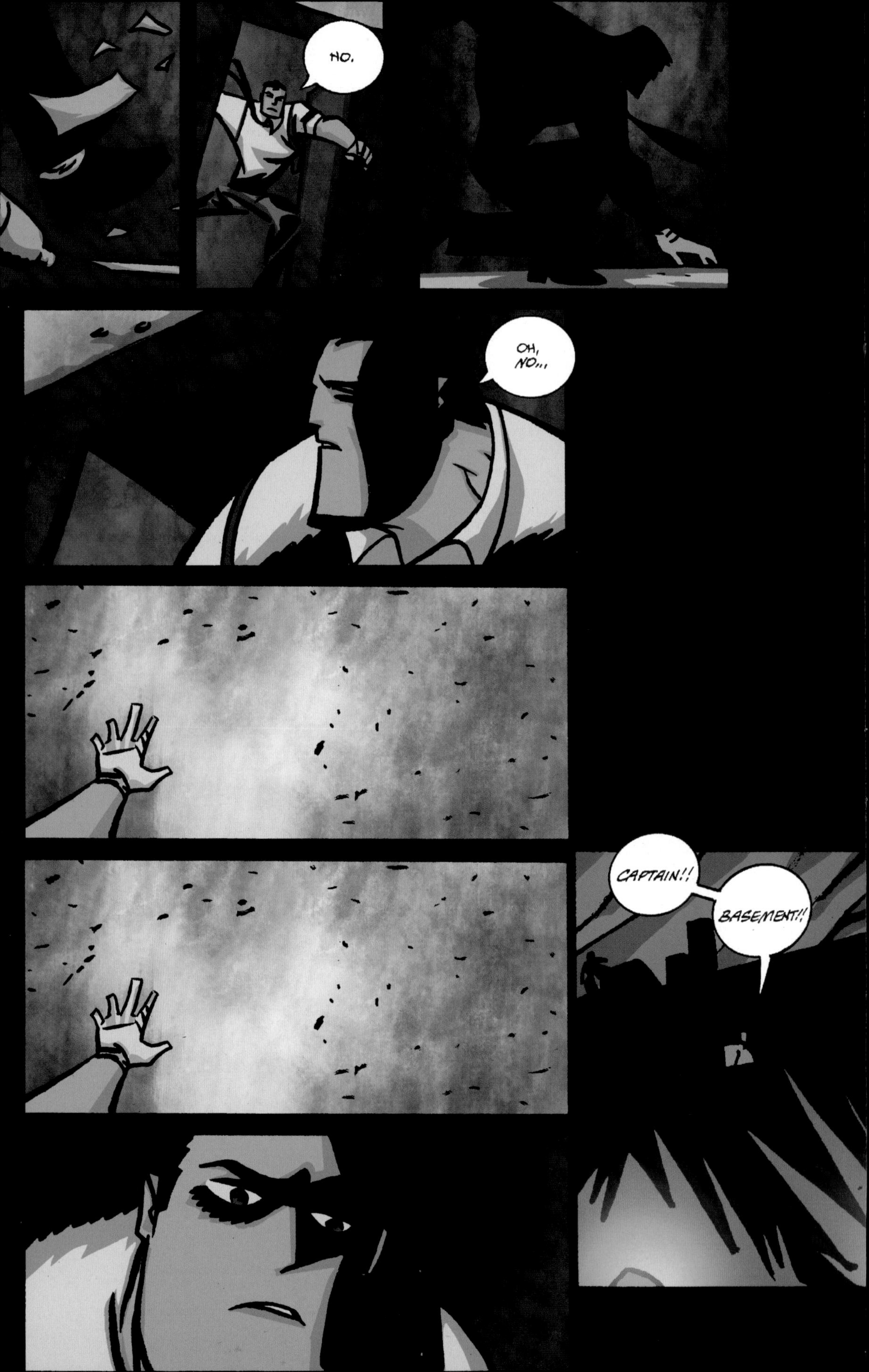
NO.
OH, NO...
CAPTAIN!!
BASEMENT!!

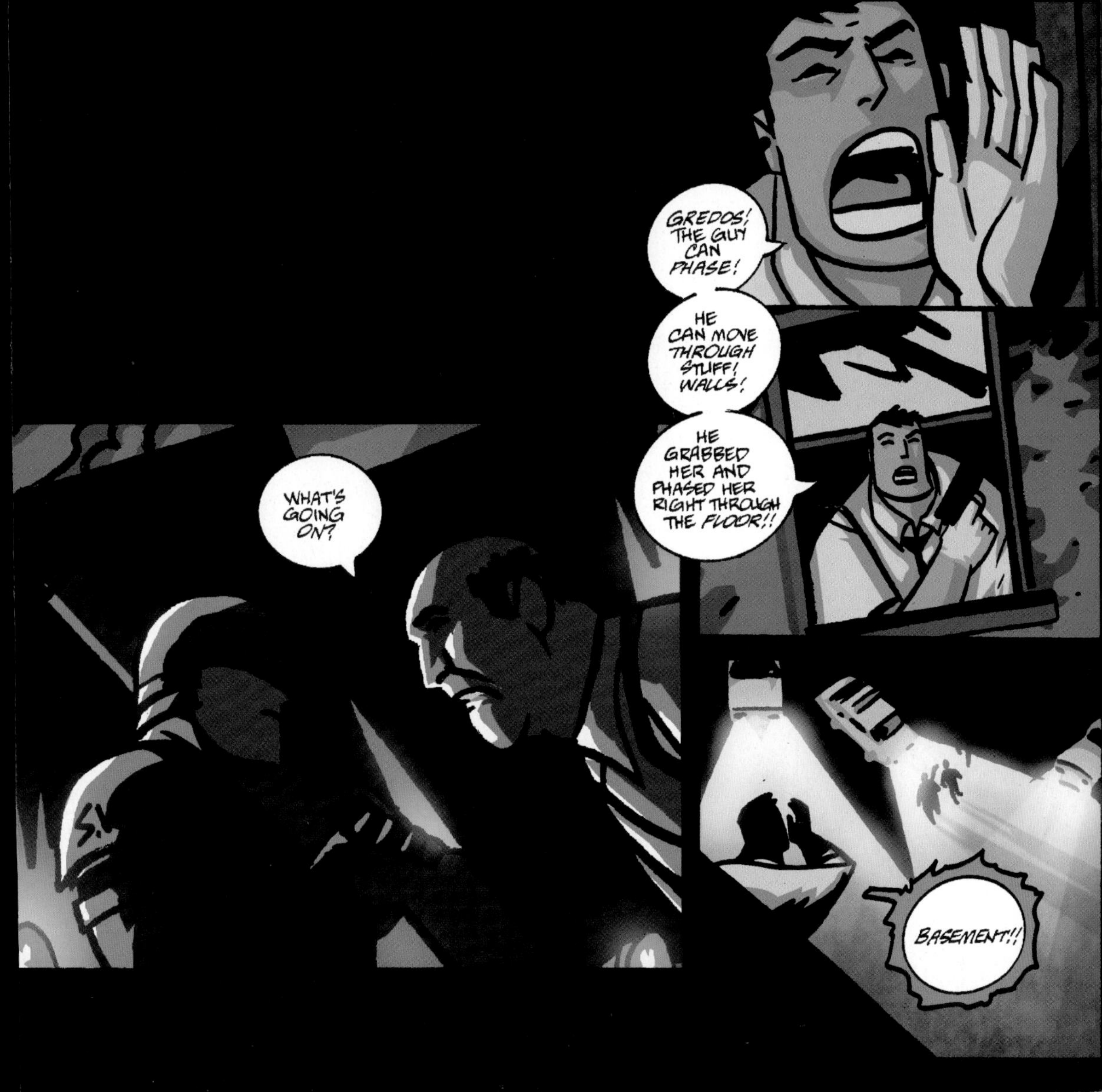
GREDOS! THE GUY CAN PHASE!
HE CAN MOVE THROUGH STUFF! WALLS!
HE GRABBED HER AND PHASED HER RIGHT THROUGH THE FLOOR!!
WHAT'S GOING ON?
BASEMENT!!

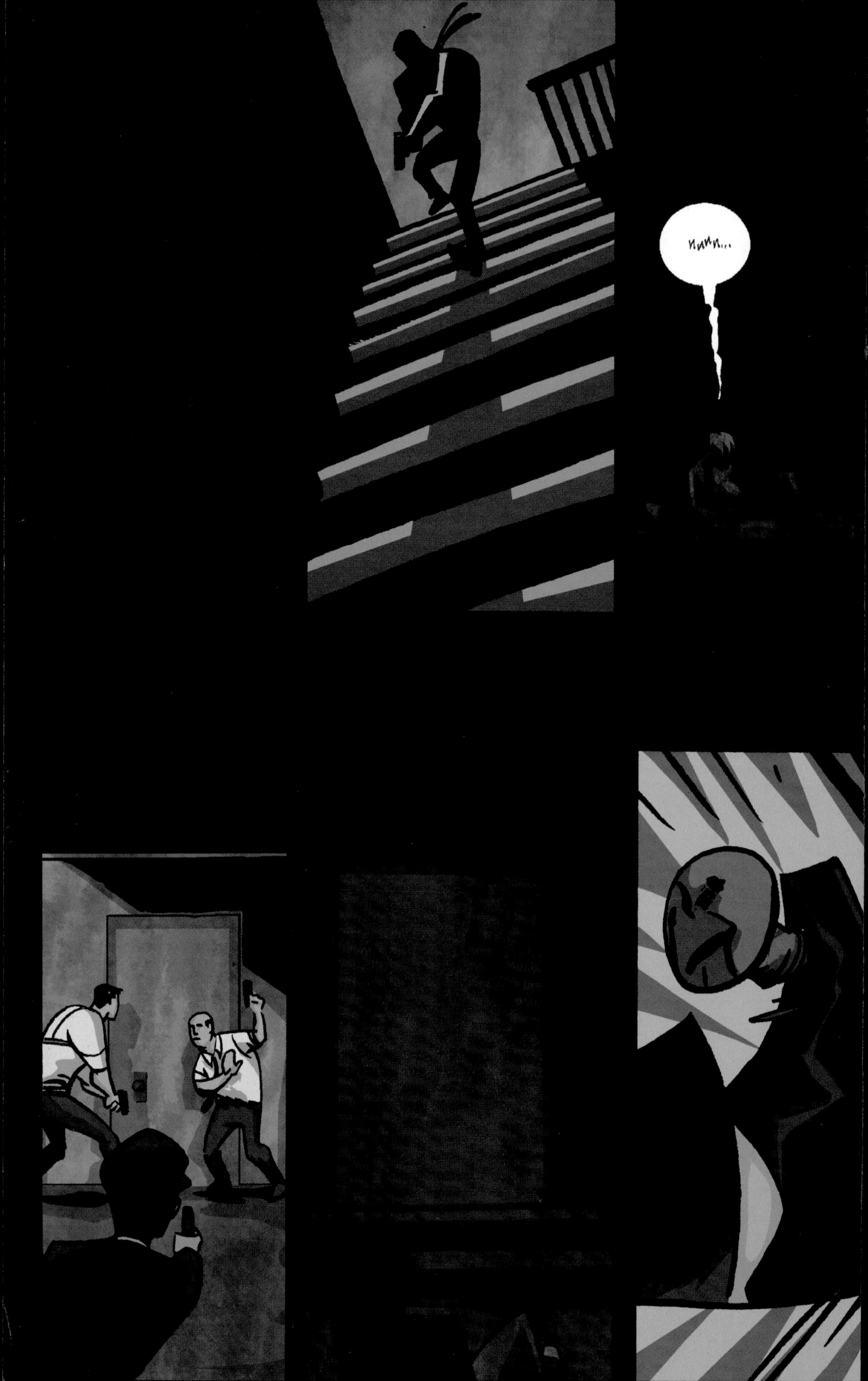
NNNN...

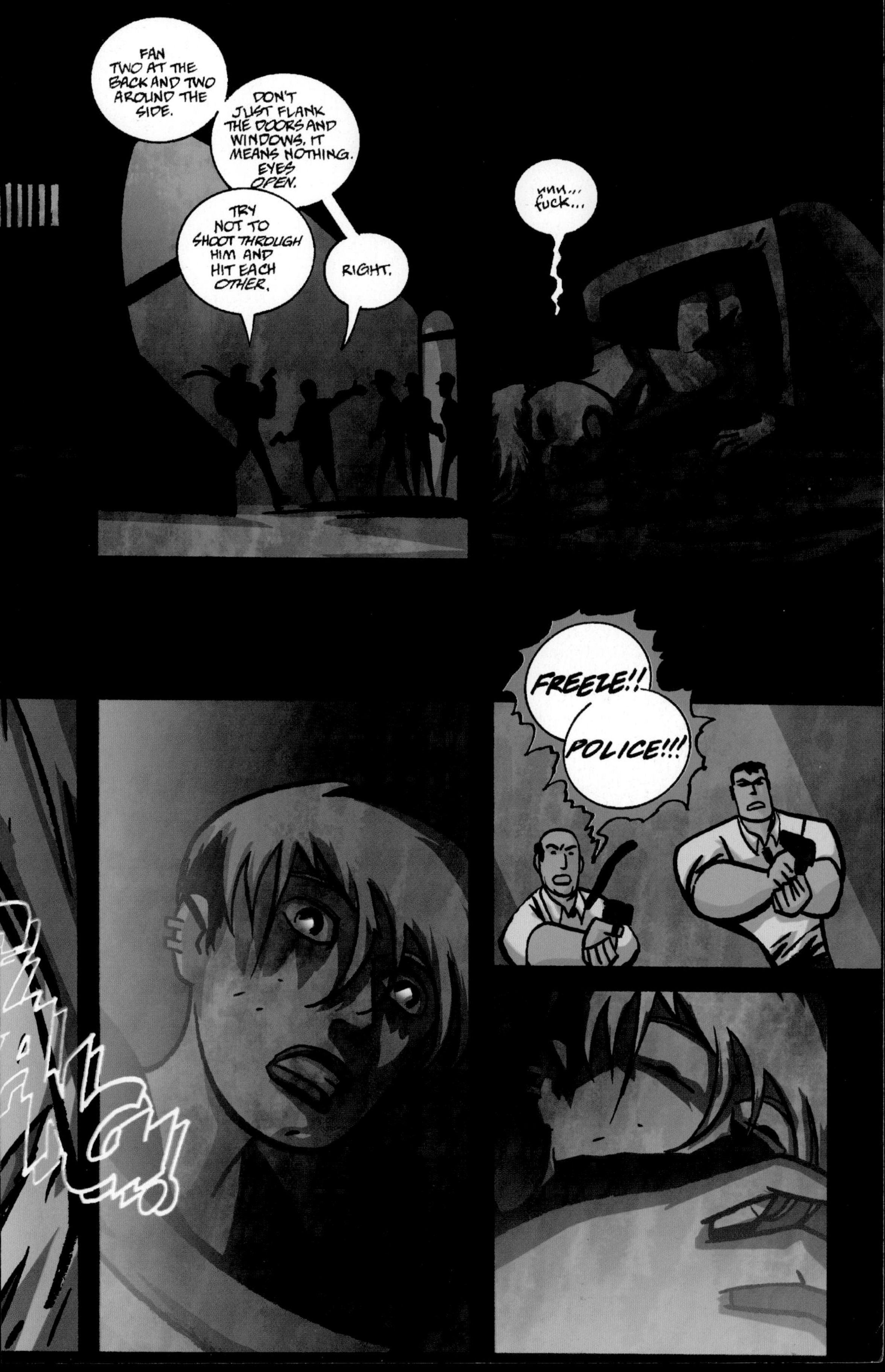
FAN TWO AT THE BACK AND TWO AROUND THE SIDE.
DON'T JUST FLANK THE DOORS AND WINDOWS, IT MEANS NOTHING. EYES OPEN.
TRY NOT TO SHOOT THROUGH HIM AND HIT EACH OTHER.
RIGHT.
nnn... fuck...
FREEZE!!
POLICE!!!

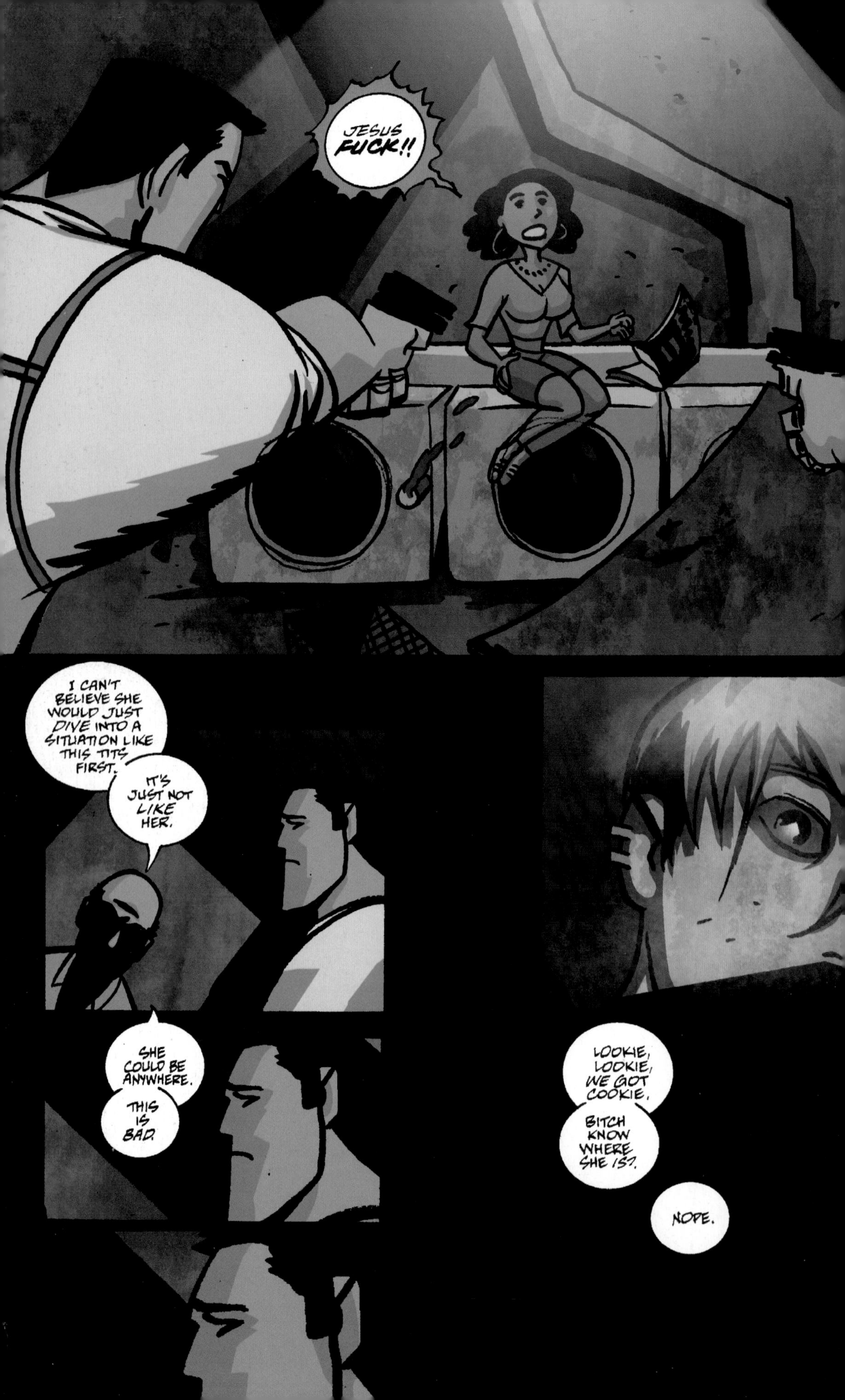
JESUS FUCK!!
I CAN'T BELIEVE SHE WOULD JUST DIVE INTO A SITUATION LIKE THIS TITS FIRST.
IT'S JUST NOT LIKE HER.
SHE COULD BE ANYWHERE.
THIS IS BAD.
LOOKIE, LOOKIE, WE GOT COOKIE.
BITCH KNOW WHERE SHE IS?
NOPE.

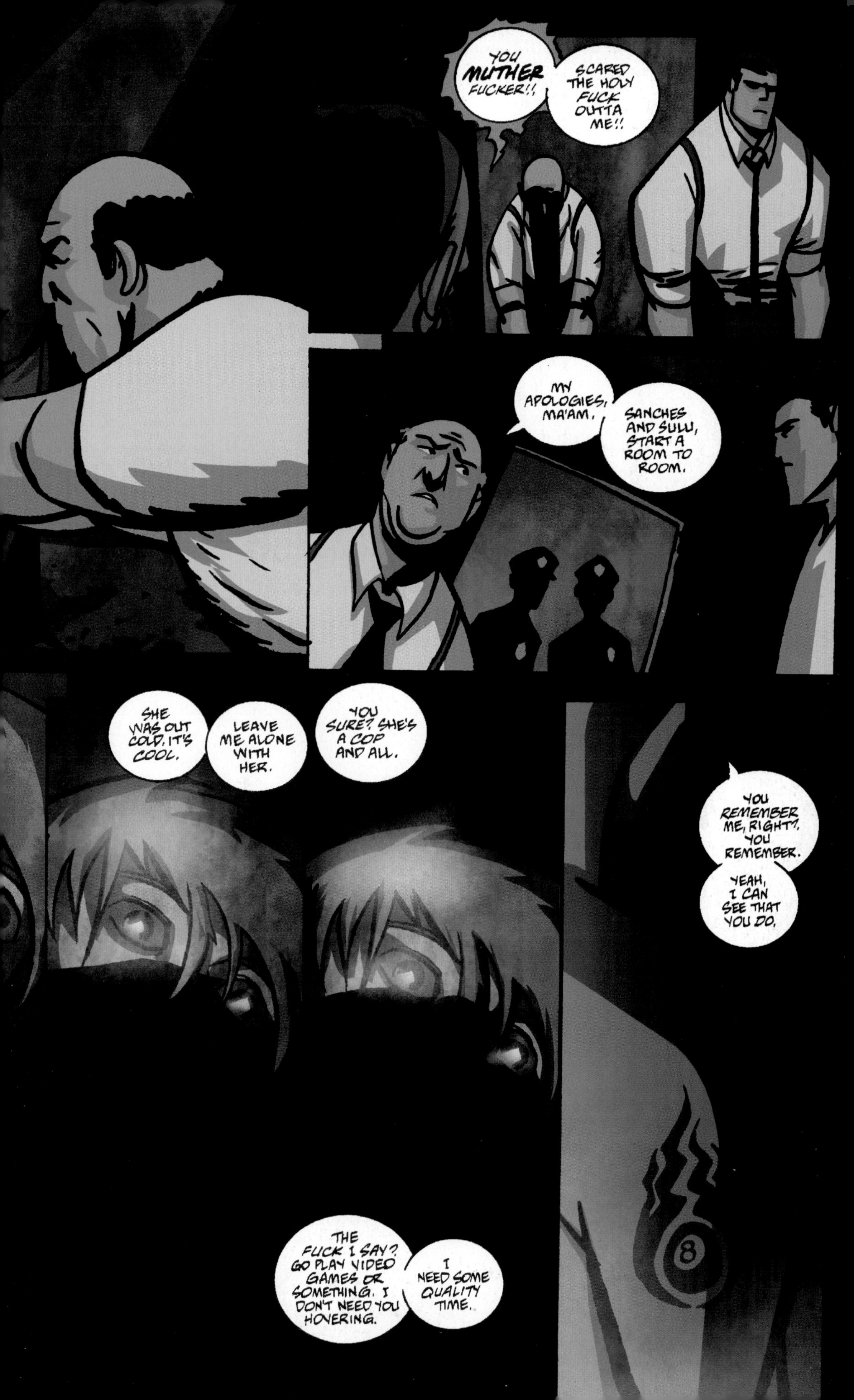
YOU MUTHER FUCKER!!
SCARED THE HOLY FUCK OUTTA ME!!
MY APOLOGIES, MA'AM.
SANCHES AND SULU, START A ROOM TO ROOM.
SHE WAS OUT COLD. IT'S COOL.
LEAVE ME ALONE WITH HER.
YOU SURE? SHE'S A COP AND ALL.
THE FUCK I SAY? GO PLAY VIDEO GAMES OR SOMETHING. I DON'T NEED YOU HOVERING.
I NEED SOME QUALITY TIME.
YOU REMEMBER ME, RIGHT? YOU REMEMBER.
YEAH, I CAN SEE THAT YOU DO.

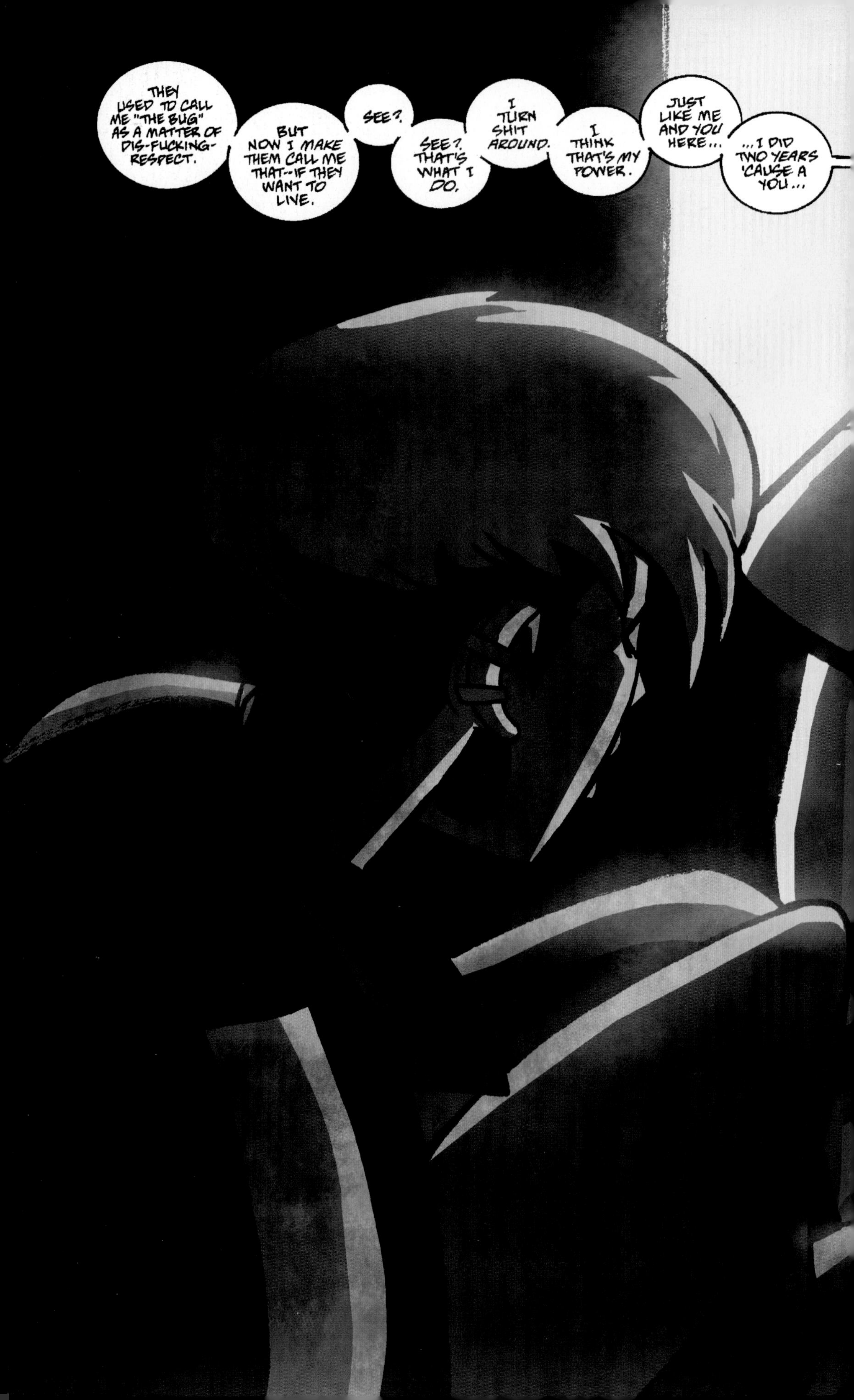
THEY USED TO CALL ME "THE BUG" AS A MATTER OF DIS-FUCKING-RESPECT.
BUT NOW I MAKE THEM CALL ME THAT--IF THEY WANT TO LIVE.
SEE?
SEE?. THAT'S WHAT I DO.
I TURN SHIT AROUND.
I THINK THAT'S MY POWER.
JUST LIKE ME AND YOU HERE...
...I DID TWO YEARS 'CAUSE A YOU...

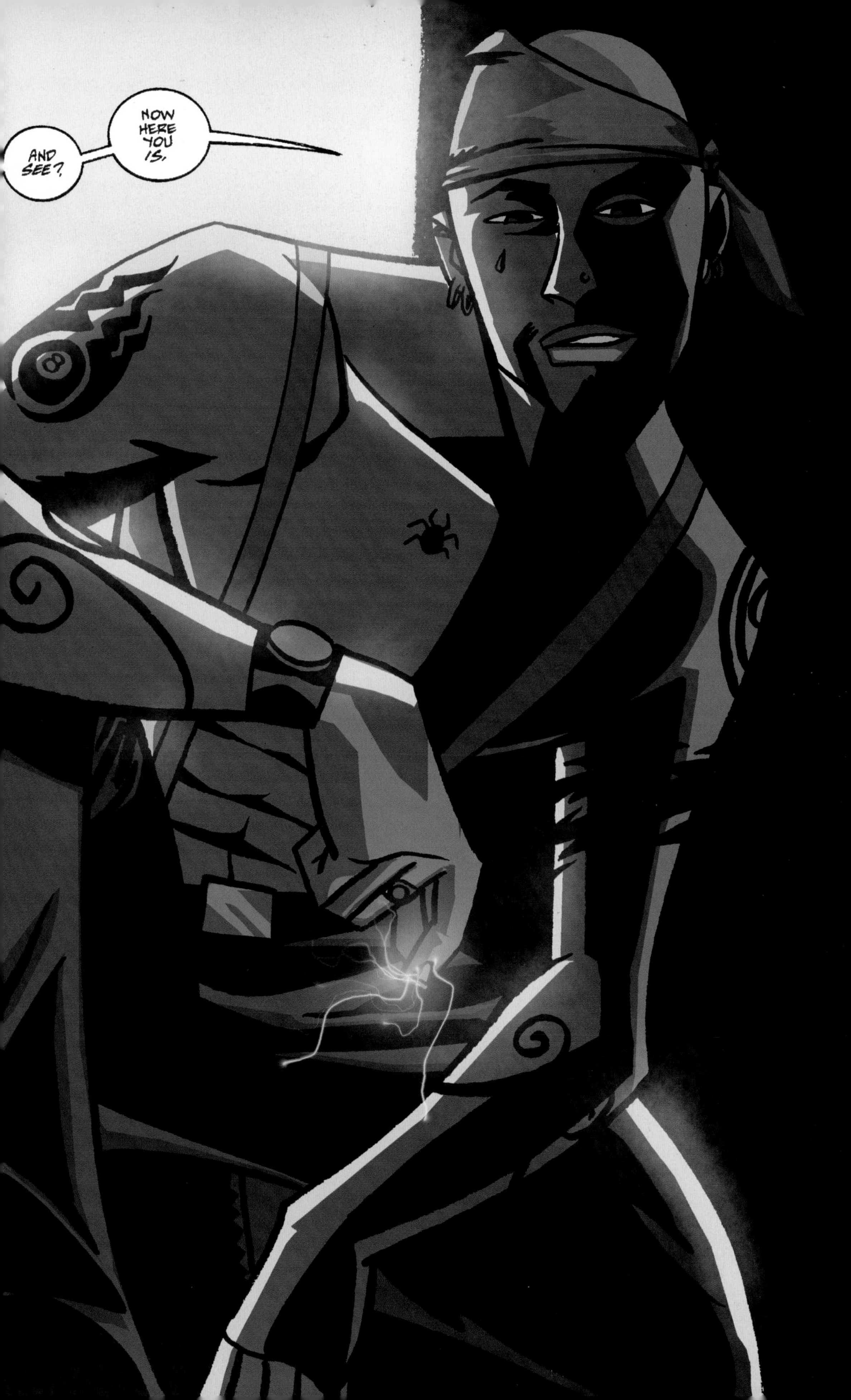

NOW HERE YOU IS,
AND SEE?

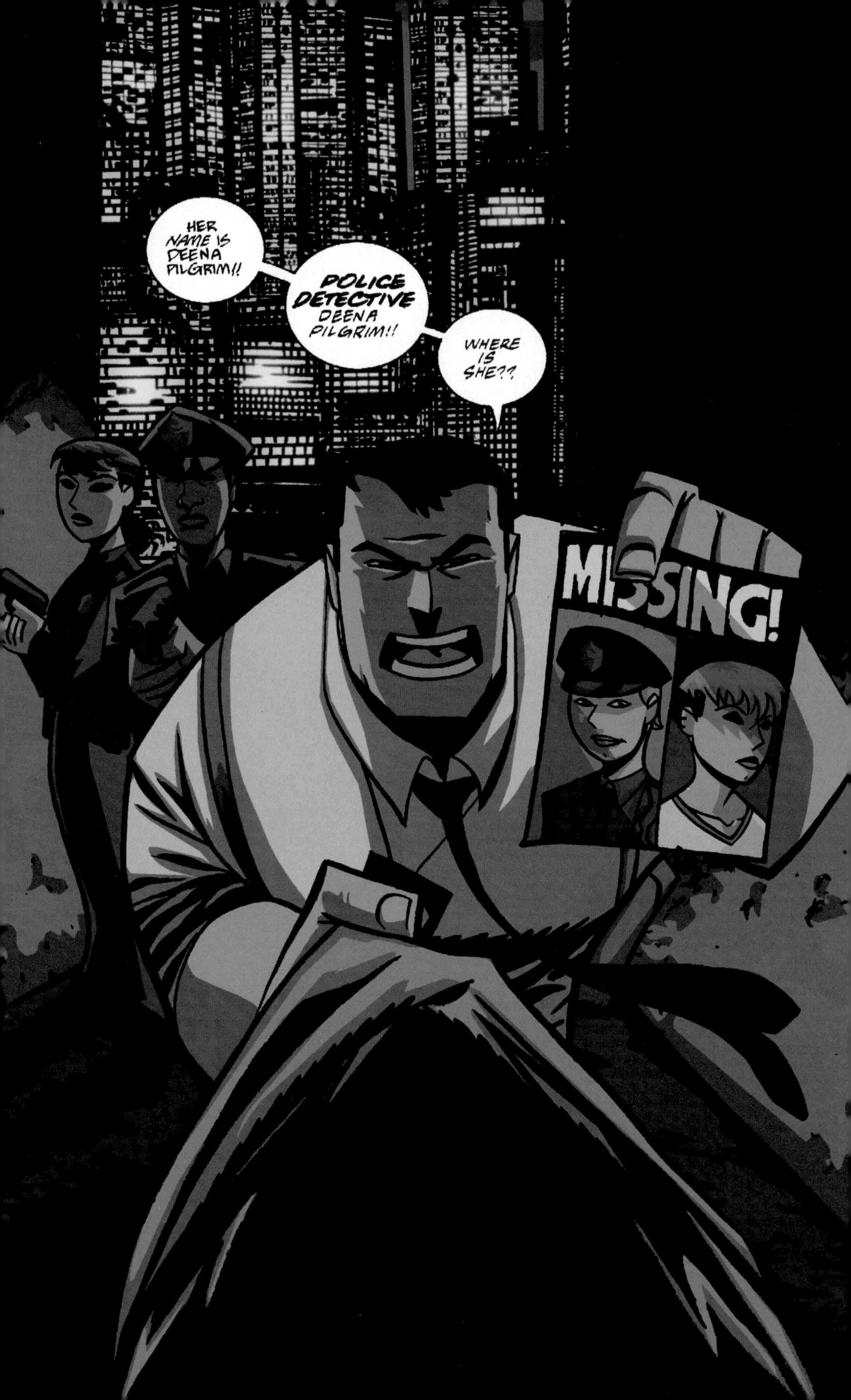
HER NAME IS DEENA PILGRIM!!
POLICE DETECTIVE DEENA PILGRIM!!
WHERE IS SHE??
MISSING!

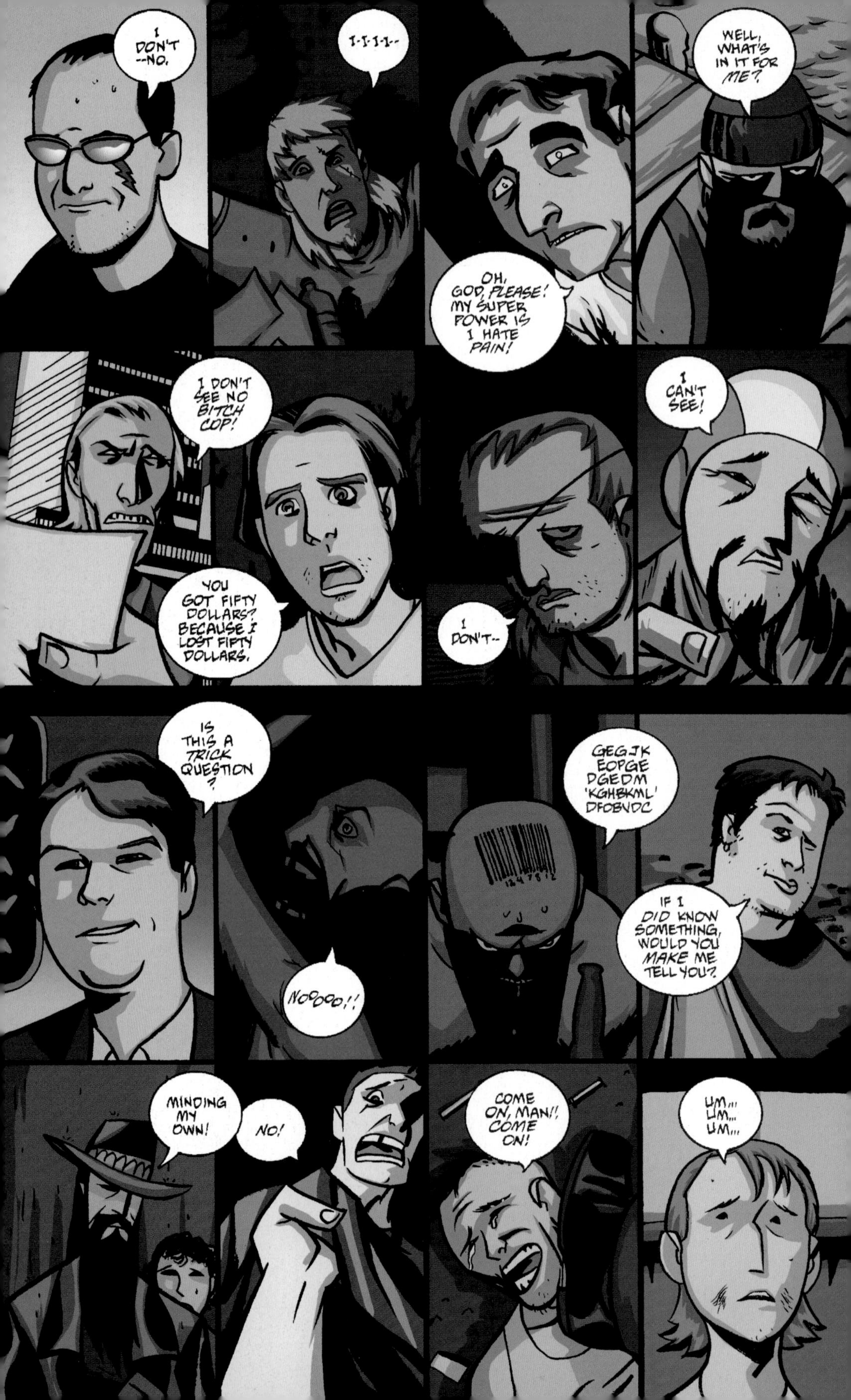
I DON'T --NO.
I-I-I-I--
OH, GOD, PLEASE! MY SUPER POWER IS I HATE PAIN!
WELL, WHAT'S IN IT FOR ME?
I DON'T SEE NO BITCH COP!
YOU GOT FIFTY DOLLARS? BECAUSE I LOST FIFTY DOLLARS.
I DON'T--
I CAN'T SEE!
IS THIS A TRICK QUESTION?
NOOOOO!!
GEGJK EOPGE DGEDM 'KGHBKML' DFOBVDC
IF I DID KNOW SOMETHING, WOULD YOU MAKE ME TELL YOU?
MINDING MY OWN!
NO!
COME ON, MAN!! COME ON!
UM... UM... UM...

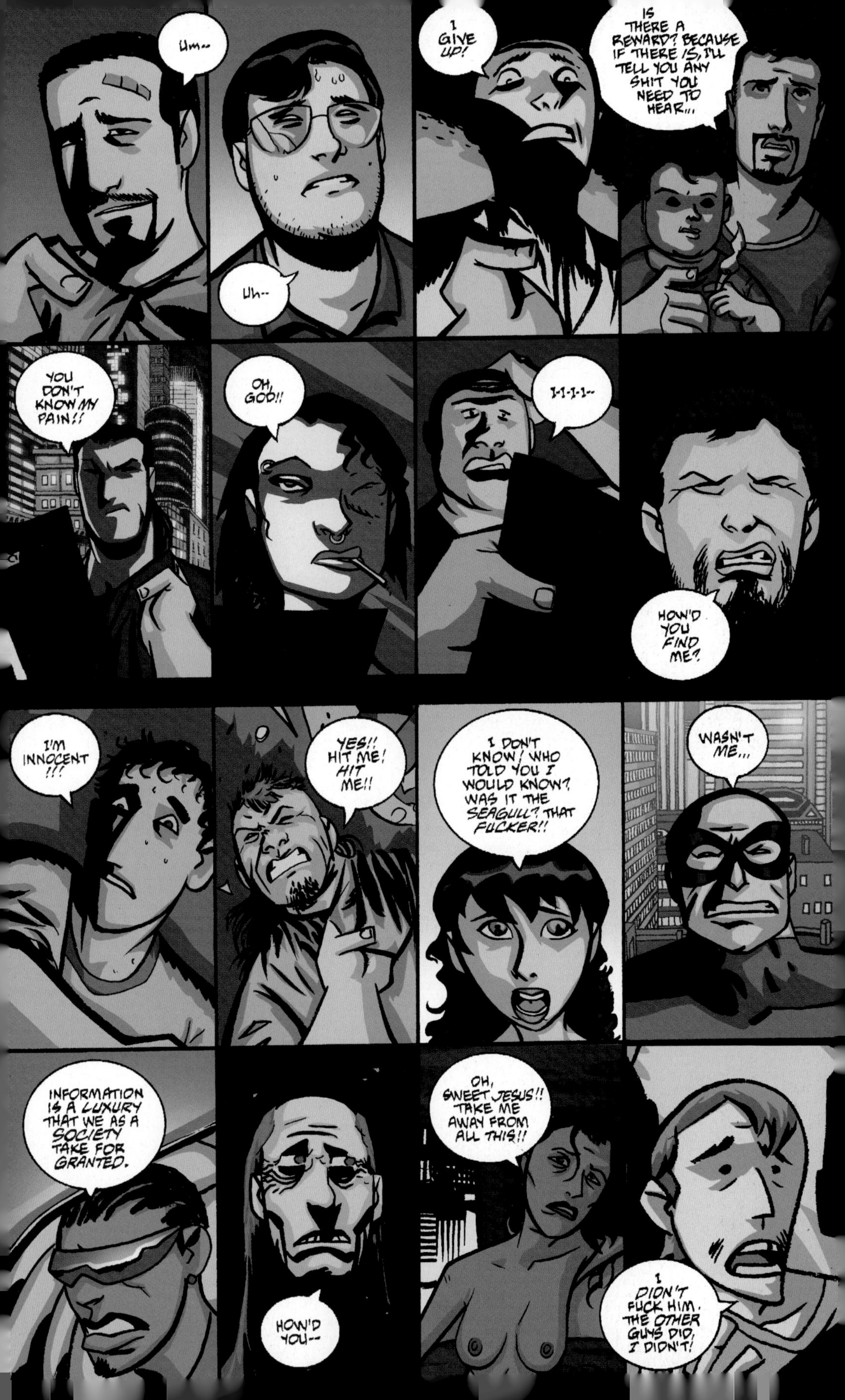
Um..
Uh--
I GIVE UP!
IS THERE A REWARD? BECAUSE IF THERE IS, I'LL TELL YOU ANY SHIT YOU NEED TO HEAR...
YOU DON'T KNOW MY PAIN!!
OH, GOD!!
I-I-I-I--
HOW'D YOU FIND ME?
I'M INNOCENT!!!
YES!! HIT ME! HIT ME!!
I DON'T KNOW! WHO TOLD YOU I WOULD KNOW? WAS IT THE SEAGULL? THAT FUCKER!!
WASN'T ME...
INFORMATION IS A LUXURY THAT WE AS A SOCIETY TAKE FOR GRANTED.
HOW'D YOU--
OH, SWEET JESUS!! TAKE ME AWAY FROM ALL THIS!!
I DIDN'T FUCK HIM. THE OTHER GUYS DID, I DIDN'T!

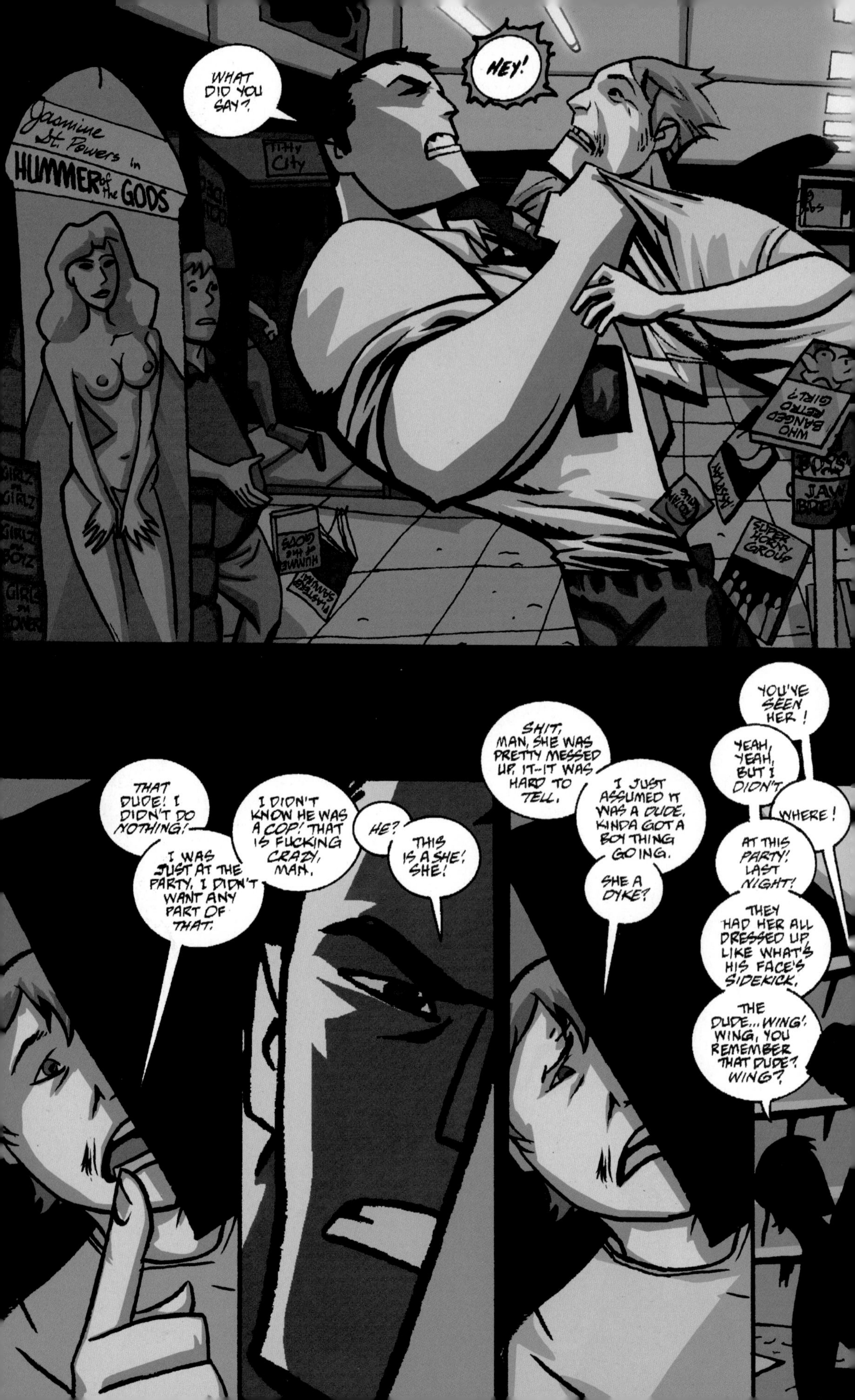

Jasmine St. Powers in
HUMMER of the GODS
Titty City
GIRLZ on GIRLZ
WHAT DID YOU SAY?
HEY!
WHO BANGED RETRO GIRL?
SUPER HORNY GROUP
THAT DUDE! I DIDN'T DO NOTHING!
I WAS JUST AT THE PARTY, I DIDN'T WANT ANY PART OF THAT.
I DIDN'T KNOW HE WAS A COP! THAT IS FUCKING CRAZY, MAN.
HE?
THIS IS A SHE! SHE!
SHIT, MAN, SHE WAS PRETTY MESSED UP, IT--IT WAS HARD TO TELL.
I JUST ASSUMED IT WAS A DUDE. KINDA GOT A BOY THING GOING.
SHE A DYKE?
YOU'VE SEEN HER!
YEAH, YEAH, BUT I DIDN'T
WHERE!
AT THIS PARTY! LAST NIGHT!
THEY HAD HER ALL DRESSED UP LIKE WHAT'S HIS FACE'S SIDEKICK.
THE DUDE... WING! WING, YOU REMEMBER THAT DUDE? WING?

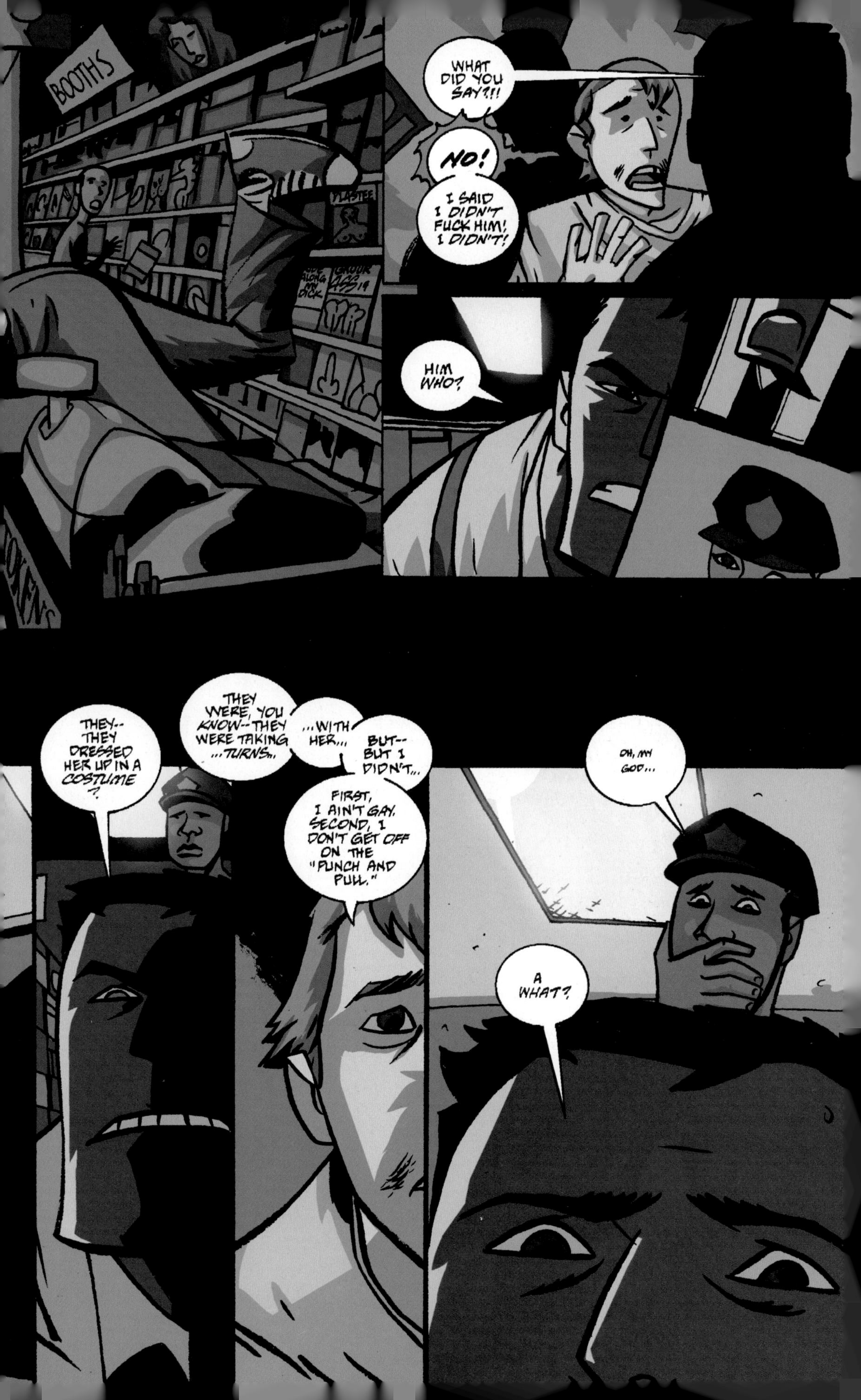
BOOTHS
WHAT DID YOU SAY?!!
NO!
I SAID I DIDN'T FUCK HIM! I DIDN'T!
HIM WHO?
THEY-- THEY DRESSED HER UP IN A COSTUME ?
THEY WERE, YOU KNOW-- THEY WERE TAKING ...TURNS...
...WITH HER...
BUT-- BUT I DIDN'T...
FIRST, I AIN'T GAY. SECOND, I DON'T GET OFF ON THE "PUNCH AND PULL."
OH, MY GOD...
A WHAT?

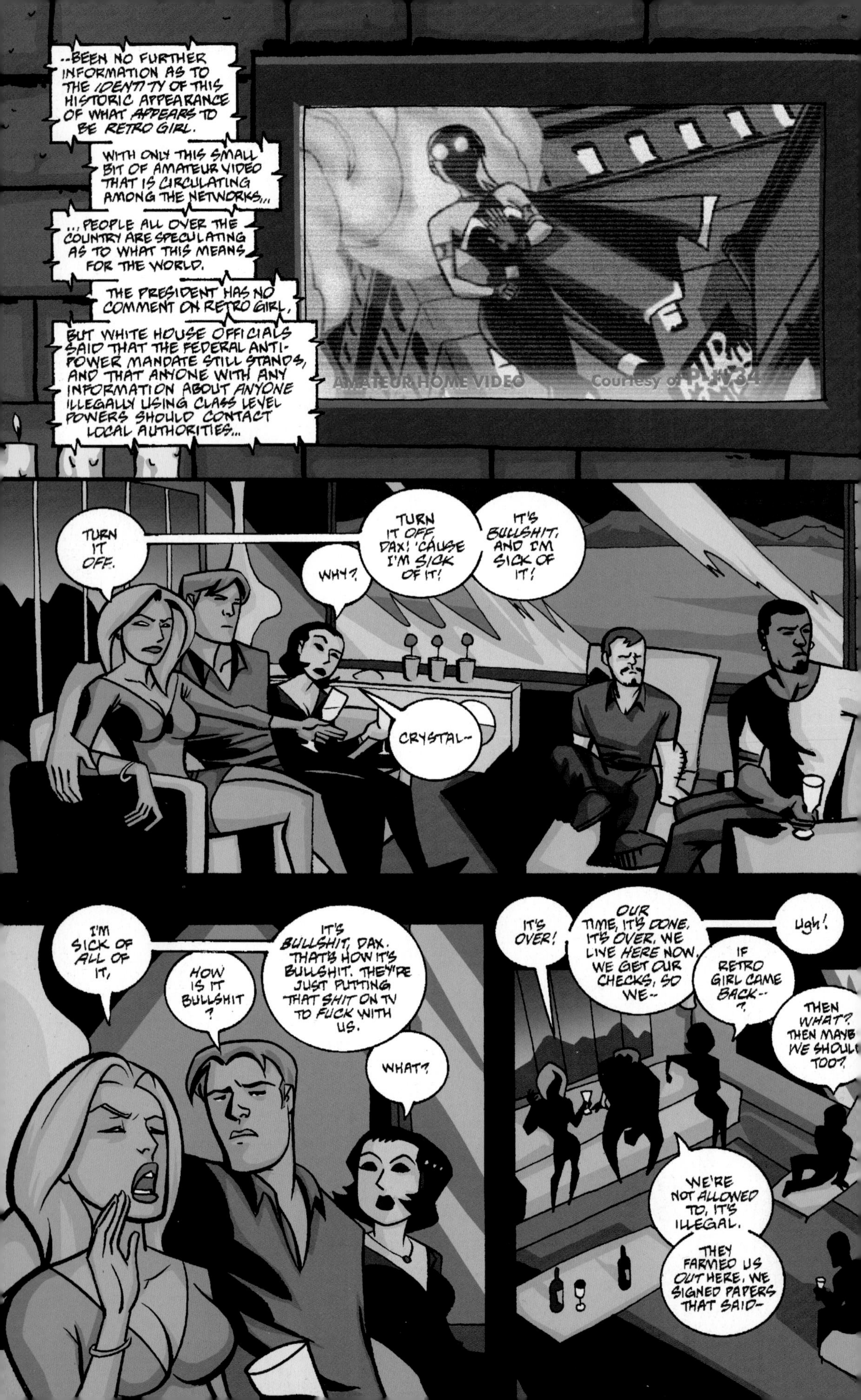

--BEEN NO FURTHER INFORMATION AS TO THE IDENTITY OF THIS HISTORIC APPEARANCE OF WHAT APPEARS TO BE RETRO GIRL.
WITH ONLY THIS SMALL BIT OF AMATEUR VIDEO THAT IS CIRCULATING AMONG THE NETWORKS...
...PEOPLE ALL OVER THE COUNTRY ARE SPECULATING AS TO WHAT THIS MEANS FOR THE WORLD.
THE PRESIDENT HAS NO COMMENT ON RETRO GIRL,
BUT WHITE HOUSE OFFICIALS SAID THAT THE FEDERAL ANTI-POWER MANDATE STILL STANDS, AND THAT ANYONE WITH ANY INFORMATION ABOUT ANYONE ILLEGALLY USING CLASS LEVEL POWERS SHOULD CONTACT LOCAL AUTHORITIES...
AMATEUR HOME VIDEO
TURN IT OFF.
WHY?
TURN IT OFF, DAX! 'CAUSE I'M SICK OF IT!
IT'S BULLSHIT, AND I'M SICK OF IT!
CRYSTAL--
I'M SICK OF ALL OF IT,
HOW IS IT BULLSHIT?
IT'S BULLSHIT, DAX. THAT'S HOW IT'S BULLSHIT. THEY'RE JUST PUTTING THAT SHIT ON TV TO FUCK WITH US.
WHAT?
IT'S OVER!
OUR TIME, IT'S DONE. IT'S OVER. WE LIVE HERE NOW. WE GET OUR CHECKS, SO WE--
UGH!
IF RETRO GIRL CAME BACK--?
THEN WHAT? THEN MAYBE WE SHOULD TOO?
WE'RE NOT ALLOWED TO, IT'S ILLEGAL.
THEY FARMED US OUT HERE. WE SIGNED PAPERS THAT SAID--

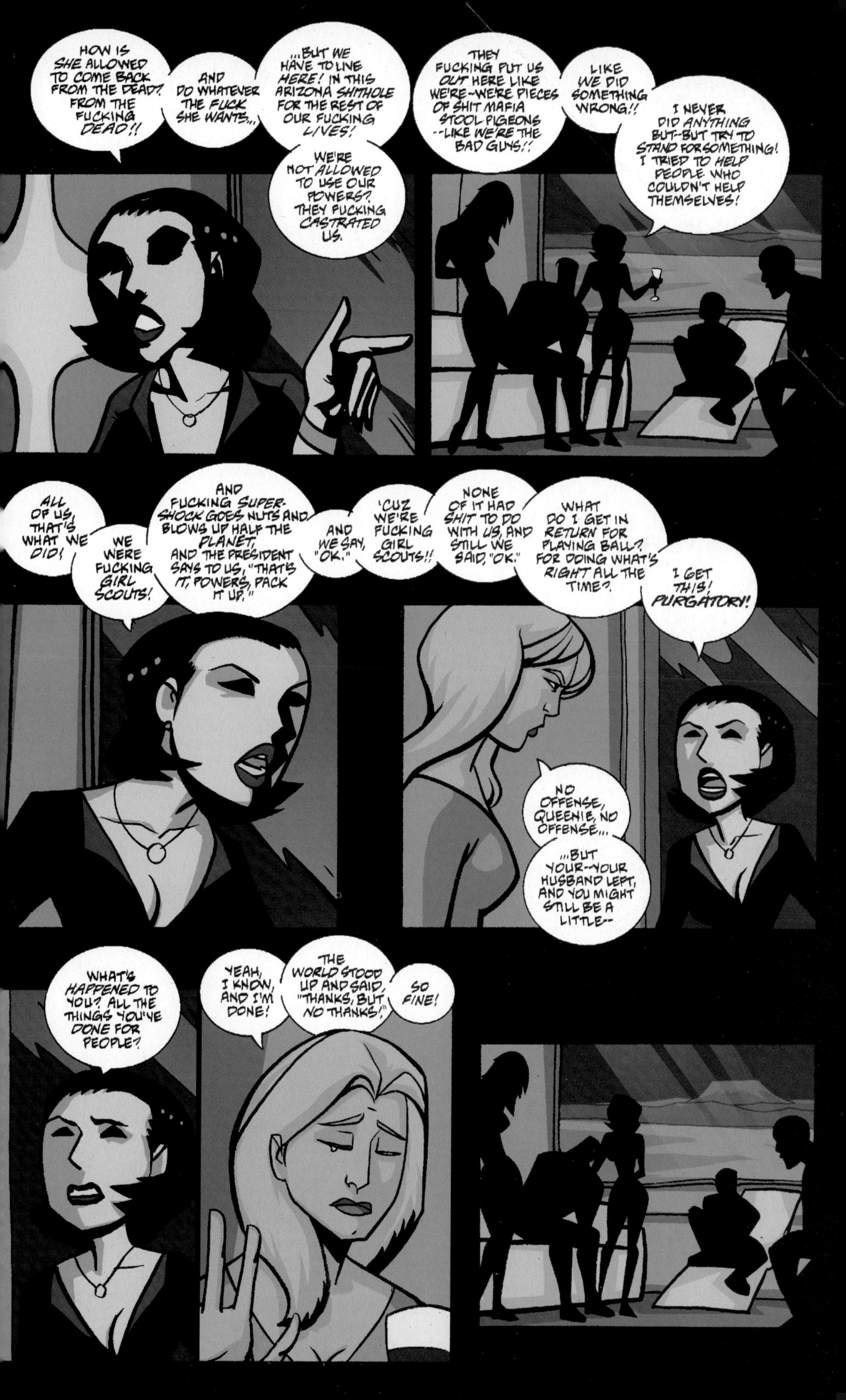
HOW IS SHE ALLOWED TO COME BACK FROM THE DEAD? FROM THE FUCKING DEAD!!
AND DO WHATEVER THE FUCK SHE WANTS...
...BUT WE HAVE TO LIVE HERE! IN THIS ARIZONA SHITHOLE FOR THE REST OF OUR FUCKING LIVES!
WE'RE NOT ALLOWED TO USE OUR POWERS? THEY FUCKING CASTRATED US.
THEY FUCKING PUT US OUT HERE LIKE WE'RE--WE'RE PIECES OF SHIT MAFIA STOOL PIGEONS --LIKE WE'RE THE BAD GUYS!!
LIKE WE DID SOMETHING WRONG!!
I NEVER DID ANYTHING BUT--BUT TRY TO STAND FOR SOMETHING! I TRIED TO HELP PEOPLE WHO COULDN'T HELP THEMSELVES!
ALL OF US, THAT'S WHAT WE DID!
WE WERE FUCKING GIRL SCOUTS!
AND FUCKING SUPER-SHOCK GOES NUTS AND BLOWS UP HALF THE PLANET, AND THE PRESIDENT SAYS TO US, "THAT'S IT, POWERS, PACK IT UP."
AND WE SAY, "OK."
'CUZ WE'RE FUCKING GIRL SCOUTS!!
NONE OF IT HAD SHIT TO DO WITH US, AND STILL WE SAID, "OK."
WHAT DO I GET IN RETURN FOR PLAYING BALL? FOR DOING WHAT'S RIGHT ALL THE TIME?
I GET THIS! PURGATORY!
NO OFFENSE, QUEENIE, NO OFFENSE...
...BUT YOUR--YOUR HUSBAND LEFT, AND YOU MIGHT STILL BE A LITTLE--
WHAT'S HAPPENED TO YOU? ALL THE THINGS YOU'VE DONE FOR PEOPLE?
YEAH, I KNOW, AND I'M DONE!
THE WORLD STOOD UP AND SAID, "THANKS, BUT NO THANKS."
SO FINE!

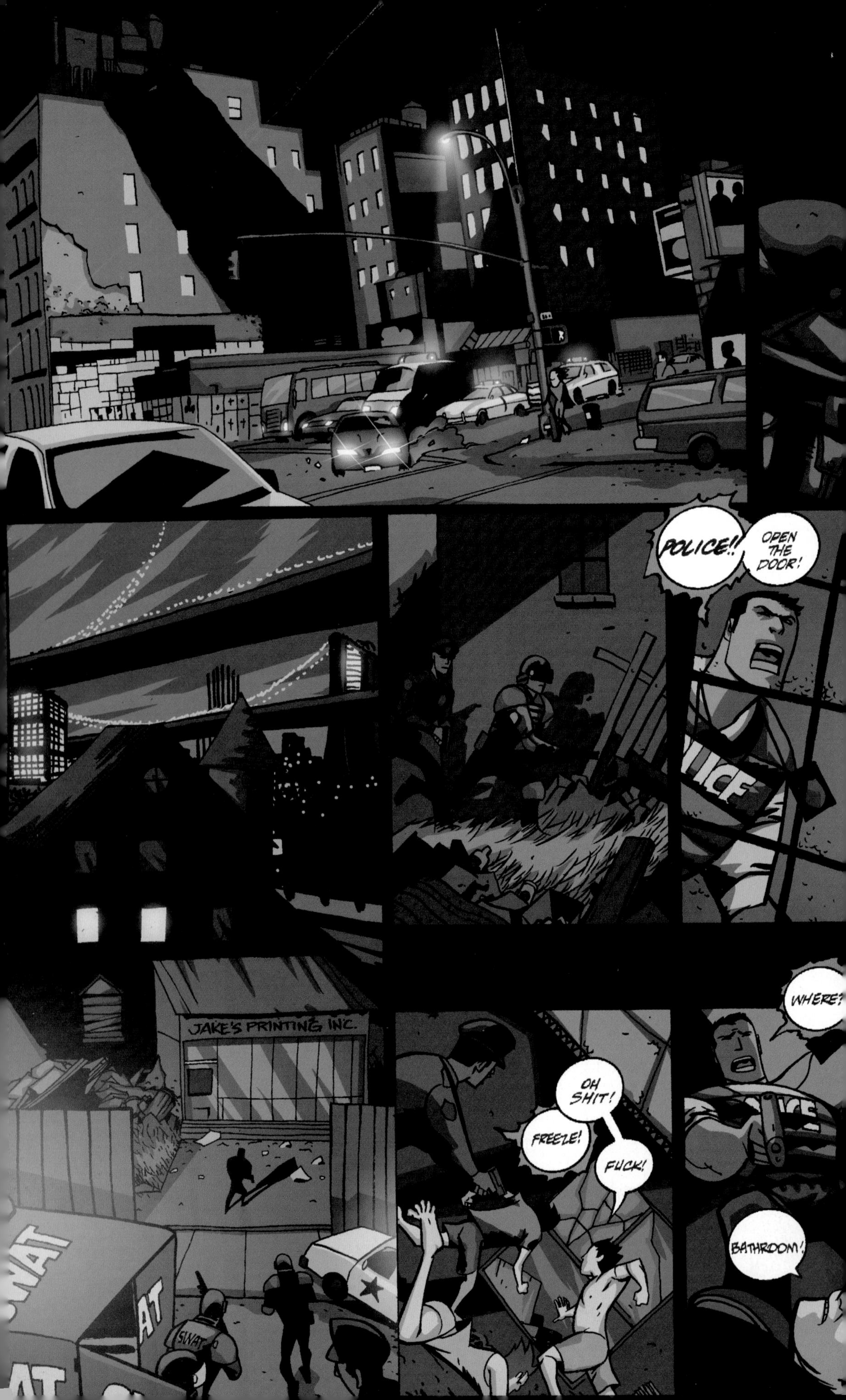
POLICE!!
OPEN THE DOOR!
POLICE
JAKE'S PRINTING INC.
SWAT
OH SHIT!
FREEZE!
FUCK!
WHERE?
BATHROOM!

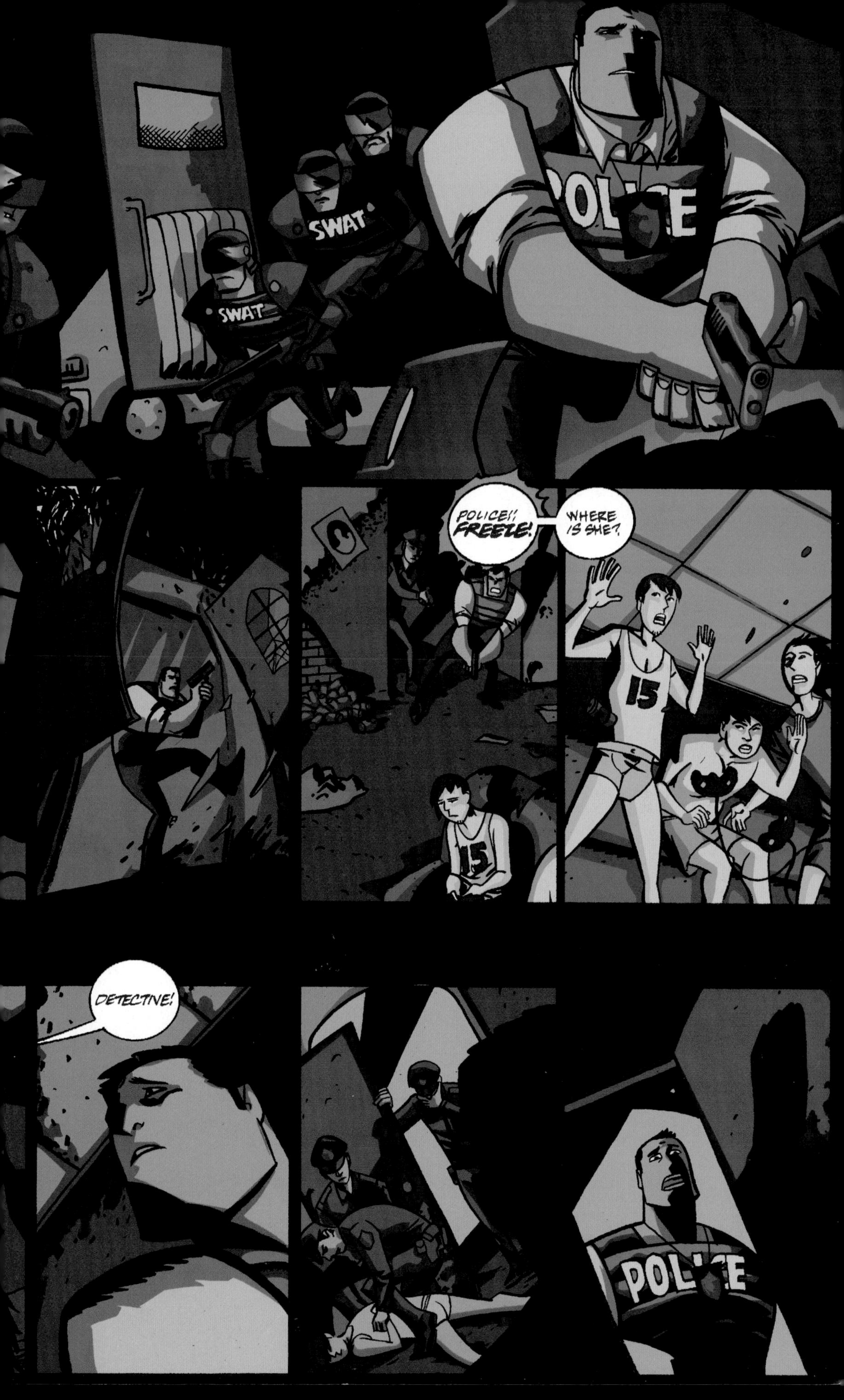
POLICE!! FREEZE!
WHERE IS SHE?
DETECTIVE!

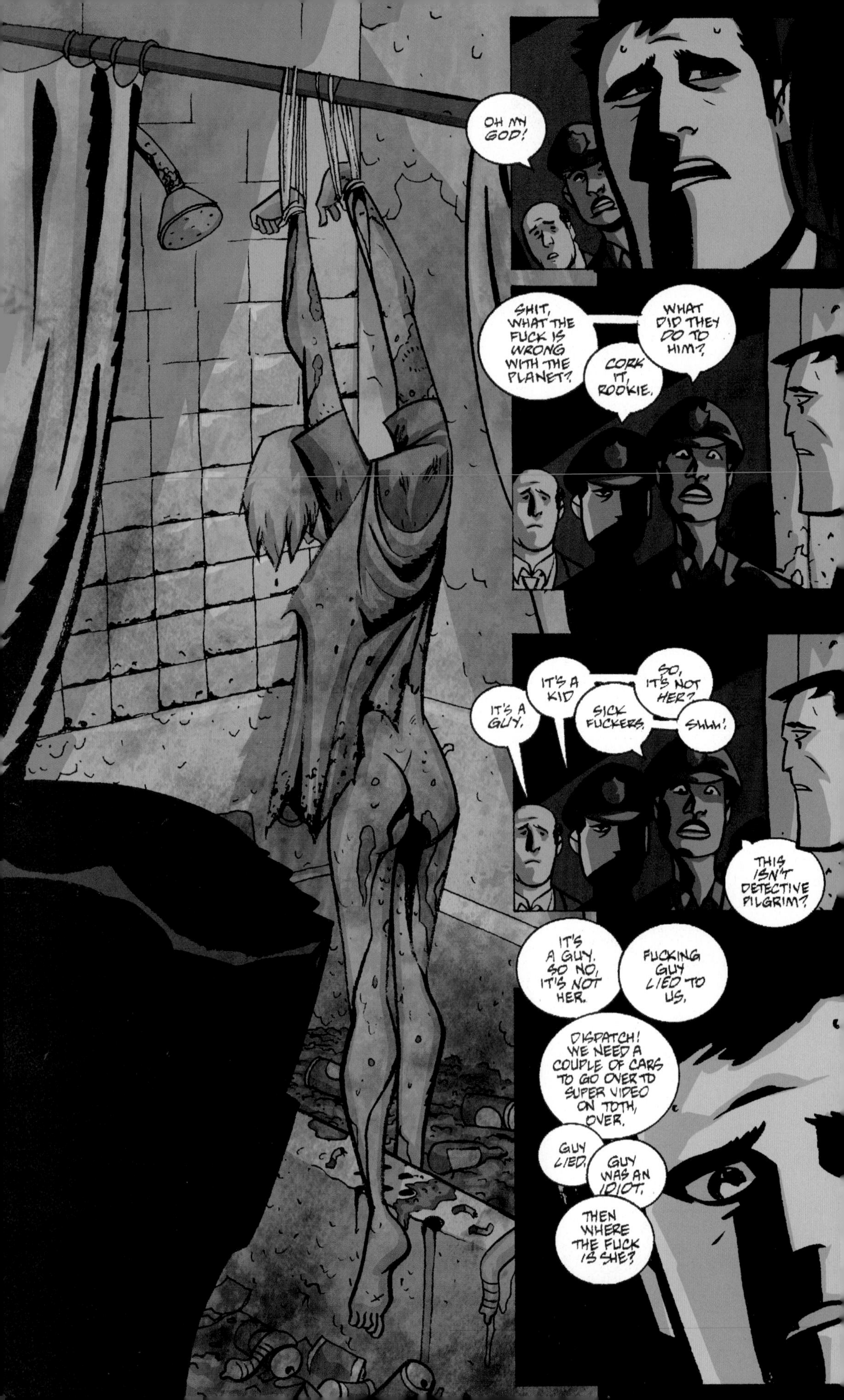
OH MY GOD!
SHIT, WHAT THE FUCK IS WRONG WITH THE PLANET?
WHAT DID THEY DO TO HIM?
CORK IT, ROOKIE.
IT'S A GUY.
IT'S A KID
SO, IT'S NOT HER?
SICK FUCKERS.
SHHH!
THIS ISN'T DETECTIVE PILGRIM?
IT'S A GUY. SO NO, IT'S NOT HER.
FUCKING GUY LIED TO US.
DISPATCH! WE NEED A COUPLE OF CARS TO GO OVER TO SUPER VIDEO ON 70TH, OVER.
GUY LIED.
GUY WAS AN IDIOT.
THEN WHERE THE FUCK IS SHE?

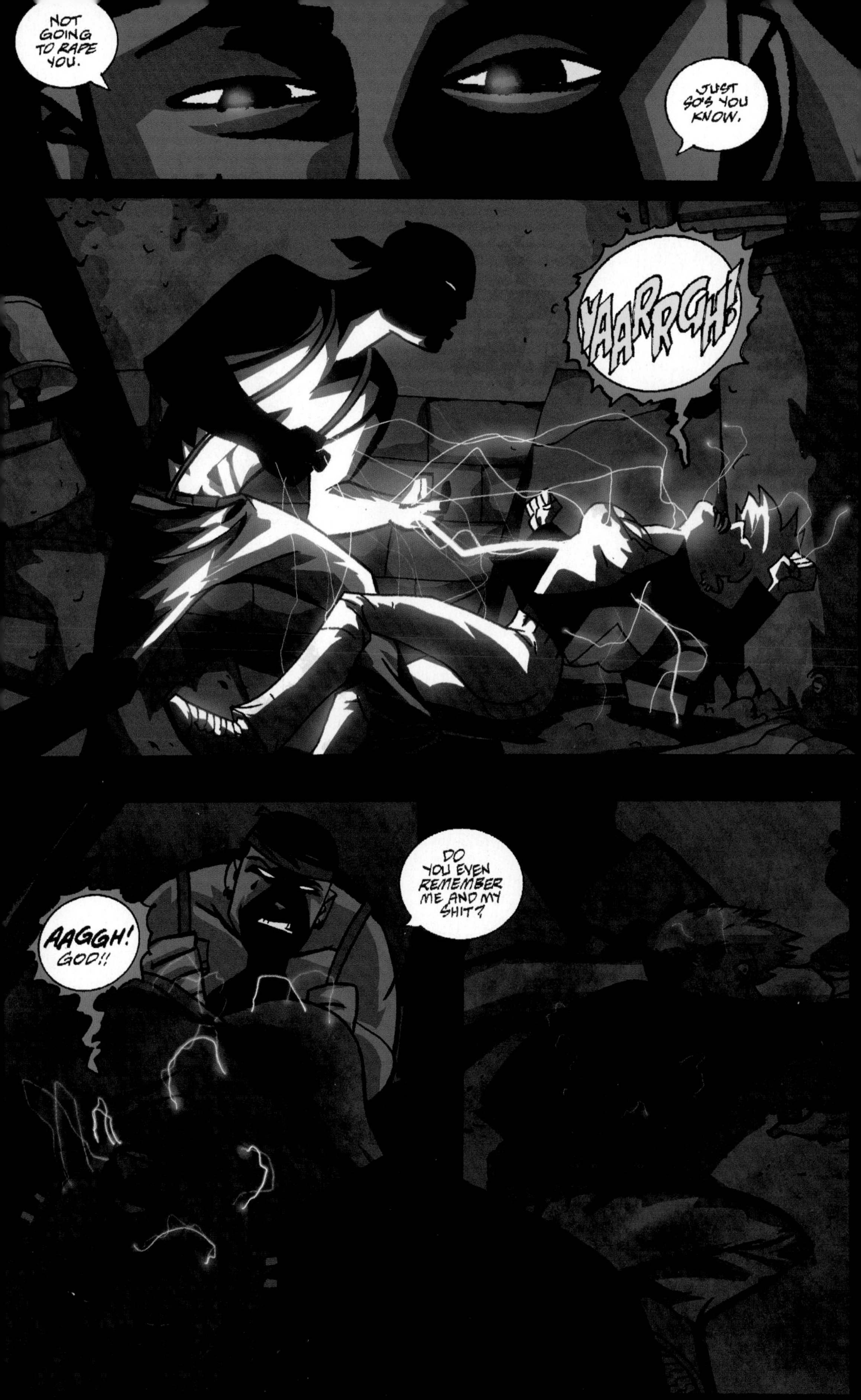
NOT GOING TO RAPE YOU.
JUST SO'S YOU KNOW.
YAARRGH!
DO YOU EVEN REMEMBER ME AND MY SHIT?
AAGGH! GOD!!

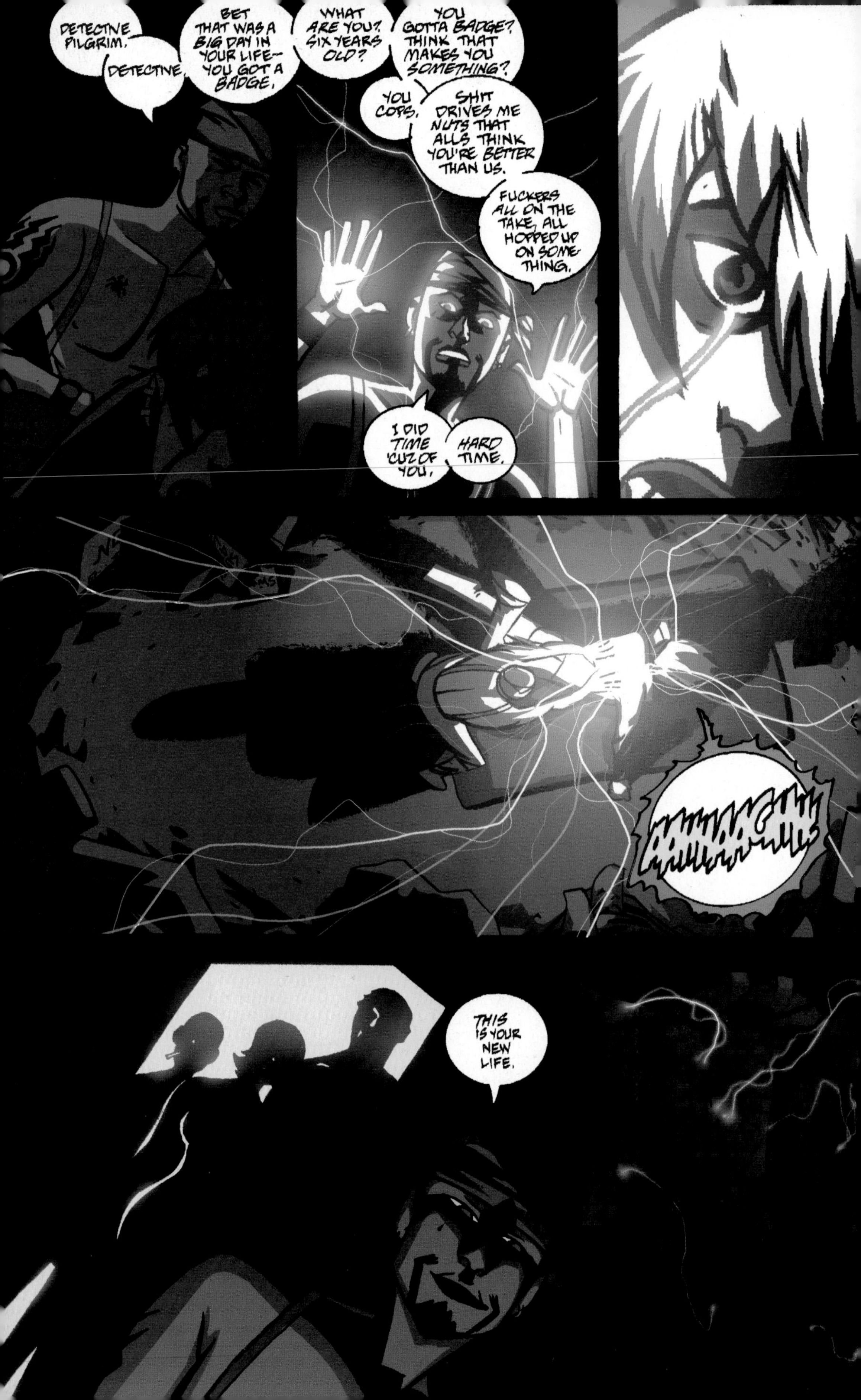
DETECTIVE PILGRIM.
DETECTIVE.
BET THAT WAS A BIG DAY IN YOUR LIFE-- YOU GOT A BADGE.
WHAT ARE YOU? SIX YEARS OLD?
YOU GOTTA BADGE? THINK THAT MAKES YOU SOMETHING?
YOU COPS.
SHIT DRIVES ME NUTS THAT ALLS THINK YOU'RE BETTER THAN US.
FUCKERS ALL ON THE TAKE, ALL HOPPED UP ON SOME-THING.
I DID TIME 'CUZ OF YOU.
HARD TIME.
AAAAAAAGH!!
THIS IS YOUR NEW LIFE.

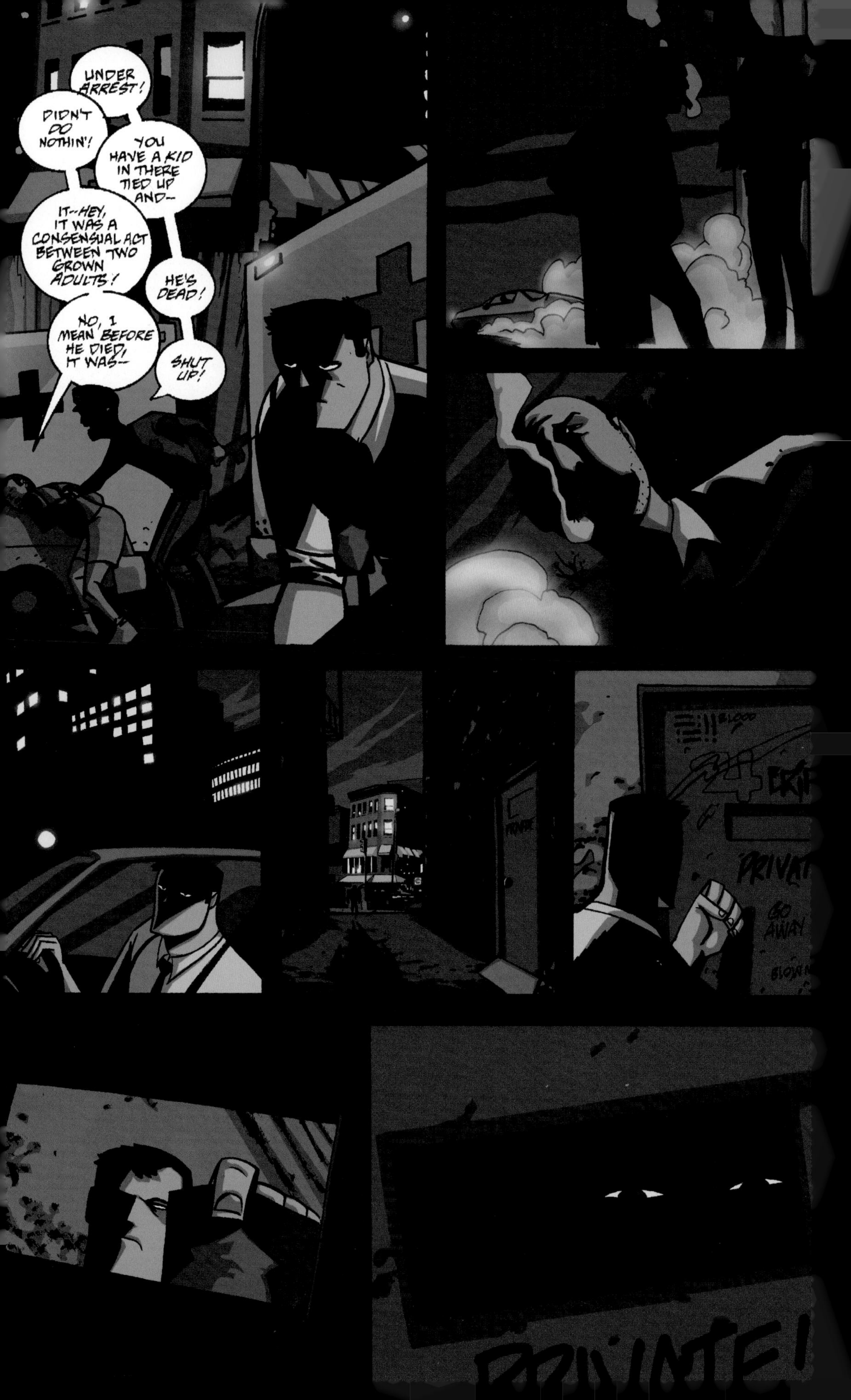
UNDER ARREST!
DIDN'T DO NOTHIN'!
YOU HAVE A KID IN THERE TIED UP AND--
IT--HEY, IT WAS A CONSENSUAL ACT BETWEEN TWO GROWN ADULTS!
HE'S DEAD!
NO, I MEAN BEFORE HE DIED, IT WAS--
SHUT UP!
GO AWAY

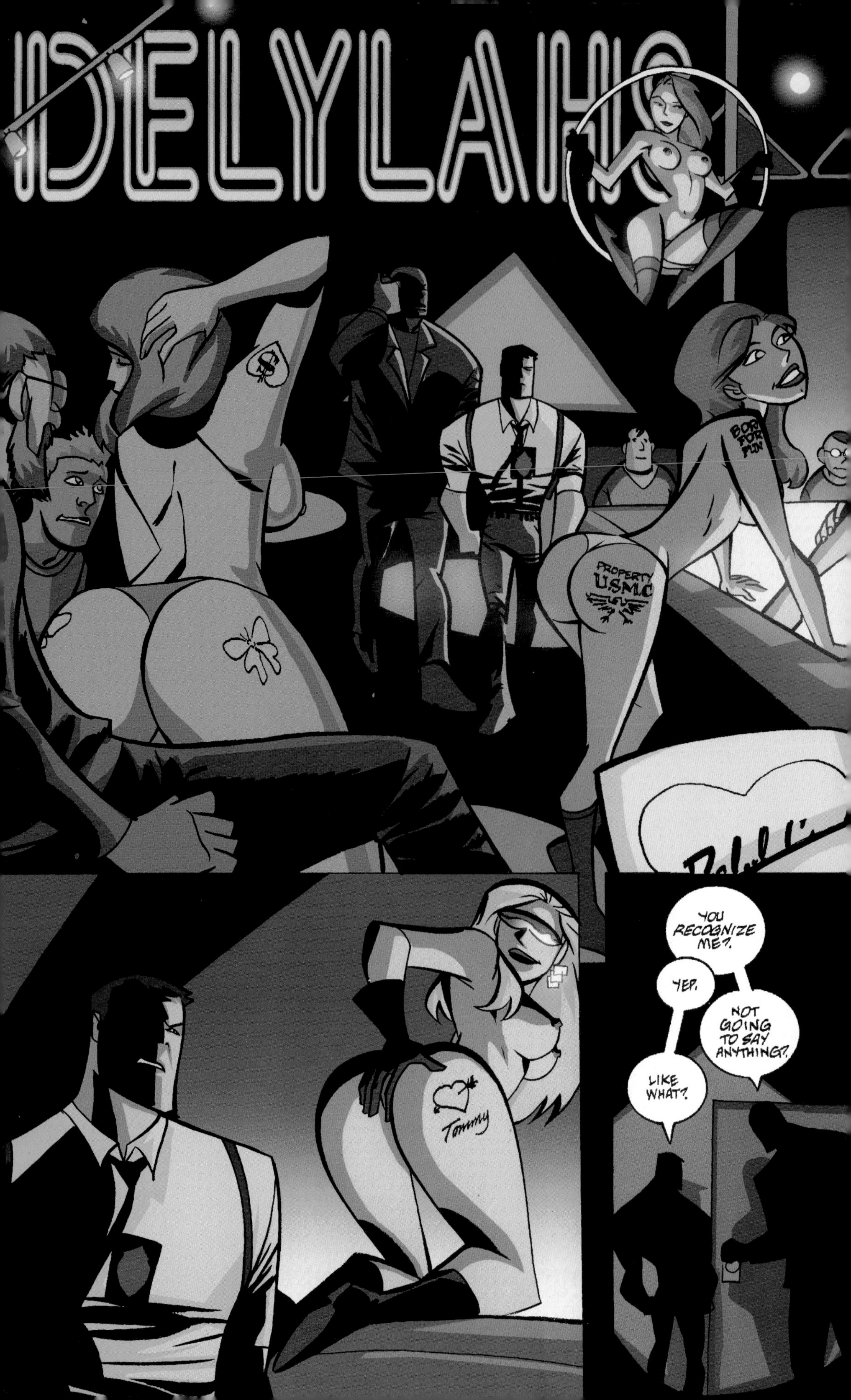
DELYLAHS
$
BORN FOR FUN
PROPERTY U.S.M.C
Tommy
YOU RECOGNIZE ME?
YEP.
NOT GOING TO SAY ANYTHING?
LIKE WHAT?

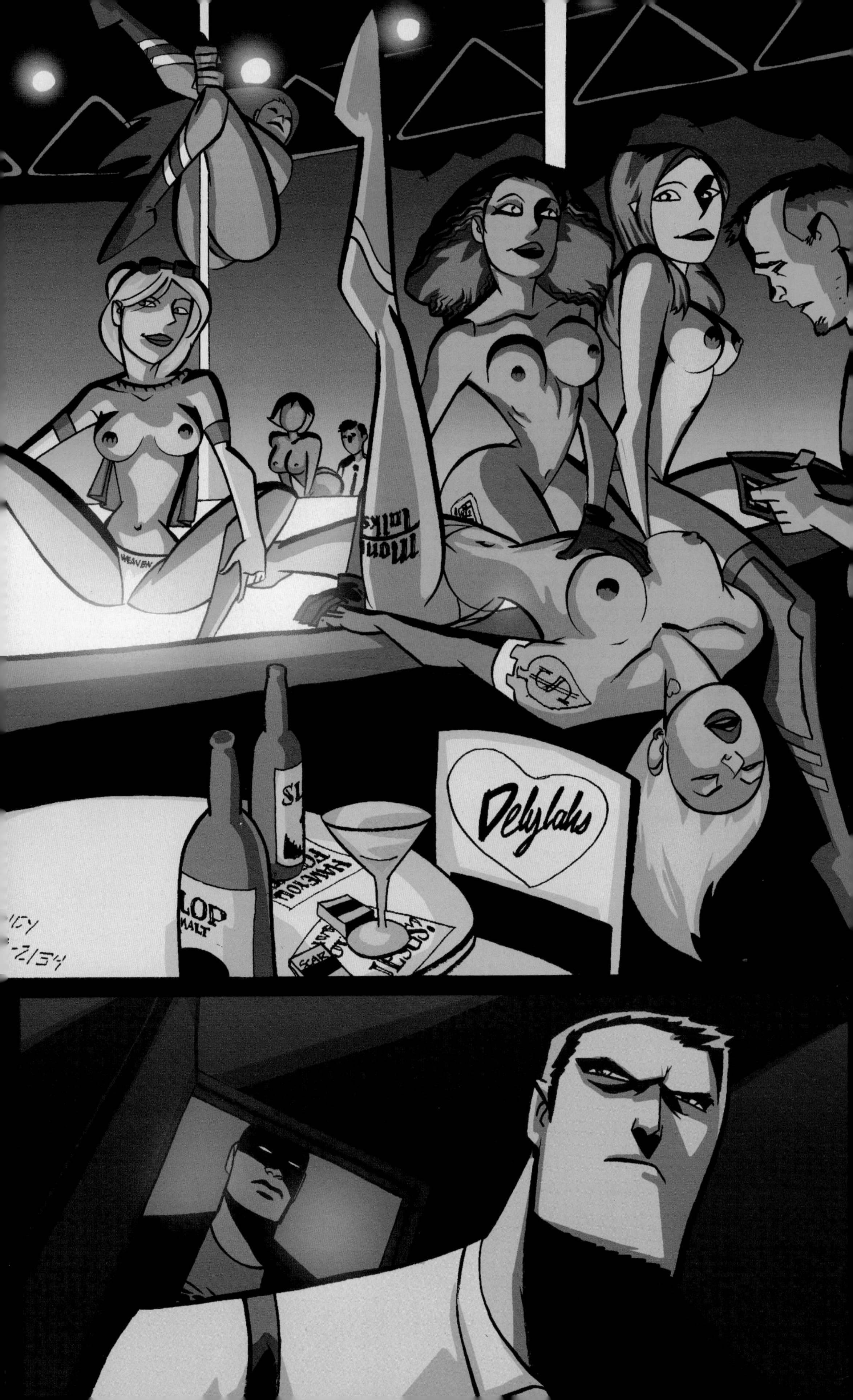

WEAVEN
Delylahs
LOP
MALT

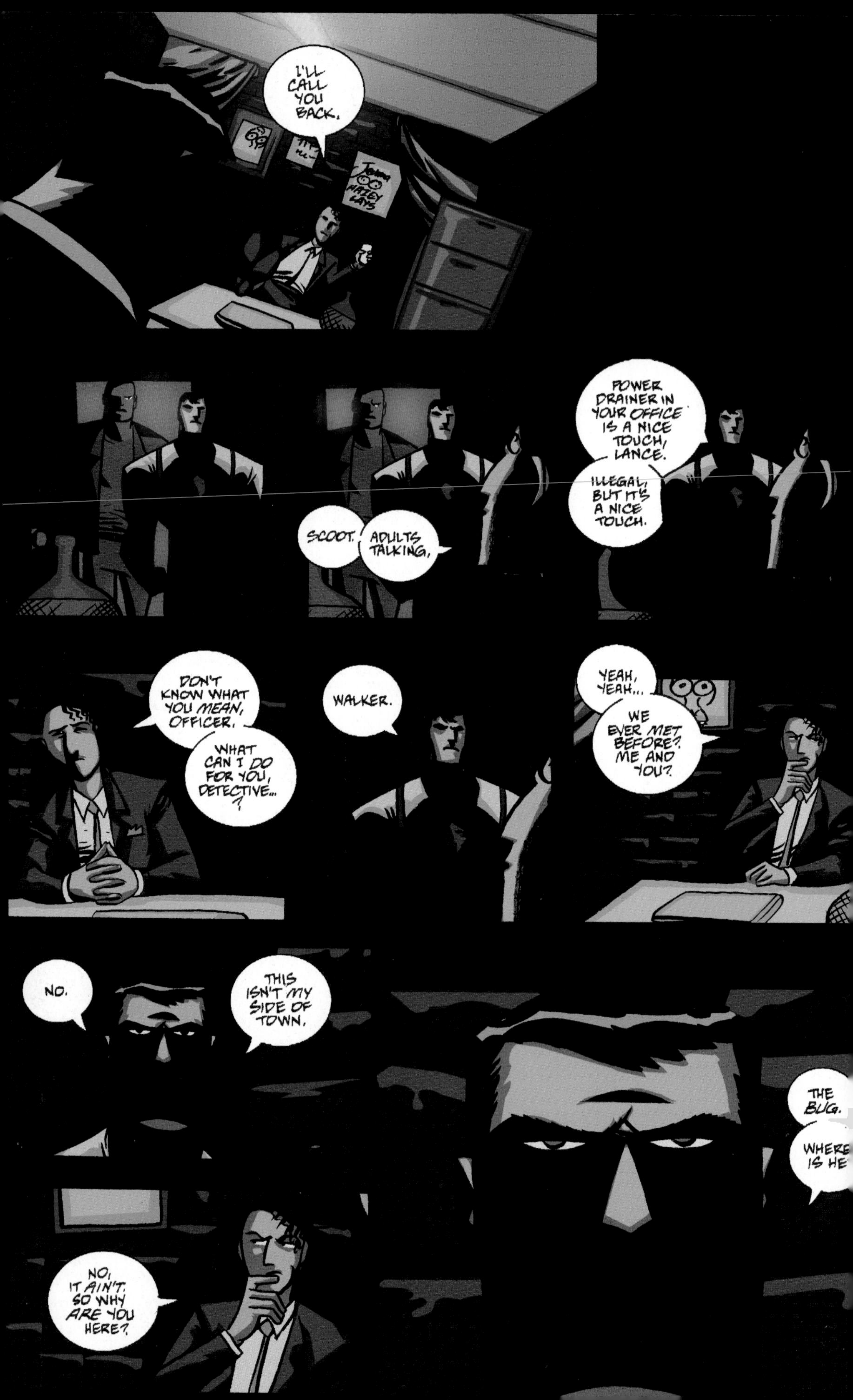

I'LL CALL YOU BACK.
SCOOT.
ADULTS TALKING.
POWER DRAINER IN YOUR OFFICE IS A NICE TOUCH, LANCE.
ILLEGAL, BUT IT'S A NICE TOUCH.
DON'T KNOW WHAT YOU MEAN, OFFICER.
WHAT CAN I DO FOR YOU, DETECTIVE...?
WALKER.
YEAH, YEAH...
WE EVER MET BEFORE? ME AND YOU?
NO.
THIS ISN'T MY SIDE OF TOWN.
NO, IT AIN'T. SO WHY ARE YOU HERE?
THE BUG.

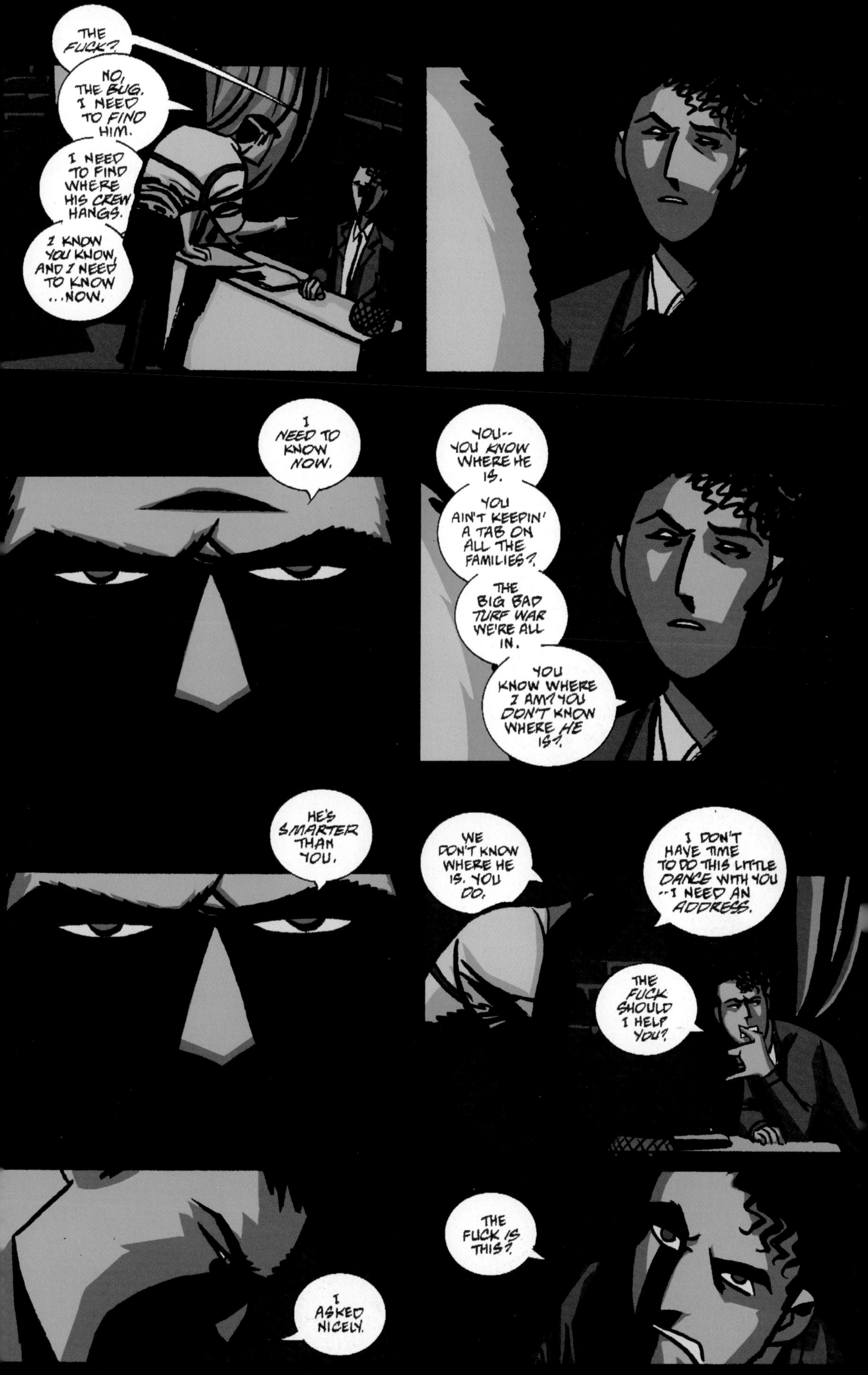
THE FUCK?
NO, THE BUG. I NEED TO FIND HIM.
I NEED TO FIND WHERE HIS CREW HANGS.
I KNOW YOU KNOW, AND I NEED TO KNOW ...NOW.
I NEED TO KNOW NOW.
YOU-- YOU KNOW WHERE HE IS.
YOU AIN'T KEEPIN' A TAB ON ALL THE FAMILIES?
THE BIG BAD TURF WAR WE'RE ALL IN.
YOU KNOW WHERE I AM? YOU DON'T KNOW WHERE HE IS?
HE'S SMARTER THAN YOU.
WE DON'T KNOW WHERE HE IS. YOU DO.
I DON'T HAVE TIME TO DO THIS LITTLE DANCE WITH YOU --I NEED AN ADDRESS.
THE FUCK SHOULD I HELP YOU?
THE FUCK IS THIS?
I ASKED NICELY.

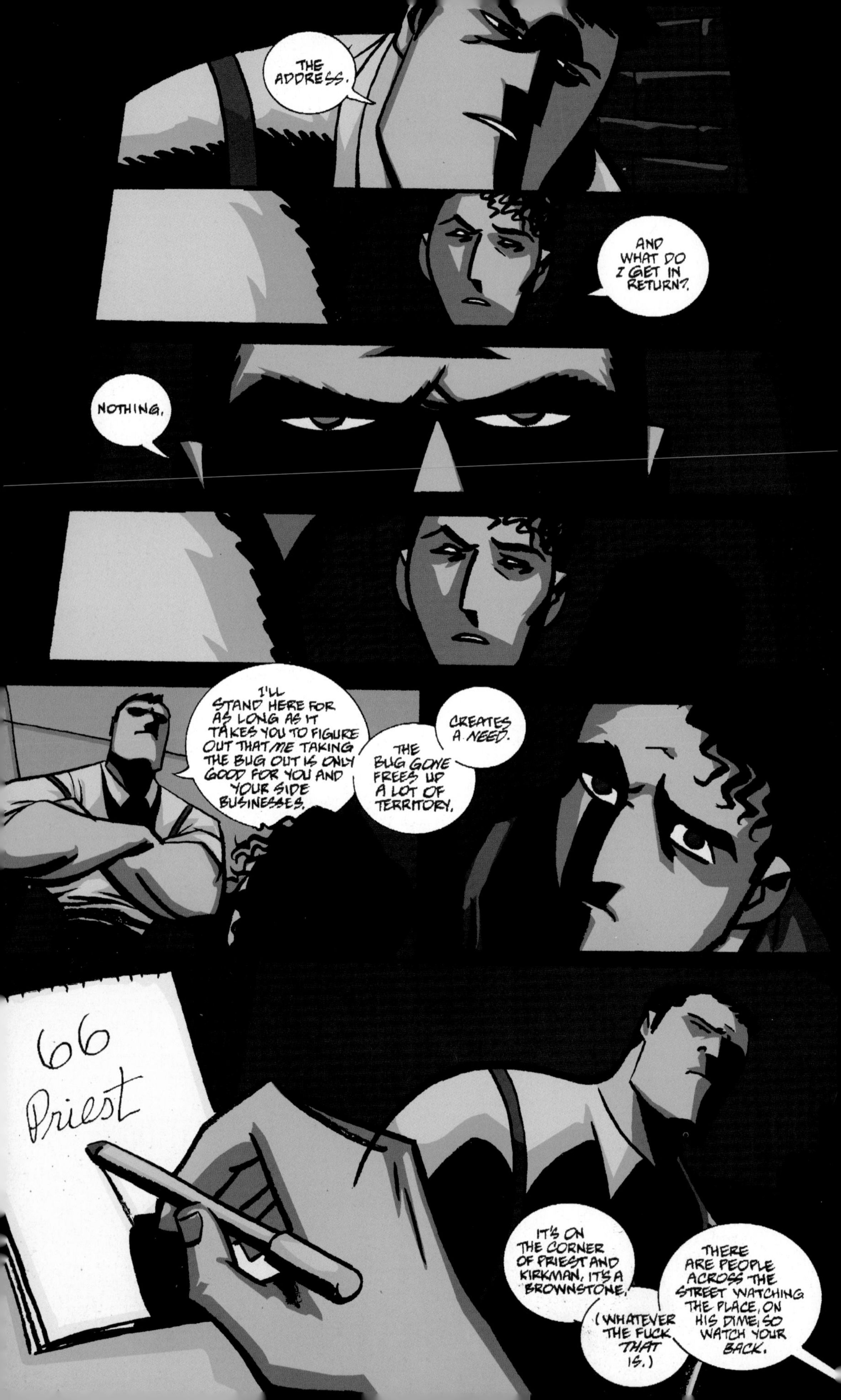

THE ADDRESS.
AND WHAT DO I GET IN RETURN?
NOTHING.
I'LL STAND HERE FOR AS LONG AS IT TAKES YOU TO FIGURE OUT THAT ME TAKING THE BUG OUT IS ONLY GOOD FOR YOU AND YOUR SIDE BUSINESSES.
THE BUG GONE FREES UP A LOT OF TERRITORY.
CREATES A NEED.
66 Priest
IT'S ON THE CORNER OF PRIEST AND KIRKMAN. IT'S A BROWNSTONE.
(WHATEVER THE FUCK THAT IS.)
THERE ARE PEOPLE ACROSS THE STREET WATCHING THE PLACE, ON HIS DIME, SO WATCH YOUR BACK.

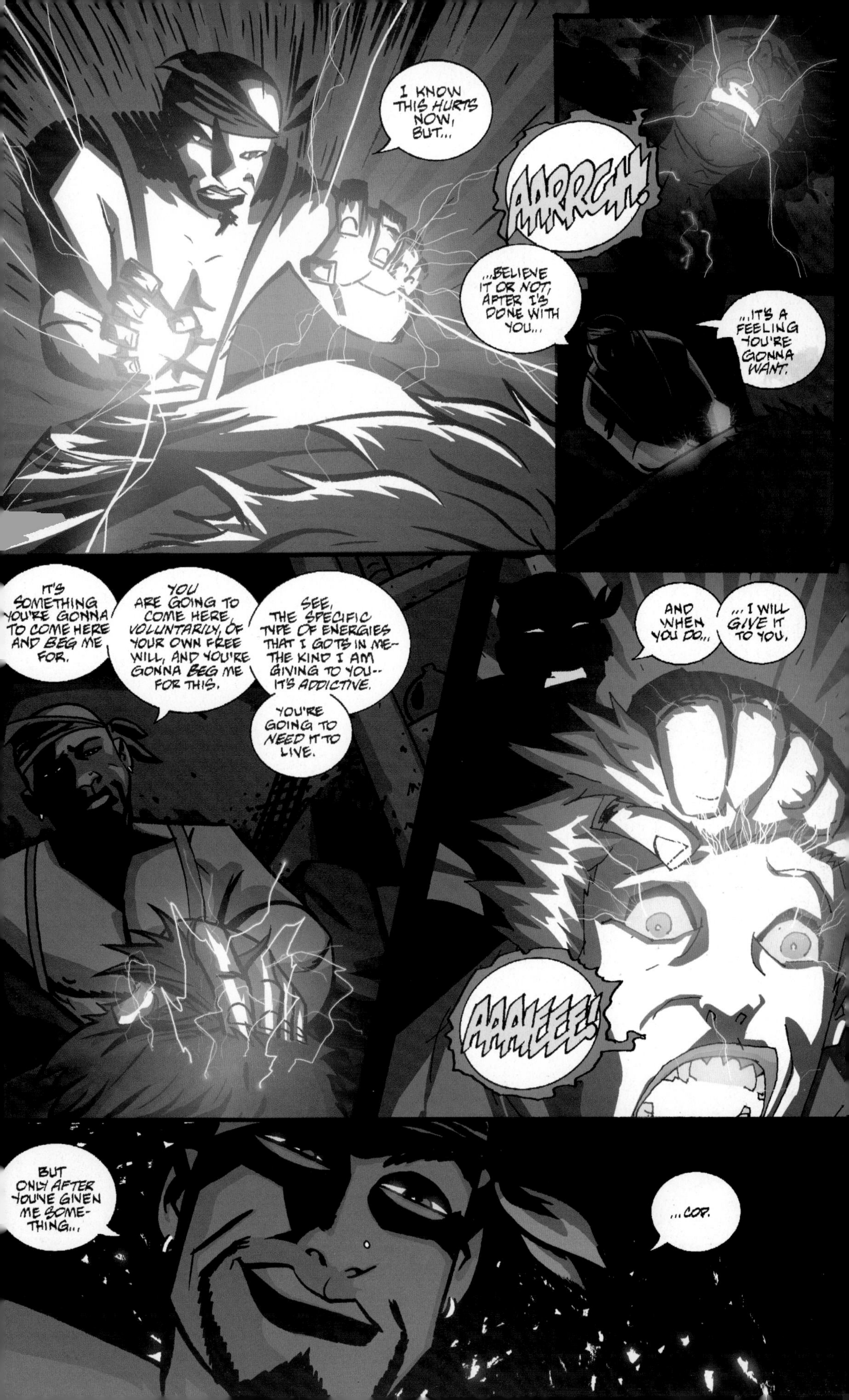
I KNOW THIS HURTS NOW, BUT...
AARRGH!
...BELIEVE IT OR NOT, AFTER I'S DONE WITH YOU...
...IT'S A FEELING YOU'RE GONNA WANT.
IT'S SOMETHING YOU'RE GONNA TO COME HERE AND BEG ME FOR.
YOU ARE GOING TO COME HERE, VOLUNTARILY, OF YOUR OWN FREE WILL, AND YOU'RE GONNA BEG ME FOR THIS.
SEE, THE SPECIFIC TYPE OF ENERGIES THAT I GOTS IN ME-- THE KIND I AM GIVING TO YOU-- IT'S ADDICTIVE.
YOU'RE GOING TO NEED IT TO LIVE.
AND WHEN YOU DO...
...I WILL GIVE IT TO YOU.
AAAIEEE!
BUT ONLY AFTER YOU'VE GIVEN ME SOME-THING...
...COP.

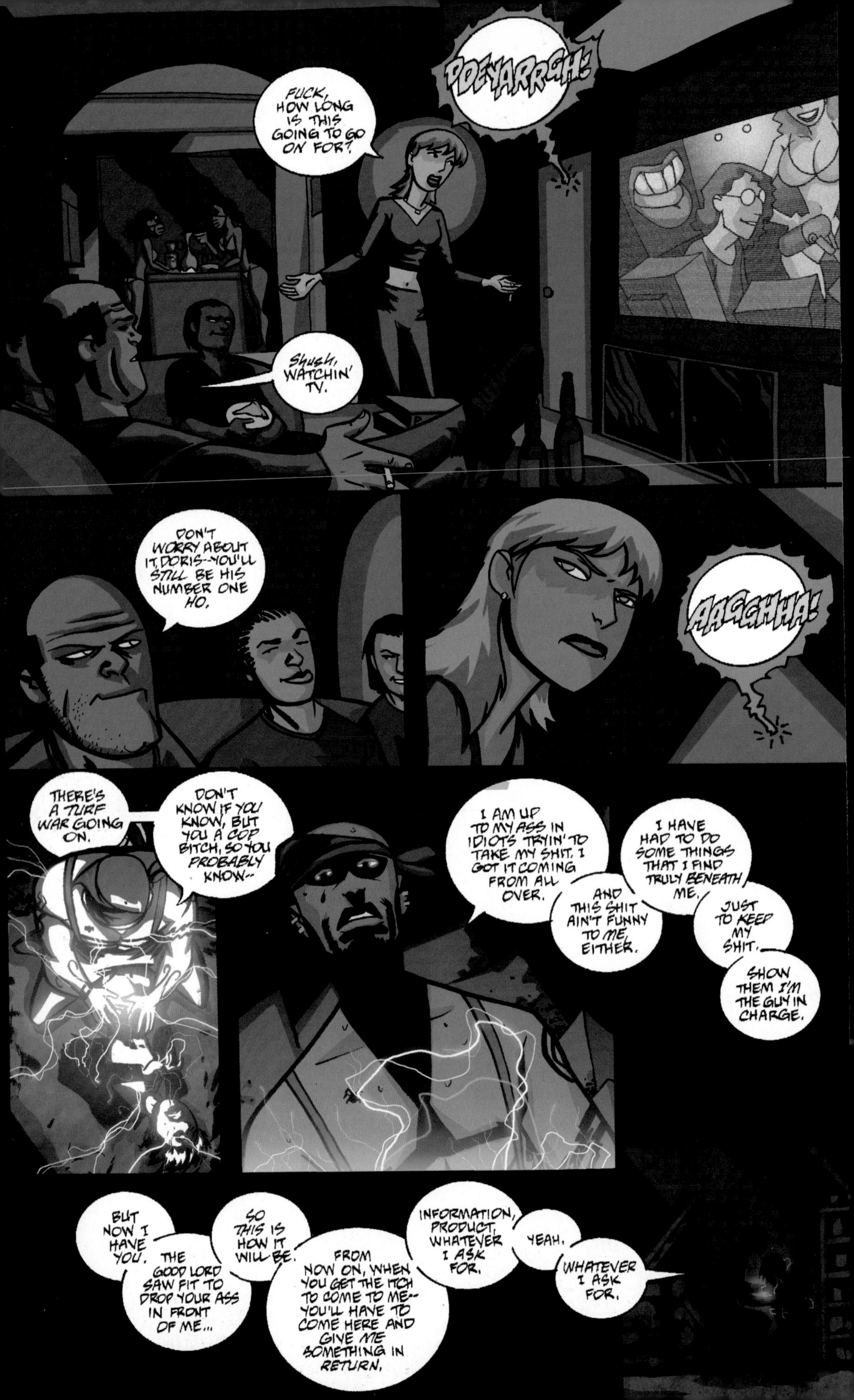

FUCK, HOW LONG IS THIS GOING TO GO ON FOR?
PDEYARRGH!
SHUSH, WATCHIN' TV.
DON'T WORRY ABOUT IT, DORIS--YOU'LL STILL BE HIS NUMBER ONE HO.
AAGGHHA!
THERE'S A TURF WAR GOING ON.
DON'T KNOW IF YOU KNOW, BUT YOU A COP BITCH, SO YOU PROBABLY KNOW--
I AM UP TO MY ASS IN IDIOTS TRYIN' TO TAKE MY SHIT. I GOT IT COMING FROM ALL OVER.
AND THIS SHIT AIN'T FUNNY TO ME, EITHER.
I HAVE HAD TO DO SOME THINGS THAT I FIND TRULY BENEATH ME,
JUST TO KEEP MY SHIT.
SHOW THEM I'M THE GUY IN CHARGE.
BUT NOW I HAVE YOU.
THE GOOD LORD SAW FIT TO DROP YOUR ASS IN FRONT OF ME...
SO THIS IS HOW IT WILL BE.
FROM NOW ON, WHEN YOU GET THE ITCH TO COME TO ME--YOU'LL HAVE TO COME HERE AND GIVE ME SOMETHING IN RETURN.
INFORMATION, PRODUCT, WHATEVER I ASK FOR.
YEAH.
WHATEVER I ASK FOR.

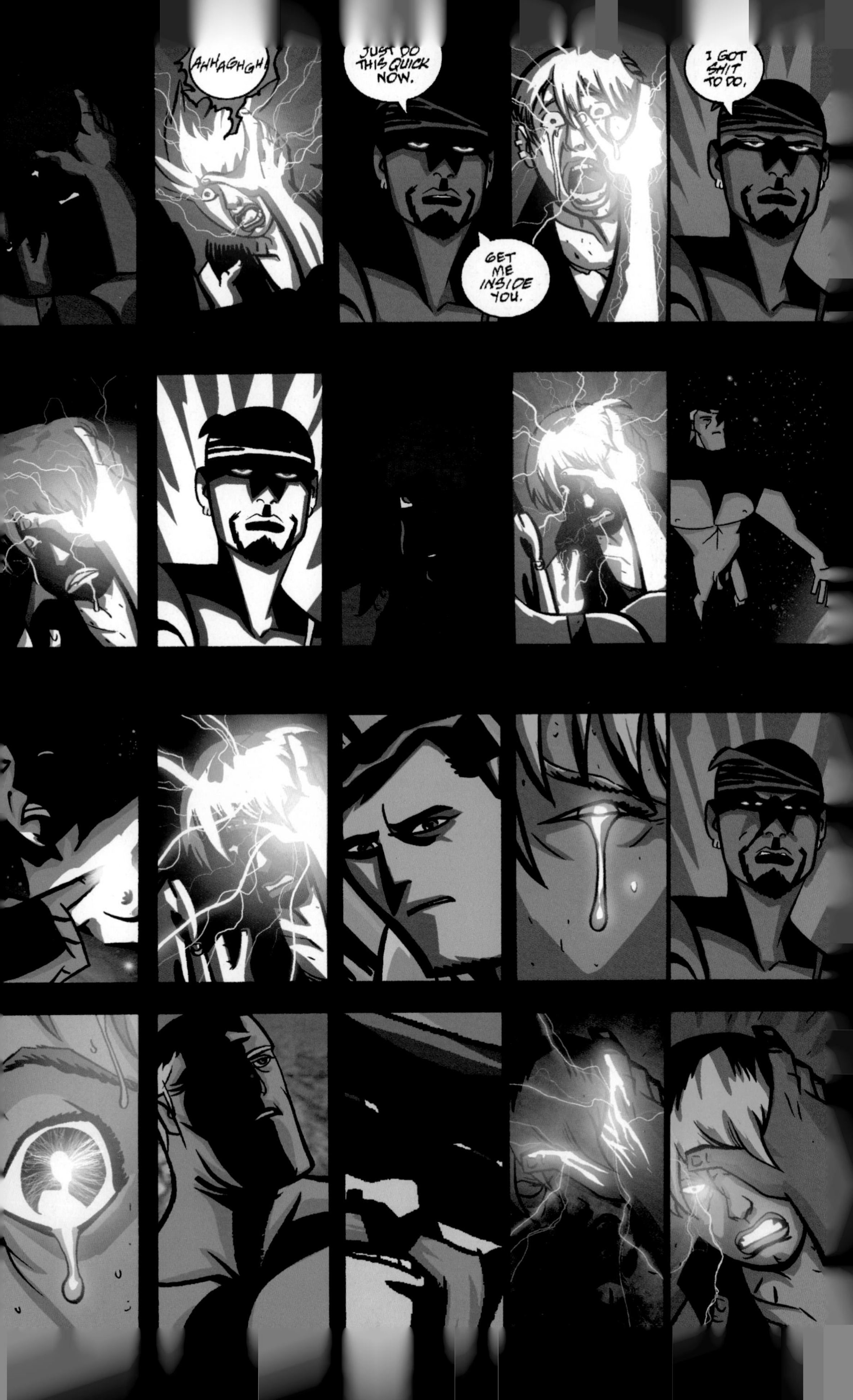
AHHAGHGH!
JUST DO THIS QUICK NOW.
GET ME INSIDE YOU.
I GOT SHIT TO DO.

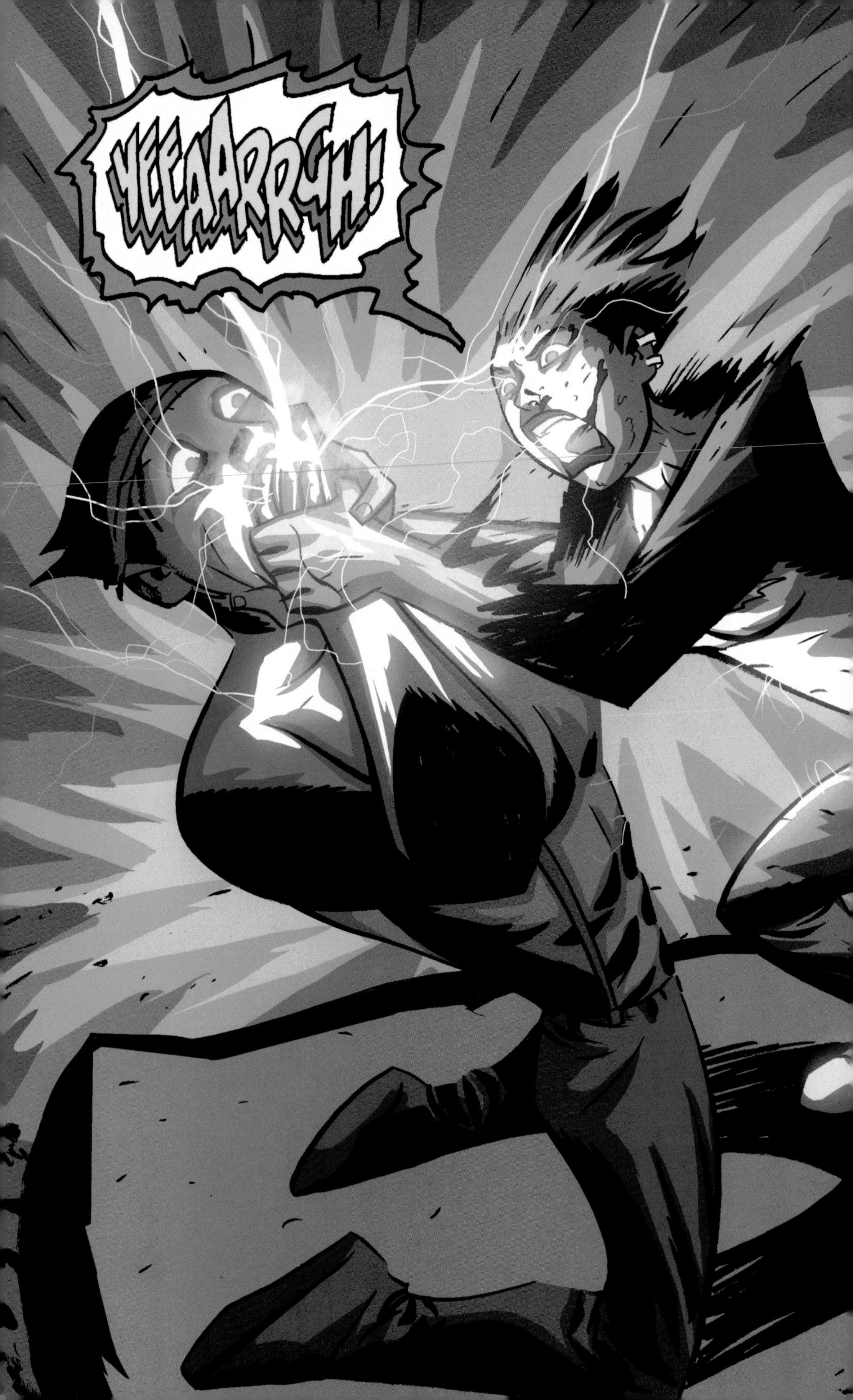
YEEAARRGH!

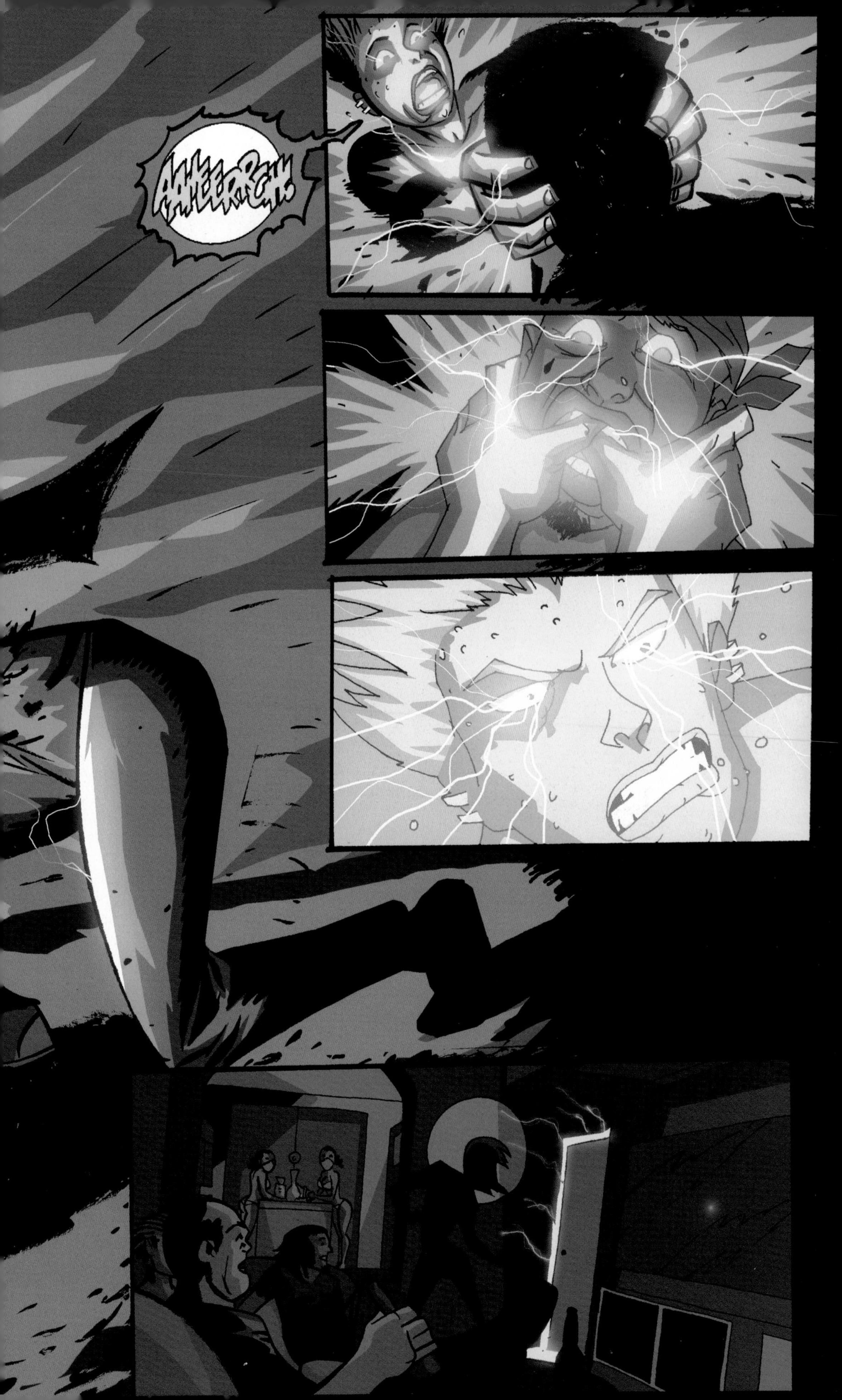
AAHEERRGH!

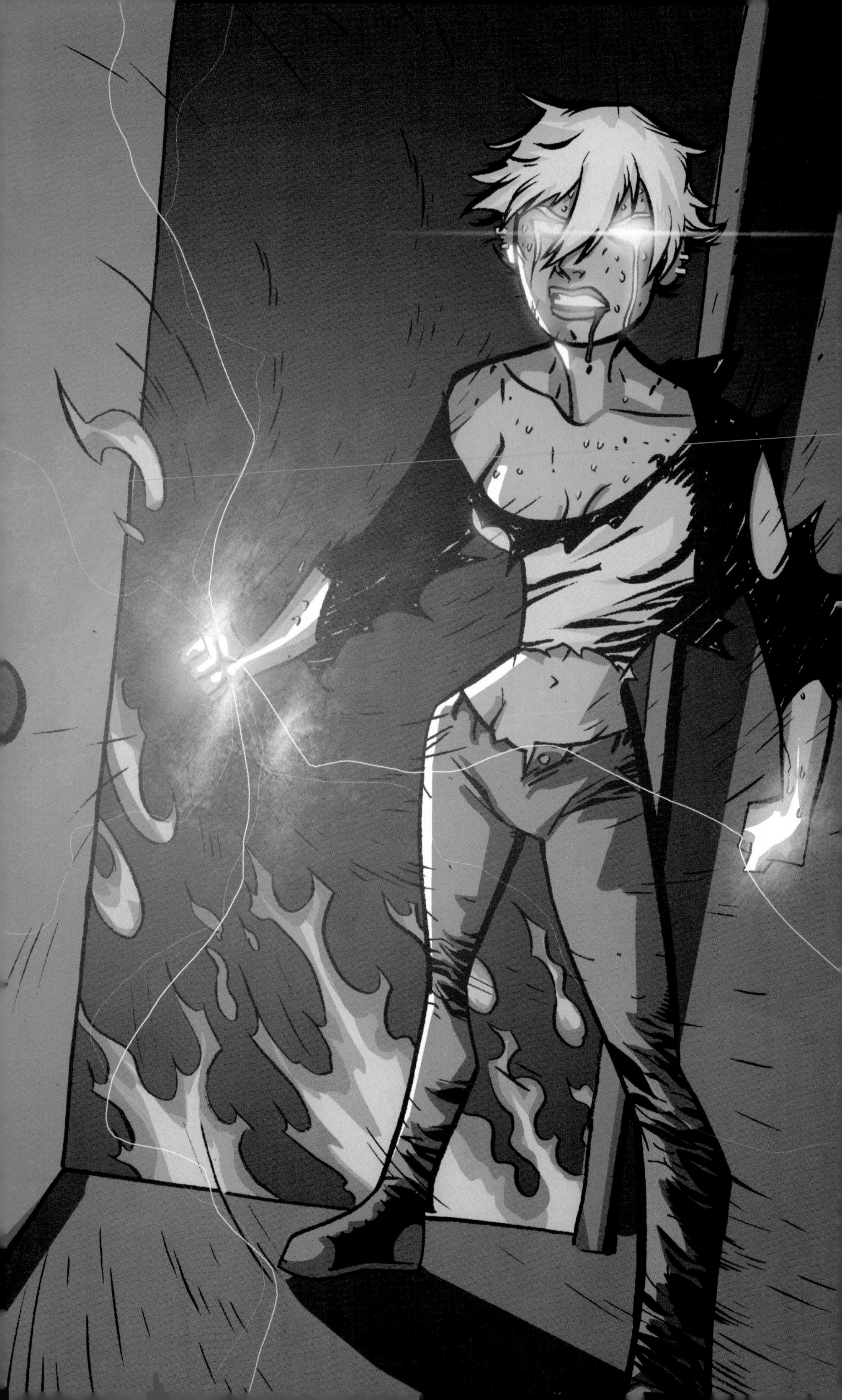

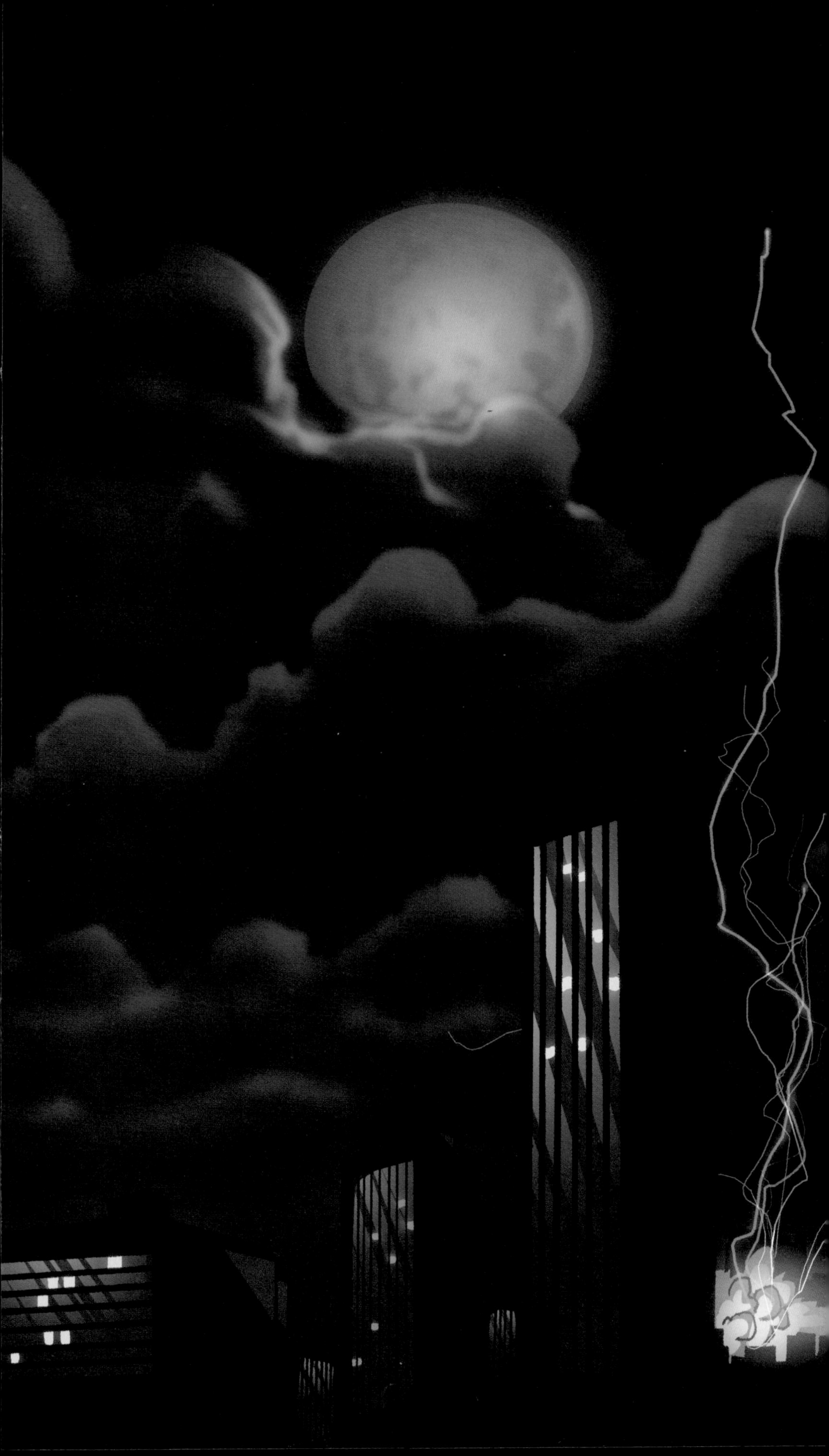

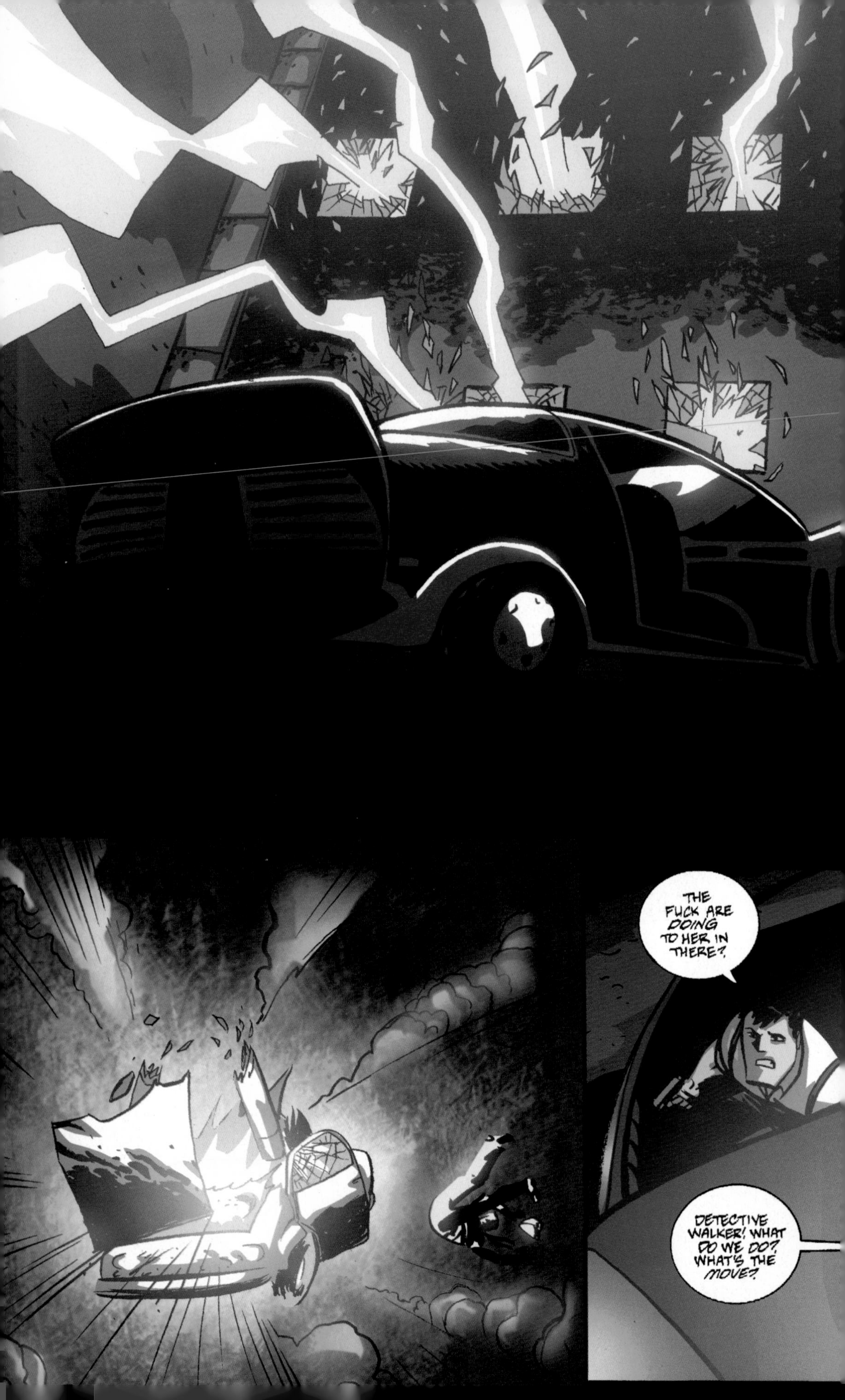
THE FUCK ARE DOING TO HER IN THERE?
DETECTIVE WALKER! WHAT DO WE DO? WHAT'S THE MOVE?

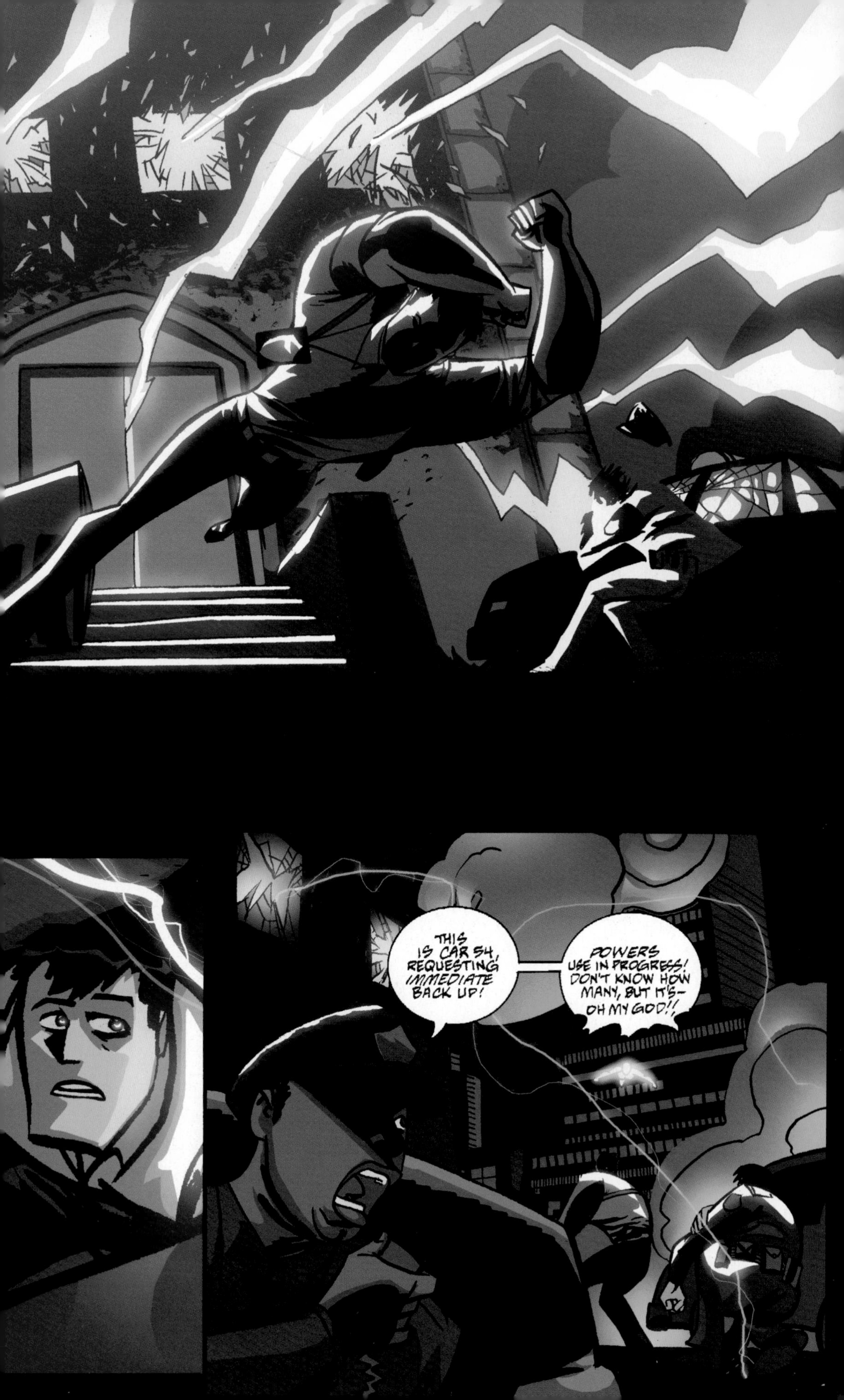
THIS IS CAR 54, REQUESTING IMMEDIATE BACK UP!
POWERS USE IN PROGRESS! DON'T KNOW HOW MANY, BUT IT'S— OH MY GOD!!

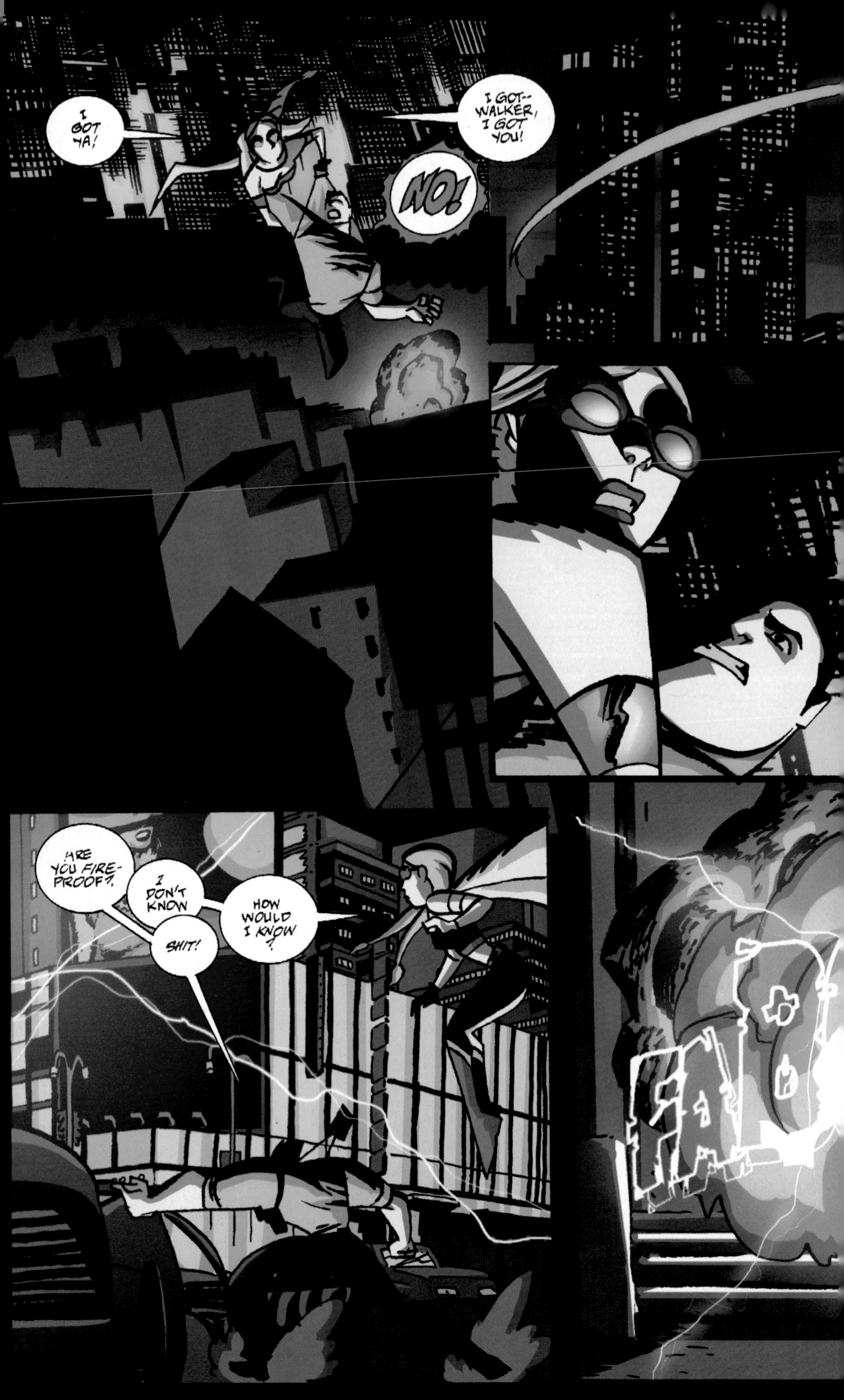
I GOT YA!
I GOT-- WALKER, I GOT YOU!
NO!
ARE YOU FIRE-PROOF?
I DON'T KNOW
SHIT!
HOW WOULD I KNOW ?

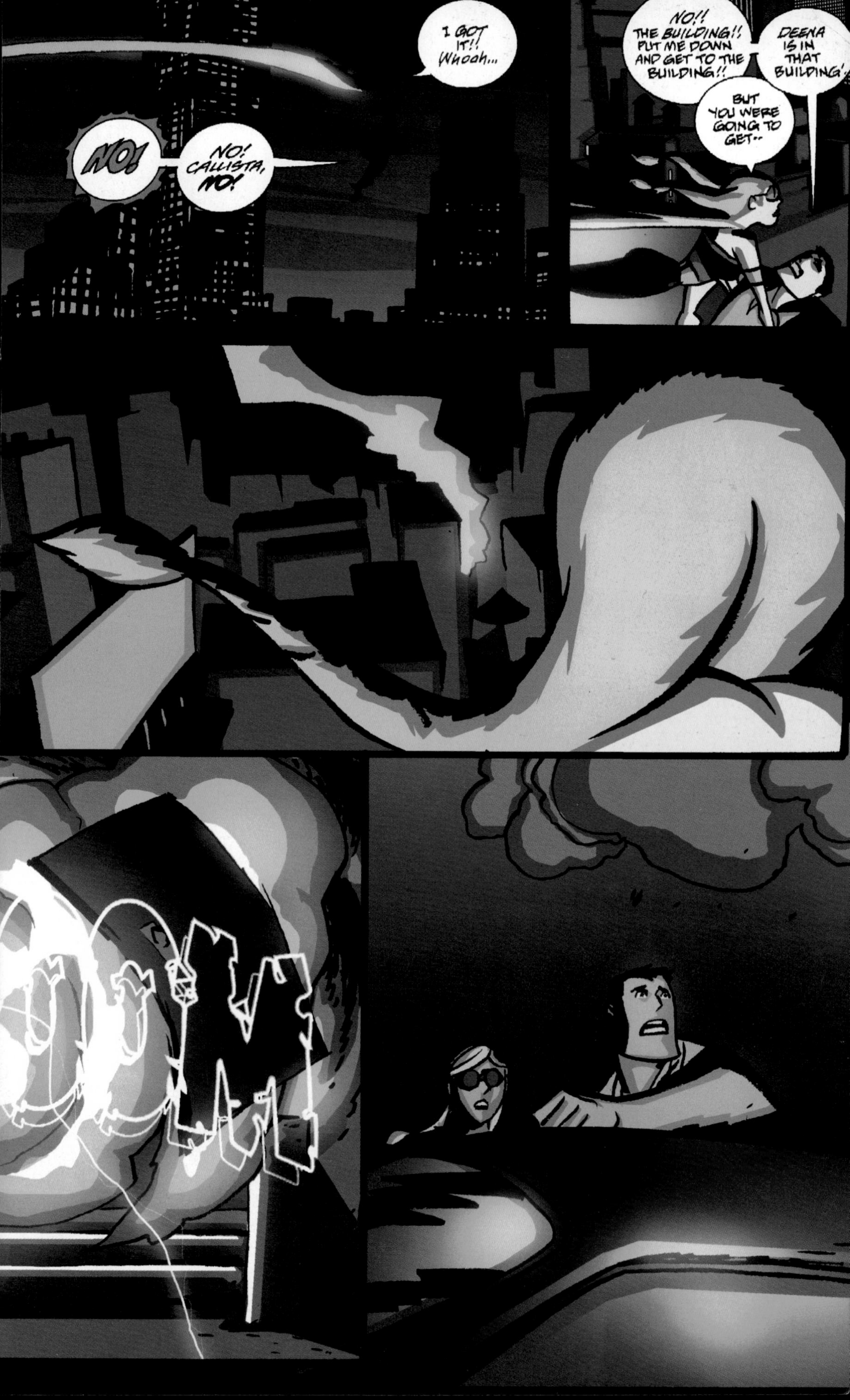
I GOT IT!! Whoah...
NO!
NO! CALLISTA, NO!
NO!! THE BUILDING!! PUT ME DOWN AND GET TO THE BUILDING!!
DEENA IS IN THAT BUILDING!
BUT YOU WERE GOING TO GET--

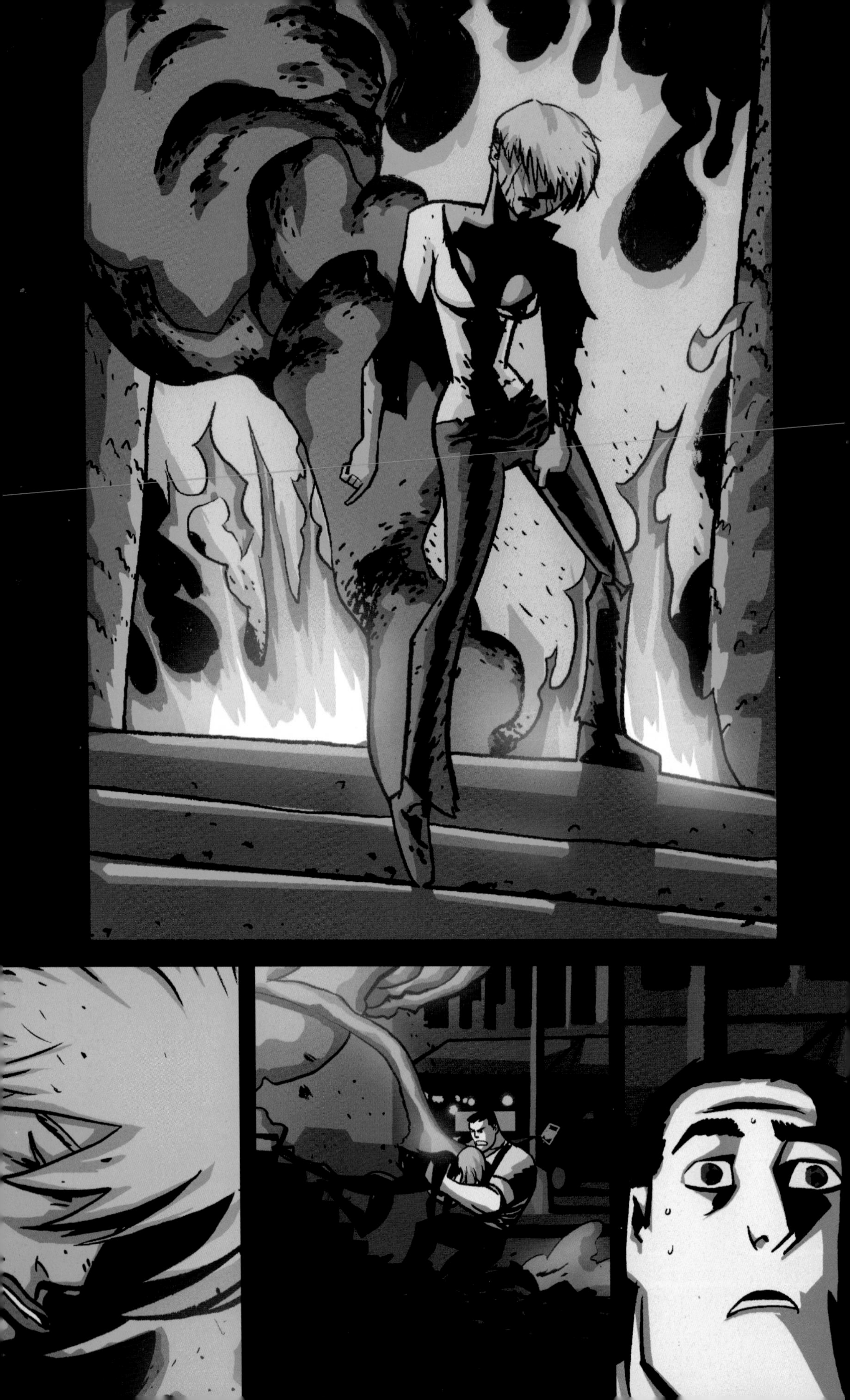

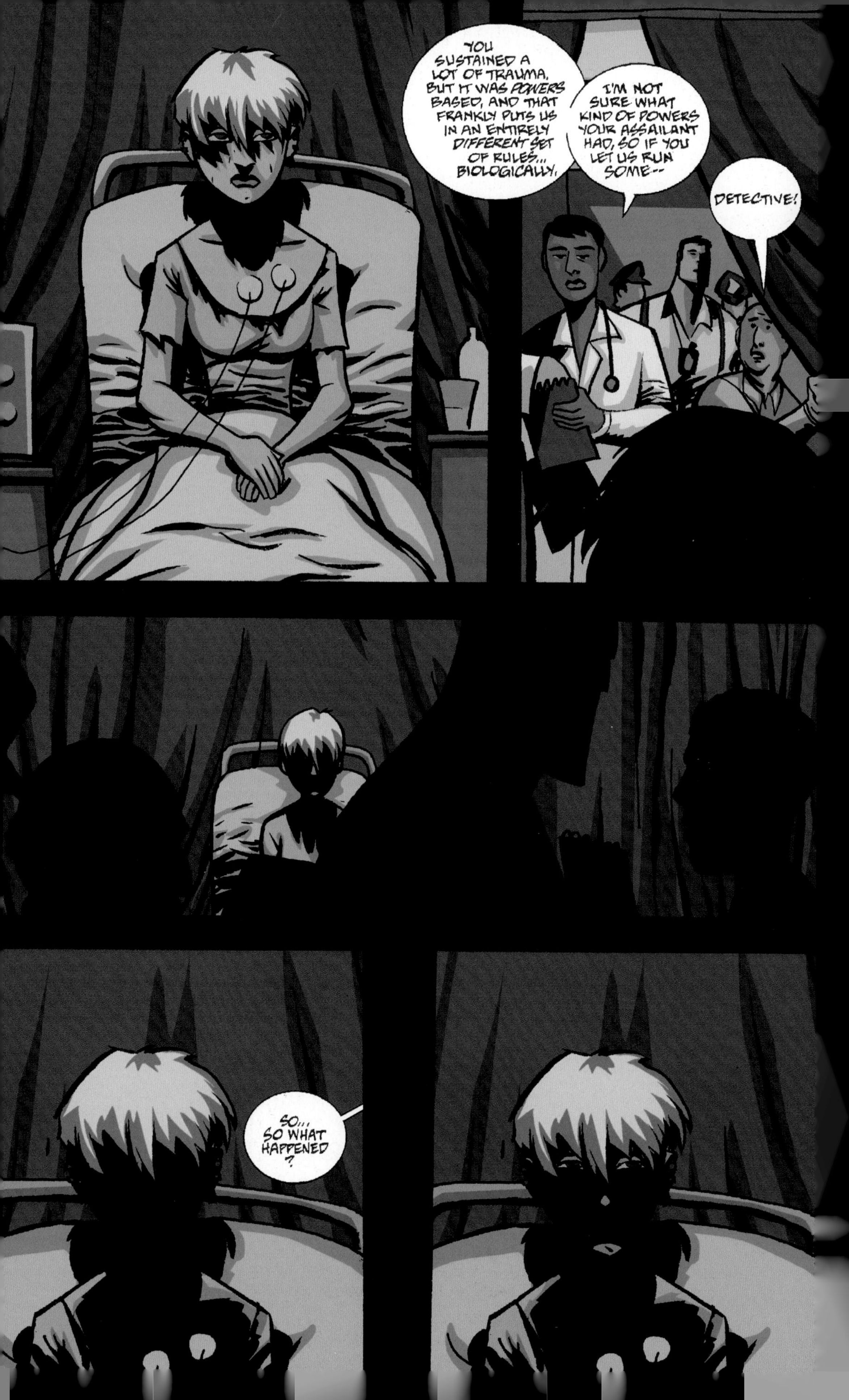
YOU SUSTAINED A LOT OF TRAUMA, BUT IT WAS POWERS BASED, AND THAT FRANKLY PUTS US IN AN ENTIRELY DIFFERENT SET OF RULES... BIOLOGICALLY.
I'M NOT SURE WHAT KIND OF POWERS YOUR ASSAILANT HAD, SO IF YOU LET US RUN SOME--
DETECTIVE!
SO... SO WHAT HAPPENED?

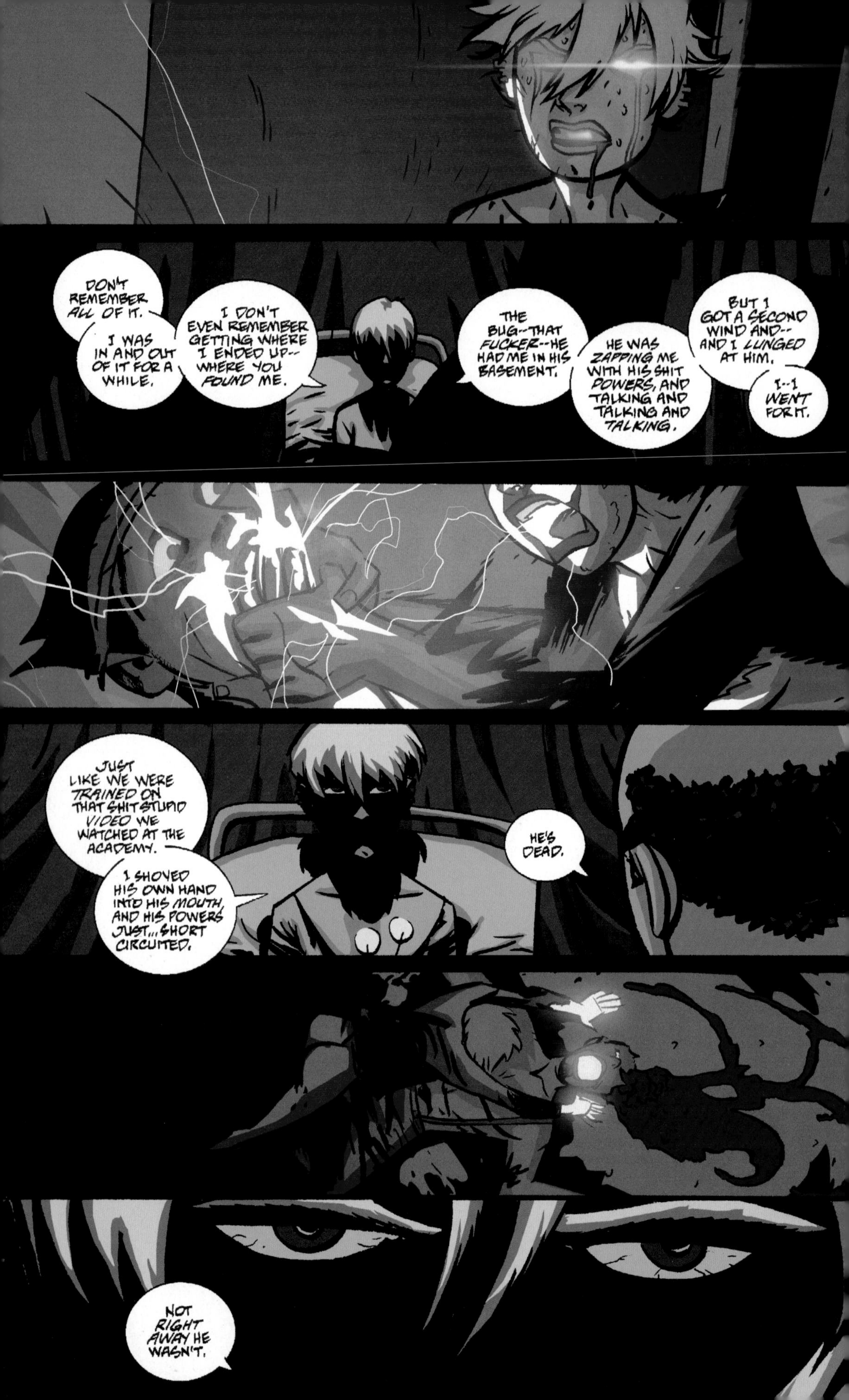
DON'T REMEMBER ALL OF IT.
I WAS IN AND OUT OF IT FOR A WHILE.
I DON'T EVEN REMEMBER GETTING WHERE I ENDED UP-- WHERE YOU FOUND ME.
THE BUG--THAT FUCKER--HE HAD ME IN HIS BASEMENT.
HE WAS ZAPPING ME WITH HIS SHIT POWERS, AND TALKING AND TALKING AND TALKING.
BUT I GOT A SECOND WIND AND-- AND I LUNGED AT HIM.
I--I WENT FOR IT.
JUST LIKE WE WERE TRAINED ON THAT SHITSTUPID VIDEO WE WATCHED AT THE ACADEMY.
I SHOVED HIS OWN HAND INTO HIS MOUTH, AND HIS POWERS JUST... SHORT CIRCUITED.
HE'S DEAD.
NOT RIGHT AWAY HE WASN'T.

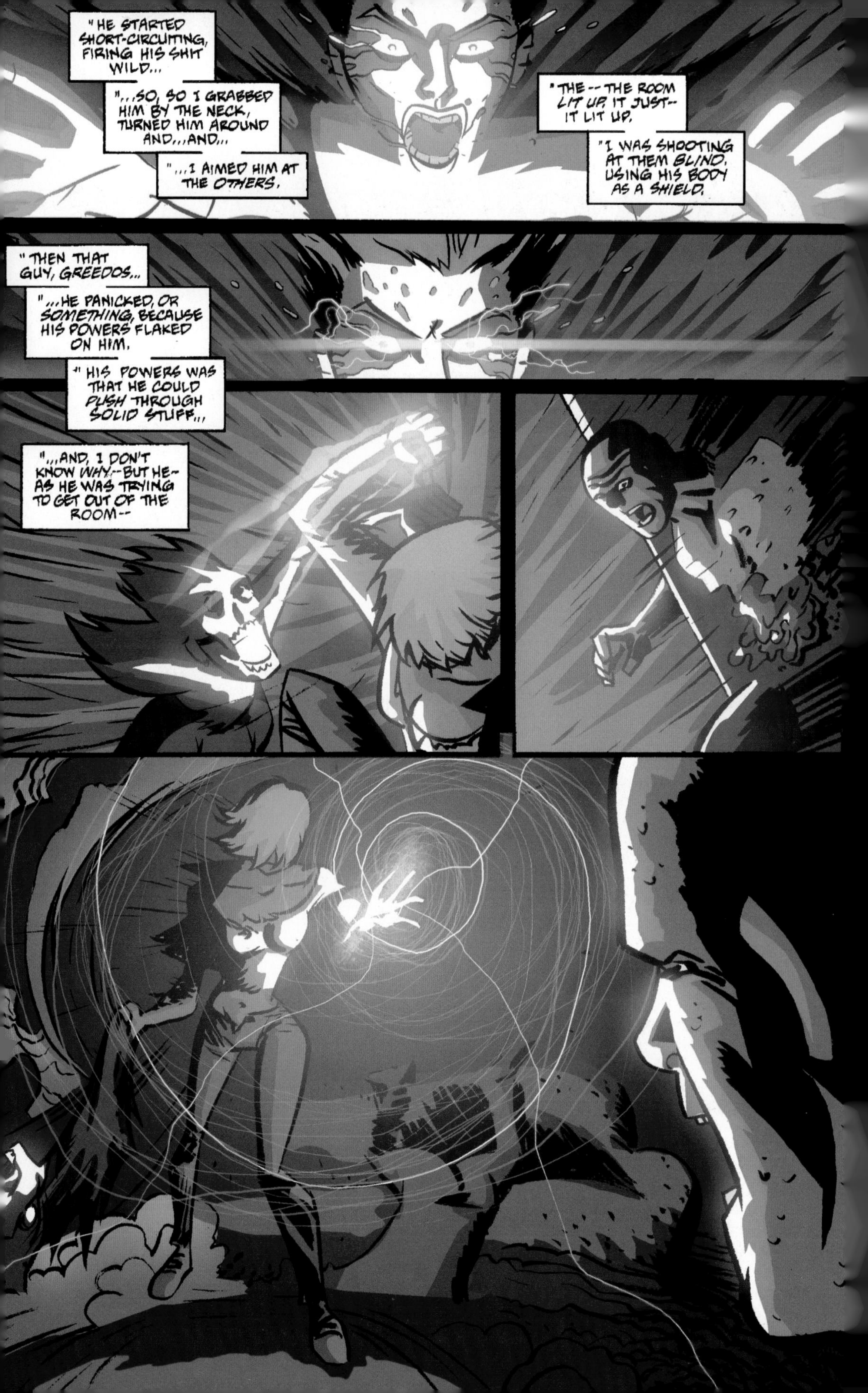
"HE STARTED SHORT-CIRCUITING, FIRING HIS SHIT WILD...
"...SO, SO I GRABBED HIM BY THE NECK, TURNED HIM AROUND AND...AND...
"...I AIMED HIM AT THE OTHERS.
"THE -- THE ROOM LIT UP. IT JUST-- IT LIT UP.
"I WAS SHOOTING AT THEM BLIND, USING HIS BODY AS A SHIELD.
"THEN THAT GUY, GREEDOS...
"...HE PANICKED, OR SOMETHING, BECAUSE HIS POWERS FLAKED ON HIM.
"HIS POWERS WAS THAT HE COULD PUSH THROUGH SOLID STUFF...
"...AND, I DON'T KNOW WHY--BUT HE-- AS HE WAS TRYING TO GET OUT OF THE ROOM--

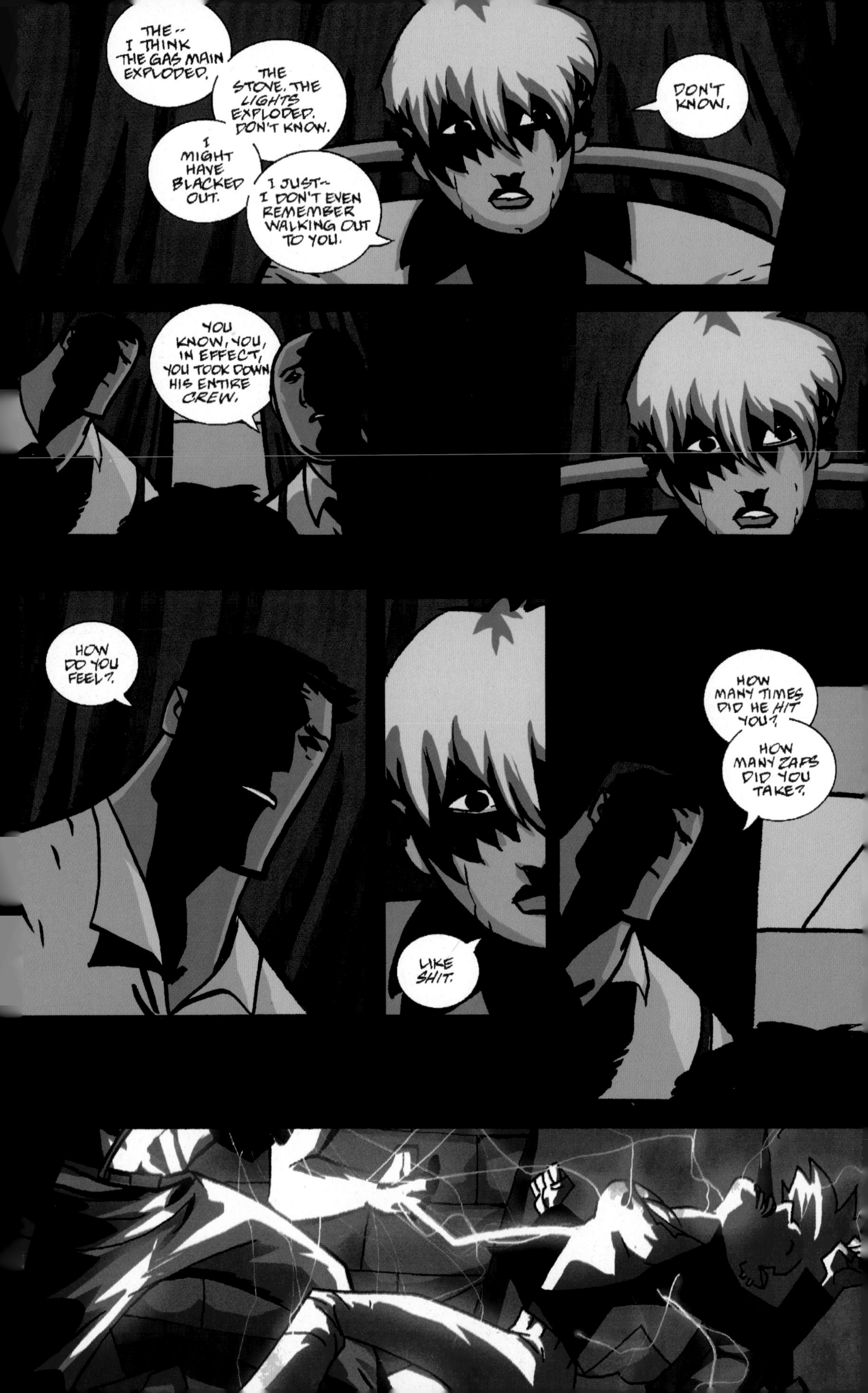
THE-- I THINK THE GAS MAIN EXPLODED.
THE STOVE. THE LIGHTS EXPLODED. DON'T KNOW.
I MIGHT HAVE BLACKED OUT.
I JUST-- I DON'T EVEN REMEMBER WALKING OUT TO YOU.
DON'T KNOW.
YOU KNOW, YOU, IN EFFECT, YOU TOOK DOWN HIS ENTIRE CREW.
HOW DO YOU FEEL?
LIKE SHIT.
HOW MANY TIMES DID HE HIT YOU?
HOW MANY ZAPS DID YOU TAKE?

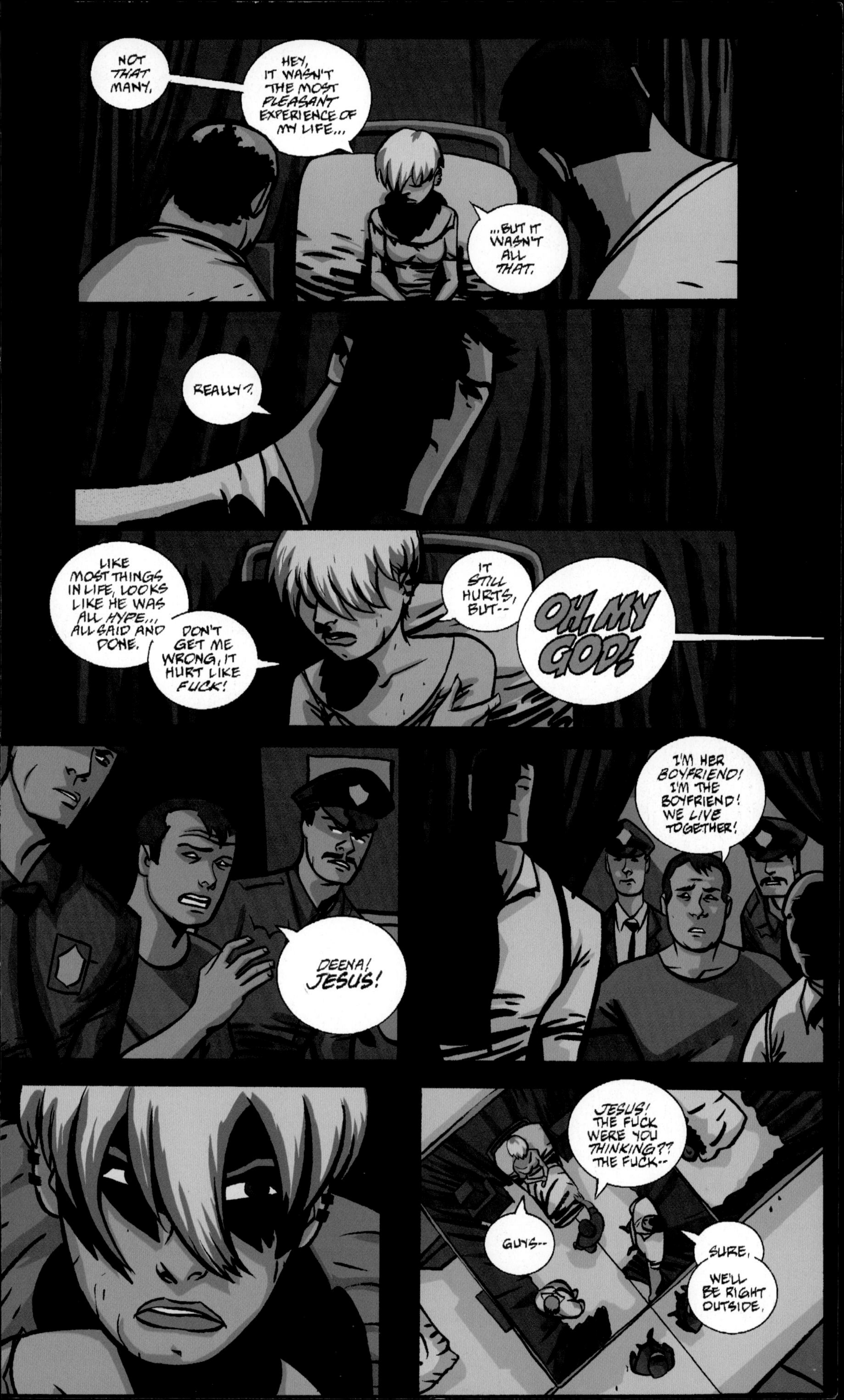
NOT THAT MANY.
HEY, IT WASN'T THE MOST PLEASANT EXPERIENCE OF MY LIFE...
...BUT IT WASN'T ALL THAT.
REALLY?
LIKE MOST THINGS IN LIFE, LOOKS LIKE HE WAS ALL HYPE... ALL SAID AND DONE.
DON'T GET ME WRONG, IT HURT LIKE FUCK!
IT STILL HURTS, BUT--
OH, MY GOD!
DEENA! JESUS!
I'M HER BOYFRIEND! I'M THE BOYFRIEND! WE LIVE TOGETHER!
JESUS! THE FUCK WERE YOU THINKING?? THE FUCK--
GUYS--
SURE. WE'LL BE RIGHT OUTSIDE.

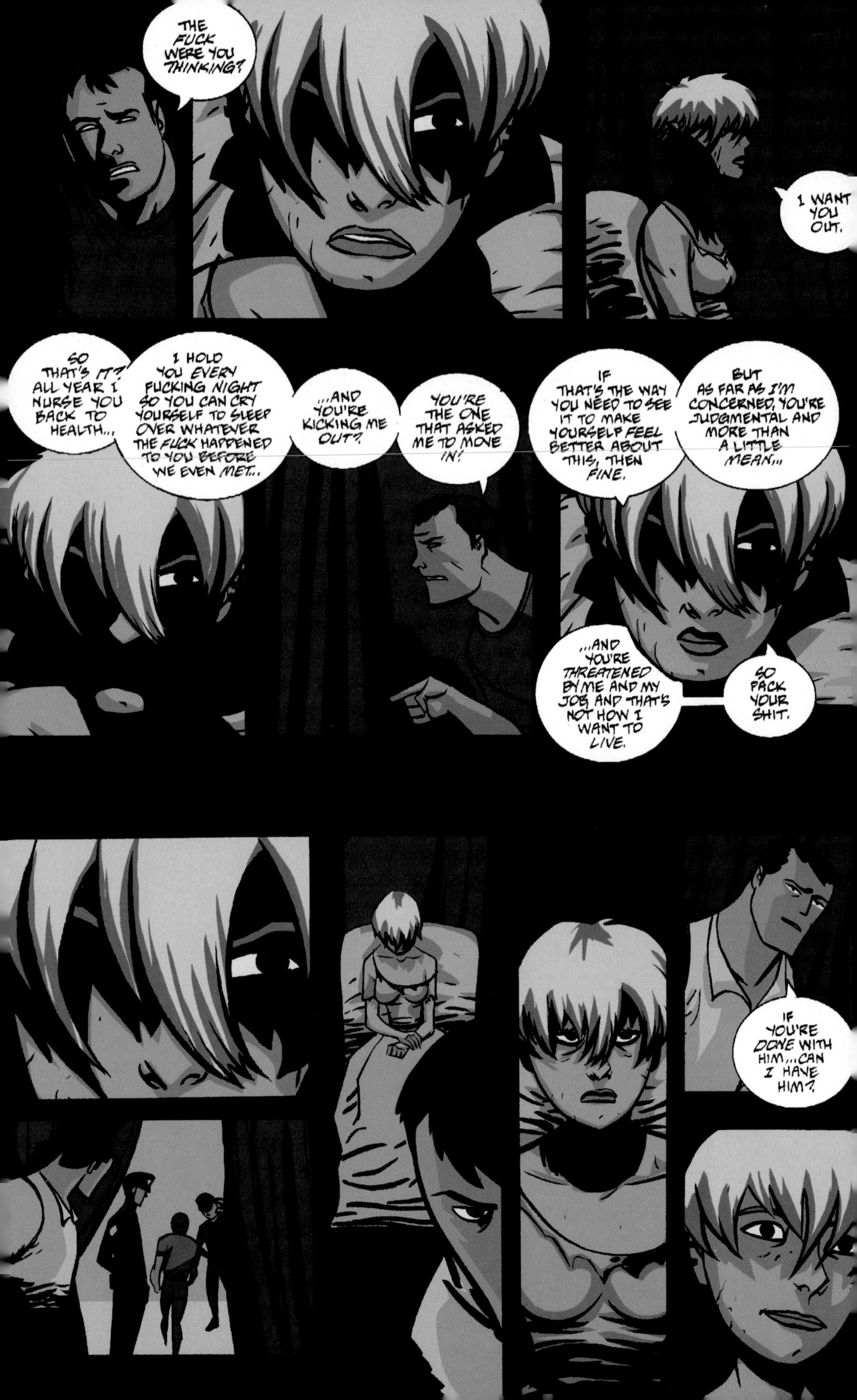
THE FUCK WERE YOU THINKING?
I WANT YOU OUT.
SO THAT'S IT? ALL YEAR I NURSE YOU BACK TO HEALTH...
I HOLD YOU EVERY FUCKING NIGHT SO YOU CAN CRY YOURSELF TO SLEEP OVER WHATEVER THE FUCK HAPPENED TO YOU BEFORE WE EVEN MET...
...AND YOU'RE KICKING ME OUT?
YOU'RE THE ONE THAT ASKED ME TO MOVE IN!
IF THAT'S THE WAY YOU NEED TO SEE IT TO MAKE YOURSELF FEEL BETTER ABOUT THIS, THEN FINE.
BUT AS FAR AS I'M CONCERNED, YOU'RE JUDGMENTAL AND MORE THAN A LITTLE MEAN...
...AND YOU'RE THREATENED BY ME AND MY JOB, AND THAT'S NOT HOW I WANT TO LIVE.
SO PACK YOUR SHIT.
IF YOU'RE DONE WITH HIM... CAN I HAVE HIM?

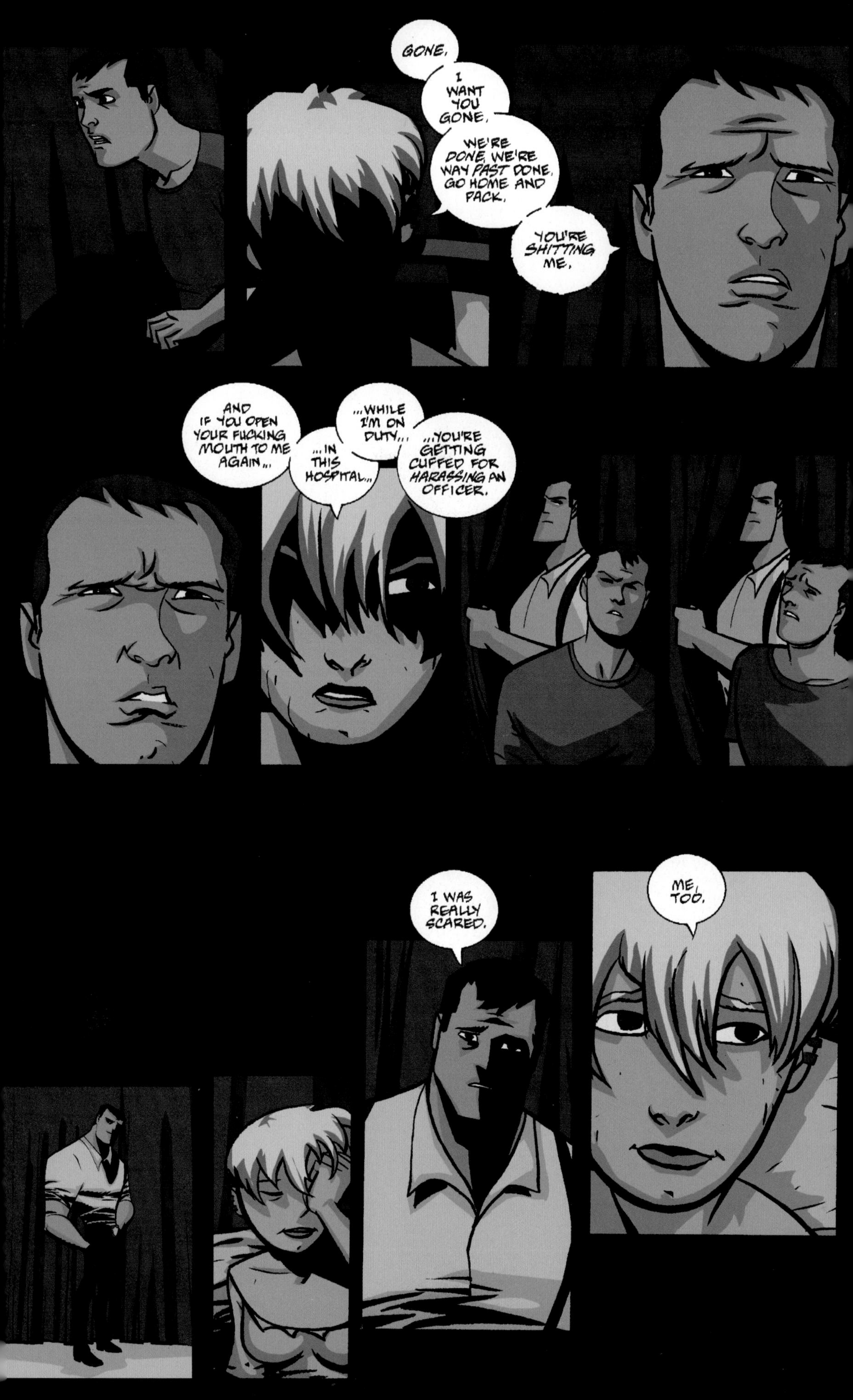

GONE.
I WANT YOU GONE.
WE'RE DONE. WE'RE WAY PAST DONE. GO HOME AND PACK.
YOU'RE SHITTING ME.
AND IF YOU OPEN YOUR FUCKING MOUTH TO ME AGAIN...
...IN THIS HOSPITAL...
...WHILE I'M ON DUTY...
...YOU'RE GETTING CUFFED FOR HARASSING AN OFFICER.
I WAS REALLY SCARED.
ME, TOO.

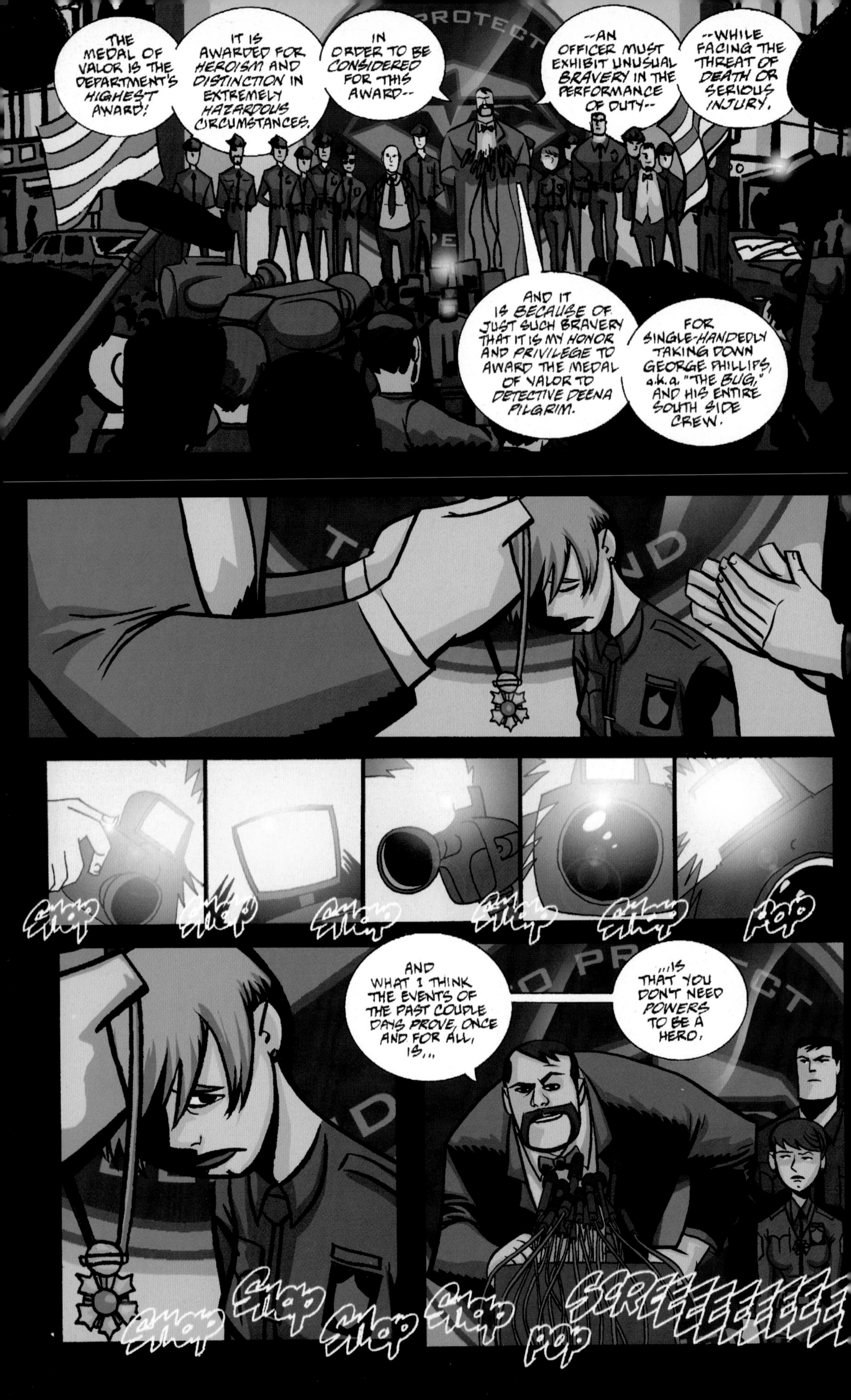
THE MEDAL OF VALOR IS THE DEPARTMENT'S HIGHEST AWARD!
IT IS AWARDED FOR HEROISM AND DISTINCTION IN EXTREMELY HAZARDOUS CIRCUMSTANCES.
IN ORDER TO BE CONSIDERED FOR THIS AWARD--
--AN OFFICER MUST EXHIBIT UNUSUAL BRAVERY IN THE PERFORMANCE OF DUTY--
--WHILE FACING THE THREAT OF DEATH OR SERIOUS INJURY.
AND IT IS BECAUSE OF JUST SUCH BRAVERY THAT IT IS MY HONOR AND PRIVILEGE TO AWARD THE MEDAL OF VALOR TO DETECTIVE DEENA PILGRIM.
FOR SINGLE-HANDEDLY TAKING DOWN GEORGE PHILLIPS, a.k.a. "THE BUG," AND HIS ENTIRE SOUTH SIDE CREW.
POP
AND WHAT I THINK THE EVENTS OF THE PAST COUPLE DAYS PROVE, ONCE AND FOR ALL, IS...
...IS THAT YOU DON'T NEED POWERS TO BE A HERO.
POP

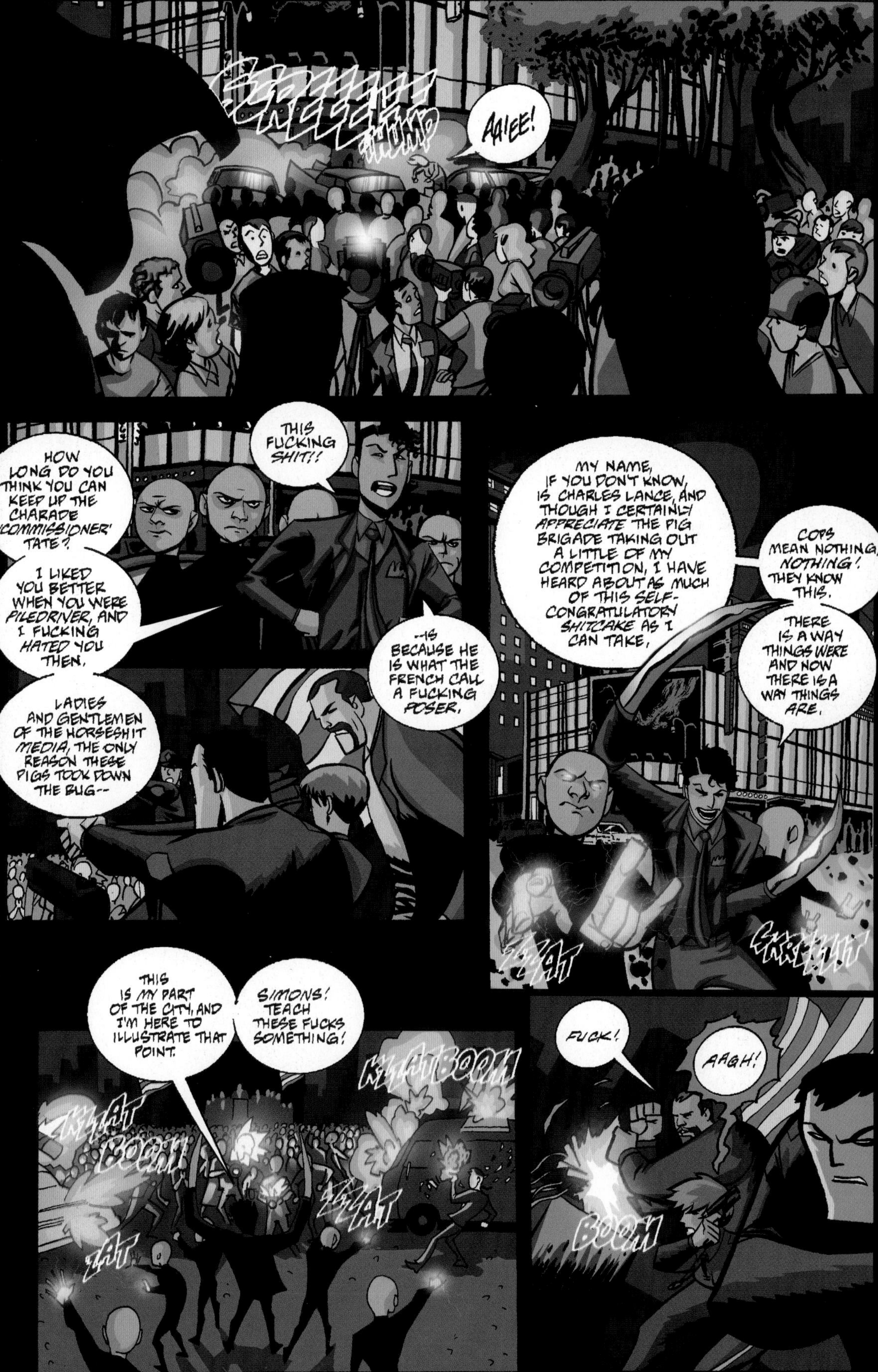

AAIEE!
HOW LONG DO YOU THINK YOU CAN KEEP UP THE CHARADE 'COMMISSIONER' TATE?
THIS FUCKING SHIT!!
I LIKED YOU BETTER WHEN YOU WERE PILEDRIVER, AND I FUCKING HATED YOU THEN.
LADIES AND GENTLEMEN OF THE HORSESHIT MEDIA, THE ONLY REASON THESE PIGS TOOK DOWN THE BUG--
--IS BECAUSE HE IS WHAT THE FRENCH CALL A FUCKING POSER.
MY NAME, IF YOU DON'T KNOW, IS CHARLES LANCE, AND THOUGH I CERTAINLY APPRECIATE THE PIG BRIGADE TAKING OUT A LITTLE OF MY COMPETITION, I HAVE HEARD ABOUT AS MUCH OF THIS SELF-CONGRATULATORY SHITCAKE AS I CAN TAKE.
COPS MEAN NOTHING, NOTHING! THEY KNOW THIS.
THERE IS A WAY THINGS WERE AND NOW THERE IS A WAY THINGS ARE.
THIS IS MY PART OF THE CITY, AND I'M HERE TO ILLUSTRATE THAT POINT.
SIMONS! TEACH THESE FUCKS SOMETHING!
BOOM
ZZAT
FUCK!
AARGH!
BOOM

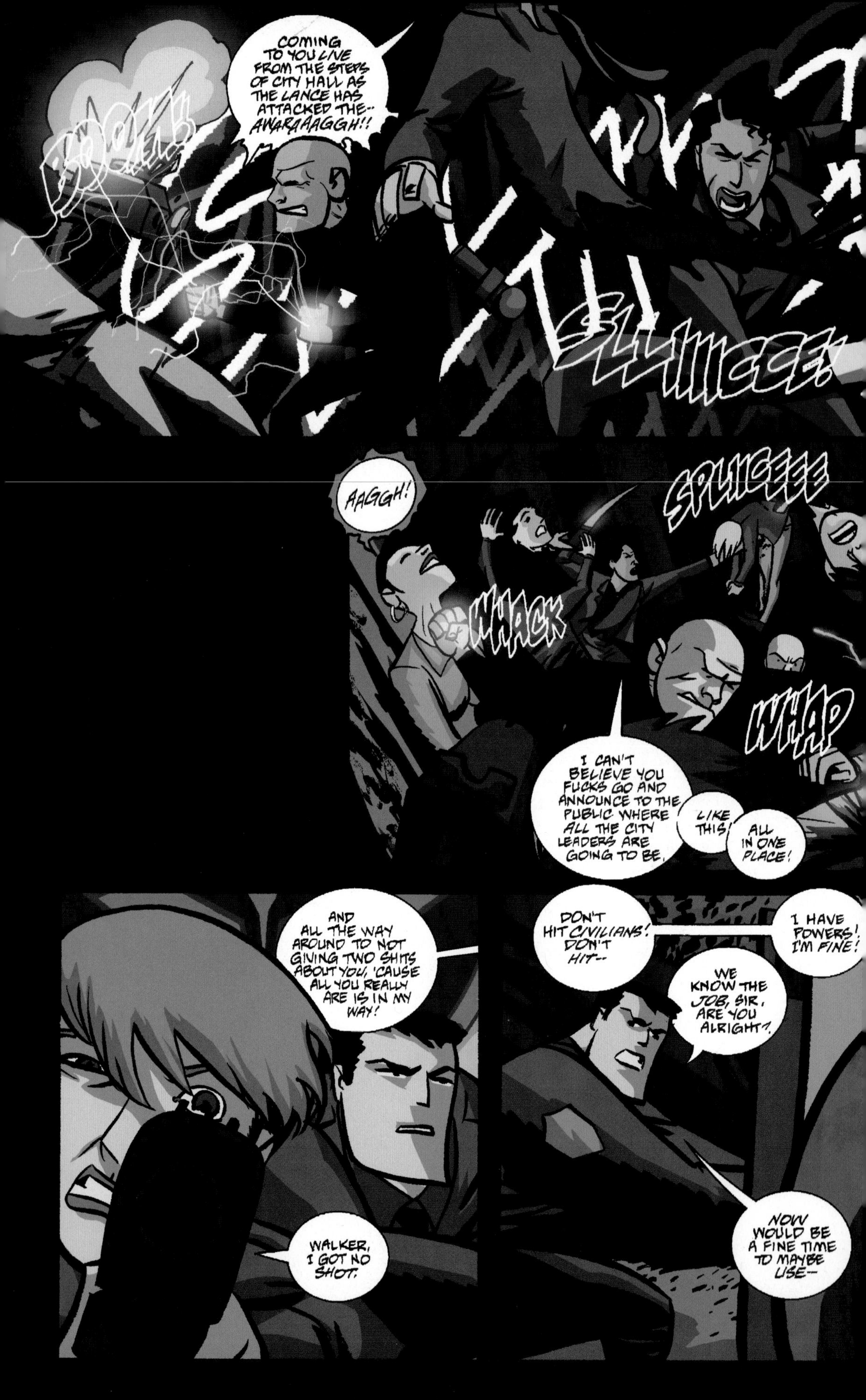
COMING TO YOU LIVE FROM THE STEPS OF CITY HALL AS THE LANCE HAS ATTACKED THE-- AWARAAAGGH!!
SLLIIICCE!
AAGGH!
SPLIICEEE
WHACK
WHAP
I CAN'T BELIEVE YOU FUCKS GO AND ANNOUNCE TO THE PUBLIC WHERE ALL THE CITY LEADERS ARE GOING TO BE.
LIKE THIS!
ALL IN ONE PLACE!
AND ALL THE WAY AROUND TO NOT GIVING TWO SHITS ABOUT YOU, 'CAUSE ALL YOU REALLY ARE IS IN MY WAY!
WALKER, I GOT NO SHOT.
DON'T HIT CIVILIANS! DON'T HIT--
I HAVE POWERS! I'M FINE!
WE KNOW THE JOB, SIR, ARE YOU ALRIGHT?
NOW WOULD BE A FINE TIME TO MAYBE USE--

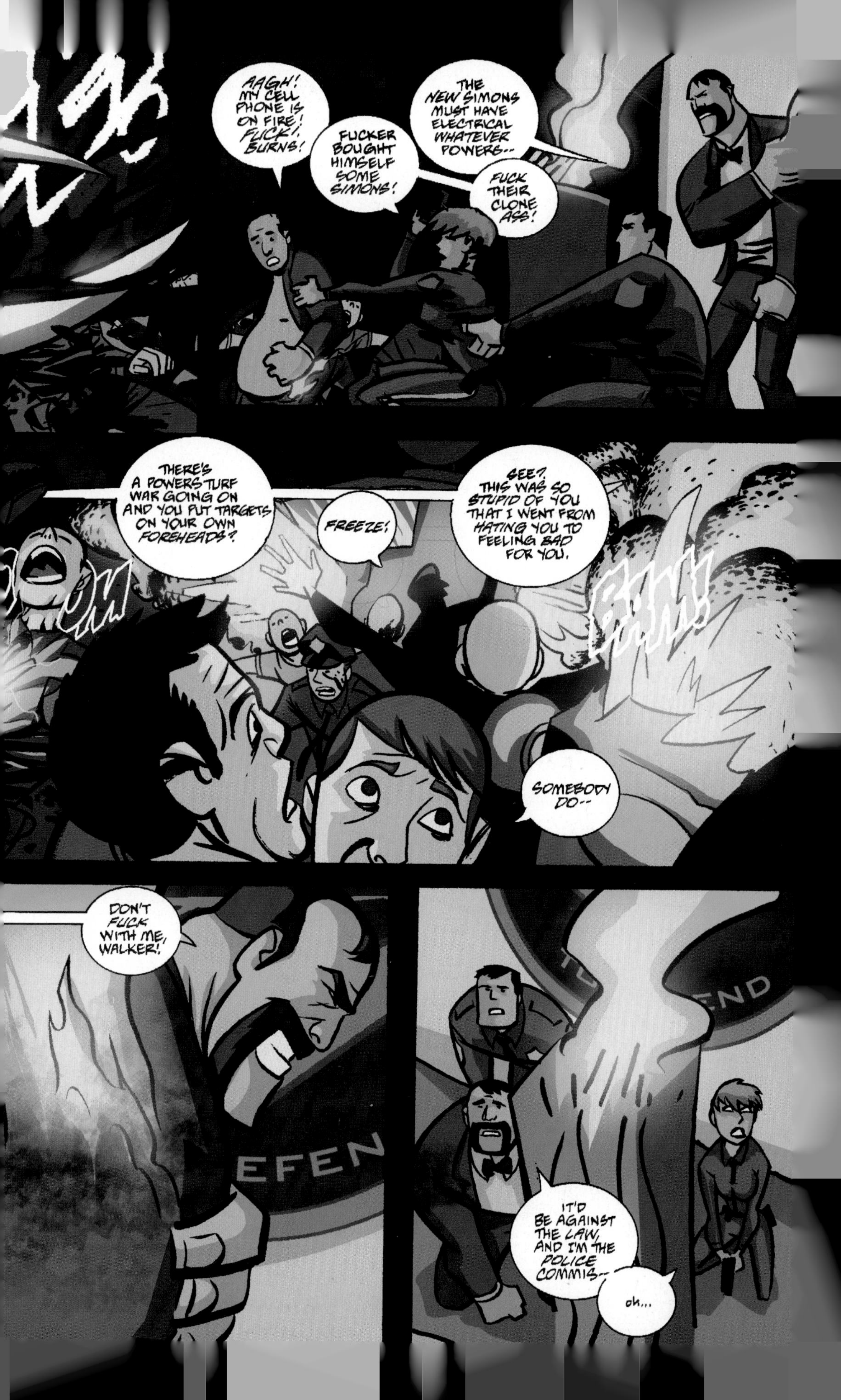
AAGH! MY CELL PHONE IS ON FIRE! FUCK! BURNS!
FUCKER BOUGHT HIMSELF SOME SIMONS!
THE NEW SIMONS MUST HAVE ELECTRICAL WHATEVER POWERS--
FUCK THEIR CLONE ASS!
THERE'S A POWERS TURF WAR GOING ON AND YOU PUT TARGETS ON YOUR OWN FOREHEADS?
FREEZE!
SEE? THIS WAS SO STUPID OF YOU THAT I WENT FROM HATING YOU TO FEELING BAD FOR YOU.
SOMEBODY DO--
DON'T FUCK WITH ME, WALKER!
IT'D BE AGAINST THE LAW, AND I'M THE POLICE COMMIS--
oh...

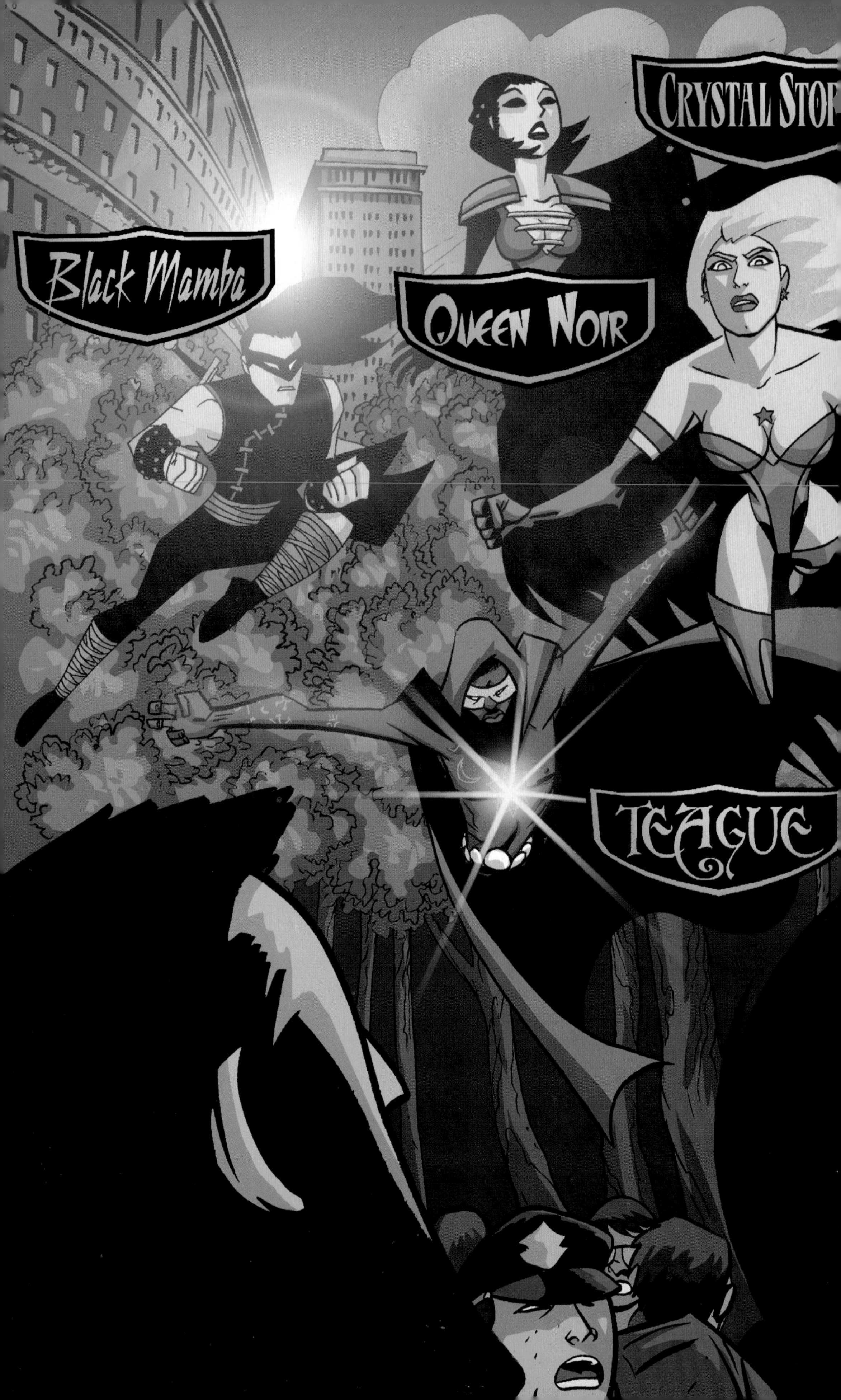
Crystal Stor
Black Mamba
Queen Noir
Teague

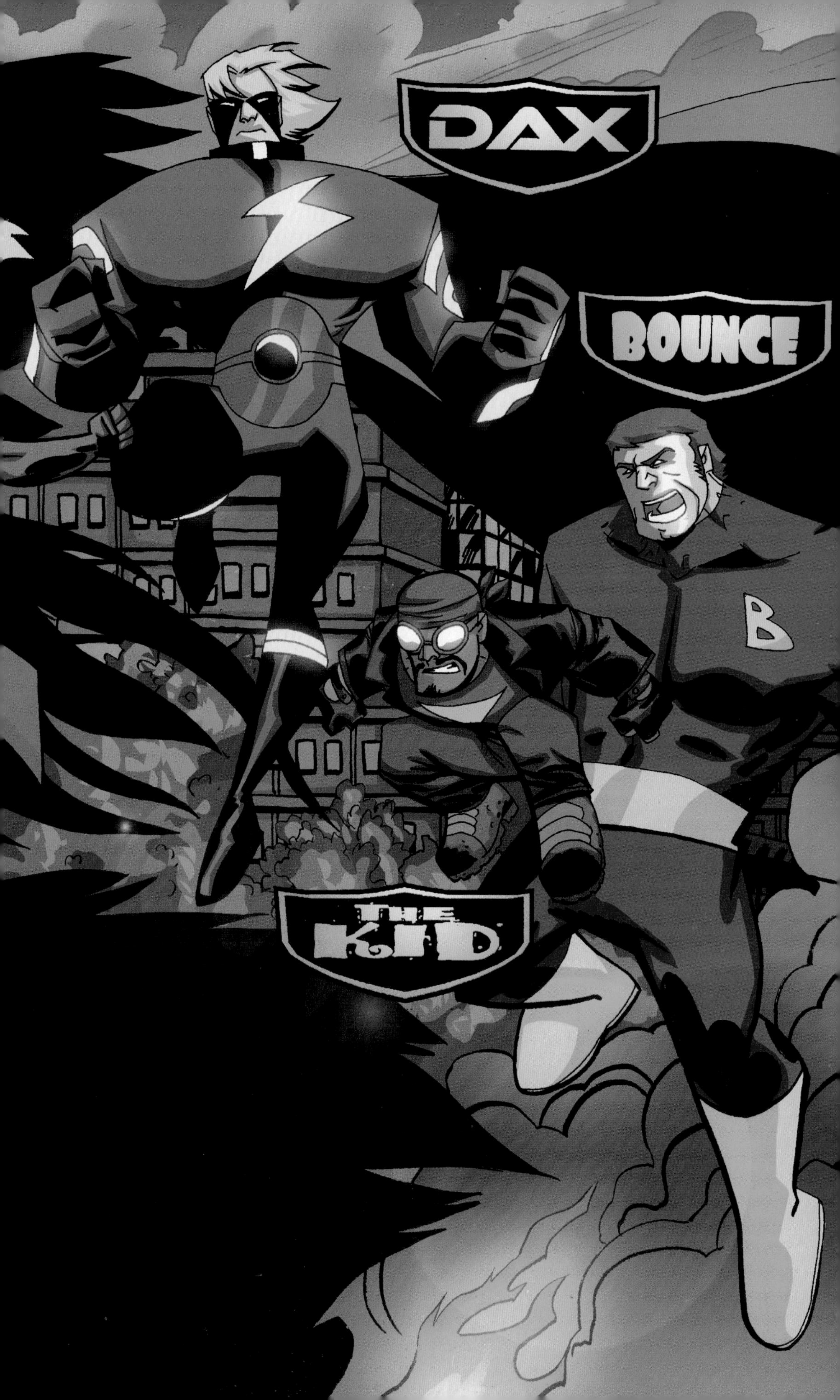
DAX
BOUNCE
B
THE KID

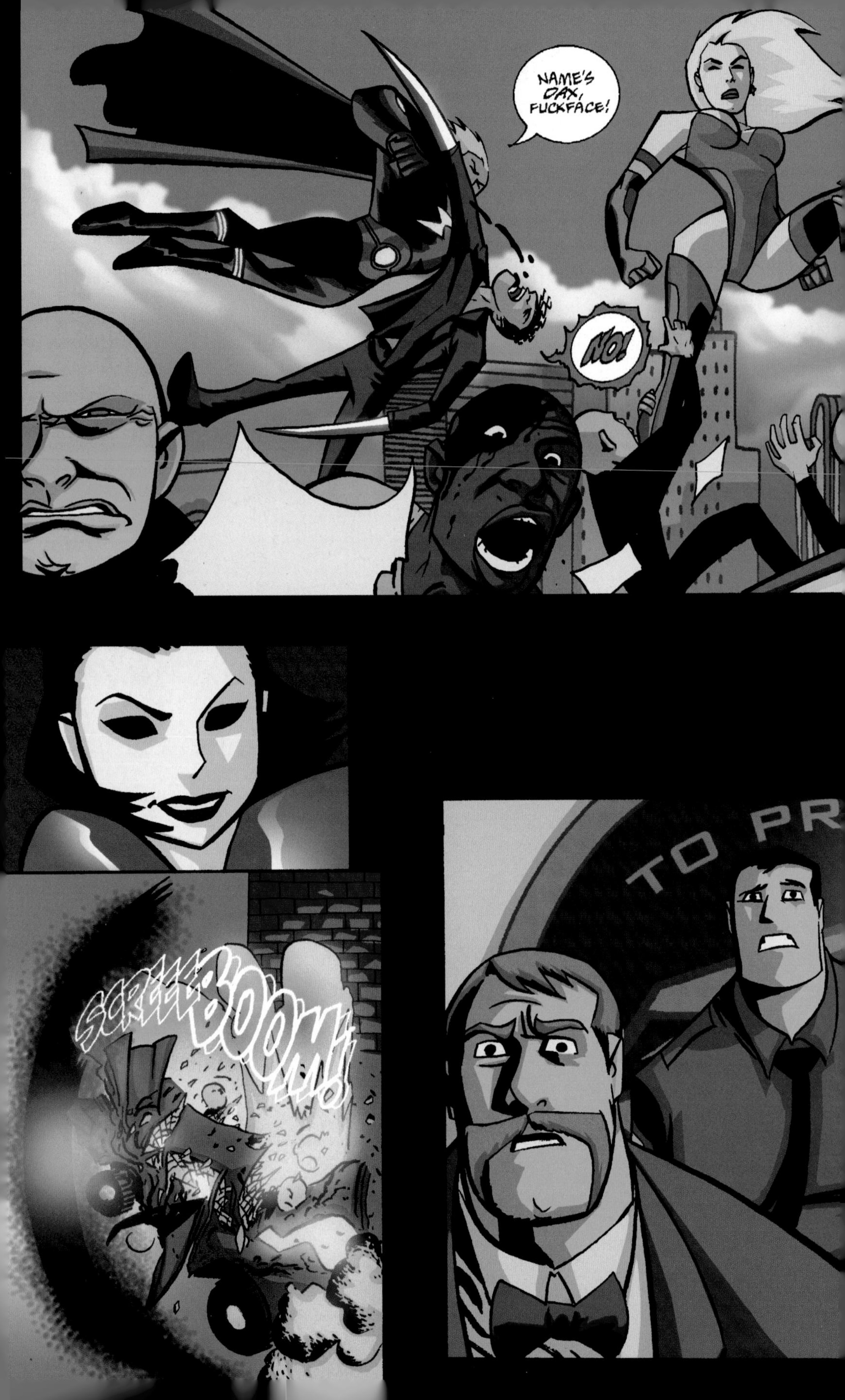
NAME'S DAX, FUCKFACE!
NO!
SCREE-BOOM!
TO PR

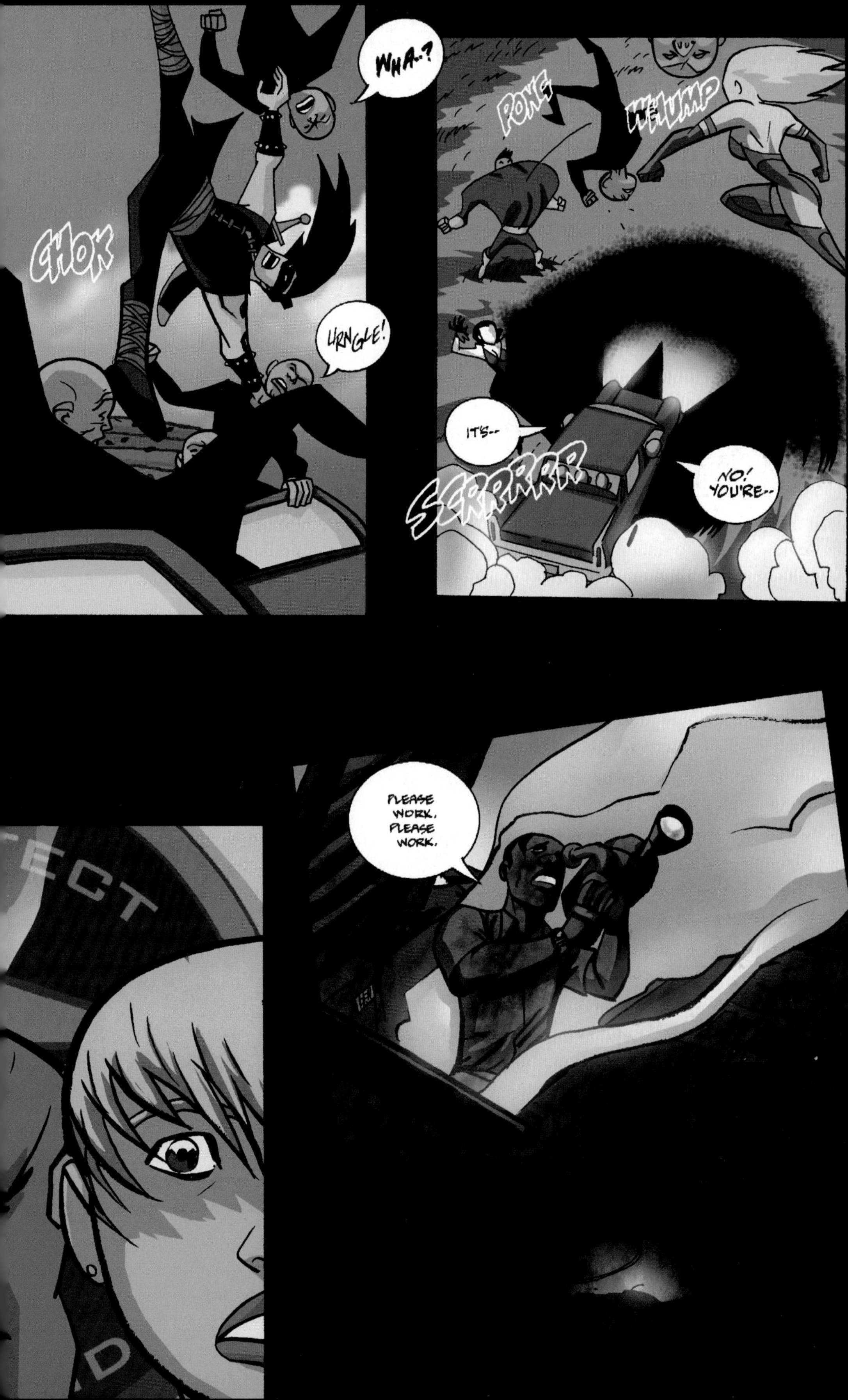
WHA..?
CHOK
URNGLE!
PONG
WHUMP
IT'S--
SCRRRRR
NO! YOU'RE--
PLEASE WORK, PLEASE WORK.

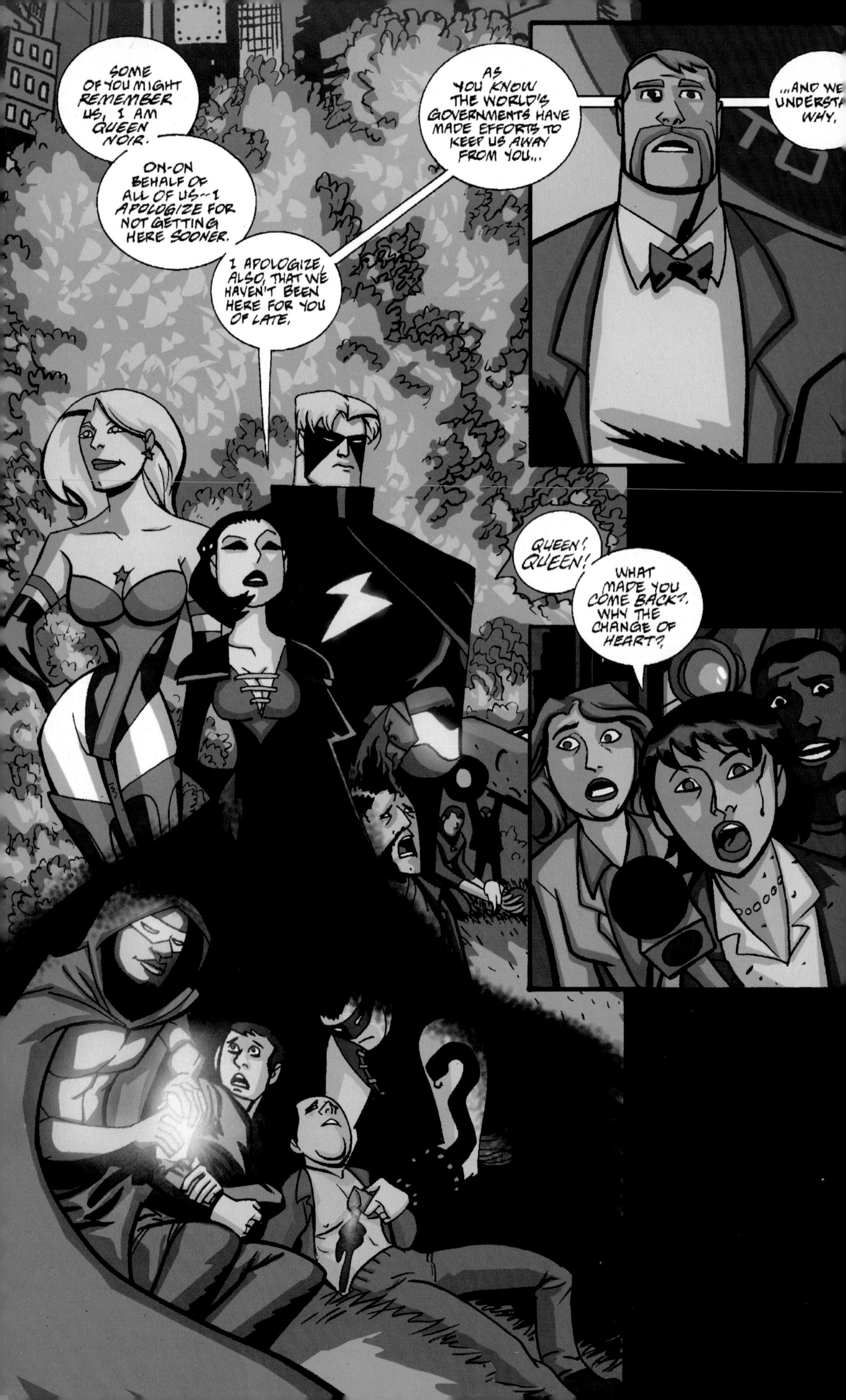
SOME OF YOU MIGHT REMEMBER US, I AM QUEEN NOIR.
ON-ON BEHALF OF ALL OF US--I APOLOGIZE FOR NOT GETTING HERE SOONER.
I APOLOGIZE, ALSO, THAT WE HAVEN'T BEEN HERE FOR YOU OF LATE.
AS YOU KNOW THE WORLD'S GOVERNMENTS HAVE MADE EFFORTS TO KEEP US AWAY FROM YOU...
...AND WE UNDERSTA WHY.
QUEEN! QUEEN!
WHAT MADE YOU COME BACK? WHY THE CHANGE OF HEART?

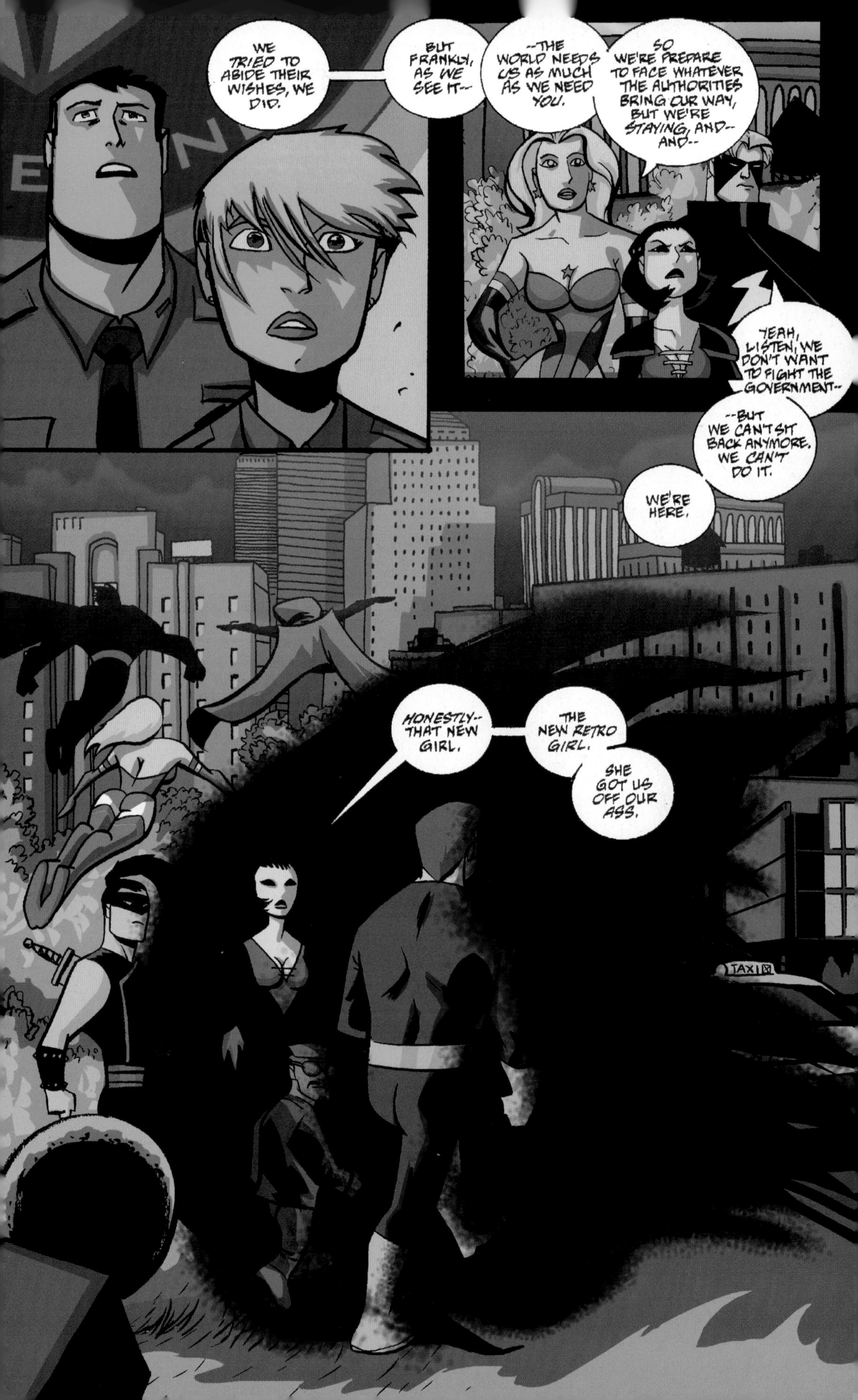
WE TRIED TO ABIDE THEIR WISHES, WE DID.
BUT FRANKLY, AS WE SEE IT--
--THE WORLD NEEDS US AS MUCH AS WE NEED YOU.
SO WE'RE PREPARE TO FACE WHATEVER THE AUTHORITIES BRING OUR WAY, BUT WE'RE STAYING, AND-- AND--
YEAH, LISTEN, WE DON'T WANT TO FIGHT THE GOVERNMENT--
--BUT WE CAN'T SIT BACK ANYMORE. WE CAN'T DO IT.
WE'RE HERE.
HONESTLY-- THAT NEW GIRL.
THE NEW RETRO GIRL.
SHE GOT US OFF OUR ASS.
TAXI

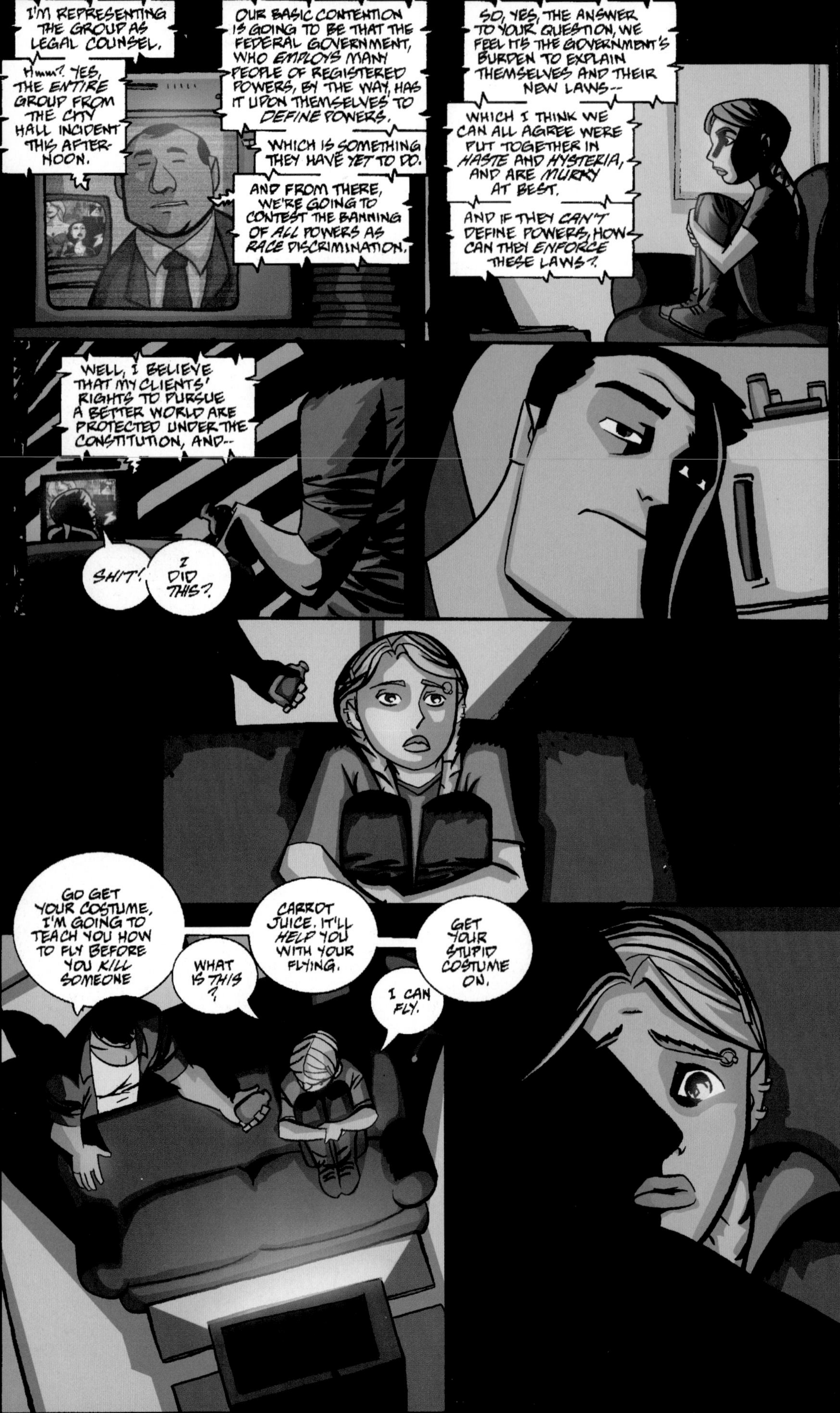

I'M REPRESENTING THE GROUP AS LEGAL COUNSEL.
Hmm? YES, THE ENTIRE GROUP FROM THE CITY HALL INCIDENT THIS AFTERNOON.
OUR BASIC CONTENTION IS GOING TO BE THAT THE FEDERAL GOVERNMENT, WHO EMPLOYS MANY PEOPLE OF REGISTERED POWERS, BY THE WAY, HAS IT UPON THEMSELVES TO DEFINE POWERS.
WHICH IS SOMETHING THEY HAVE YET TO DO.
AND FROM THERE, WE'RE GOING TO CONTEST THE BANNING OF ALL POWERS AS RACE DISCRIMINATION.
SO, YES, THE ANSWER TO YOUR QUESTION, WE FEEL IT'S THE GOVERNMENT'S BURDEN TO EXPLAIN THEMSELVES AND THEIR NEW LAWS--
WHICH I THINK WE CAN ALL AGREE WERE PUT TOGETHER IN HASTE AND HYSTERIA, AND ARE MURKY AT BEST.
AND IF THEY CAN'T DEFINE POWERS, HOW CAN THEY ENFORCE THESE LAWS?
WELL, I BELIEVE THAT MY CLIENTS' RIGHTS TO PURSUE A BETTER WORLD ARE PROTECTED UNDER THE CONSTITUTION, AND--
SHIT!
I DID THIS?
GO GET YOUR COSTUME, I'M GOING TO TEACH YOU HOW TO FLY BEFORE YOU KILL SOMEONE
WHAT IS THIS?
CARROT JUICE. IT'LL HELP YOU WITH YOUR FLYING.
I CAN FLY.
GET YOUR STUPID COSTUME ON.

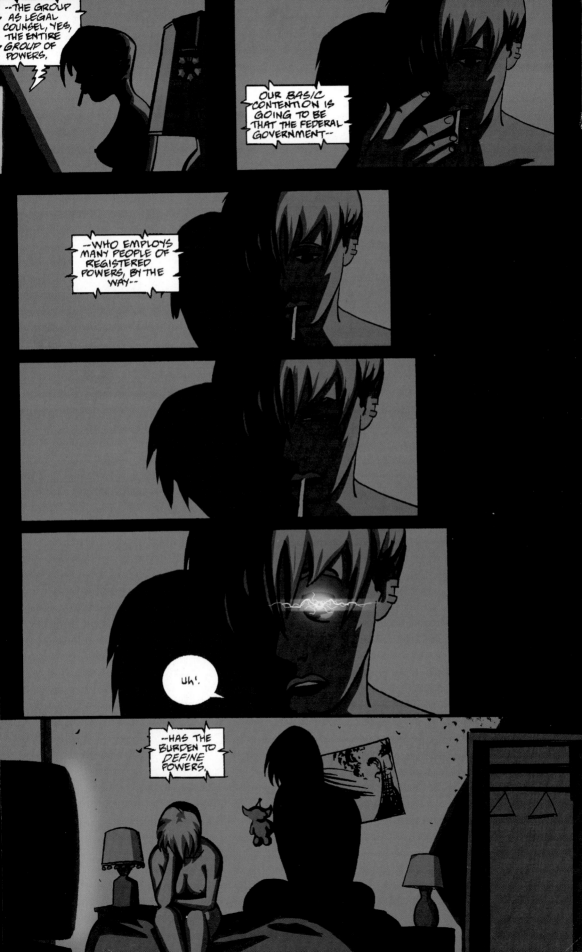

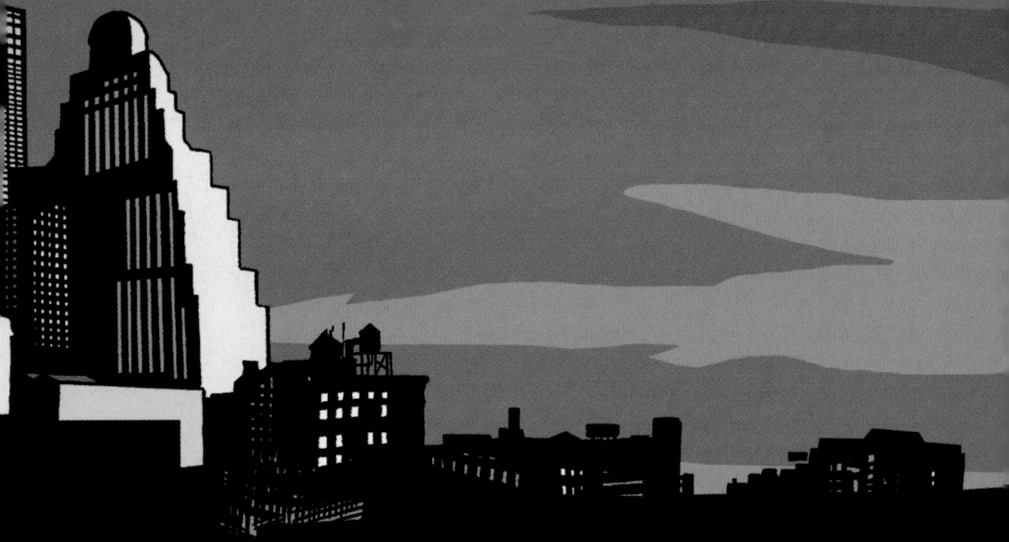

POWERS

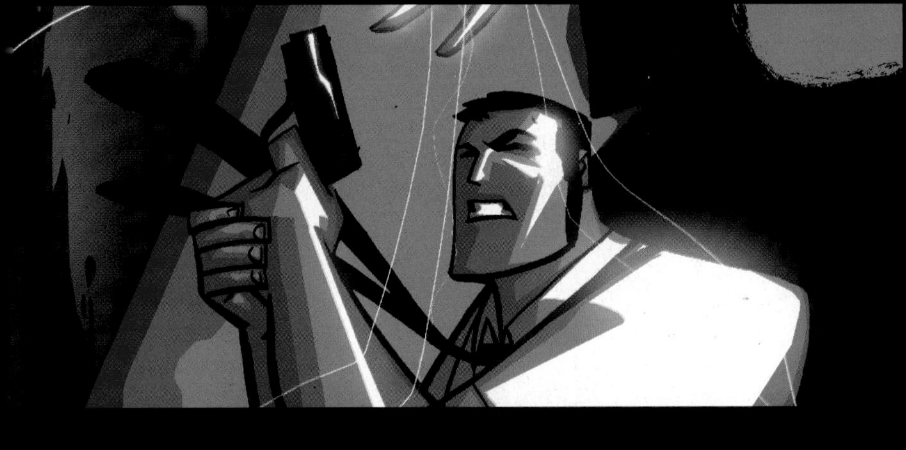

COVER GALLERY

First draft for the cover of our first Icon issue.

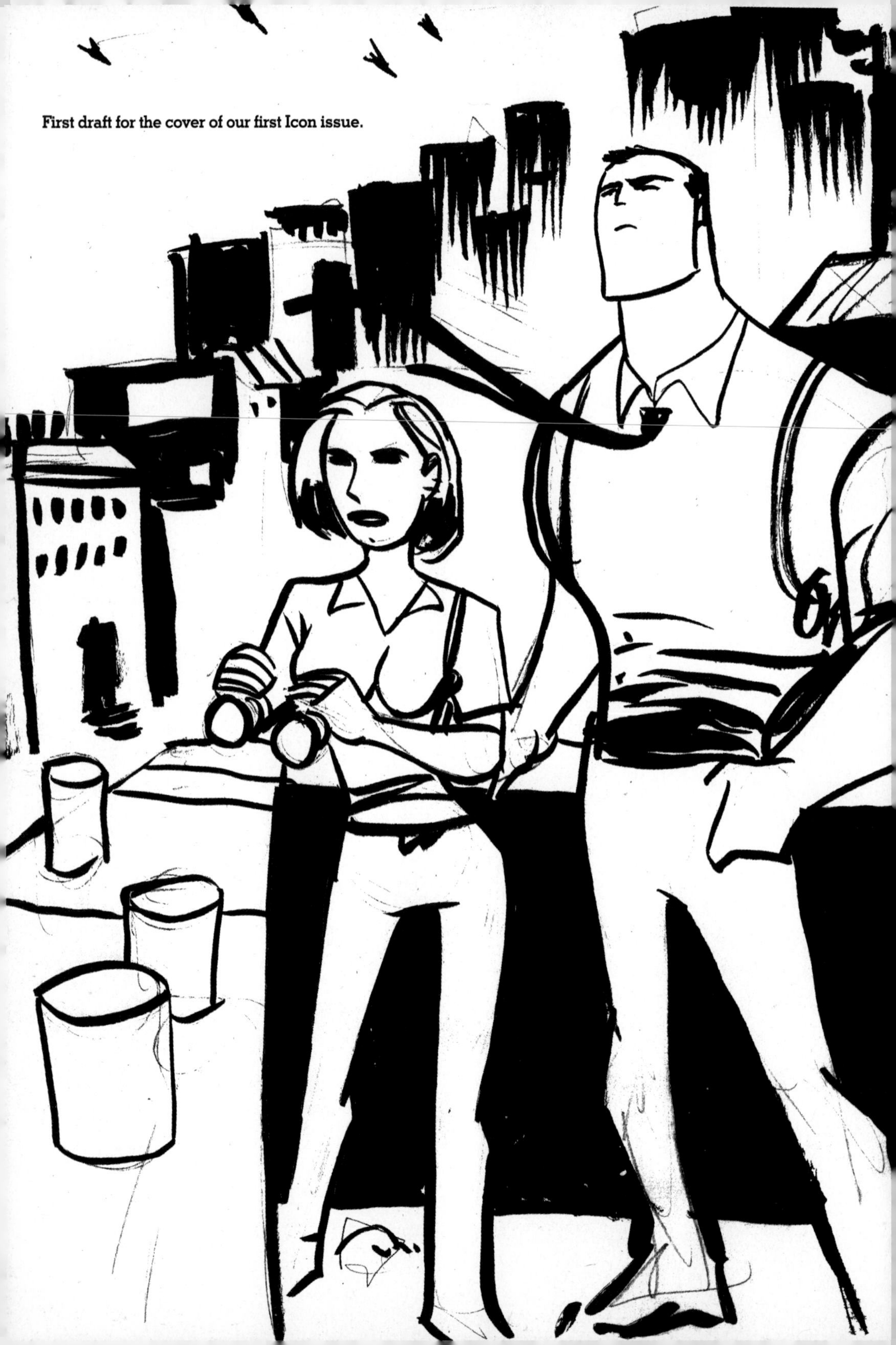

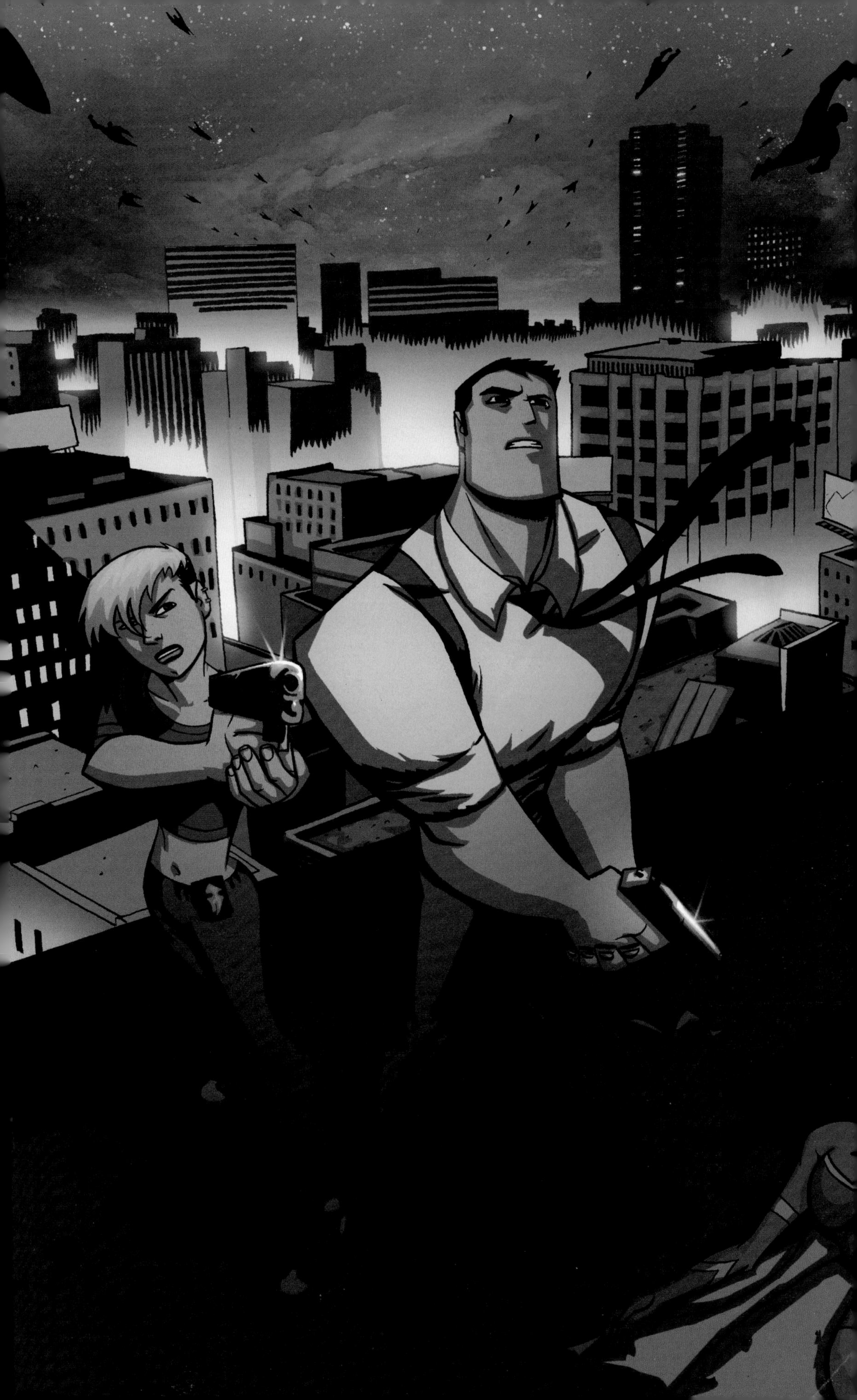

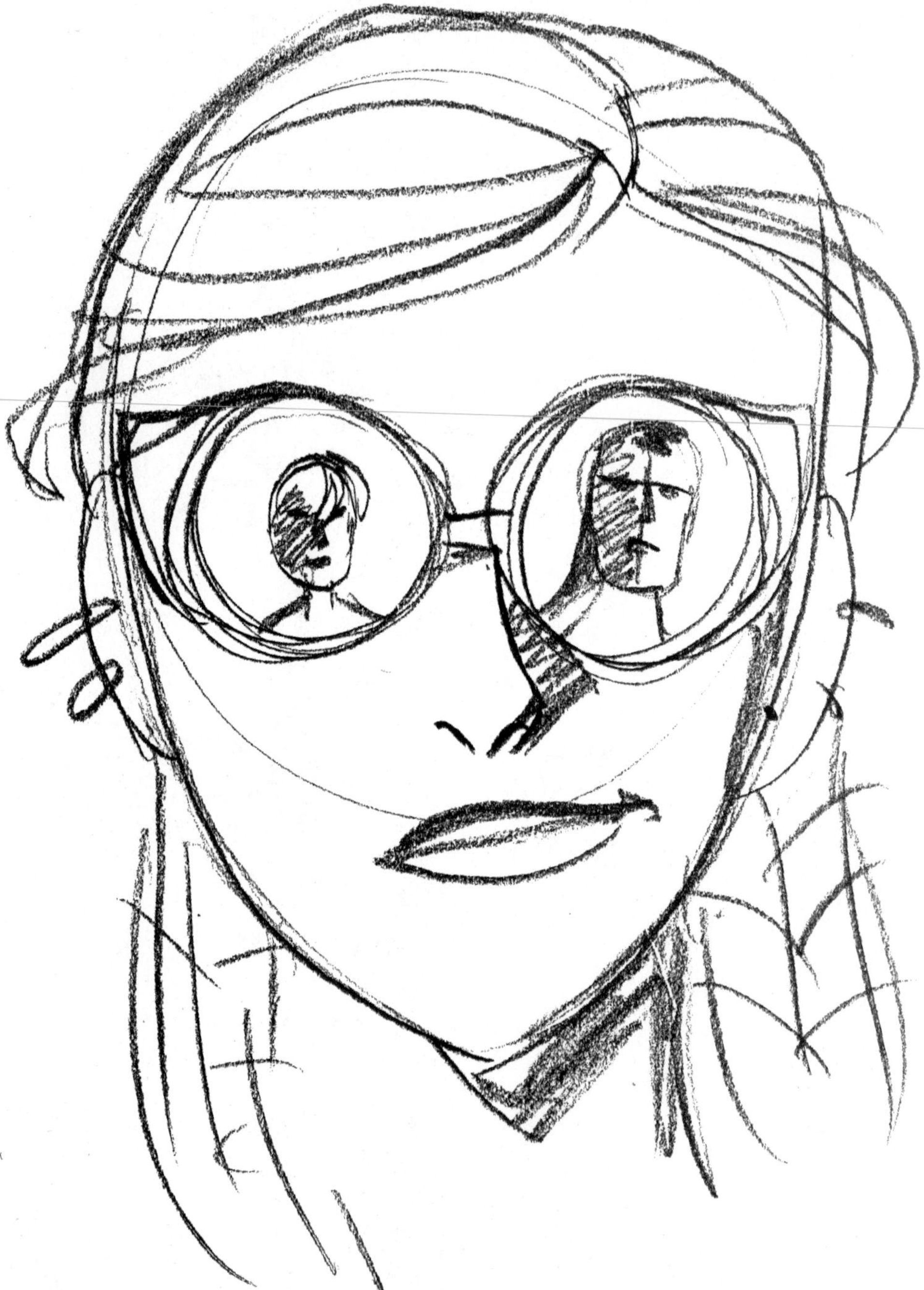

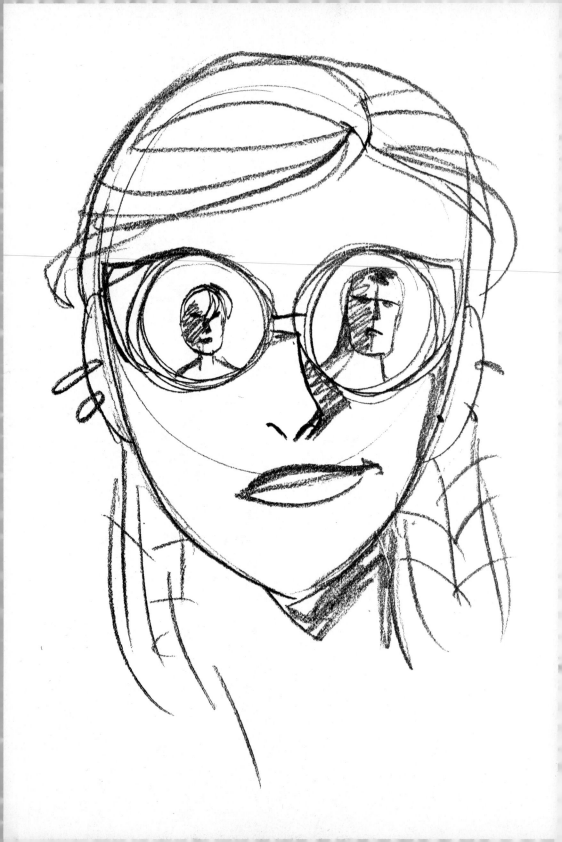

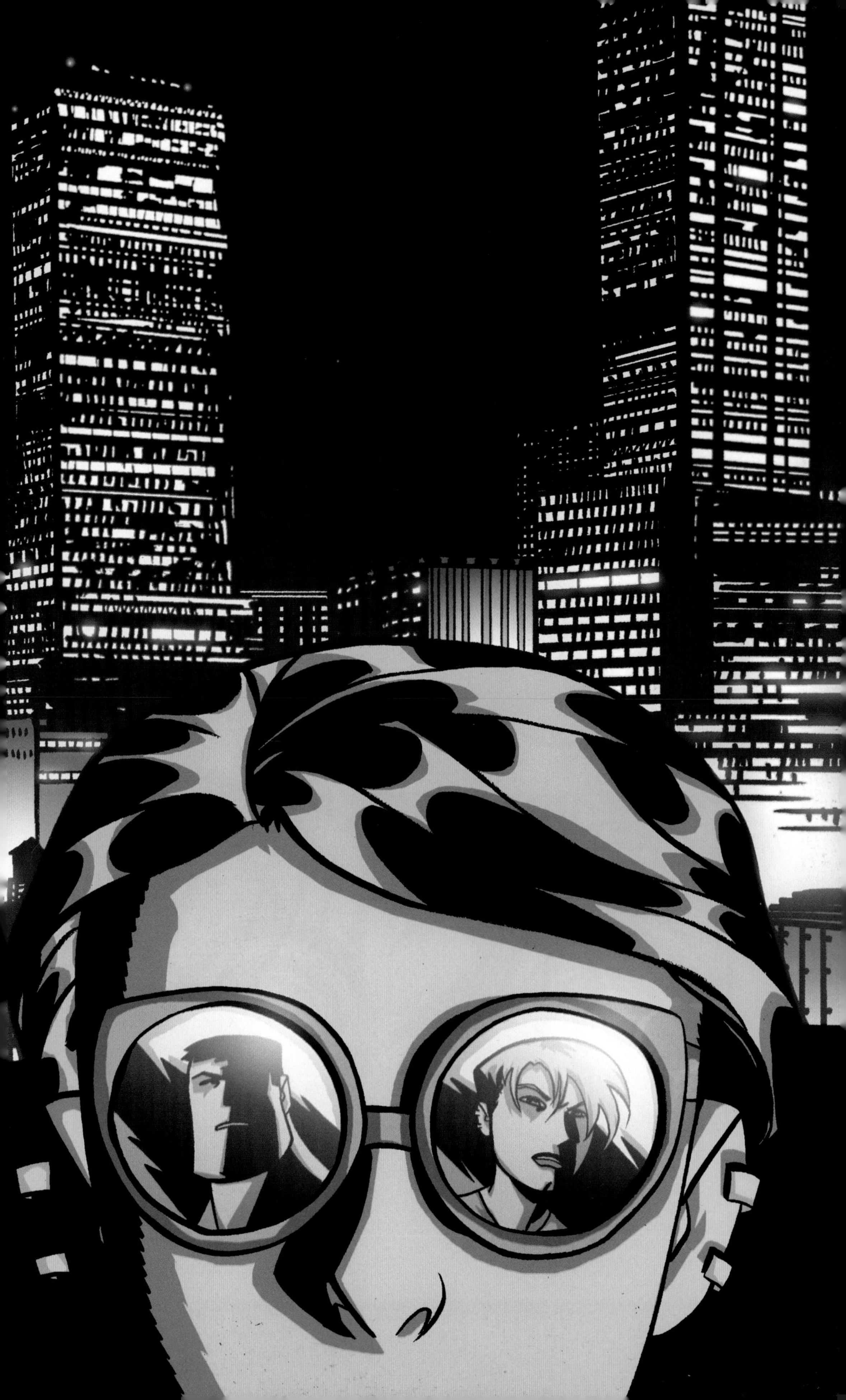

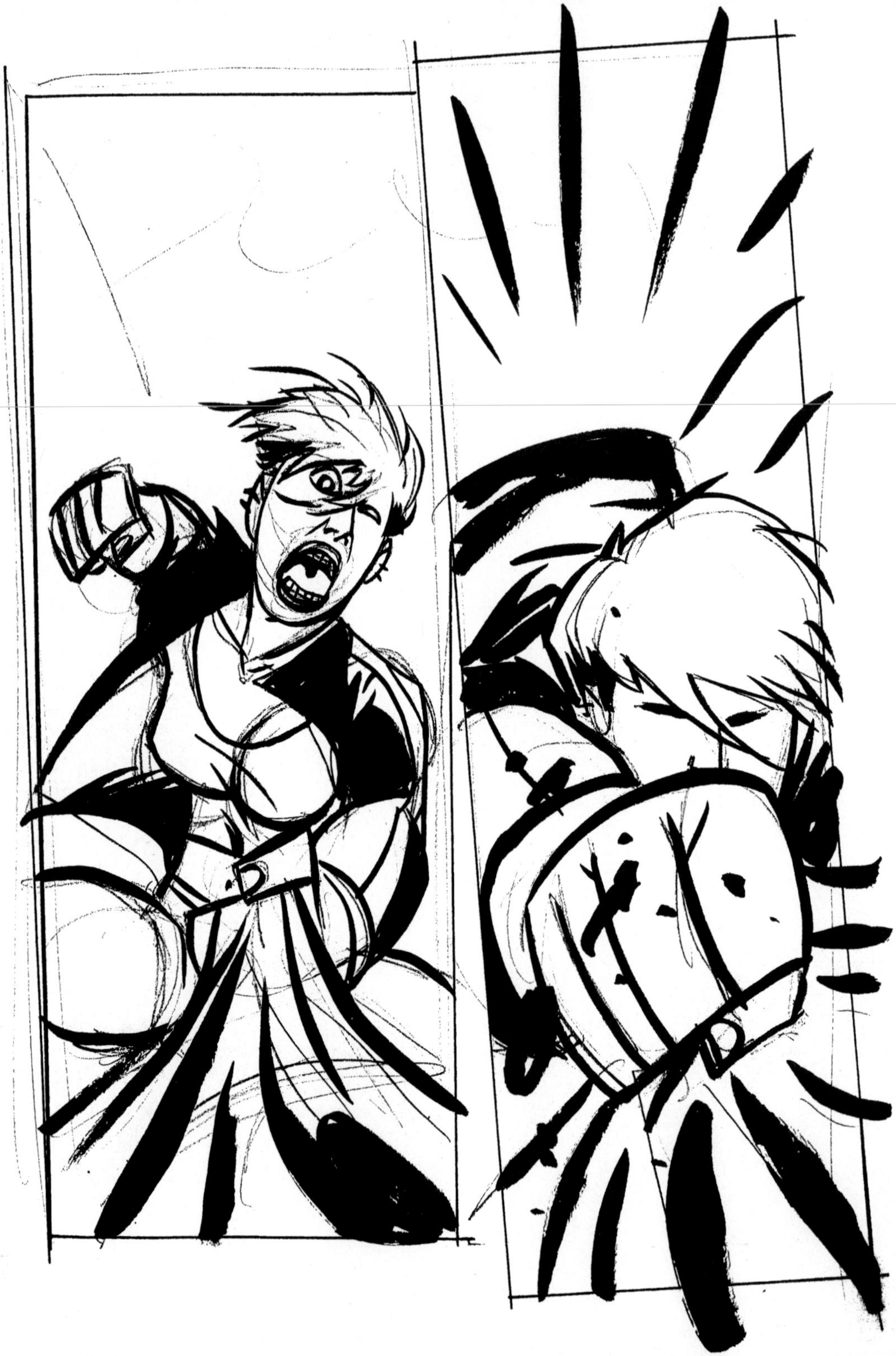

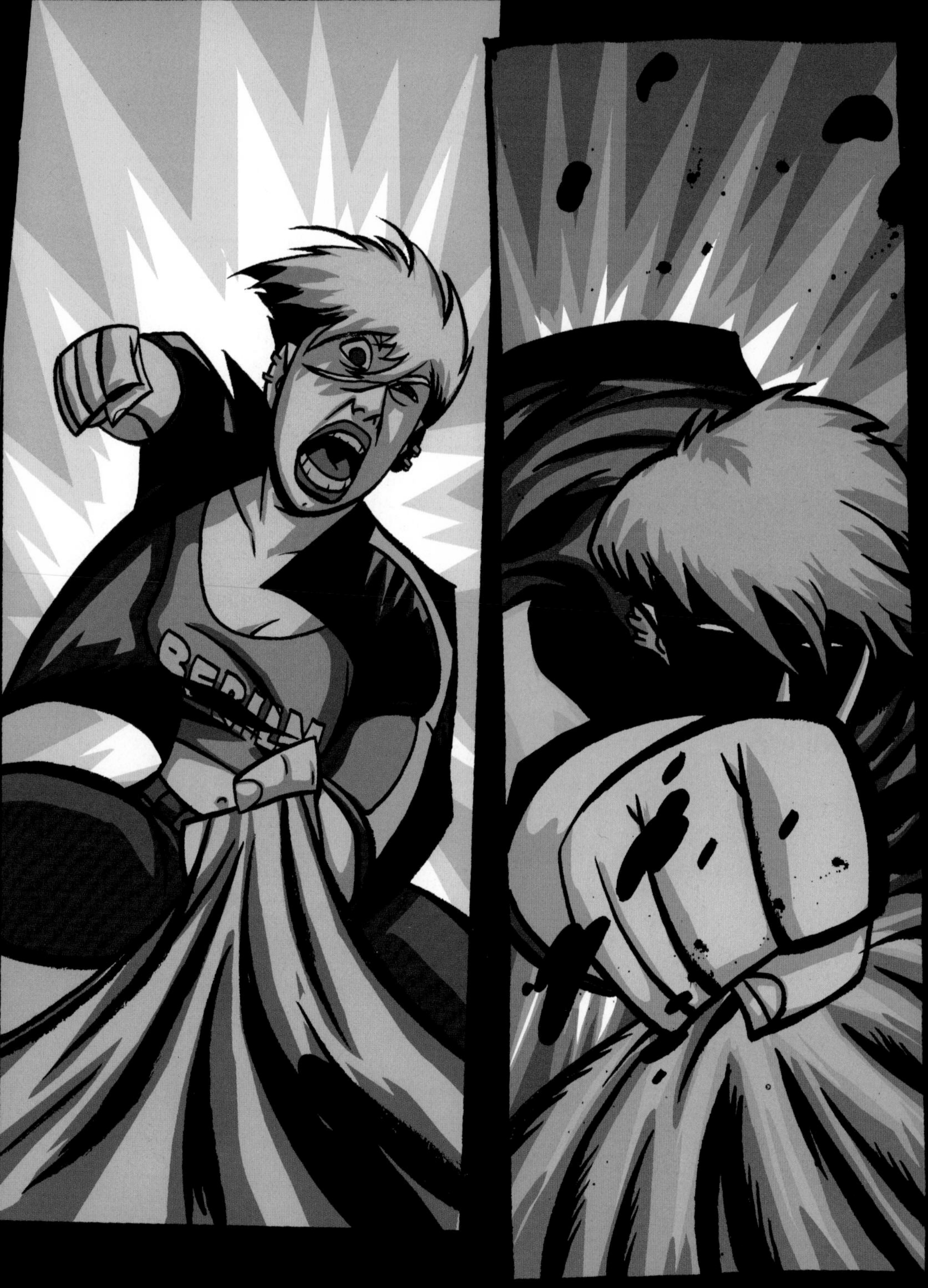

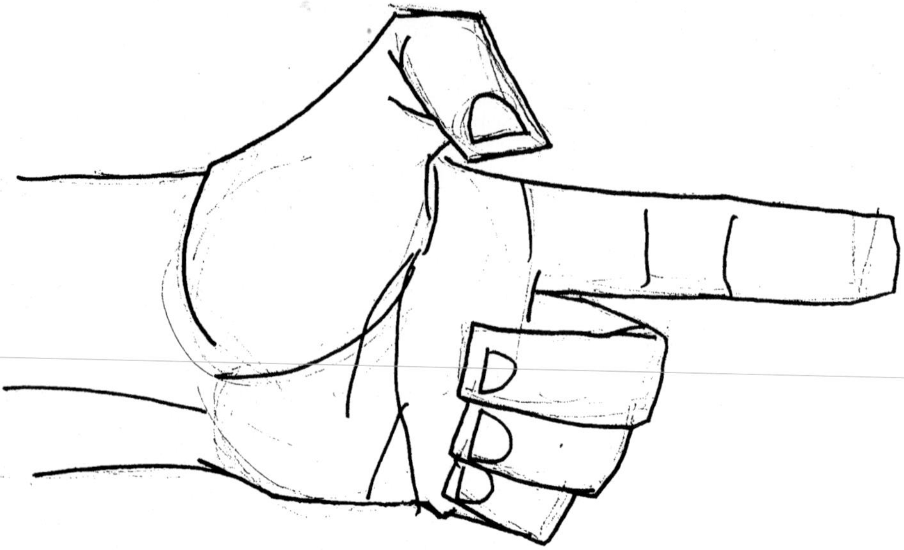

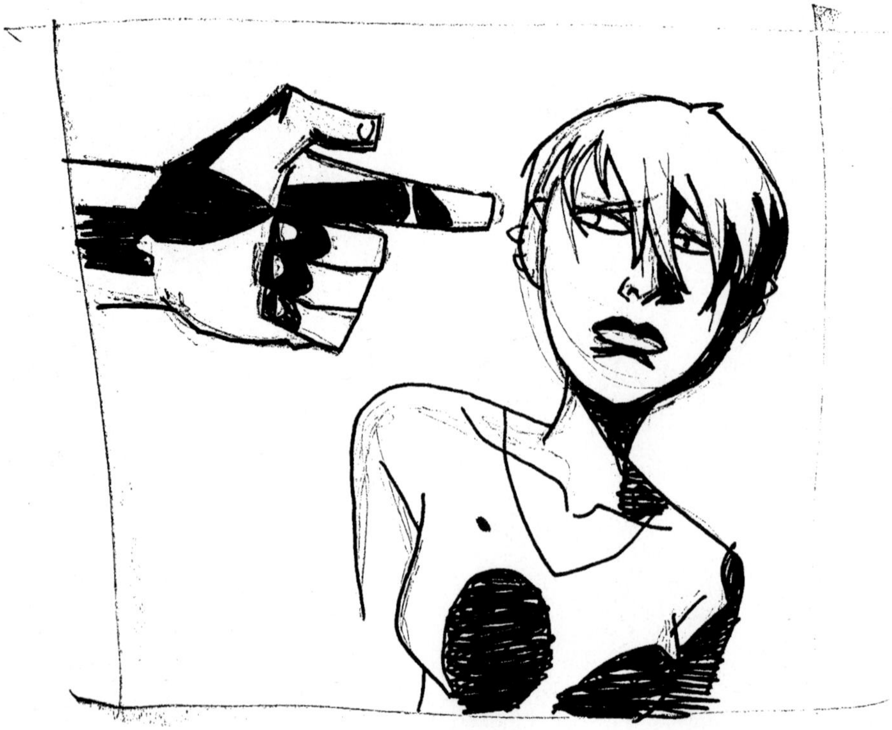

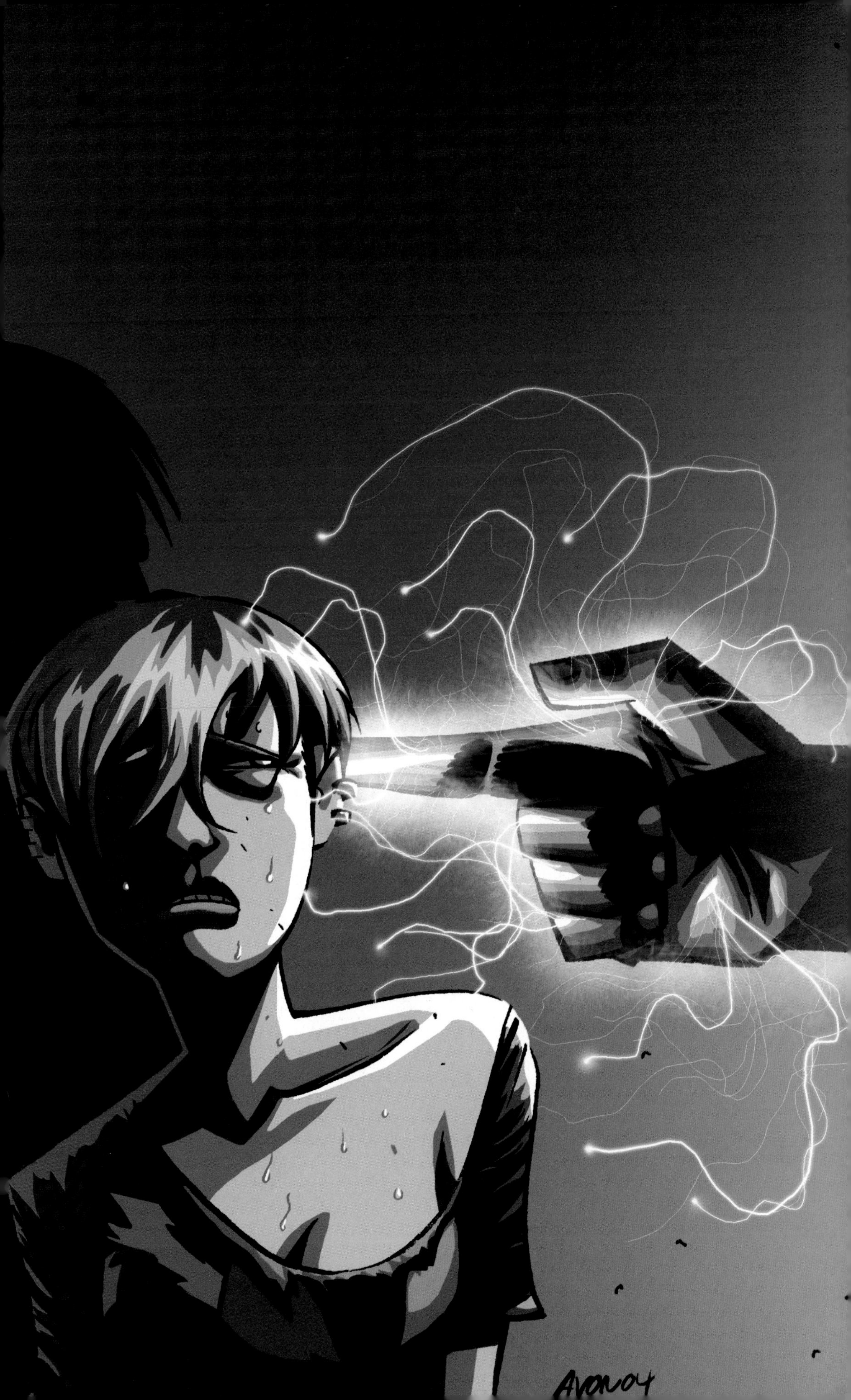
AVON04

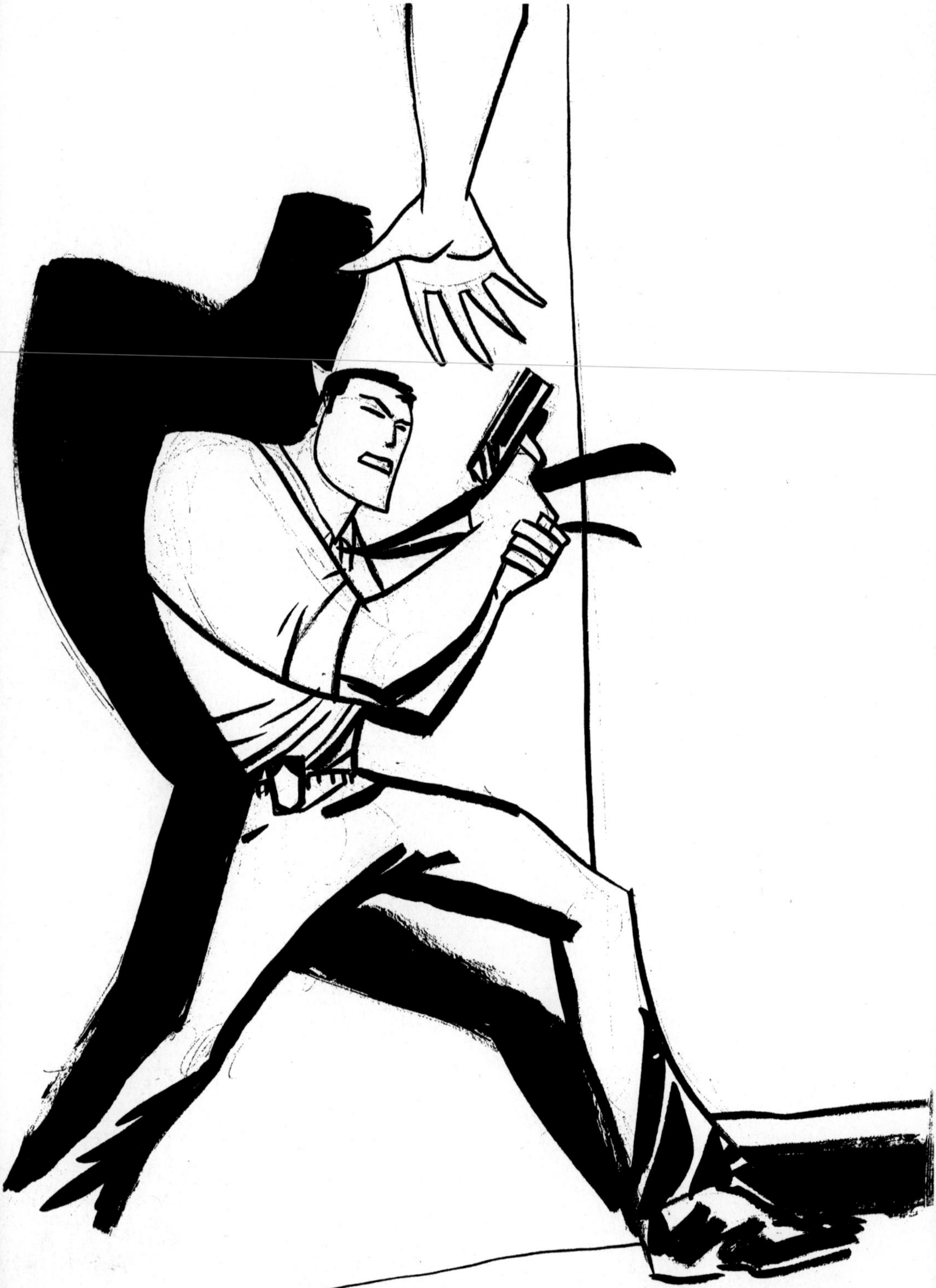

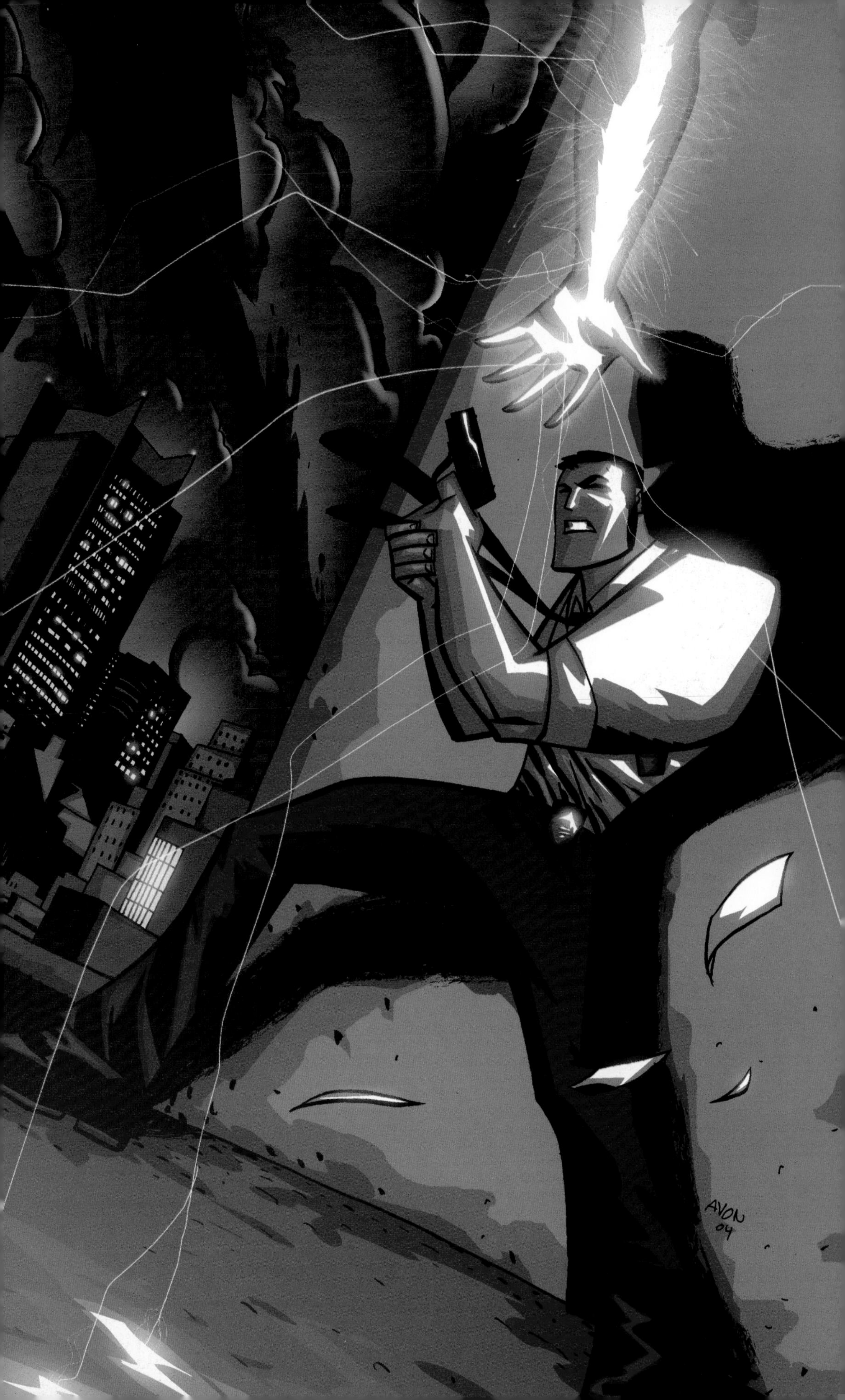
AVON
04

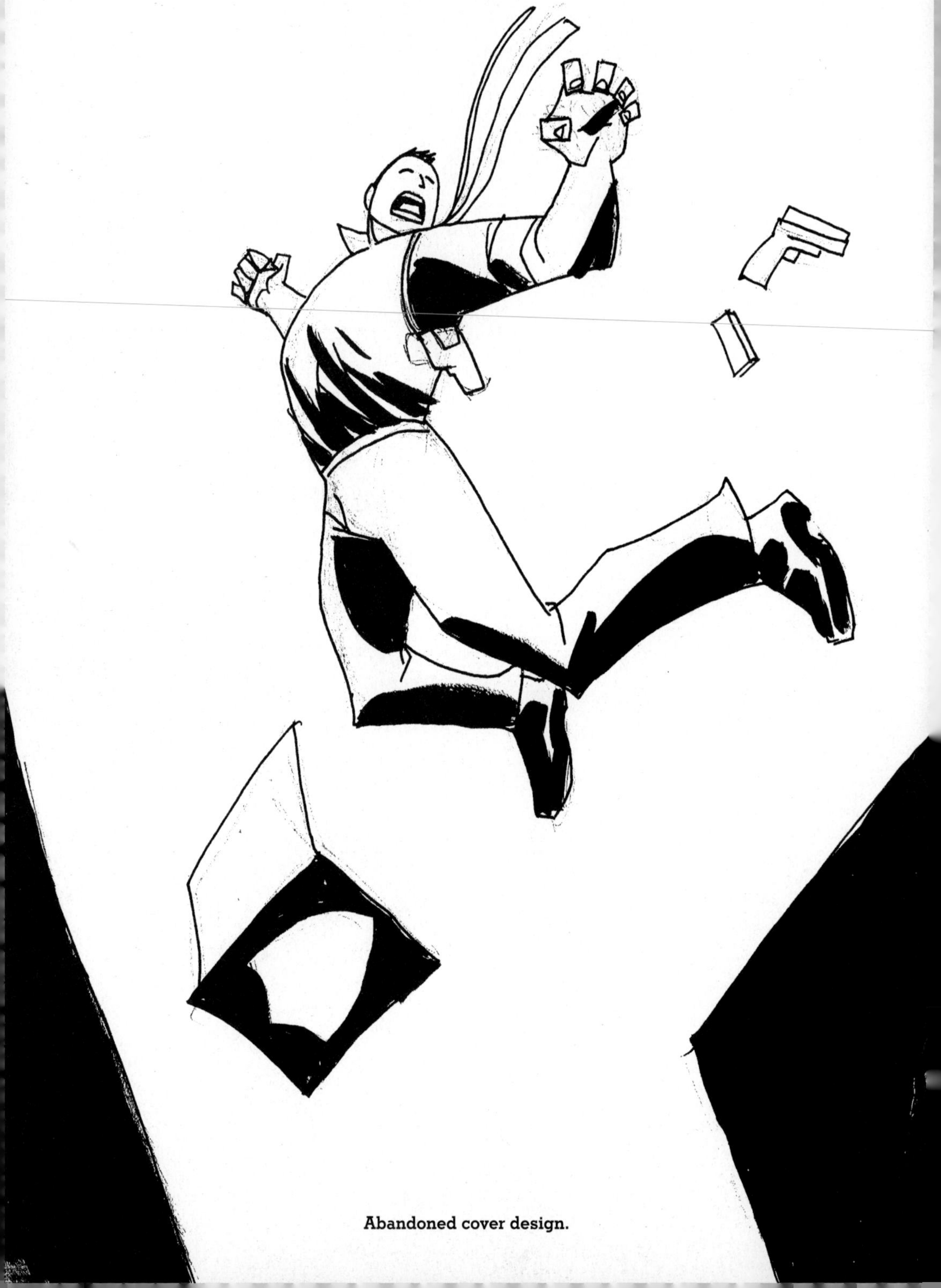

Abandoned cover design.

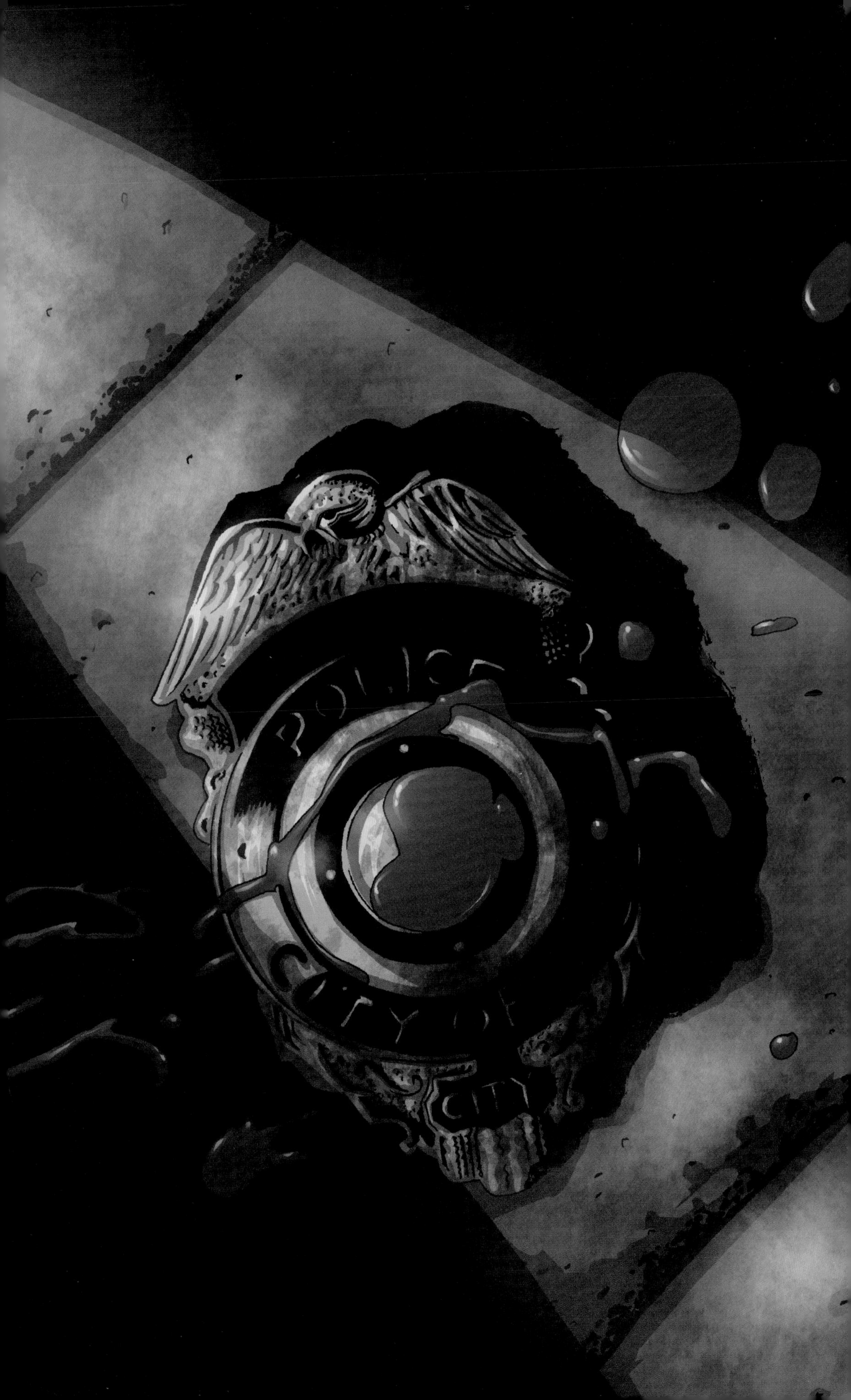
CITY OF
CITY

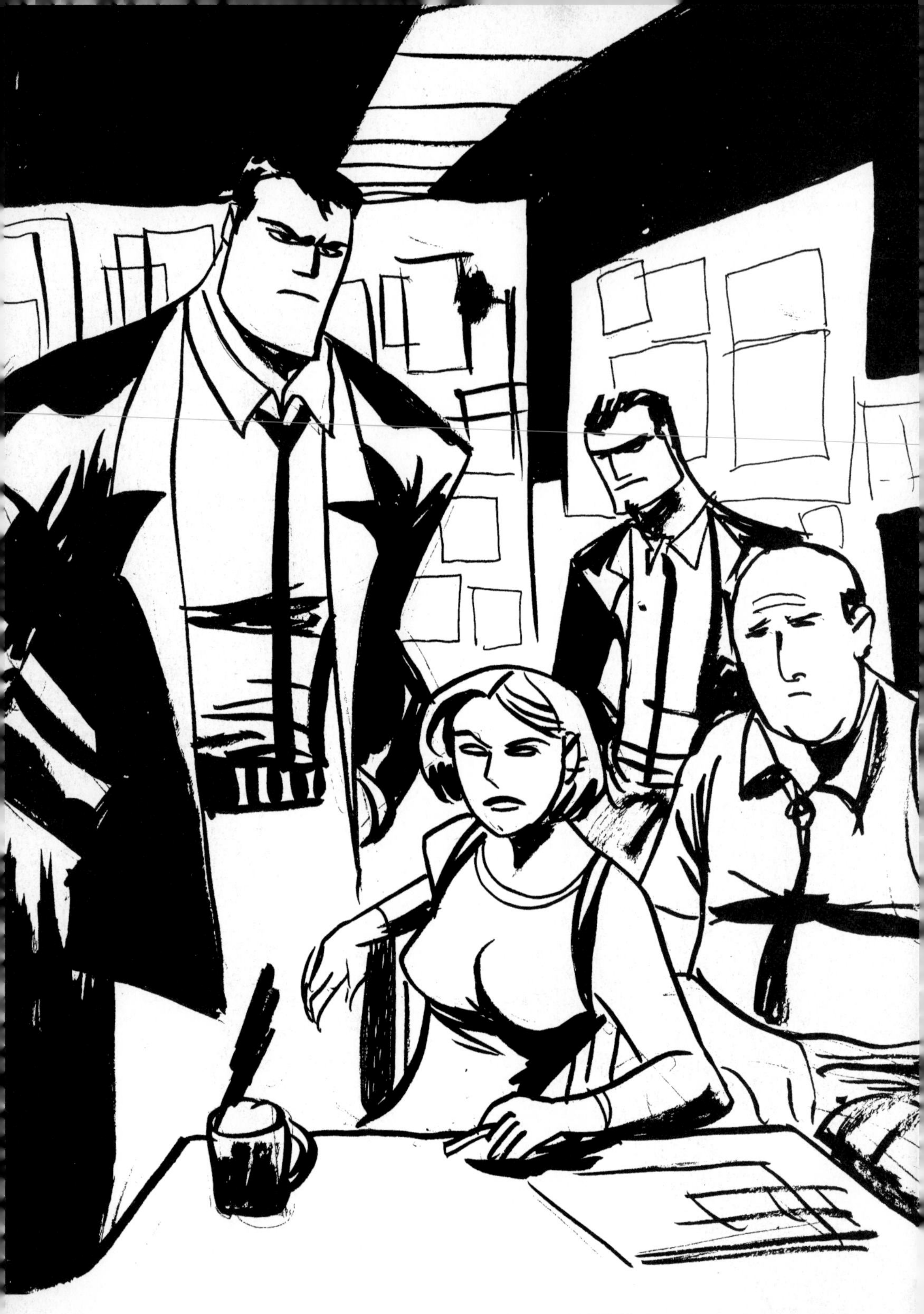

This is the original art to the Dynamic Forces alternate cover to POWERS #1. I don't even know if this ever shipped. Notice deena's hair--we ditched that new do quick. It just didn't seem Deena- ish.

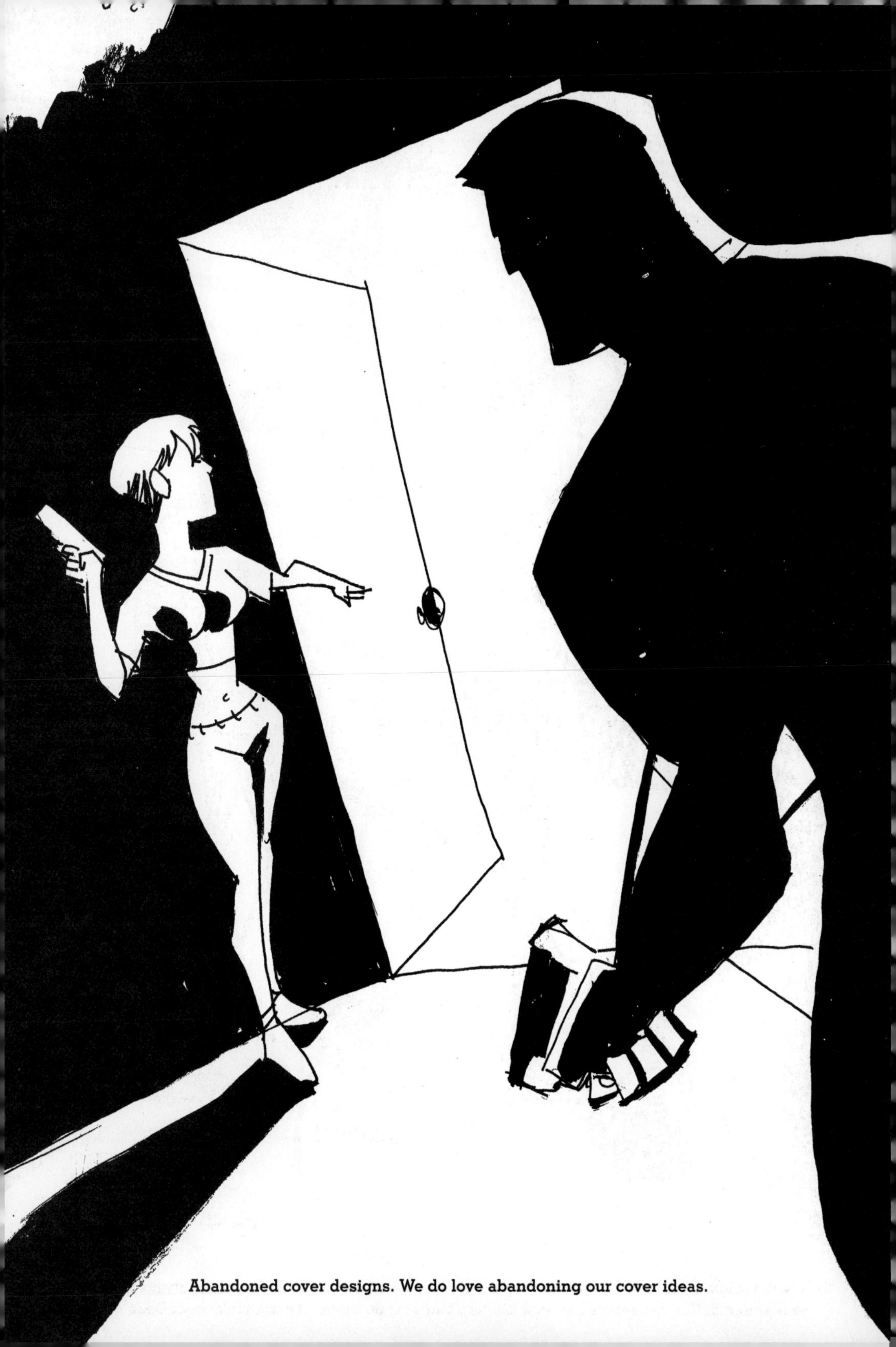

Abandoned cover designs. We do love abandoning our cover ideas.

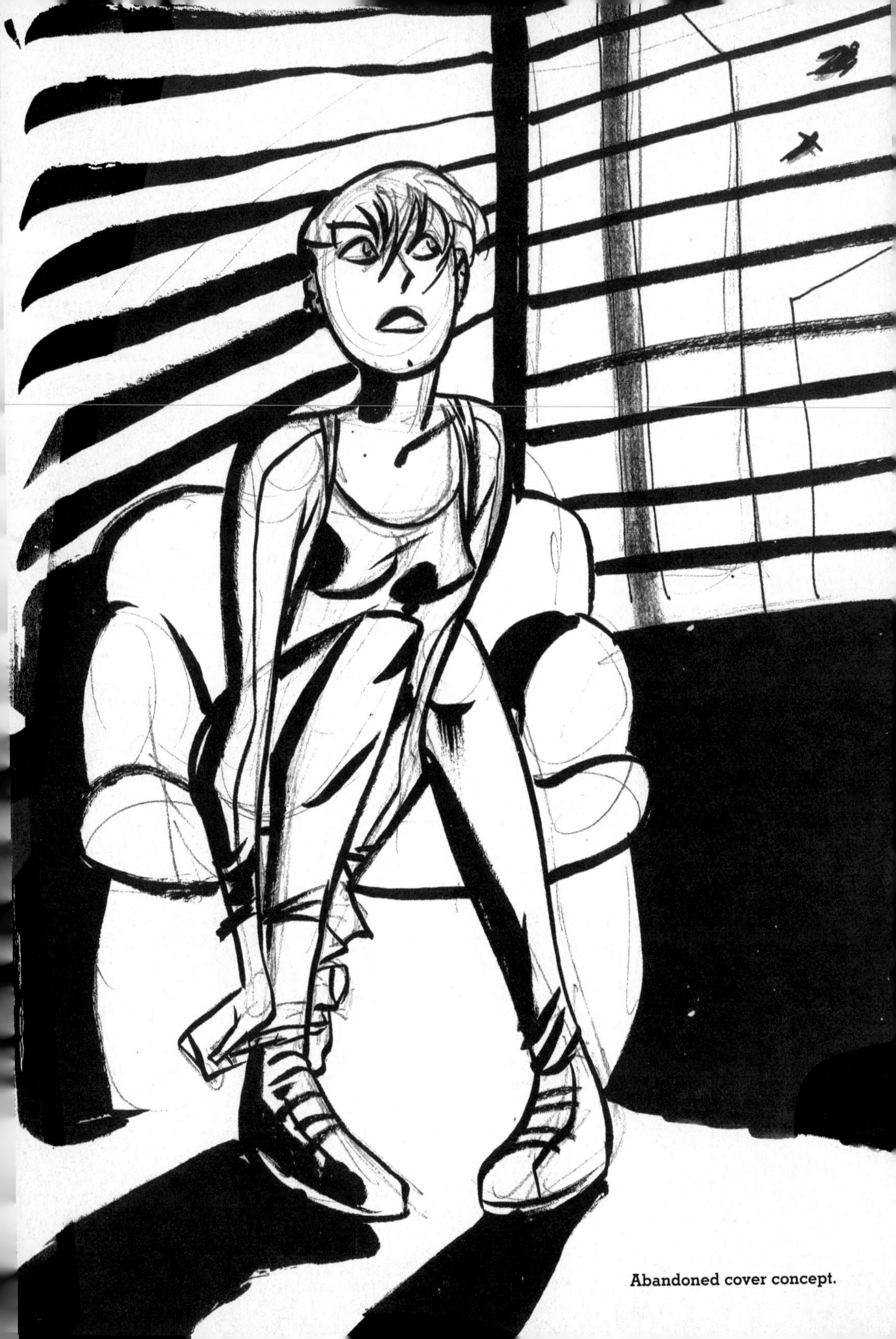

Abandoned cover concept.

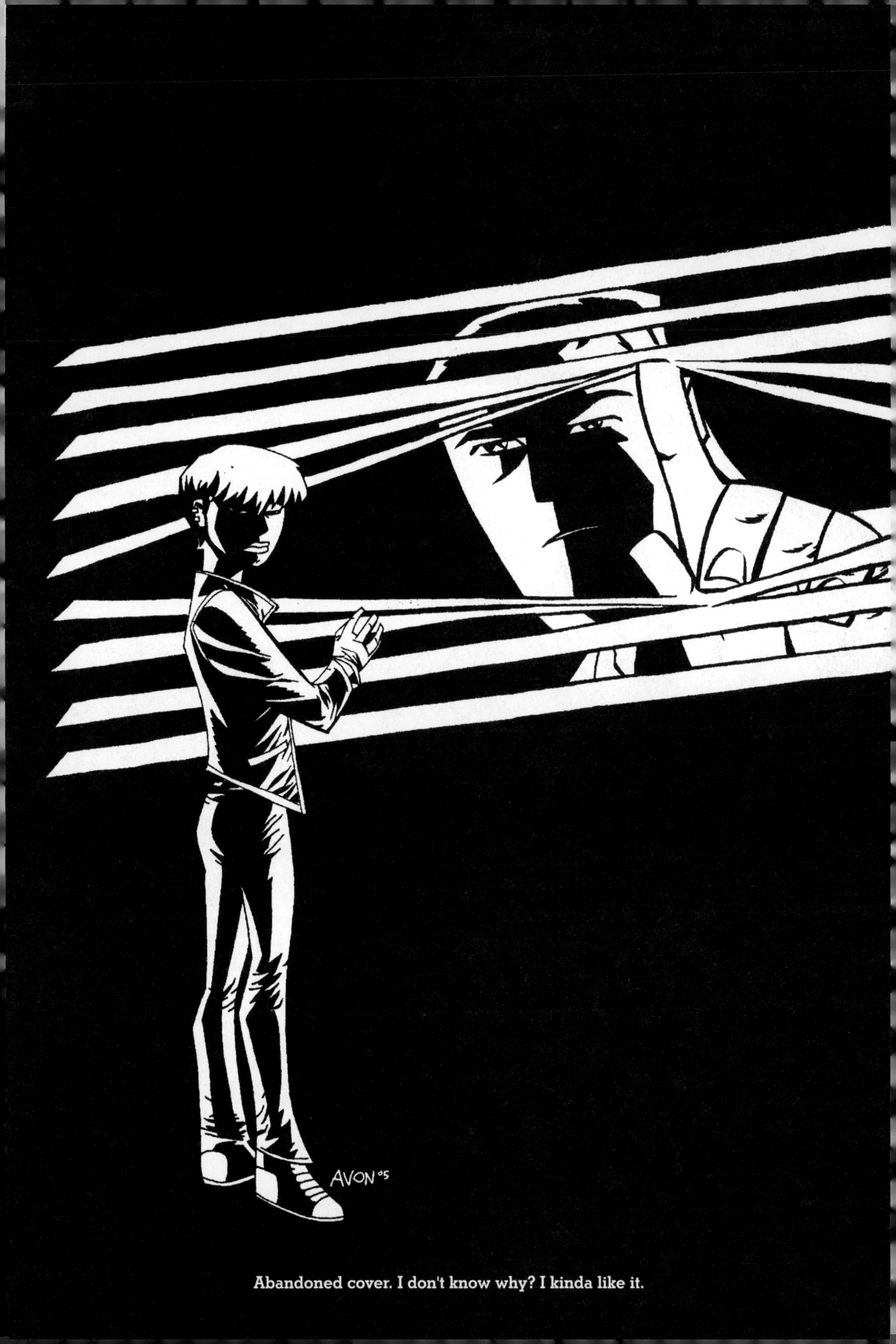
AVON '05

Abandoned cover. I don't know why? I kinda like it.

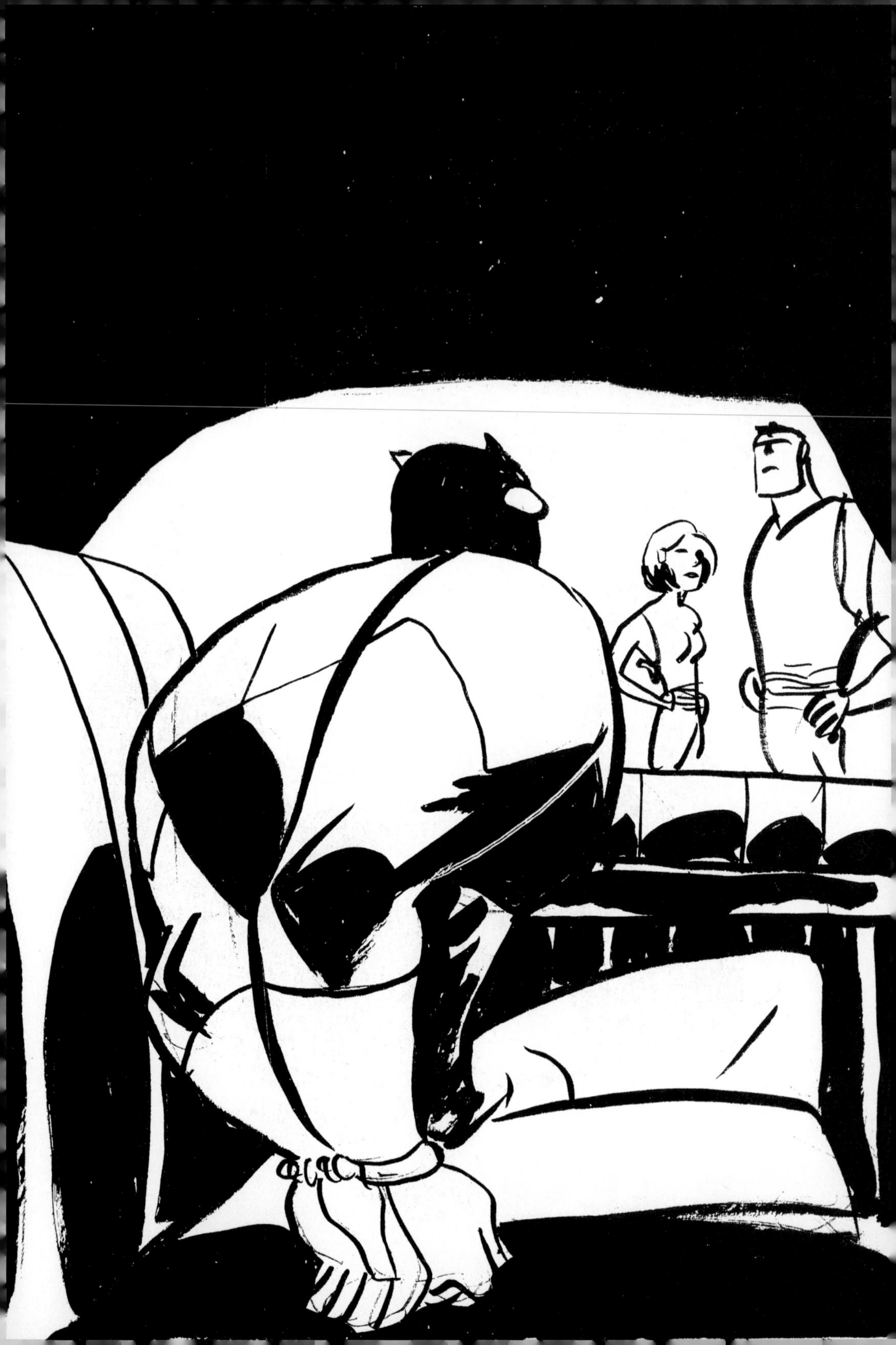

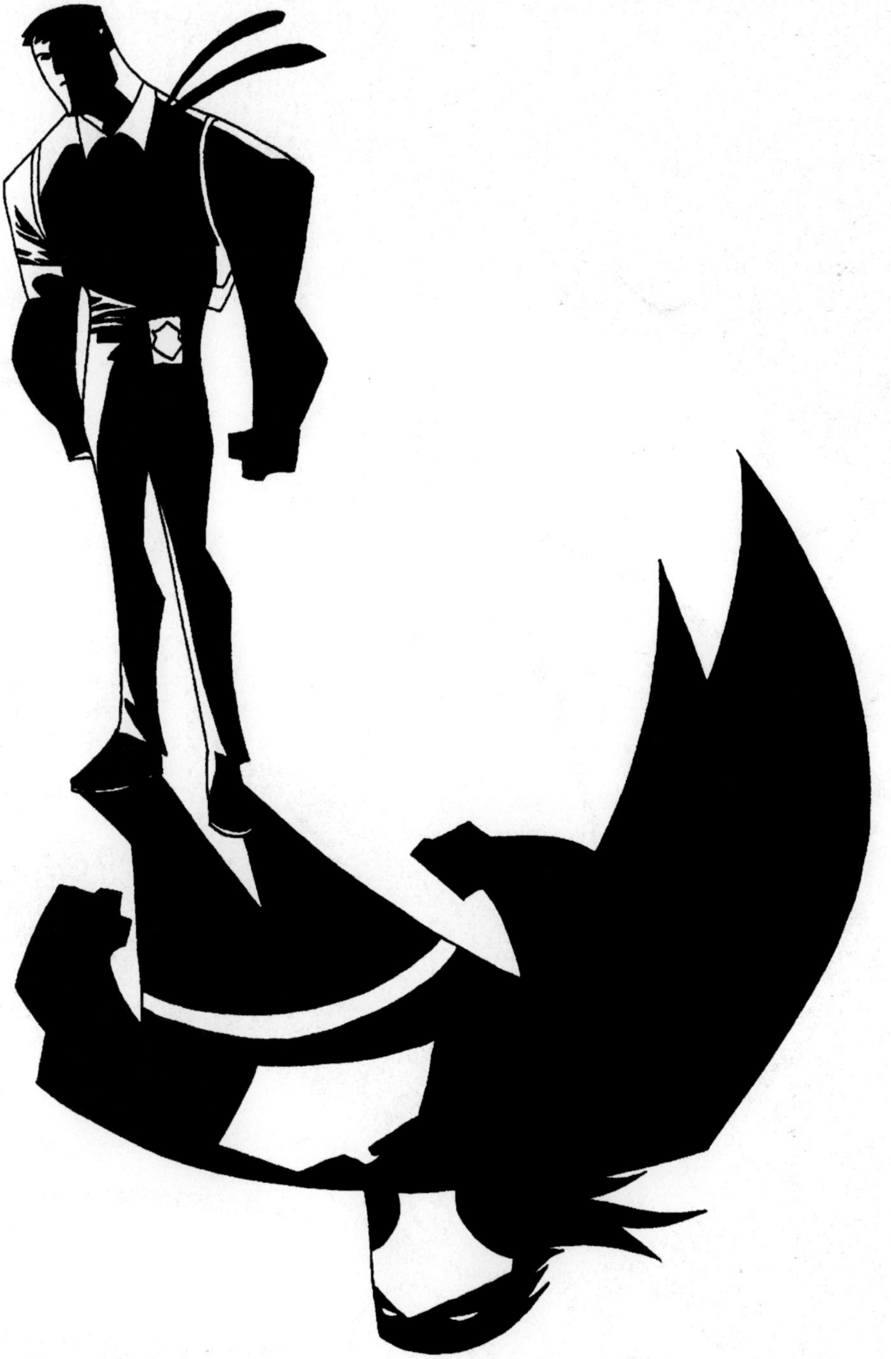

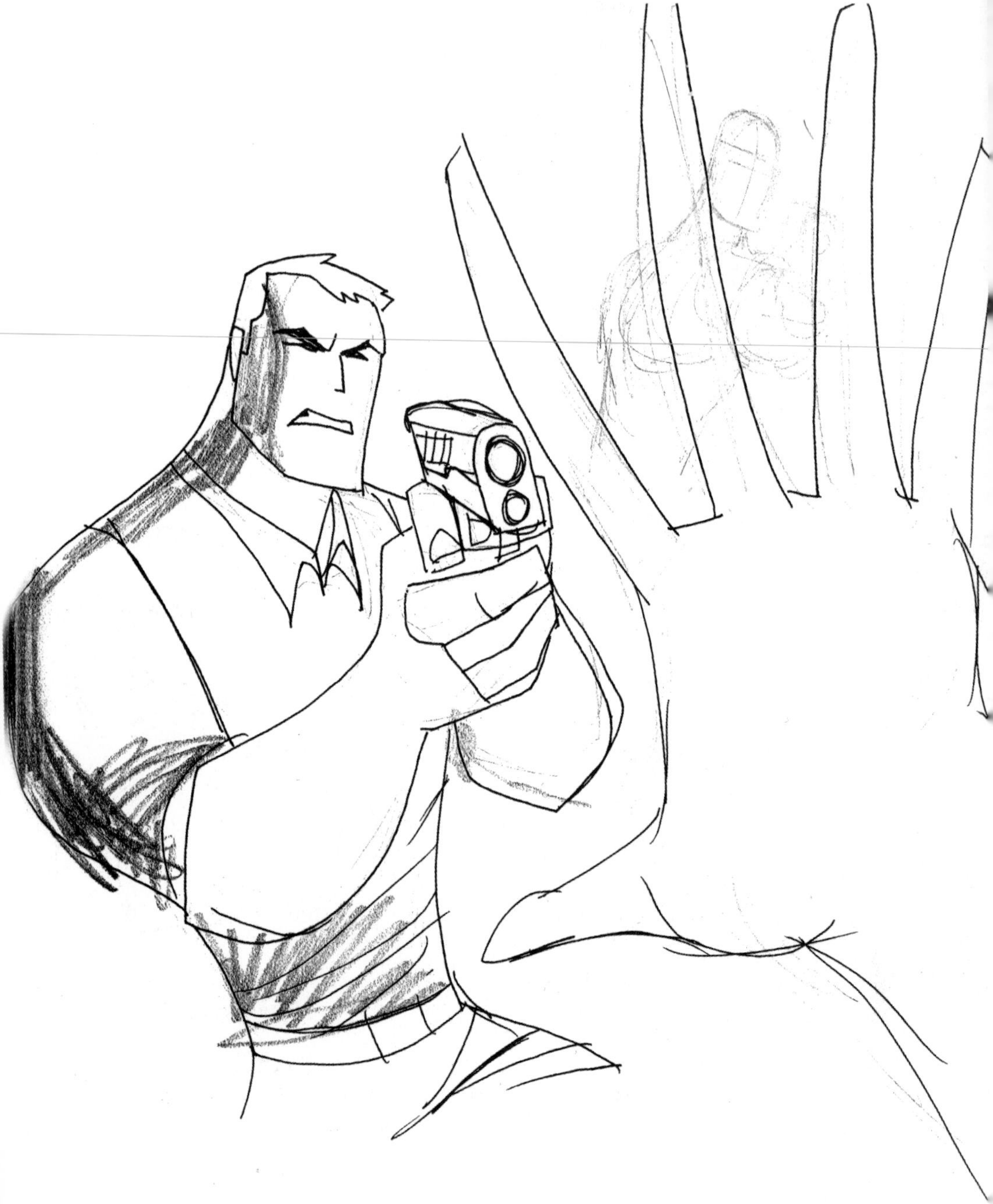

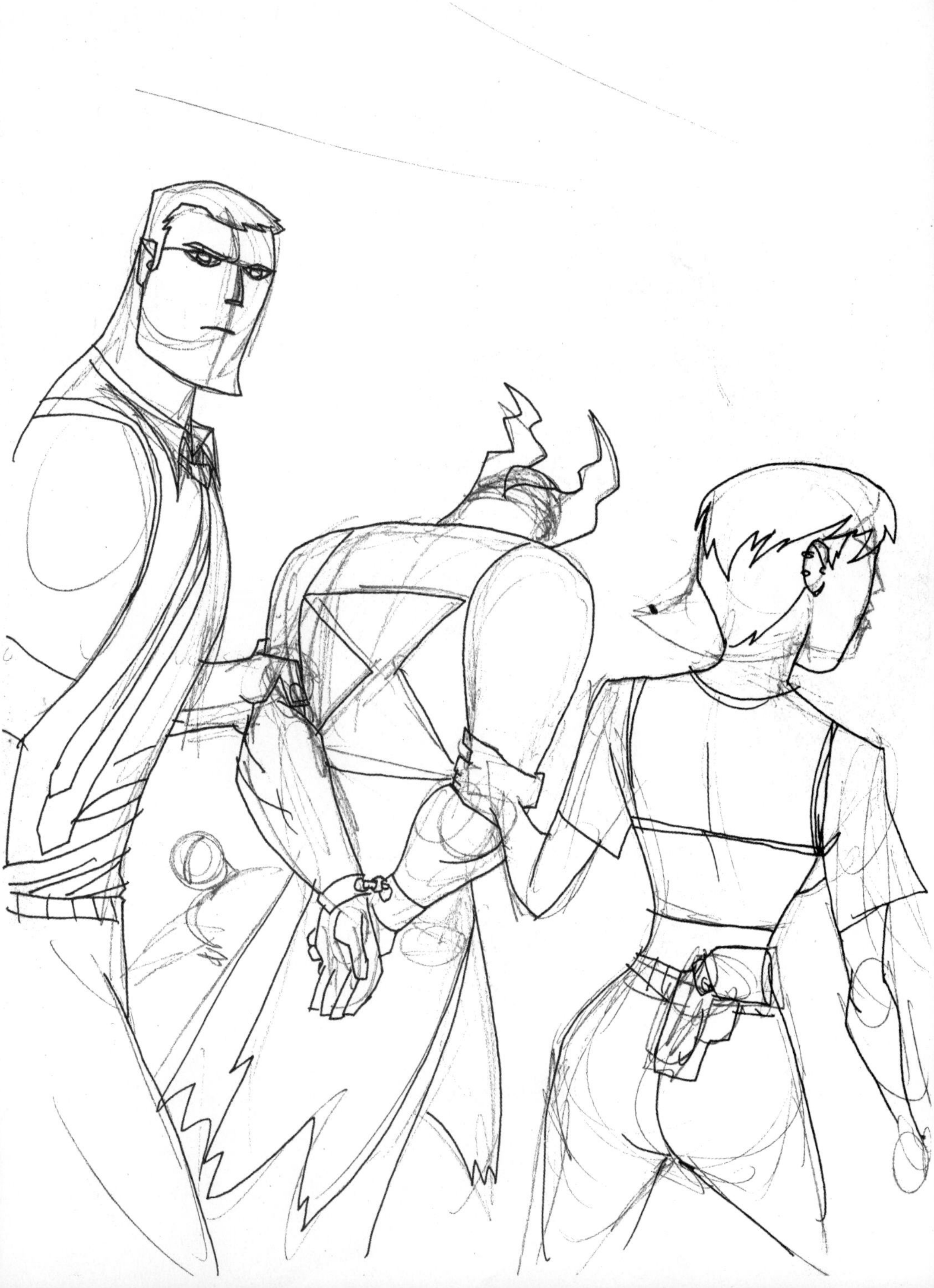

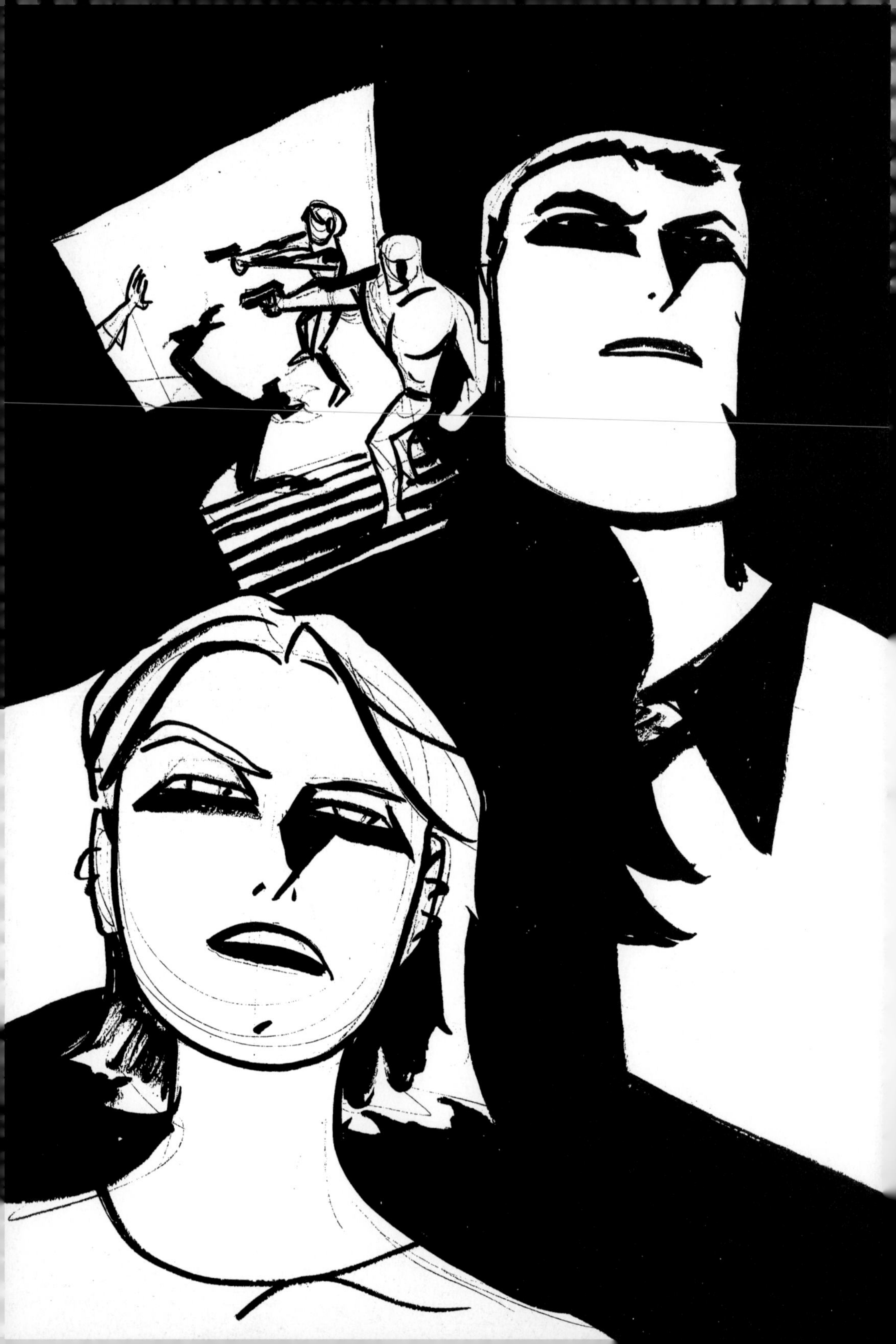

THE GALLERY

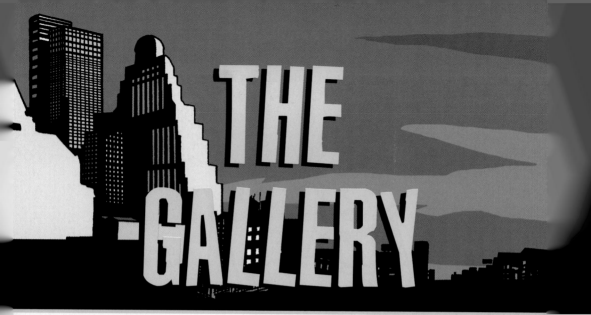

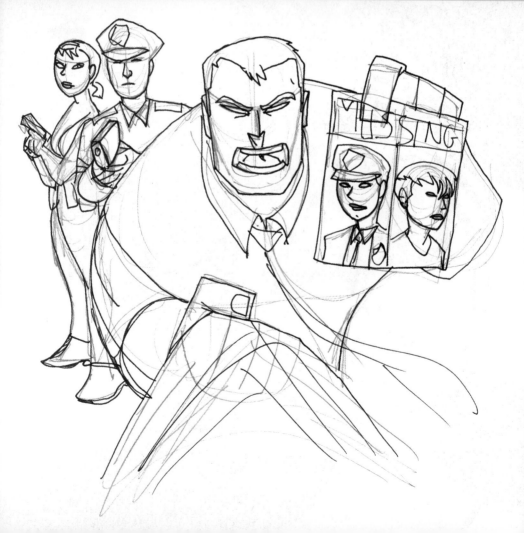

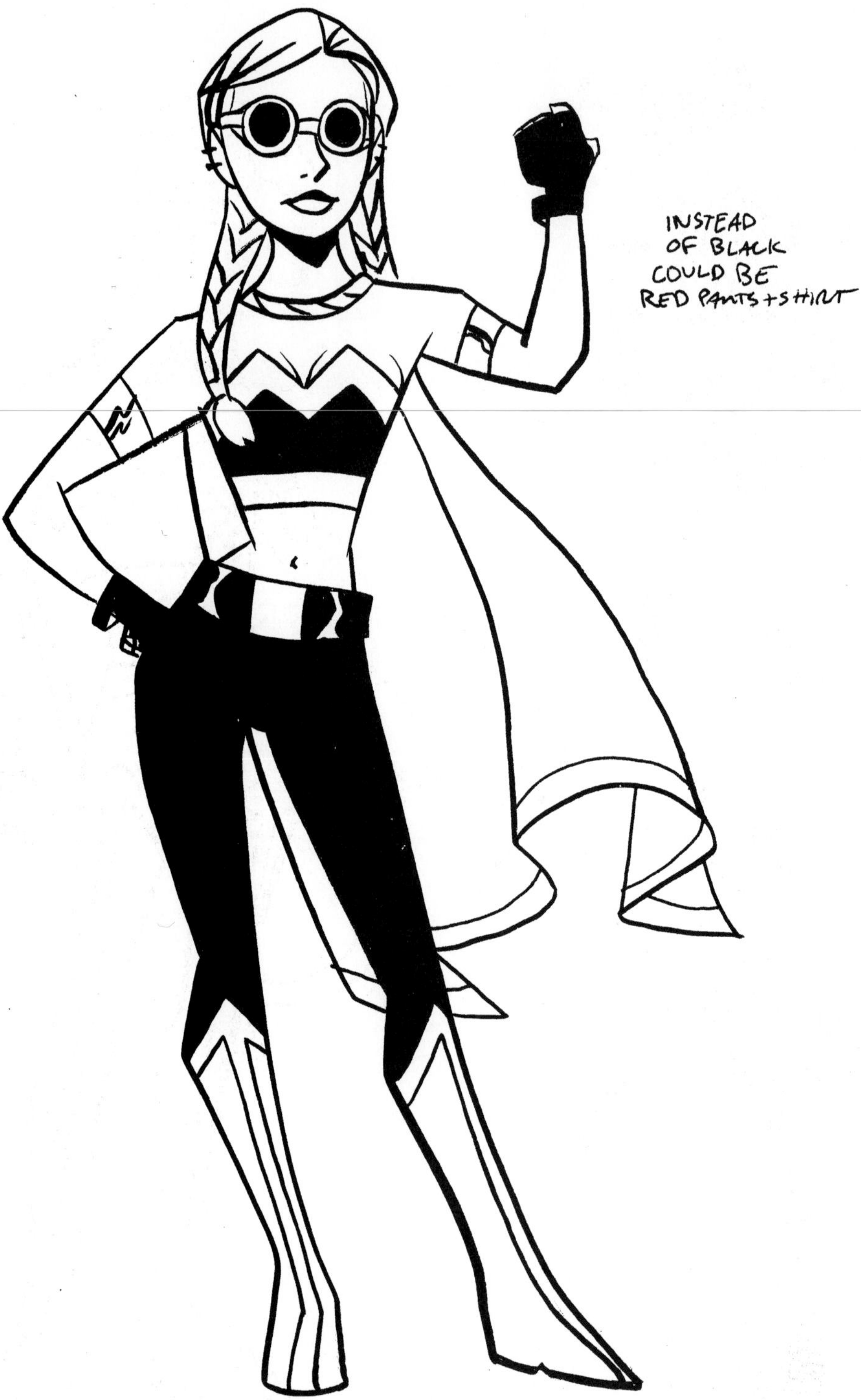
INSTEAD OF BLACK COULD BE RED PANTS+SHIRT

The new Retro Girl design. We picked and picked at this one. It had to be new and perfect.

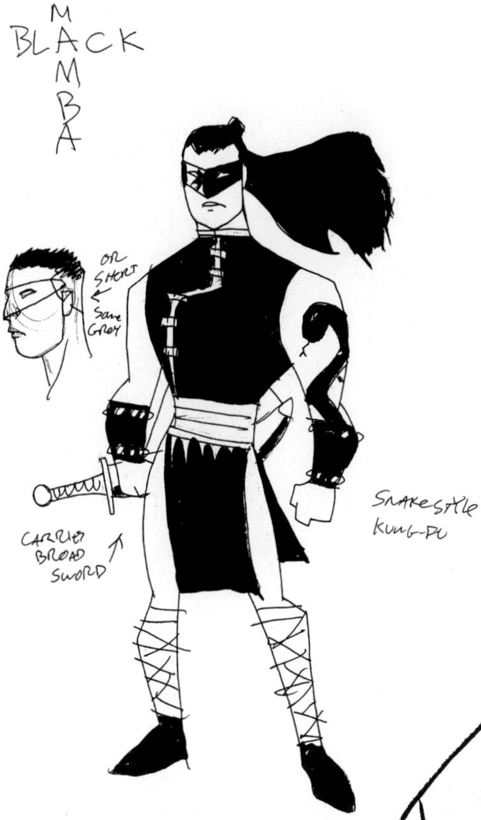
BLACK MAMBA
OR SHORT
Same Grey
CARRIES BROAD SWORD
SNAKE STYLE KUNG-FU

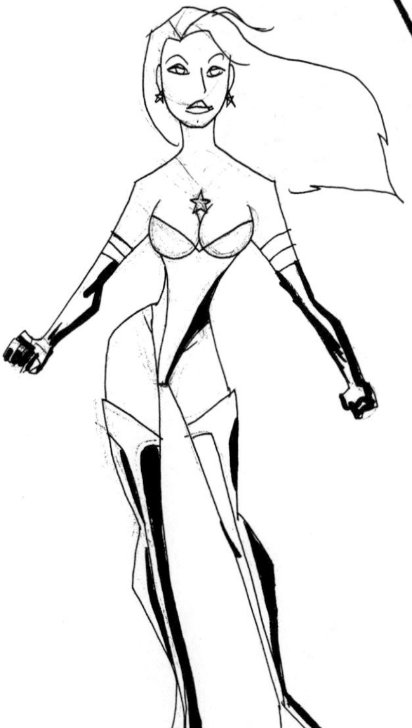

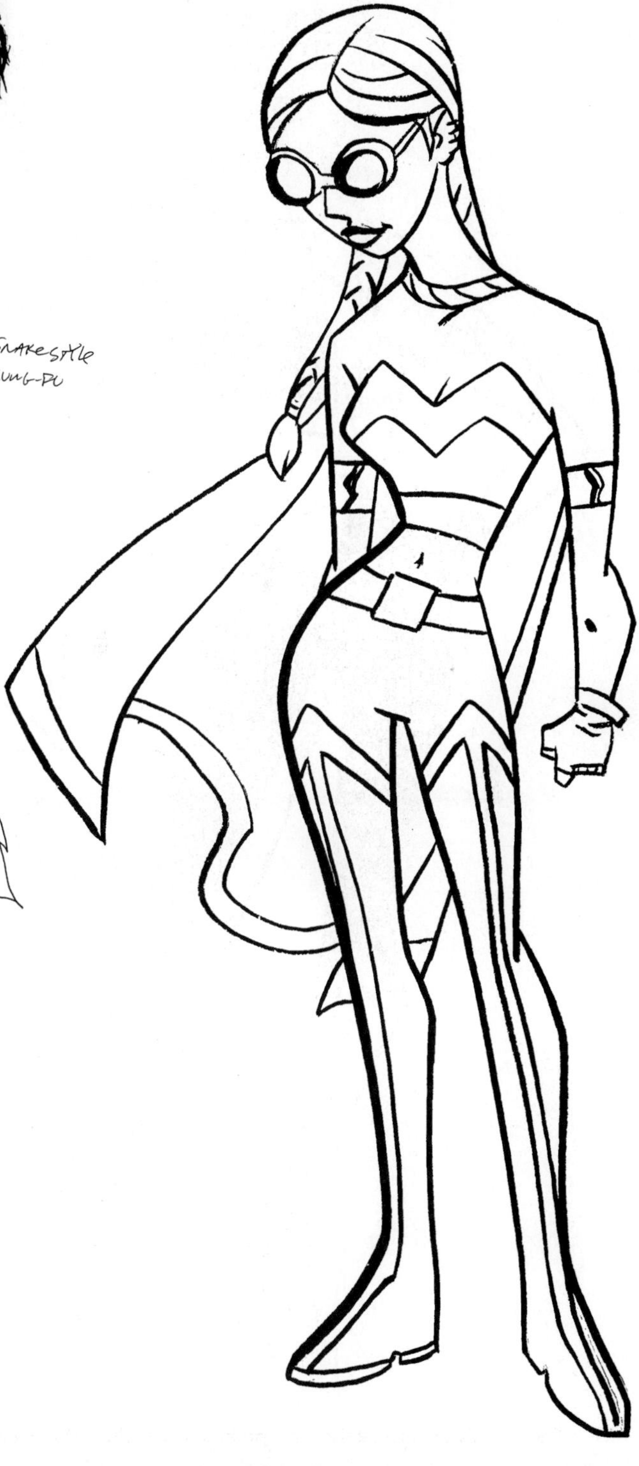

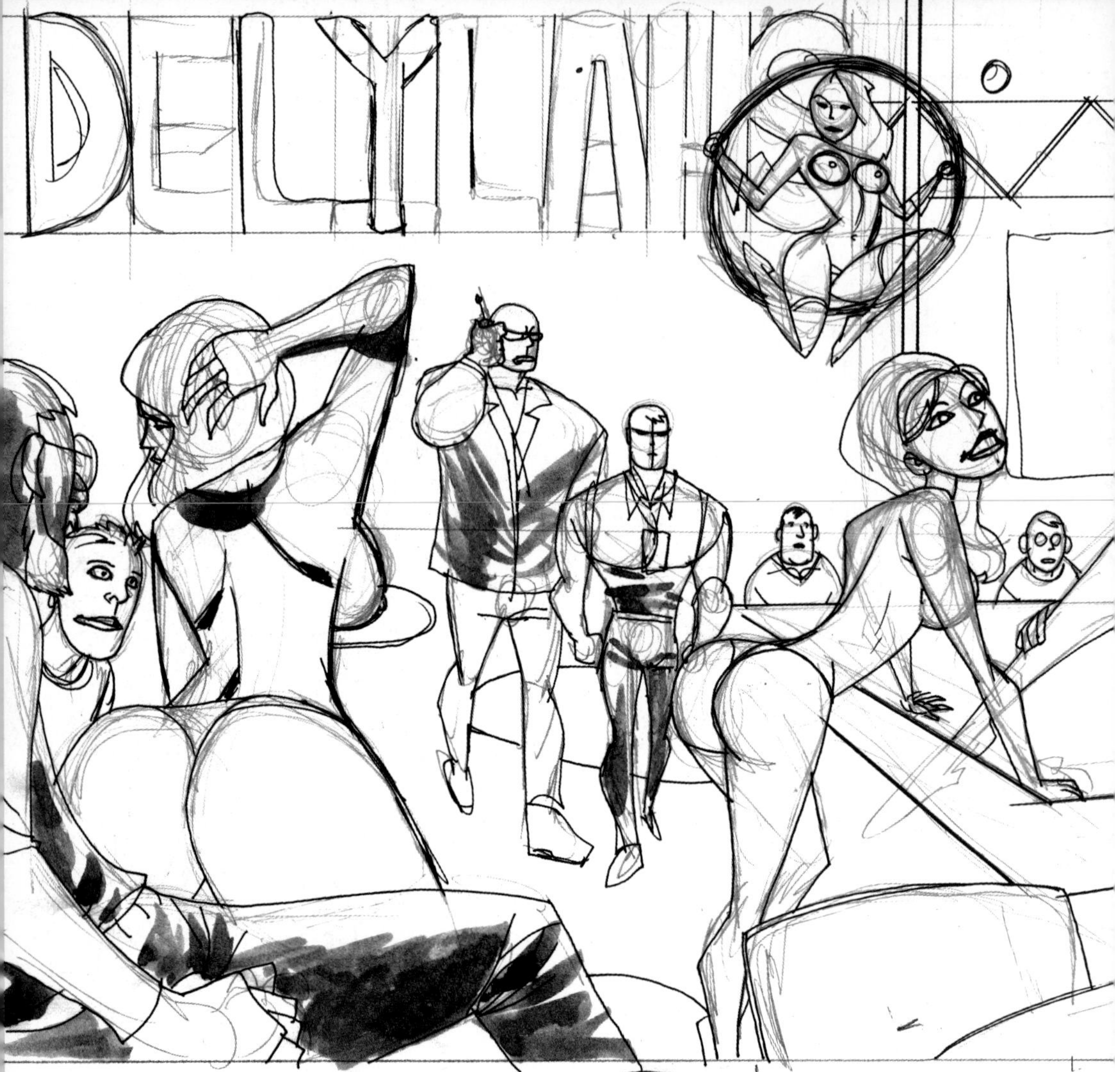
DELYLAH

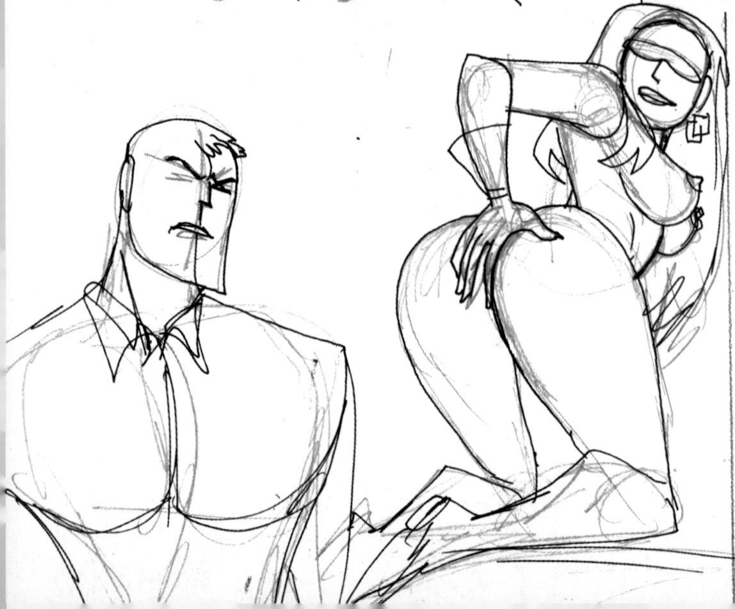

Yes, at first glance this strip club scene might seem gratuitous but if Oeming isn't given an ass shot to draw every 125 pages or so he just starts putting them into the book whether I ask for them or not, so it's best to get them out of the way so he can get back to work.

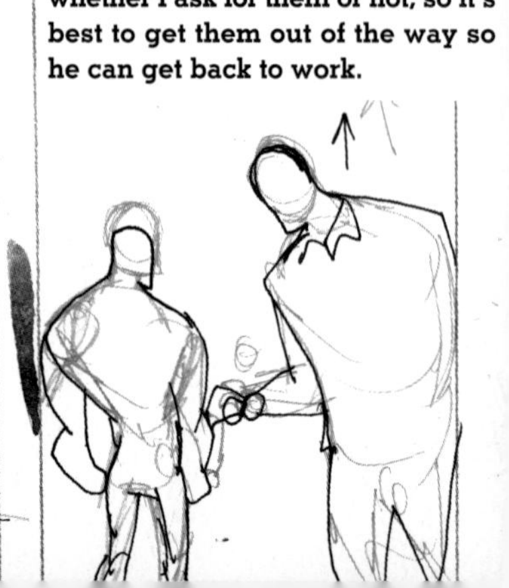

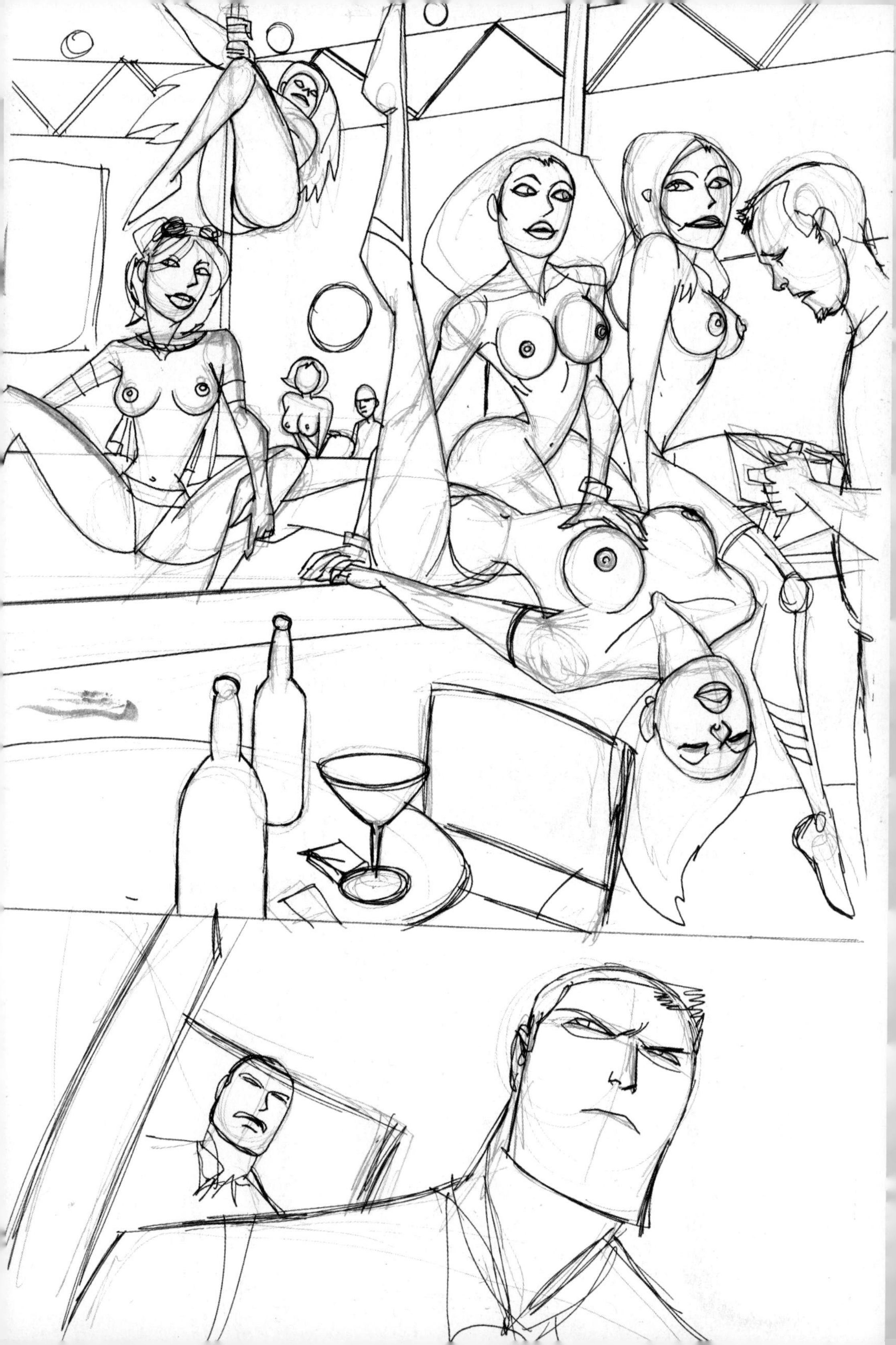

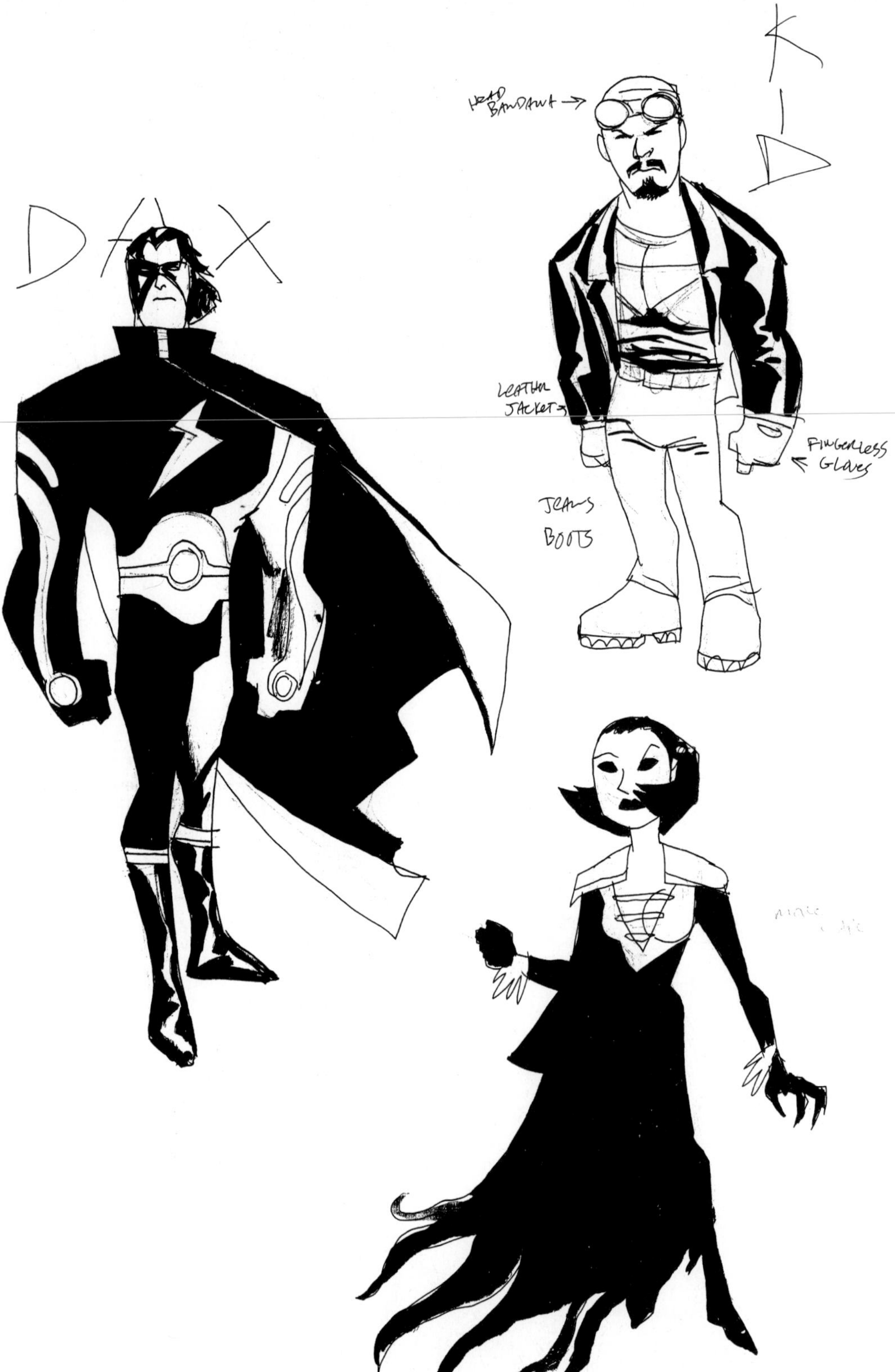
DAX
KID
HEAD BANDANA →
LEATHER JACKET →
FINGERLESS GLOVES
JEANS
BOOTS

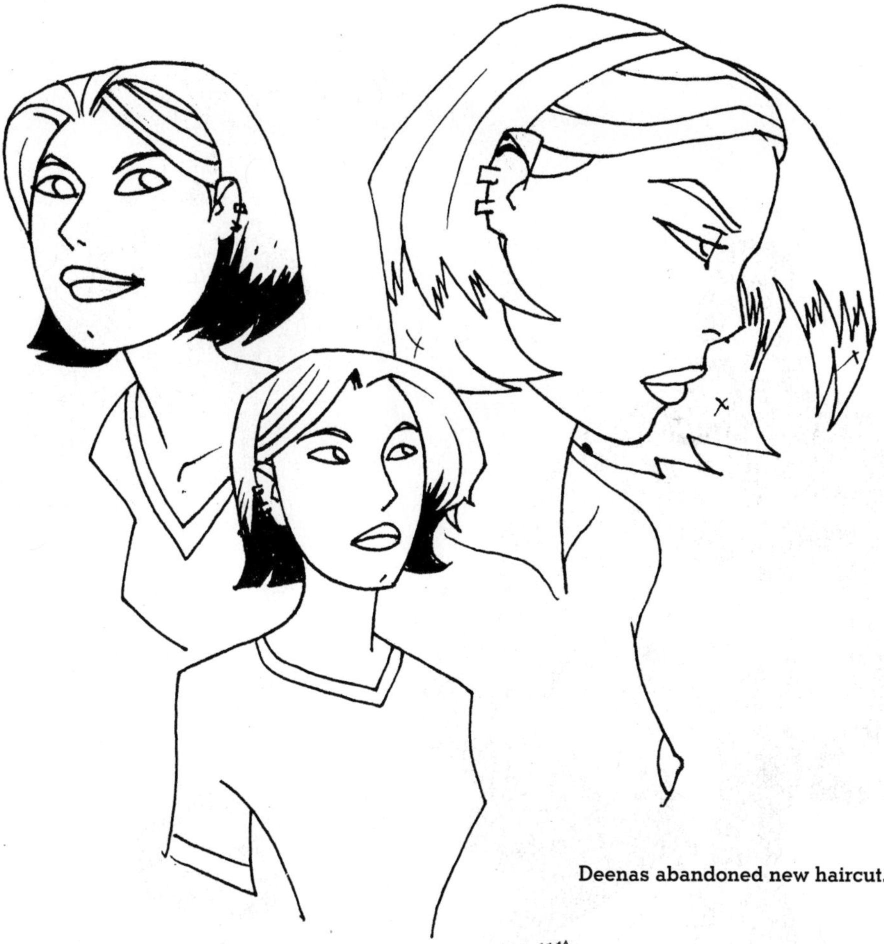

Deenas abandoned new haircut.

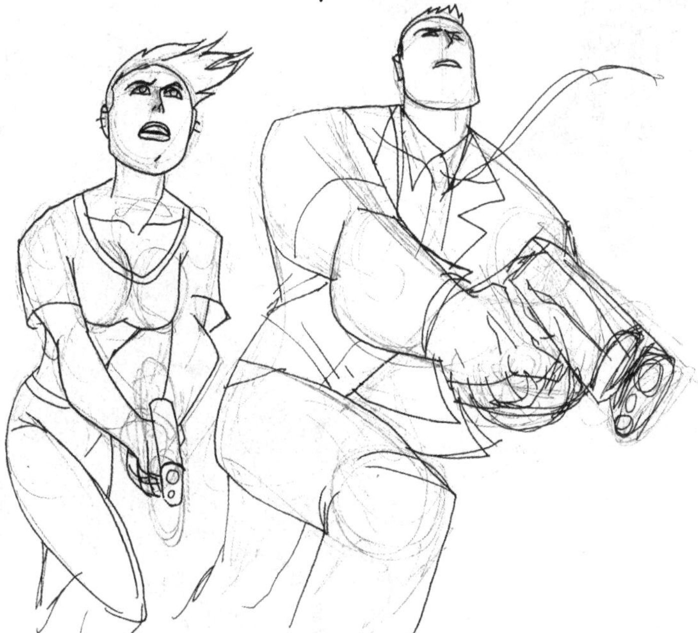

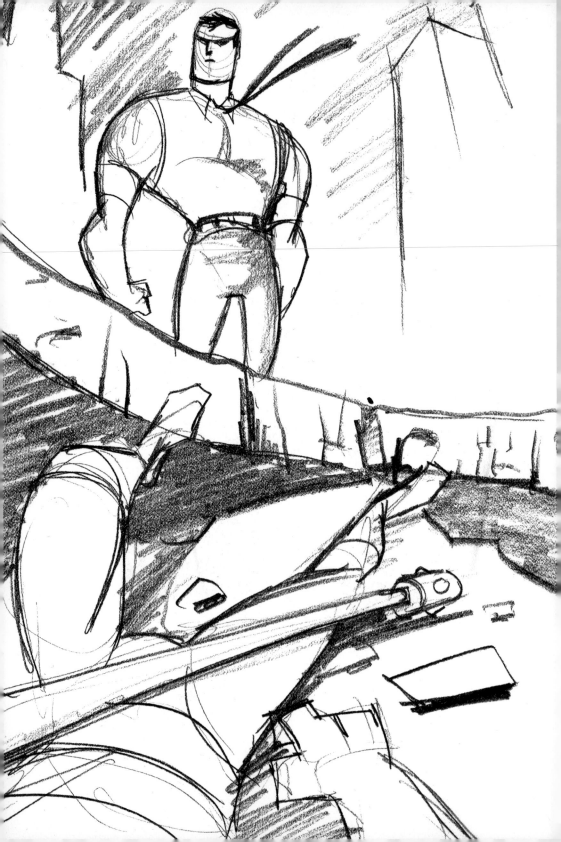

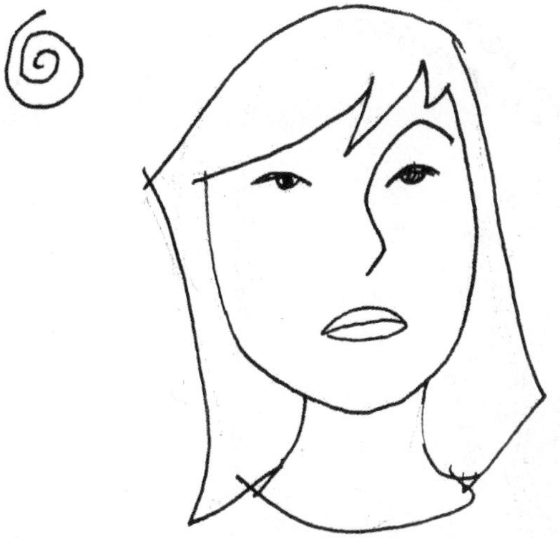

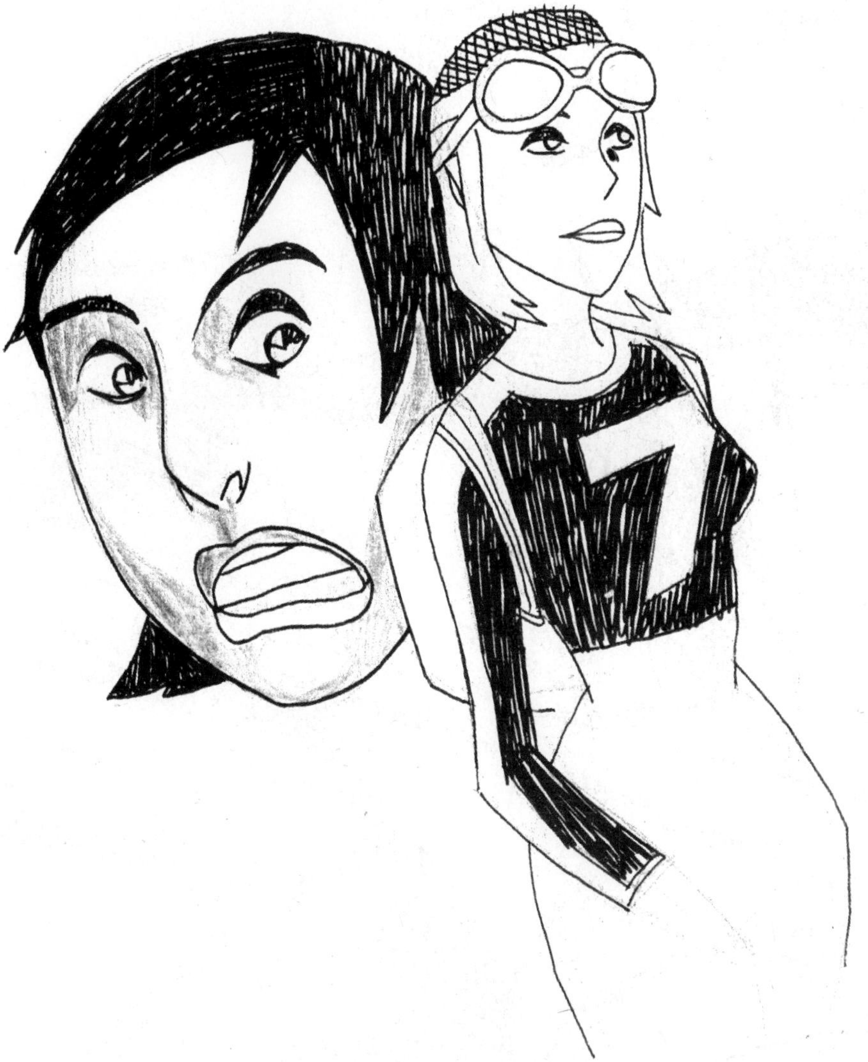
7

TEAGUE

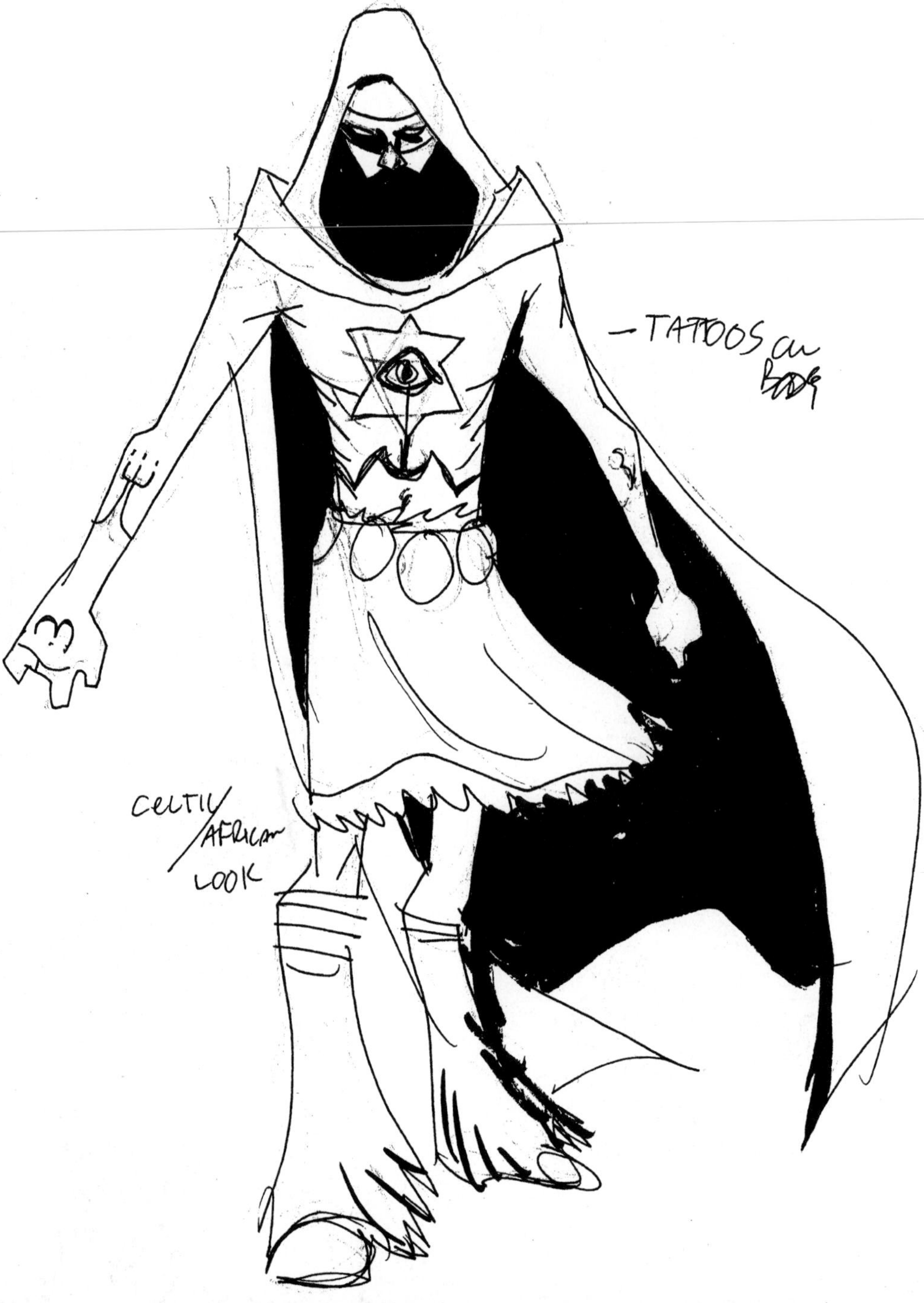

-TATTOOS ON BODY
CELTIC/AFRICAN LOOK

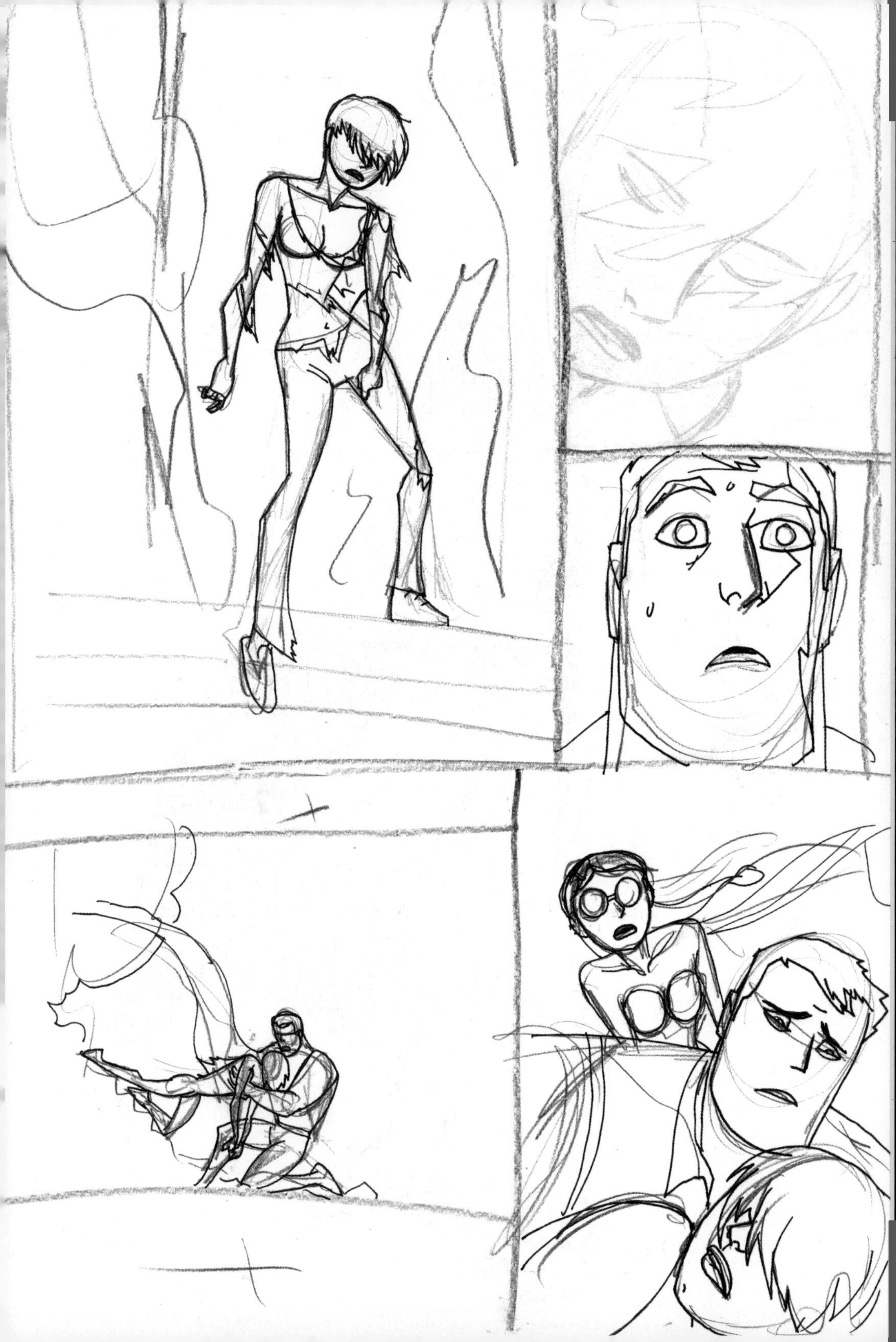

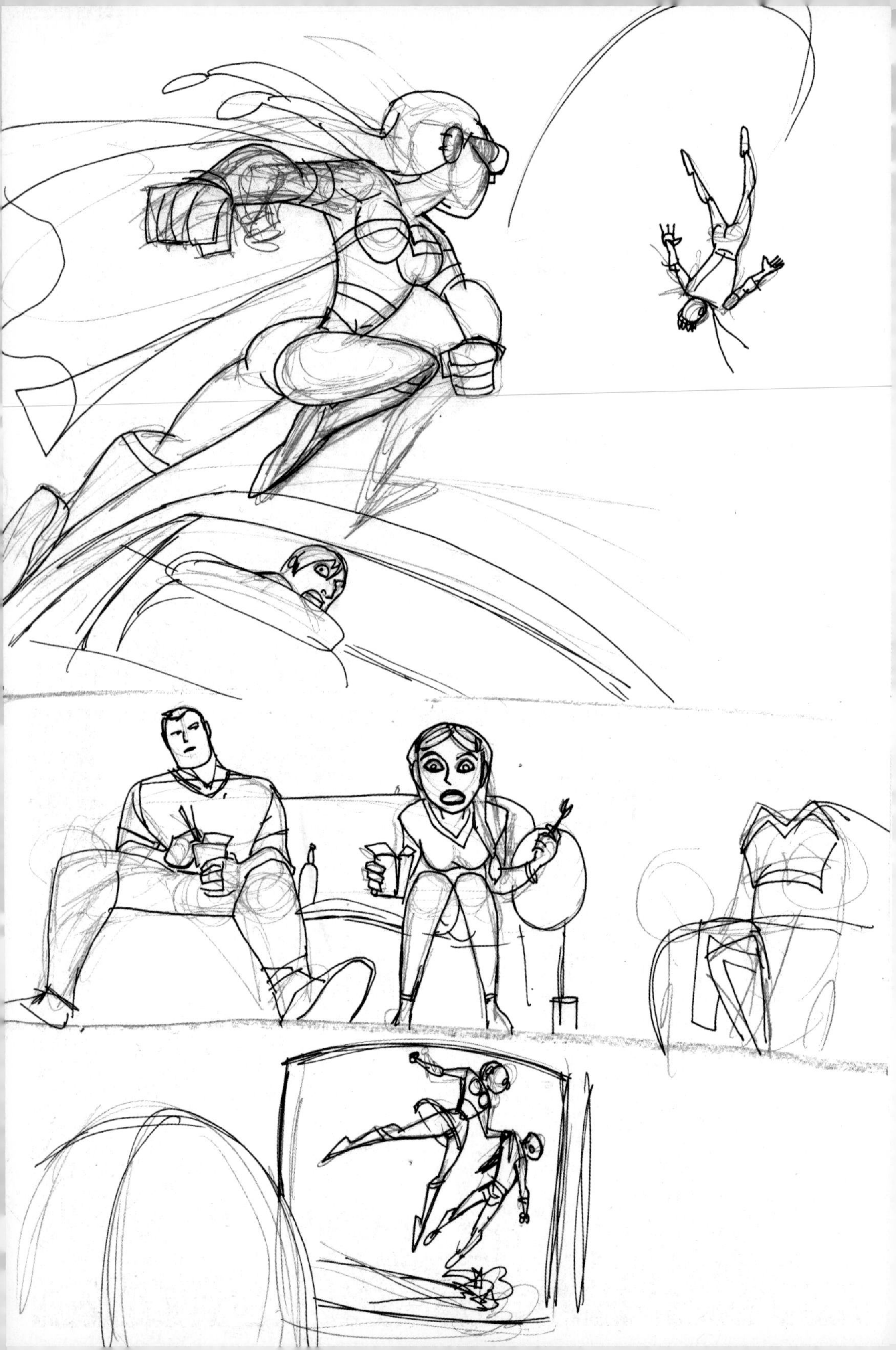

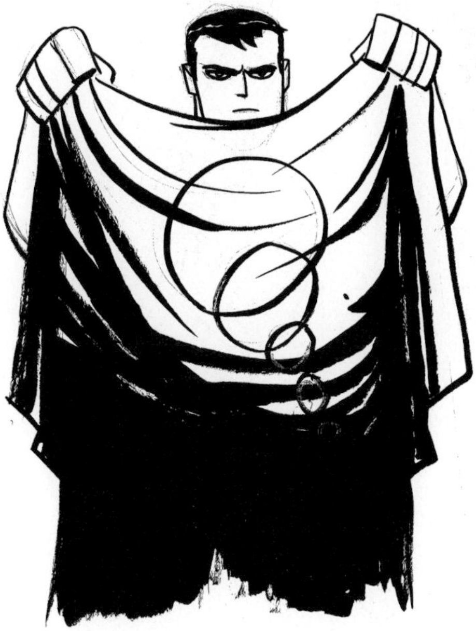

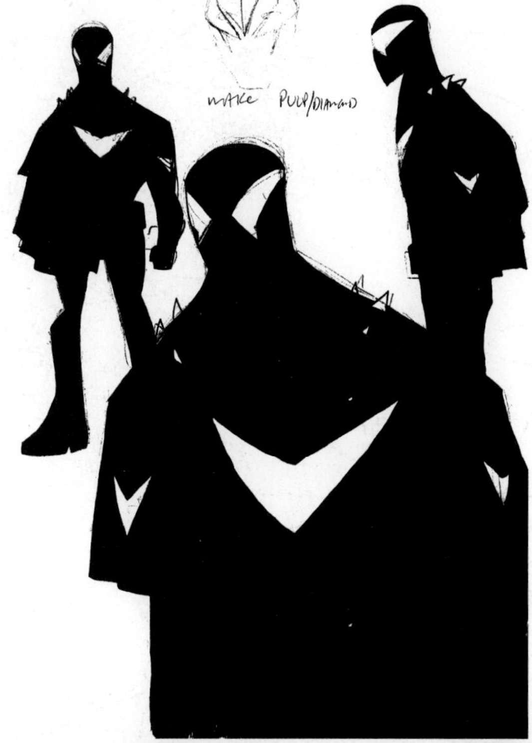
BLACK GAUNA
MAKE PULP/DIAMOND

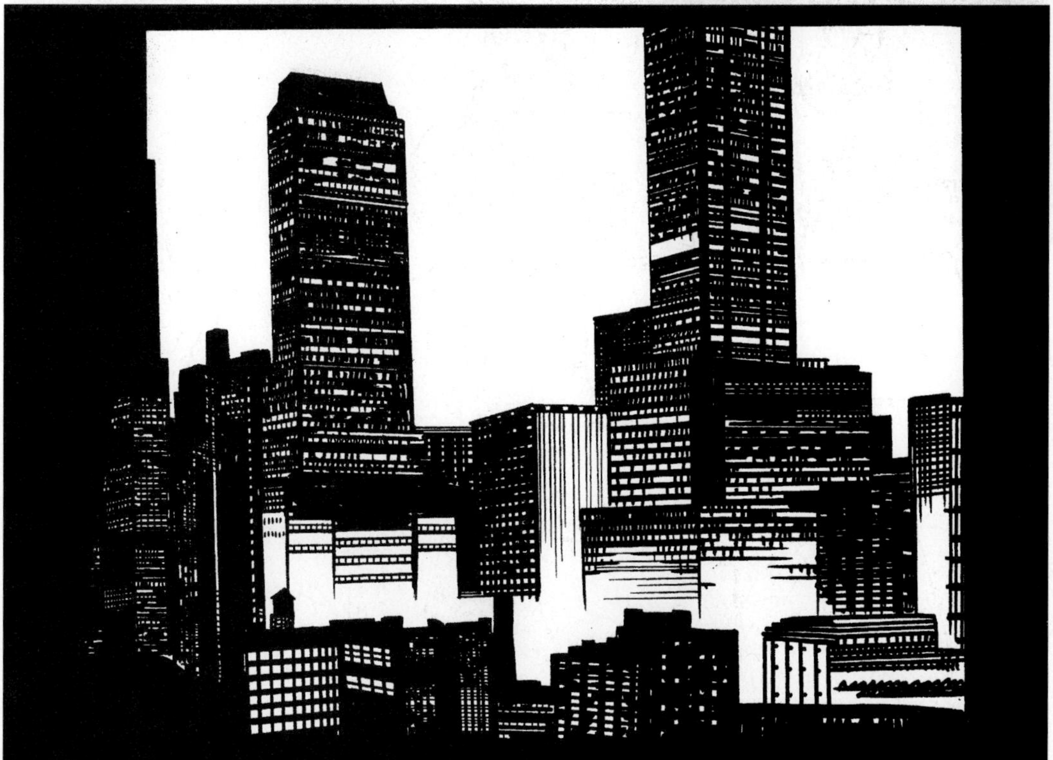

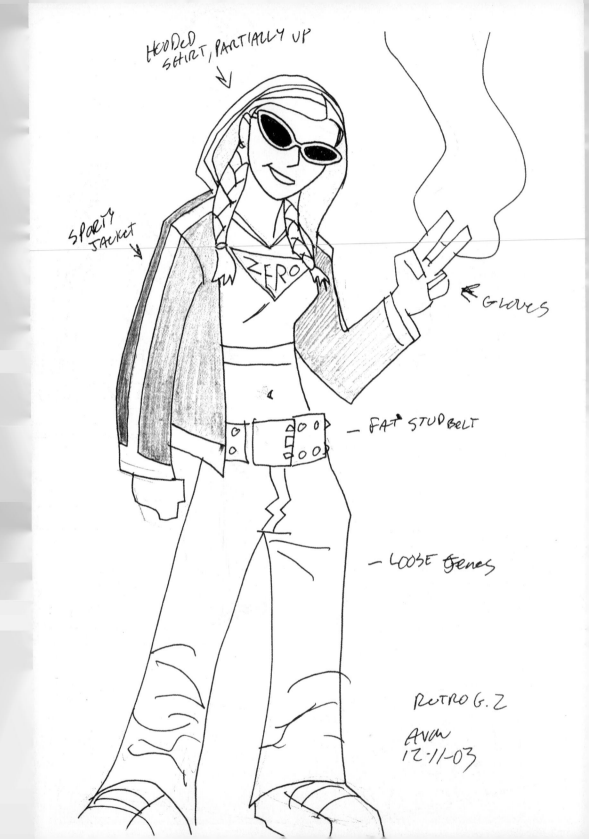

HOODED SHIRT, PARTIALLY UP

SPORTY JACKET

ZERO

GLOVES

FAT STUDBELT

LOOSE Jenes

RETRO G. Z

Avon
12-11-03

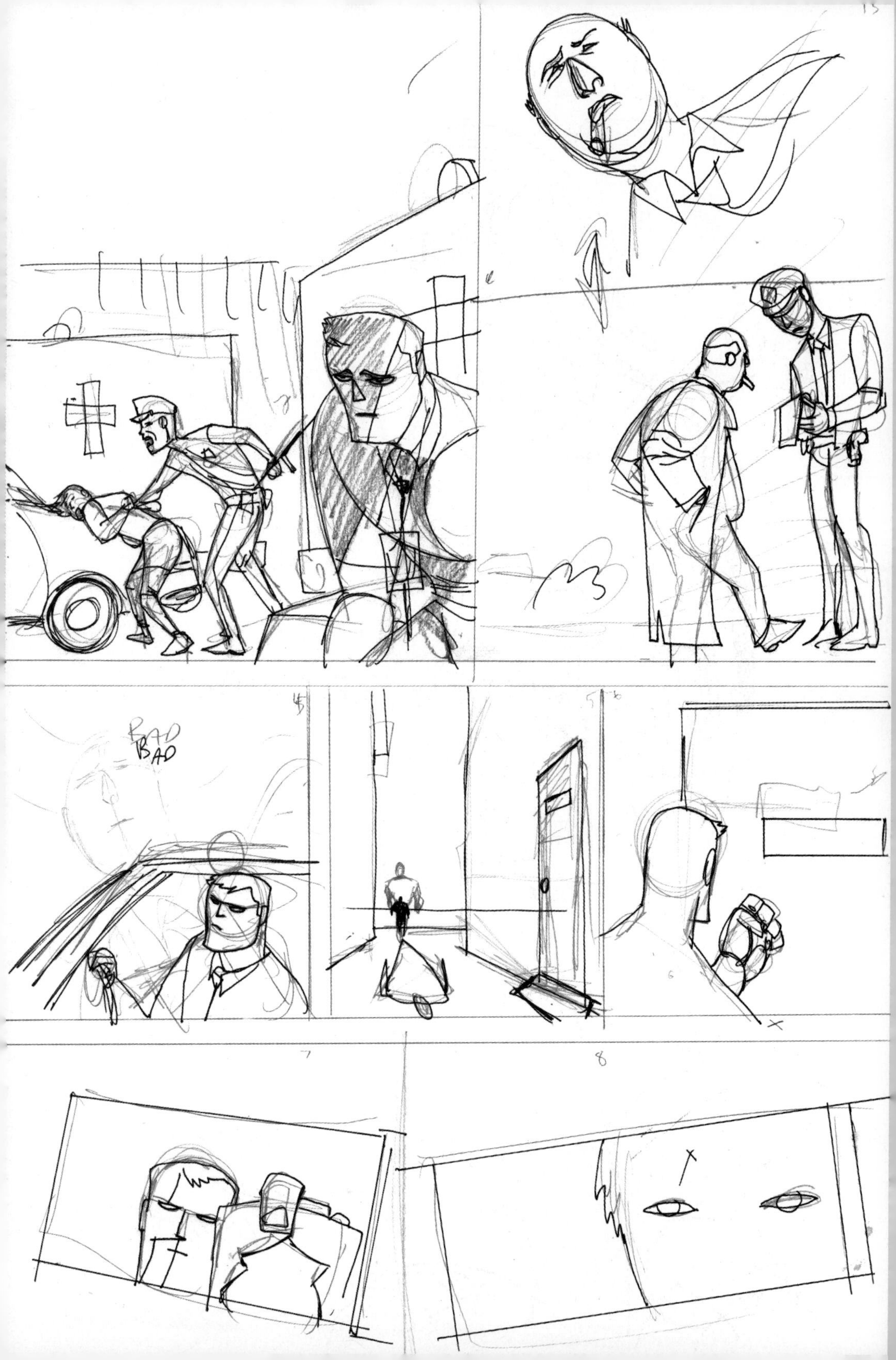
BAD

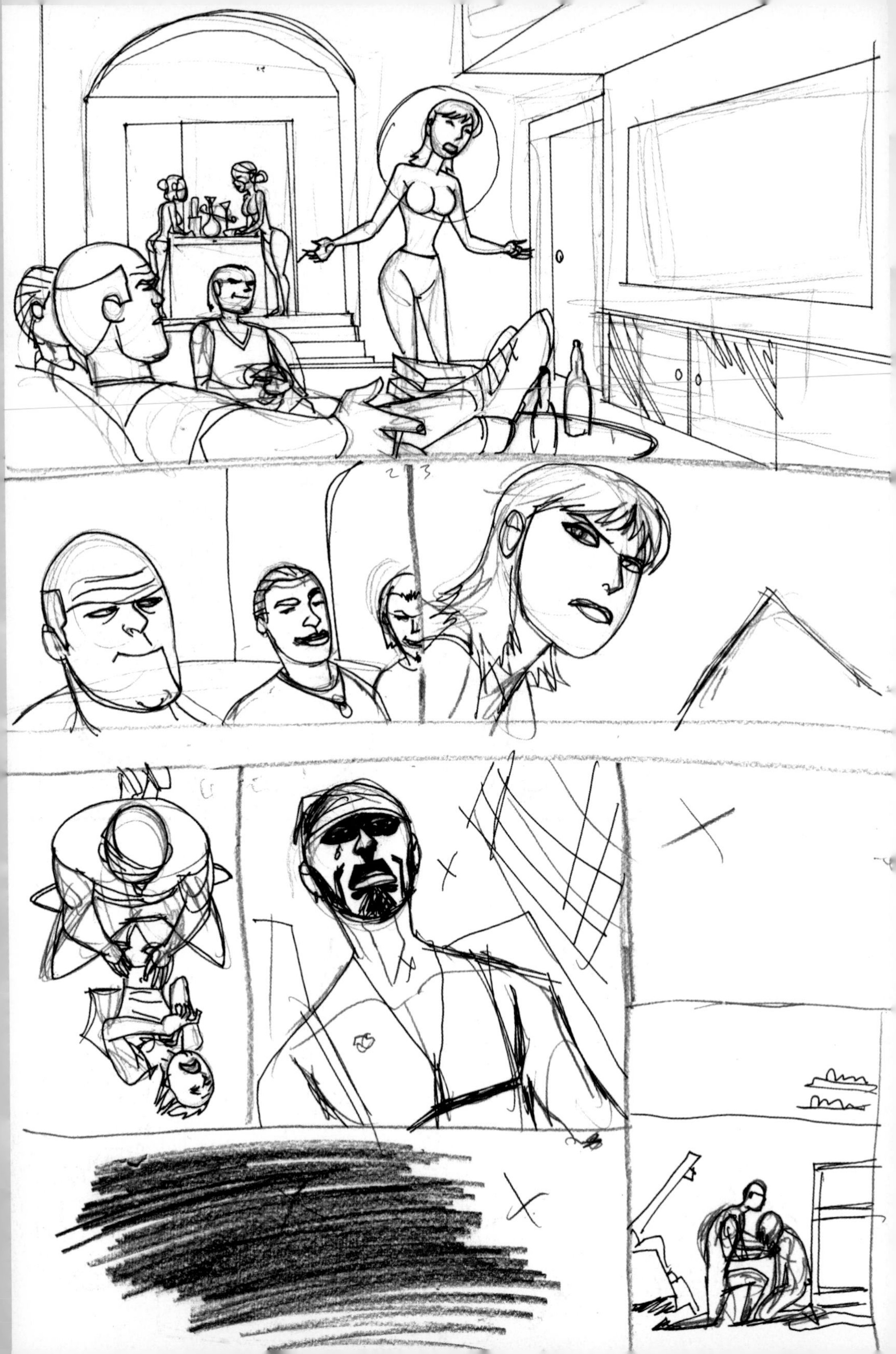

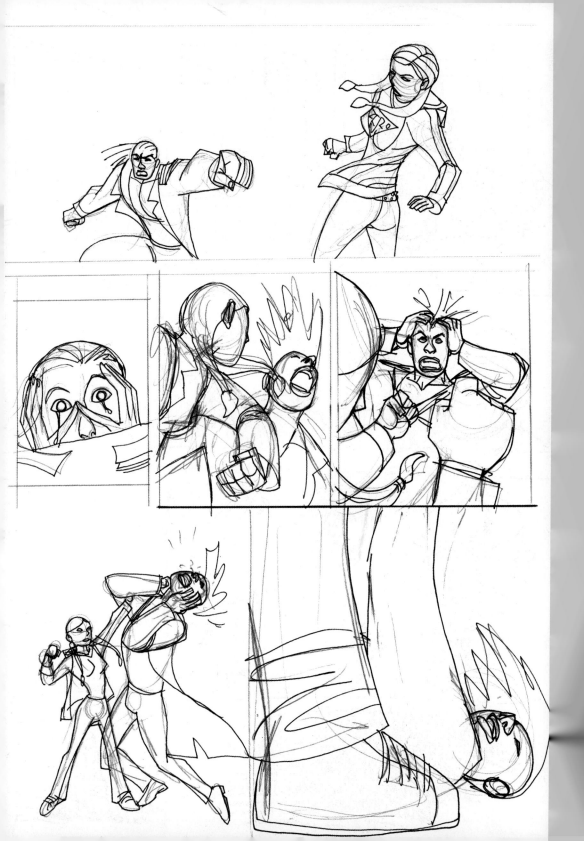

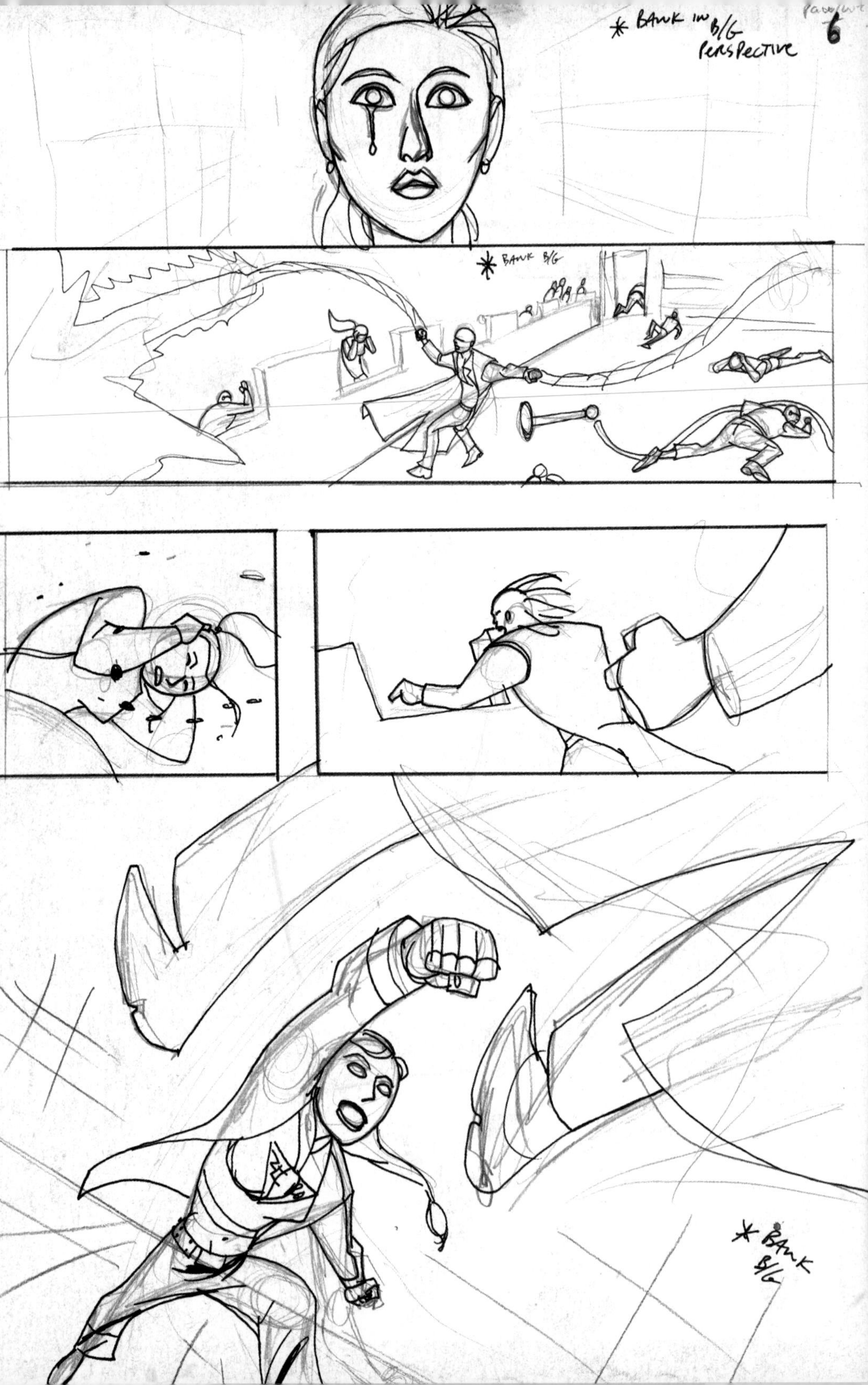
* BANK IN B/G PERSPECTIVE
6
* BANK B/G
* BANK B/G

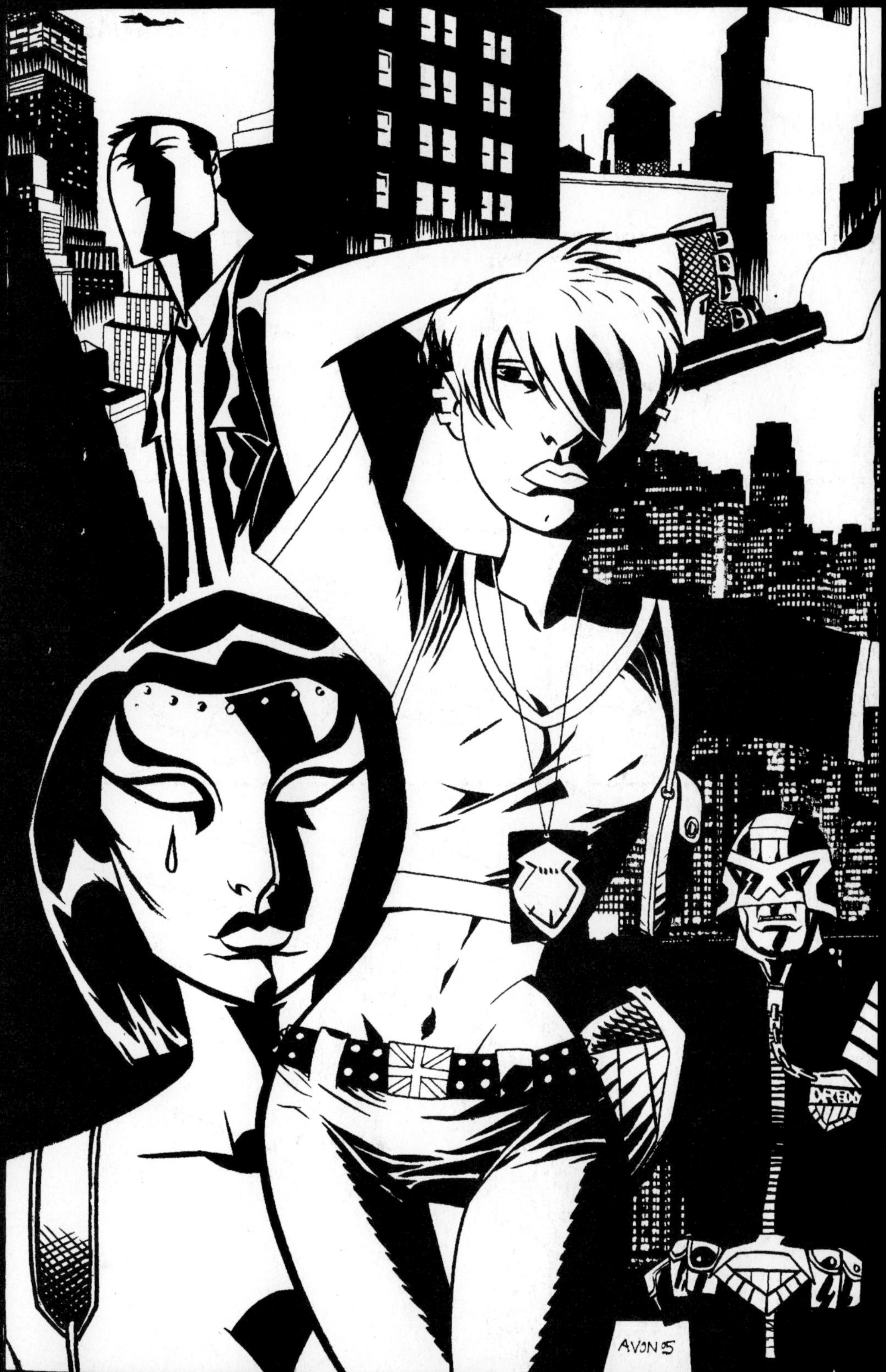
AVON 05

By the authors...

POWERS
- Who Killed Retro Girl?
- Roleplay
- Little Deaths
- Supergroup
- Anarchy
- The Sellouts
- Forever
- Powers Script Book
- Powers Coloring/
  Activity Book
- Powers Annual

By Bendis...

- Jinx
- Goldfish
- Fortune and Glory
- Torso
- Alias
- The Pulse
- Secret War
- Ultimate Spider-Man
- Daredevil
- Avengers
- Total Sell Out

By Oeming...

- The Six Samurai
- Bastard of the Gods
- Hammer of the Gods
- Ship of Fools
- Parliament of Justice

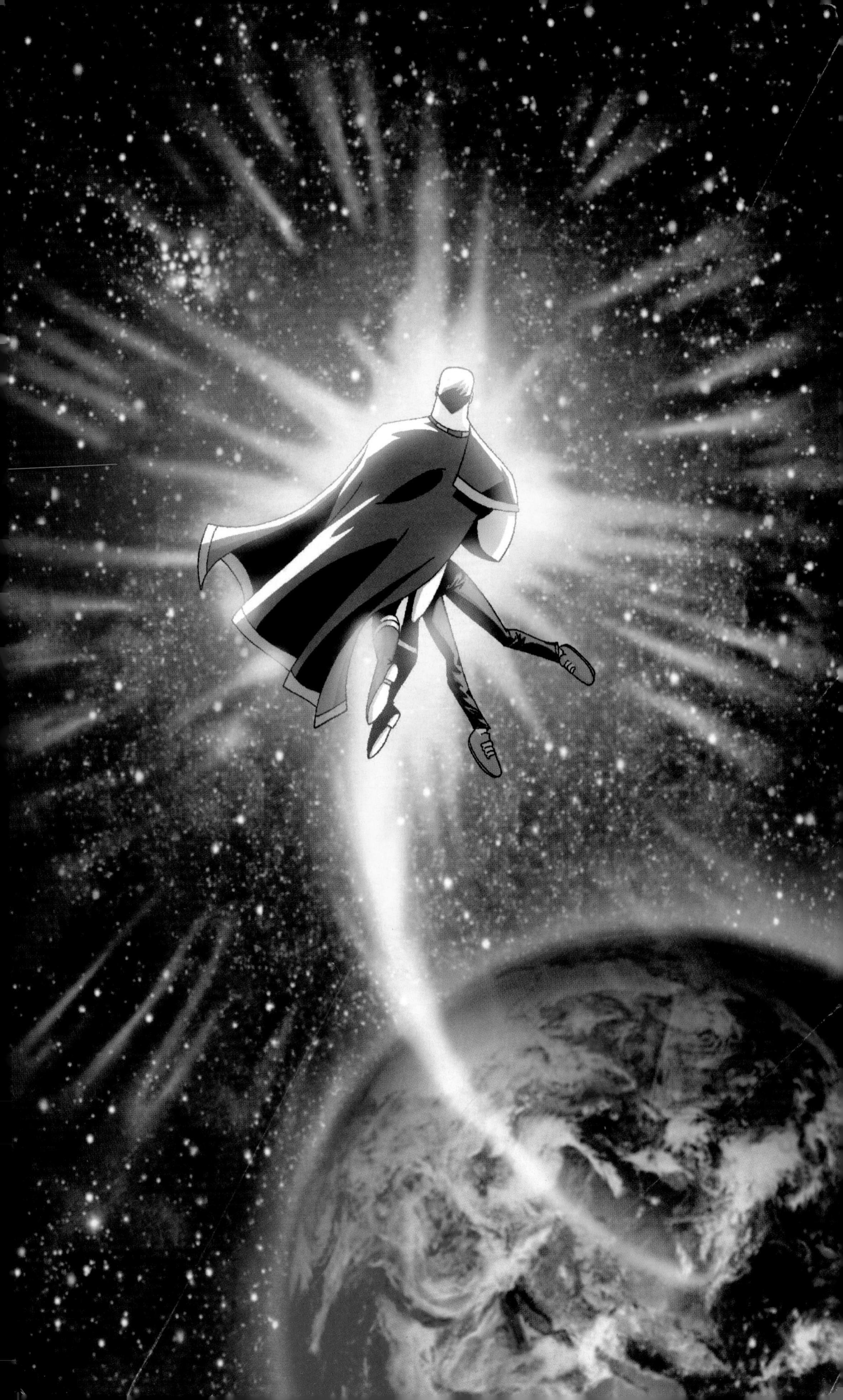